European Yearbook of International Economic Law

Special Issue

The European Yearbook of International Economic Law (EYIEL) is an annual publication in International Economic Law, a field increasingly emancipating itself from Public International Law scholarship and evolving into a fully-fledged academic discipline in its own right. With the yearbook, the editors and publisher intend to make a significant contribution to the development of this "new" discipline and provide an international reference source of the highest possible quality. The EYIEL covers all areas of IEL, in particular WTO Law, External Trade Law for major trading countries, important Regional Economic Integration agreements, International Competition Law, International Investment Regulation, International Monetary Law, International Intellectual Property Protection and International Tax Law. In addition to the regular annual volumes, EYIEL Special Issues routinely address specific current topics in International Economic Law.

Mariela de Amstalden • Niall Moran •
Henok Asmelash
Editors

International Economic Law

New Approaches and Issues

Springer

Editors
Mariela de Amstalden
Exeter Law School
University of Exeter
Exeter, UK

Niall Moran
School of Law and Government
Dublin City University
Dublin, Ireland

Henok Asmelash
Birmingham Law School
University of Birmingham
Birmingham, UK

ISSN 2364-8392 ISSN 2364-8406 (electronic)
European Yearbook of International Economic Law
ISSN 2510-6880 ISSN 2510-6899 (electronic)
Special Issue
ISBN 978-3-031-41995-9 ISBN 978-3-031-41996-6 (eBook)
https://doi.org/10.1007/978-3-031-41996-6

This Springer imprint is published by the registered company Springer Nature Switzerland AG
The registered company address is: Gewerbestrasse 11, 6330 Cham, Switzerland

Paper in this product is recyclable.

Foreword

One of the most impactful events organized each year under the aegis of the Society of International Economic Law (SIEL) is the International Conference of the Postgraduate and Early Career Professionals/Academics Network. The PEPA Network, as it is commonly referred to, aims at fostering collaboration and mentoring opportunities for emerging academics and professionals in the field of international economic law and it has been very successful in doing so. In June 2022, the PEPA Network organized its 11th International Conference at the University of Birmingham Law School. Over 50 young academics and professionals participated in the Conference. This book on *International Economic Law: New Approaches and Issues* contains 14 of the best papers presented at the Conference.

As befits young academics and professionals, who will be tomorrow's leaders in the field of international economic law, the authors of the selected papers explore emerging issues and problems in international economic law as well as new approaches to issues and problems which have been haunting us since long. Reflecting the diversity of the SIEL membership, the authors of the selected papers come from all corners of the world and present in their papers a wide range of views.

The papers included in this book are organized in four parts, which each look at issues and problems in international economic law from a different angle. After an insightful introduction to the book by its editors and main organizers of the Conference, Mariela de Amstalden of the University of Exeter, Henok Asmelash of the University of Birmingham and Niall Moran of the Dublin City University, the first part of the book deals with new approaches to international economic law and addresses topics such as the depoliticization of investment disputes; the OECD Good Regulatory Practices' Toolbox; the role of multilateral institutions in the perpetuation of climate breakdown and vulnerability; and a Third World approach to international law (TWAIL) in reforming the international investment regime. The second part of the book, which deals with technology and innovation in international economic law, includes papers on 3D printing and the rules of origin conundrum; digital cultural goods and services and international trade law; and e-commerce provisions in regional trade agreements and their impact on African MSMEs. The third part of the book deals with public policy and international economic law. This part contains papers on geopolitics, geo-economics, and international economic law; the problematic interpretation of the MFN treatment provision in an agreement on the avoidance of double taxation and the prevention of fiscal evasion; the proposed anti-coercion instrument of the European Union; and the role of the principle of autonomy of EU law as an EU public policy exception in the context of investor-State dispute settlement. The fourth and last part of the book deals with international trade regulation and includes papers on provisions on biodiversity in EU free trade agreements; energy transit under GATT Article V and energy trade dispute resolution in the WTO; and special and differential treatment in WTO law and EU economic partnership agreements.

While I found myself in (occasionally strong but always wholesome) disagreement with the authors of some of the papers included in this book, all of the papers have brought me new insights and much food for thought. I therefore wholeheartedly congratulate the editors and the authors on this book, which I strongly recommend to known and aspiring experts in international economic law.

World Trade Institute, University of Bern, Bern, Switzerland

Peter Van den Bossche

Preface

The Society of International Economic Law (SIEL) hosted its 11th International Conference of the Postgraduate and Early Career Professionals/Academics of the Society of International Economic Law (PEPA/SIEL) at the University of Birmingham, Birmingham Law School from 8–10 June 2022. Of the 12 panels and over 50 speakers, 14 of the best papers presented have been selected to form this edited collection. This volume considers novel emerging issues in international economic law (IEL), as well as new methodological approaches to more familiar topics. It brings together a diverse range of contributors from five continents, with invaluable perspectives from all geographic areas.

This volume aims to delve deeply into some of the most challenging emerging areas in international economic law. These questions are approached from an interdisciplinary perspective, bringing together legal, economic, and political analysis. It is aimed at academics and practitioners at all stages of their careers. Many of the areas considered in this volume are either entirely new or are being returned to after decades of dormancy. It is our hope that these contributions will bring fresh insight into these new and old areas of IEL.

We consider diversity and inclusivity foundational values in IEL. The richness of original and significant ideas presented throughout this volume present us with an opportunity to appreciate different facets in originality and rigour in legal academic writing, further highlighting the wealth of methodological and stylistic preferences of emerging legal scholars in IEL.

The conference convenors received a considerable number of abstracts that underwent a double-blind peer-review process. Forty emerging IEL scholars were selected to present their papers, receiving feedback from senior members of the SIEL community and beyond. The discussions were lively, stimulating, and enriching, leading the conference conveners to propose the compilation of selected papers into a published book.

As a result, this volume is divided into four parts. Part I focuses on new approaches to IEL. Chapter 1 starts the conversation about the dominant depoliticization narrative in contemporary investor-state dispute settlement system (ISDS), examining the shift from early gunboat diplomacy to present economic statecraft through a procedural justice lens. Chapter 2 posits that effective policy-making in nation-states necessarily requires an awareness and assessment of transnational legal processes, best achieved by implementing good regulatory practices (GRP), as exemplified by Brazil. Chapter 3 critically examines whether multilateral institutions play a role in the exacerbation of inequality and anthropogenic climate breakdown by encouraging extractive activity and industrial production, with the effect of perpetuating vulnerabilities in Third World peoples. Chapter 4 follows on by drawing from Third World Approaches to International Law (TWAIL) to propose reform of international investment regimes by addressing inequities and biases against newly emergent nation-states.

Technology and innovation in IEL is examined in the contributions included in Part II. Contributions focus on potential innovations in trade rules relating to 3D printing and video games, while a third chapter considers the potential impact e-commerce provisions may have for African MSMEs. A common thread running through the papers is the examination of the role of Regional Trade Agreements: Chap. 5 considers preferential rules of origin and how firms may strategically locate 3D files in the context of 3D printing; Chap. 6 looks at digital trade rules, innovations under recent RTAs, and diverging approaches in the USA, EU, and China; Chap. 7 examines the e-commerce chapters of four major recent trade agreements and how they will impact WTO and AfCFTA negotiations, as well as African MSMEs more generally.

Public policy and IEL is the focus of Part III. A variety of topics are covered including the use of policy instruments to achieve geopolitical goals, the EU's Anti-Coercion Instrument, the autonomy of EU law in ISDS, and MFN provisions in taxation treaties. The first two chapters delve into the increasing shift towards unilateral measures in international economic law. Chapter 8 examines the pursuit of geopolitical interests through trade and investment policies and the effects of this on international economic law; this sets the stage for Chap. 9 which examines how the EU can square its proposed Anti-Coercion Instrument with its multilateralist DNA, and the legality of this instrument under WTO rules. The second two chapters of Part III concern the interplay between domestic and international law in relation to the interpretation of international treaties. Chapter 10 considers public policy exceptions in international investment law, the principle of autonomy of EU law, and whether a harmonious interpretation of this principle can be arrived at in EU law and international law. The author puts forth the view that the autonomy of EU law is undermined where the EU is unable to operate according to its constitutional structure under general exceptions in investment protection agreements. Chapter 11 considers the interpretation of the MFN clause under the Dutch-India Double Taxation Avoidance Agreement. This chapter focuses on the aftermath of the *Concentrix* ruling before the Delhi High Court and the questions it raises for those drafting and interpreting international treaties.

Finally, Part IV focuses on emerging issues and trends in international trade regulation. Chapter 12 considers the regulation of energy transit in the multilateral trading system. It assesses the adequacy of extant trade rules that govern transit in facilitating the transit of energy products and the appropriateness of the WTO dispute settlement system to resolve energy transit-related disputes. Chapter 13 examines the interplay between trade and environment through the prism of biodiversity-related provisions in 'new generation' FTAs. Focusing on recent EU trade agreements, the chapter investigates the impact of international trade on biodiversity and the role of sustainability chapters contained in such agreements to counteract the adverse effects of trade on biodiversity. The final chapter of Part IV, Chap. 14, uses the concept of 'community interest' to explore the emergence and operation of special and differential treatment regimes in multilateral and plurilateral trade agreements. It offers valuable insights into whether and how community interest informs the special and differential treatment regimes of the WTO and EU-African Economic Partnership Agreements (EPAs).

The editors wish to convey their heartfelt gratitude to all those who contributed to the success of the Conference and this volume. We would like to extend our sincere thanks to Prof. Peter Van den Bossche for his Closing Remarks during the Conference and for generously providing a Preface to this edited collection, as well as the numerous IEL scholars who reviewed abstracts and participated as discussants at the Conference. Their comments and feedback played a crucial role in shaping the chapters presented in this volume. We are also grateful to the Society of International Economic Law (SIEL) and the University of Birmingham Law School for their unwavering support in organizing and hosting the Conference. The editors would also like to express their appreciation to all the conference participants who attended and contributed to the event. The hybrid format of the Conference allowed for a diverse range of participants from around the world to attend and contribute to the conference. Finally, we thank Eliana Baey for outstanding research assistance during the compilation and editing of this volume. The rich insights presented through a variety of methodological lenses in this volume reflect the vibrant and dynamic nature of IEL as a distinct field of law, while celebrating the diversity in scholarship, in content and form, from the expanding IEL community. In a spirit of inclusiveness, it is our hope that this collection will serve as a platform to showcase emerging IEL talent that is as diverse as the discipline itself, to continue constructive dialogue in this ever-changing area of law.

Exeter, UK — Mariela de Amstalden
Dublin, Ireland — Niall Moran
Birmingham, UK — Henok Asmelash

Contents

Contributors

Christiana Agbo-Ejeh Baze University, Faculty of Law, Abuja, Nigeria

Alexandros Bakos City Law School, City, University of London, London, UK

Magali Favaretto Prieto Fernandes Fundação Getúlio Vargas (FGV), São Paulo School of Law, Sao Paulo, Brazil

Cornelia Furculita Speyer, Germany

Sean Madden Birmingham Law School, University of Birmingham, Birmingham, UK

Gautam Mohanty Kozminski University and Jindal Global Law School, Warsaw, Poland

Justine Muller Arles, France

Martin Luther Munu Maastricht University, Institute for Globalisation and International Regulation (IGIR), Faculty of Law, Maastricht, The Netherlands

Olufunmilola Olabode Olabisi Onabanjo University, Ago-Iwoye, Nigeria

Mukesh Rawat Hemvati Nandan Bahuguna Garhwal University, Garhwal, Uttarakhand, India

Saurabh Sharma Rajiv Gandhi National University of Law, Patiala, Punjab, India

Trajan Shipley Brussels, Belgium

Michail Skouzes I. Vassardanis & Partners Law Firm, Patras, Greece

Diana Elizabeth Wade Department of Legal Studies, Università Commerciale Luigi Bocconi, Milano, Italy

Najibullah Zamani Radboud University, Nijmegen, The Netherlands

Siqi Zhao KU Leuven, Leuven, Belgium

Abbreviations

3D/3DP	Three-dimensional printing
AB	Appellate Body
ACI	Anti-Coercion Instrument
ACP	African, Caribbean and Pacific
AfCFTA	African Continental Free Trade Area
AGOA	Africa Growth and Opportunity Act
AIIB	Asian Infrastructure Investment Bank
ASEAN	Association of Southeast Asian Nations
ATEC	US-Brazil Agreement on Trade and Economic Cooperation
BEPS	Base Erosion and Profit Shifting
BIT	Bilateral Investment Treaty
BRICS	Brazil, Russia, India, China and South Africa bloc
BUSBC	Brazil-US Business Council
BWI	Bretton Woods Institutions
CAD	Computer-aided design
CAMEX	Brazilian Foreign Trade Board
CBA	Cost–Benefit Analysis
CBDT	Central Board of Direct Taxes
CD	Compact Disc
CETA	Comprehensive Economic and Trade Agreement
CITES	Convention on International Trade in Endangered Species of Wild Fauna and Flora
CJEU	Court of Justice of the EU
CMAP	Brazil's Council for the Monitoring and Evaluation of Public Policies
CNI	Brazil's National Confederation of Industry
CO2	Carbon Dioxide
CPC	Central Provisional Classification
CPTPP	Comprehensive and Progressive Agreement for Trans-Pacific Partnership
CTH	Change of Tariff Heading

DoC	Brazil Department of Commerce
DSB	Dispute Settlement Body
DSU	Dispute Settlement Understanding
DTAA	Double Taxation Avoidance Agreement
DVD	Digital Video Disc
EC	European Commission
EC Treaty	The Treaty establishing the European Community
ECOWAS	Economic Community of West African States
ECT	Energy Charter Treaty
EDF	European Development Fund
EP	European Parliament
EU	European Union
FET	Fair and Equitable Treatment
FDI	Foreign Direct Investment
GATS	General Agreement on Trade in Services
GATT	General Agreement on Tariffs and Trade
GE	General Electric
GHG	Greenhouse Gas
GRP	Good regulatory practices
GSP	Generalized System of Preferences
GTI	Inter-Ministerial Working Group (Brazil)
GVC	Global Value Chain
HS	Harmonized System
IBA	International Bar Association
ICSID	International Centre for Settlement of Investment Disputes
IEL	International Economic Law
IIR	International Investment Regime
ILC	International Law Commission
IMF	International Monetary Fund
INTA	European Parliament's Committee on International Trade
IoT	Internet of Things
IPR	Intellectual Property Right
IRA	Independent Regulatory Agencies
IRC	International Regulatory Cooperation
iREG	Indicators of Regulatory Policy and Governance
ISDS	Investor-state dispute settlement
ITA	International Trade Association (Brazil)
IUU	Illegal, Unreported, and Unregulated
JSI	Joint Statements Initiative
MDIC	Ministry of Development, Industry and Foreign Trade (Brazil)
MFN	Most-Favoured-Nation
MLI	Multilateral Convention to Implement Tax Treaty Related Measures to Prevent Base Erosion and Profit Shifting
MLI	Multilateral Institutions

MoU	Memorandum of Understanding
MSME	Micro, Small and Medium Enterprise
NAFTA	North American Free Trade Agreement
NFT	Non-fungible Token
NIEO	New International Economic Order
NPI	Net positive Impact
NPM	New Public Management
NT	National Treatment (WTO)
NYC	New York Convention for the Recognition and Enforcement of Arbitral Awards
OECD	Organisation for Economic Co-operation and Development
OIRA	Office of Information and Regulatory Affairs (Brazil)
PDR	People's Democratic Republic (Lao)
PEPA	Postgraduate and Early Career Professionals/Academics (SIEL)
PMR	Product Market Regulation
PRO-REG	Program for Strengthening the Institutional Capacity for Regulatory Management (Brazil)
PTA	Preferential Trade Agreement
PUMA	Public Management Committee
R&D	Research and development
RCEP	Regional Comprehensive Economic Partnership
RIA	Regulatory Impact Assessment
RoO	Rules of Origin
RTA	Regional Trade Agreement
SAP	Structural Adjustment Programme
SDG	Sustainable Development Goal
SDT	Special and Differential Treatment
SIEL	Society of International Economic Law
SME	Small and medium-sized enterprises
SOE	State-Owned Enterprise
TCA	UK-EU Trade and Cooperation Agreement
TEU	Treaty on European Union
TFEU	Treaty on the Functioning of the European Union
TiSA	Trade in Services Agreement
TNC	Transnational Corporations
TPP	Trans-Pacific Partnership
TSD	Trade and Sustainable Development
TTIP	Transatlantic Trade and Investment Partnership
TV	Television
TWAIL	Third World Approaches to International Law
UNCITRAL	United Nations Commission on International Trade Law
UNCLOS	United Nations Convention on the Law of the Sea
UNCTAD	United Nations Conference on Trade and Development
UNECA	United Nations Economic Commission for Africa

UNESCO	United Nations Educational, Scientific and Cultural Organisation
US	United States
USMCA	United States Mexico Canada Agreement
USTR	United States Trade Representative
VCLT	Vienna Convention on the Law of Treaties
WB	World Bank
WCO	World Customs Organization
WTO	World Trade Organization

Part I
New Approaches to International Economic Law

The Depoliticization of Investment Disputes: How Deep Does the "Rabbit Hole" Go?

Gautam Mohanty and Alexandros Bakos

Contents

Abstract Despite the original aim of investor-state dispute settlement (ISDS) to establish a neutral and non-political forum for resolving disputes, recent scholarly debates demonstrate an increasing level of politicisation. However, as this article demonstrates, complete depoliticisation was never either the intention of ISDS or a realistic possibility—at least substantially. Investment protection standards, for example, serve as safeguards against political risk. In this context, the article demonstrates that it is the adherence to procedural international rule of law elements that can actually counter the growing politicisation and maintain ISDS's neutrality. The first section explores the desirability of depoliticisation in ISDS, distinguishing between procedural and substantive aspects. The second section delves into the parameters of procedural depoliticisation, highlighting the tools employed and identifying instances of its strongest implementation. The paper concludes by explaining the impracticality and undesirability of achieving complete substantive depoliticisation.

The authors are grateful to Prof. David Collins, Prof. Yuka Fukunaga, Prof. Markus Wagner, Dr. Mariela de Amstalden, and Dr. Lijun Zhao for their comments on this paper. The authors are also grateful to Mr. Arnav Doshi for his editorial assistance. All the mistakes are, of course, the authors' own.

G. Mohanty (✉)
Kozminski University and Jindal Global Law School, Warsaw, Poland

A. Bakos
City Law School, City, University of London, London, UK

M. de Amstalden et al. (eds.), *International Economic Law*, Special Issue,
https://doi.org/10.1007/978-3-031-41996-6_1

1 Introduction

One of the founding narratives of international investment law and arbitration is the depoliticization of the contemporary investor-state dispute settlement system (ISDS).[1] Essentially, investors who are aggrieved by host state measures (or the lack of such measures in certain cases) would benefit from a third-party dispute settlement mechanism, normally *via* arbitration (pinning that investor, as a claimant, against the host state, as a respondent).[2]

From a theoretical standpoint, this arbitration mechanism supposedly removes the influence of politics from the disputes between the foreign investor and the host state of the investment.[3] From a historical perspective, the transition to a "(quasi-) judicialized" form of settlement of disputes between foreign investors and host states was almost revolutionary (although explainable in the context of multilateral reforms in the twentieth century, especially since the end of the Cold War).[4] This is why commentators argue that the mechanism is a depoliticized one,[5] seeing how initially investor-state disputes would be settled politically in most cases.

Traditionally, the foreign investor would be under the protection of its home state.[6] If the host state adopted measures that aggrieved that investor, there was a risk that the home state of the foreign investor would intervene.[7] In fact, intervention by the home state would normally be the only way in which an aggrieved investor could safeguard its interests, once a conflict with the host state of the investment occurred. This intervention would sometimes be diplomatic,[8] and sometimes even forceful or threatening the use of force.[9] It was one of the most common examples of one state exercising its political might and influence over another—in order for the former to allegedly protect the interests of its nationals.[10]

---

[1]On depoliticization, as one of the founding narratives of international investment law and arbitration, *see*, generally, Shihata (1986), pp. 1–25, Kozawa (2002) and Bjorklund (2010), p. 211, Paparinskis (2012), p. 271, Titi (2015), p. 261, Kriebaum (2019), pp. 23–40, Mehranavar and Johnson (2022), p. 264.

[2]Mehranavar and Johnson (2022), pp. 265–266.

[3]Ibid.

[4]Cutler (2018), pp. 73–78; Alter et al. (2019), pp. 453, 458; Basedow (2022), p. 1374; Voeten (2022), p. 14.; Kozawa (2002), p. 828.

[5]*Supra* n 1.

[6]Cutler (2018), pp. 73–74.

[7]Kriebaum (2019), pp. 24–25.

[8]Diplomatic protection meant that the home state could protect its nationals since their property were also part of the former's. For more details, *see* Dolzer et al. (2022), p. 2. *See* also Mavrommatis Palestine Concessions (Greece v. U.K.), 1924 P.C.I.J. (ser. B) No. 3 (Aug. 30), p. 12.

[9]Dolzer et al. (2022), p. 2. *See* also, Bjorklund (2010), p. 239.

[10]Shihata (1986), p. 19.

This would come to be known as *gunboat diplomacy*, [11] something which clearly made it very difficult for smaller (or weaker), capital-importing (or which held resources desirable to foreign powers), states to exercise their sovereignty when this exercise of sovereignty conflicted with the economic interests of foreign investors, and/or those of their home state. Perhaps one of the most relevant examples refers to the Opium Wars occurring in the nineteenth century, where Great Britain used force against China in order to, among others, engage in opium-based trade activities from Chinese territory (and while investment and trade are distinct, great power politics such as this dominated international relations in that period, irrespective of whether commercial activities involved investment or trade).[12]

In present-day international economic affairs, outright force-based triggers to commerce might not constitute the norm anymore. However, what in the past stood for *gunboat diplomacy* got replaced by *economic statecraft* or "*economic gunboat diplomacy*", especially with state-controlled enterprises investing in foreign territories.[13]

Seen in this light, politicization has over the time become synonymous with a host of negative aspects revolving around ISDS and foreign investor-state relations, in general. The negative aspects, *inter alia*, include the geopolitical influence exercised by the home state of the foreign investor, unpredictability of outcome for the investor (the investor would never know how its dispute would be settled in a specific context, owing to its lack of control over the politically-charged issues), decrease in investment that would further prevent development (it is well-known that political risk is one of the major obstacles to foreign investment).[14]

All these effects of politicization run counter to the major premises of, and promises that, ISDS set out to deliver. For starters, ISDS was conceived as a neutral, objective, and predictable dispute resolution system.[15] Furthermore, removing (great power) politics—to the extent possible, at least from an institutional point of view when it comes to settlement of disputes—from the ambit of ISDS meant that the investor, the actor around which the whole mechanism was built, takes centre stage.[16]

But this goes far beyond the pure interests of the investor. It actually enables economic globalisation—with private initiative percolating through the entire investor-state relation,[17] even at the eventual dispute settlement stage (further enabling private initiative by raising the individual to an almost independent actor

[11] Dautaj (2021), pp. 288–293.

[12] Philips (2011), p. 20.

[13] *See*, generally, Duanmu (2014), p. 1044. *See*, also Boute (2019), p. 383, especially at pp. 398–415.

[14] *See* Kriebaum (2019), pp. 24–30.

[15] Vicuña (2010), p. 67. *See*, also Peters (2016), p. 291.

[16] Idem, pp. 63–64.

[17] Slobodian (2018), pp. 93, 129–131.

in international relations,[18] eventually equipping him with a remedy to obtain redress to alleged wrongs of the host state).

Against this backdrop, this chapter sets out to explore the depoliticization narrative, while also demonstrating that ISDS has never completely removed politics from the system. As already mentioned, depoliticization has been seen as an enabler of ISDS and of its success so far. Basically, removing the political influence (either from the home state, or from the host state, mostly) enables judicialization of investment disputes.[19]

In other words, international investment arbitration can exist precisely because it is an alternative to the political settlement of disputes. The latter characterises great power politics and not an independent, neutral, and objective dispute settlement mechanism. While far from perfect, ISDS offers a solution to the immediate interests, and fears, of the investors. And even acts as a key in the multilateral, rules-based, economic order characterising the twentieth century (and still—at least somewhat—characterising present times).[20]

However, we suggest a different understanding of this depoliticization narrative. The article proposes that we should conceive of depoliticization as existing, and manifesting itself, in two different realms. One realm characterizes the procedural and, to a certain extent, institutional aspect of ISDS (procedural rules and guarantees, such as those ensuring independence and impartiality of arbitrators, the dispute settlement mechanism etc.). Here, depoliticization should be understood as the decluttering of political interference of host, and home, state institutions within the governance of arbitral proceedings.

When it comes to the substantive sphere (which characterises the merits of the dispute, including the actual relationship between the investor and the host state), this chapter will go beyond and demonstrate that not only has depoliticization never completely occurred in this realm, but that a certain degree of politicization is, actually, beneficial to ISDS (or to international investment law, in general).

Other authors have expressly acknowledged the existence of politicisation existing in investor-state relations to a certain extent.[21] But this article goes further and brings forward a model to actually explain why depoliticisation should be conceived as having occurred to different degrees based on the realms in which it manifested itself—procedurally, or substantively. Moreover, we also apply John Rawls' theory concerning procedural justice to explain how procedural depoliticization (establishing the right procedures), as a *systemic good*, is enough to address most concerns existing with regards to the fairness of the final outcome in what

[18] Peters (2016), *supra* n 18, pp. 289–293. However, for the theory that any procedural rights accruing to an individual in international (investment) law are a by-product of rights that are originally those of the home state's (also known as "*delegated rights*"), *see* Paparinskis (2013), pp. 625, 627.

[19] *Supra* n 4.

[20] *Cf.* Slobodian (2018).

[21] For instance, *see* generally, Titi (2015), p. 261; Mehranavar and Johnson (2022), pp. 293, 296, 299.

would otherwise be an unpredictable, politically-charged, environment in which the foreign investor would find itself.

As such, the analysis proceeds as follows. Section 2 explores the depoliticization narrative in ISDS and how it has become widely accepted that depoliticization is desirable. This part also introduces a distinction between procedural depoliticization and substantive depoliticization. Here, we argue that international investment arbitration, in its procedural (and institutional) dimension, indeed leads to depoliticization. But this is only a partial form of depoliticization, when looking at investor-state relations globally. Substantively, however, as already mentioned, investment disputes have never been completely depoliticized.

Thus, we posit a paradigm shift that avoids evaluating investment disputes in terms of being politicized or not. We suggest, instead, a two-pronged approach that assumes (1) a (almost) complete procedural, and institutional, depoliticization and (2) a partial substantive depoliticization. That means that the questions and mechanisms used to assess those two dimensions will, of course, be different. More specifically, while procedurally one should expect depoliticization, substantively one should examine it in terms of degrees of (de)politicization, with a degree of political influence when it comes to the substance of investment disputes being acceptable—and also realistic.

Section 3, then, explores in depth the parameters of procedural depoliticization, in order to highlight tools used for this purpose, and to clarify where ISDS has attained the strongest form of depoliticization. Finally, Sect. 4 explains how, substantively, there has never been a complete depoliticization—and why that is not even desirable and also not practicable.

2 What Do We Talk About When We Talk About "Depoliticization"?

Perhaps the strongest catalyst to depoliticization was the negotiation and ratification of the Convention on the Settlement of Investment Disputes between States and Nationals of Other States (ICSID Convention) in 1965, [22] which has acquired an almost *quasi-constitutional-like* status in international investment law.[23] Almost all treaties providing for ISDS refer to ICSID as a go-to forum for the settlement of

[22] Convention on the Settlement of Investment Disputes Between States and Nationals of Other States (International Centre for Settlement of Investment Disputes [ICSID]) 575 UNTS 159.

[23] If one conceives of the ICSID dispute settlement system (seen together with the substantive provisions of applicable investment treaties in any given dispute), then functionally this framework replaced domestic, and even constitutional, rules that foreign investors distrusted when it came to committing their capital to the territory of the host state. Seen in this light, the ICSID Convention holds central stage in this *de facto* quasi-constitutional framework. *See*, for instance, Kleinheisterkamp (2015), p. 811.

investment disputes.[24] A bare reading of the *travaux préparatoires* of the ICSID Convention highlights that the Convention was introduced with an aim to insulate "*disputes from the realm of politics and diplomacy*".[25] This can be seen as a form of institutional and procedural depoliticisation.

Notably, the ICSID Convention only focused on the institutional and procedural aspects of dispute settlement. Nonetheless, it represented great progress. It is believed that investment protection treaties, containing substantial standards of protection, complement the procedural role played by international instruments such as the ICSID Convention in terms of depoliticization of investment disputes.[26] However, this complementarity is not necessarily as straightforward as it may seem at first, as will be further illustrated in Parts II and III of this article.

The term "*depoliticization*" in the context of investment arbitration is often understood as "autonomous",[27] "immune from political considerations",[28] and "detaching politics from law".[29] Aron Broches, the principal architect of the ICSID Convention, has stressed that the Convention aimed to "*remove investment disputes from the intergovernmental political sphere*"[30] and that the Convention offered "*a means of settling directly, on the legal plane, investment disputes between the State and foreign investor, which would insulate such disputes from the realm of politics and diplomacy.*"[31]

Another widespread understanding of "*depoliticization*" is the focus on the removal of the home state's political influence in the affairs between the host state and the foreign investor.[32] This was ensured by removing the possibility of the home state in exercising diplomatic protection as regards the foreign investor.[33] The transition from diplomatic protection to investment arbitration has invariably ensured the removal of two major disadvantages of diplomatic protection:

---

[24] Dolzer et al. (2022), p. 12.

[25] Convention on the Settlement of Investment Disputes between States and Nationals of Other States, Documents Concerning the Origin and the Formulation of the Convention (History of the Convention), Vol. II, Part 1, 464.

[26] Dolzer et al. (2022), p. 30.

[27] Ginsburg (2013), p. 484.

[28] Ibid.

[29] Odumosu (2007), pp. 271–272.

[30] Broches (1995), p. 163.

[31] International Centre for Settlement of Investment Disputes, History of the ICSID Convention. Documents Concerning the Origin and Formulation of the Convention on the Settlement of Investment Disputes between States and Nationals of Other States, Vol II-1 (ICSID Publication 1968), p. 242 & p. 303, Available at: https://icsid.worldbank.org/sites/default/files/publications/History%20of%20the%20ICSID%20Convention/History%20of%20ICSID%20Convention%20-%20VOLUME%20II-1.pdf.

[32] Dolzer et al. (2022), p. 30.

[33] *See* Kriebaum (2019), p. 25.

(1) removal of the discretion of the home state to pursue the claim,[34] and (2) removal of the obligation addressed to the investor to exhaust all local remedies before diplomatic protection can be pursued.[35]

However, not even in this case was there a complete removal of that political influence. For example, Article 27 of the ICSID Convention, which prohibits the diplomatic espousal of the investor's claim by its home state, removes this barrier if, following an eventual award, the host state fails to comply with it.[36] In a way, this may be technically seen as an instance of repoliticization. After all, it allows the home state to intervene in the dispute, post-award, through diplomatic espousal of the investor's claim.

However, from an effectiveness and rule of law perspective, the investor's potential lack of recourse to any mechanism that could safeguard its interests and ensure the payment of a legally rendered arbitral award makes it necessary for this type of intervention by the home state. Nonetheless, Article 27 only applies if there is a failure to enforce an ICSID Award under the normal procedure provided by Article 54 of the Convention. This provision encompasses the obligation on any state party to the treaty to enforce an ICSID Award as if such an arbitral award was a final domestic judgment of that state's own courts.[37]

Paradoxically, this form of repoliticization, tolerated through Article 27 of the ICSID Convention, is necessary to ensure that the legal-arbitral mechanism which was introduced to replace the influence of great power politics functions smoothly—essentially, allowing recourse to diplomatic protection as an alternative to traditional ways of enforcement and also seen as a recourse against the violation of the ICSID Convention by the state which failed to comply with the award.[38] Repoliticization is permitted so that, in the future, *too much politicization* is prevented.[39]

---

[34] Barcelona Traction, Light and Power Company Limited (Belgium v. Spain), Judgment, I.C.J. Reports 1970, para. 79.

[35] Article 14, para. 1 of the International Law Commission (2006), Draft Articles on Diplomatic Protection, Official Records of the General Assembly, Sixty-first Session, Supplement No. 10, UN Doc A/61/10.

[36] Article 27 of the ICSID Convention:

(1) No Contracting State shall give diplomatic protection, or bring an international claim, in respect of a dispute which one of its nationals and another Contracting State shall have consented to submit or shall have submitted to arbitration under this Convention, unless such other Contracting State shall have failed to abide by and comply with the award rendered in such dispute.
(2) Diplomatic protection, for the purposes of paragraph (1), shall not include informal diplomatic exchanges for the sole purpose of facilitating a settlement of the dispute.

[37] Reinisch (2022), pp. 1498–1506

[38] Malintoppi (2022), pp. 649–650.

[39] More specifically, as mentioned earlier, diplomatic protection here serves as an alternative to enforcement. If proper enforcement of an eventual award cannot be pursued in this situation, then diplomatic protection becomes the only solution. Removing it even in this case may have negative systemic consequences, rendering the arbitration mechanism ineffective. Long term, this creates the risk that the users and the stakeholders of ISDS will perceive it as unsuitable for its purpose and

Furthermore, rules governing non-ICSID arbitration proceedings (and eventual recognition and enforcement proceedings) seem to not contain any prohibition concerning diplomatic protection at all—thus making it even more likely that a complete depoliticization in this regard has never occurred.

However, the influence of politics in investment arbitration is not limited to the role that the home state of the investor plays whenever a dispute between the host state and the foreign investor occurs. In fact, such a skewed view risks perpetuating a myth that only serves to create an illusion: that the influence of politics is limited only to the relations between the home state and the host state. Relations between the foreign investor and the host state can also have a political element, just like those between the host state and the home state.

After all, politicization is, in a way, a form of decision-making that is taken by a political (collective in nature) body, including the government (administration).[40] Seen in this light, investor-state relations always have the potential to be politicized, as they are based mainly on the investor's relations with the public administration.

It is also pertinent to add that Ibrahim Shihata, former Secretary-General of ICSID, wrote one of the most famous articles on the depoliticization of investment disputes through ICSID, wherein he admitted that one of the aims of ICSID was to "depoliticize" the settlement of investment disputes. Importantly, he observed that.

> [t]he International Centre for the Settlement of Investment Disputes (. . .) was created by the Convention on the Settlement of Investment Disputes (. . .) to provide a forum for conflict resolution in a framework which carefully balances the interests and requirements of all the parties involved, and attempts in particular to 'depoliticize' the settlement of investment disputes.[41]

Nowhere was it mentioned that this attempt at depoliticization was limited only to removing the political influence of the home state in the dispute.[42] Of course, if it is the *settlement* of investment disputes that is to be depoliticized, then what Shihata (and, more to the point, ICSID's drafters) had in mind must have been the arbitral process itself. *That* should be depoliticized.

However, Shihata also mentions that the aim is the depoliticization of *disputes*.[43] It is doubtful if this has been achieved in its entirety, especially if one looks at an investment dispute from the point of view of the very facts that occur between the investor and the host state on the latter's territory—all the way to the enforcement of an eventual award.

---

would, eventually, resort to what existed before it—settlement of disputes *via* political means. Plainly speaking, less politicisation at this point, within a controlled (quasi-)judicialized framework, prevents the chaos and unpredictability of a complete influence of politics on the settlement of disputes between foreign investors and host states.

[40] Landwehr (2017), p. 51.

[41] Shihata (1986), p. 4.

[42] Ibid.

[43] Ibid, p. 25.

For instance, one commentator refers to sovereign immunity as a barrier to the enforcement of investor-state arbitral awards.[44] In this context, she refers to *depoliticization* not simply as an attempt to remove the great powers politics that may arise between the home state of the investor and the host state.[45] But also to "*rein in untoward political pressures stemming both from states hosting investment and from the investors' home states*" (both through the drafting of the ICSID Convention, but also through the vast network of investment protection treaties).[46]

Nonetheless, while she does admit that ISDS has never been completely depoliticized, there is no detailed explanation about the degree to which this depoliticization actually occurred.[47] There is mention, however, of the fact that doing away with diplomatic protection is only one side of the story.[48] Even the practice of major players in investment arbitration, such as the United States of America, seems to confirm that ISDS was concerned with a general depoliticization of the dispute settlement system and not simply an avoidance of diplomatic espousal that could lead to great power politics.[49]

It is also interesting to note that most of the literature on depoliticization of investment disputes focuses on how this benefits the investor and/or how this avoids great power politics/conflicts (occasionally, commentators might also focus on the benefits to the system itself).[50] However, a perusal of the existing literature indicates that there is little to no focus on how arbitral tribunals, for example, after assuming jurisdiction over certain investment disputes are actually entering into the political realm,[51] and whether this constitutes a politicization of the arbitral process itself[52]—

[44] *See* generally, Bjorklund (2010).

[45] For such a view, *see* for example, Kriebaum (2019), pp. 24–27. For a different, broader view, of depoliticization, *see* generally, Titi (2015), pp. 261–288.

[46] Bjorklund (2010), p. 214 (fn 20).

[47] Ibid.

[48] Ibid, p. 214 (fn 20), p. 240.

[49] *Republic of Ecuador v. United States of America*, UNCITRAL, PCA Case No 2012-5, Award (29 September 2012), para. 201.

[50] For instance, *see* Shihata (1986), p. 31; Kriebaum (2019), pp. 26–30; Mehranavar and Johnson (2022), pp. 265–266.

[51] This could be the case in most instances where a tribunal questions policy decisions of home states, especially those in areas of high importance to the home state (e.g. health matters, macroeconomic decisions, security and military aspects) [*see* Titi (2015), p. 265]. As such, tribunals have developed a doctrine of restraint, or deference, but there seems to be no consensus as to the exact scope of this doctrine (*see*, generally Henckels (2015)). Moreover, it is not only in investment arbitration that tribunals assuming jurisdiction over certain disputes might antagonise states which accepted the jurisdiction of an international court or tribunal. The European Court of Human Rights has faced this issue with the United Kingdom, for example [*see*, generally, Graham (2020)].

[52] One of the difficulties with limiting the involvement of an international (arbitral) tribunal with certain types of disputes because they might turn out to be too politically charged is that it is exceedingly onerous to measure, in the abstract, which dispute (or which state measure leading to a dispute) is *too* politically charged and goes beyond any acceptable threshold. After all, what has a major political impact in a specific situation depends on the factual nexus and also on the context of

something that would run contrary to the interests of host states and would raise questions of legitimacy of arbitral decision-making.[53]

In this case, depoliticization does not only mean (*quasi-)judicialization* of investment disputes.[54] Ideally, this would also mean the existence of certain limits to this *judicialization*; with arbitral tribunals refraining from acting in a certain way if, and when, certain disputes are brought to their consideration.

Unfortunately, as already pointed out,[55] it is difficult to clearly separate, substantively, the types of disputes that exceed the "*politicization threshold*" and those over which an arbitral tribunal should assume jurisdiction. Thus, the best way to ensure desired, and realistic, levels of depoliticization, as it will be shown below, [56] is through guarantees of procedural fairness, such as impartiality, independence, and a clear adherence to rule of law principles in terms of the dispute resolution process. This could partially explain why, within UNCITRAL's Working Group III,[57] discussions concerning the reform of ISDS mostly revolve around procedural issues (notwithstanding the difficulty in reaching consensus on substantive ones).[58]

---

the dispute (both historical and geographical). To give an example, a dispute concerning sovereignty over maritime features in international law might seem to demand that the adjudicator conducts a technical, clear, and predictable exercise in most cases. However, when it comes, for instance, to the South China Sea and Chinese demands, this is often seen as the highest form of lawfare (using the law, and legal means and institutions, for purely political purposes) [*see* generally, Guilfoyle (2019)]. Furthermore, simply applying an abstract model to evaluate a dispute for its level of politicisation might actually end up being a useless exercise. Simply put, theory only states that politicisation occurs when a collective body engages in decision-making (*see*, *supra*, n 43). Applying this without further consideration would lead to an absurd result—all ISDS disputes are virtually politicised. If one applies a simple narrative that ISDS should be completely depoliticised then a paradoxical outcome is reached—ISDS cannot exist anymore because it contradicts itself, with tribunals assuming competence over politicized (or politicizable) disputes. This is another reason why the main argument made in this article turns on procedural depoliticization as the way to achieve what the founders of investment arbitration envisioned in the first place. As it will be explained in Parts II and III, a fair and just outcome is reached by focusing on procedural depoliticization. This accepts the reality that, to an extent, the substance of investment disputes will always entertain a degree of politicization and that it is impossible to pinpoint exactly where the line should be drawn between permissible politicization in ISDS and impermissible politicization. As such, there is an institutional-procedural mechanism which leads to fair results without having to undertake a surgically precise transformation when it comes to the substance of foreign investment disputes.

[53] On how depoliticisation can contribute to the legitimacy of ISDS, *see* Haljan (2019), pp. 252–253.

[54] *Supra* n 4.

[55] *Supra* n 52.

[56] *See*, *infra*, Part II.

[57] United Nations Commission on International Trade Law Working Group III (Investor-State Dispute Settlement Reform) Fifty-first session, Report of Working Group III (Investor-State Dispute Settlement Reform) on the work of its thirty-fourth session (Vienna, 27 November – 1 December 2017), A/CN.9/930/Rev.1, para.20.

[58] *See*, *infra*, Part II.

Notwithstanding the above, the benefits of depoliticization (broadly speaking) are somewhat intuitive, as they are desirable. Firstly, this process removes the rather arbitrary and, perhaps, unfair influence of powerful states in international economic affairs. In other words, ISDS was aimed at ensuring a transition from great power politics in the international investment arena to a (partial [59]) judicialization of this area.

It is only partial because ISDS relies on a series of factors, including an arbitration mechanism and a legal trigger for this mechanism (normally an investment protection treaty whereby the host state extends an offer to arbitrate in case of future disputes with a foreign investor, with the latter taking up that offer by initiating investment proceedings). [60] Lack of such mechanisms may mean that the aforementioned judicialization cannot take place.

Also, most treaties dealing with international investment do not regulate the admission of investments,[61] which could, and sometimes even is, heavily influenced by (geo)political considerations. For instance, screening of foreign investment for security reasons can be heavily influenced by geopolitical considerations, as is the case with some Western states that are adamant to admit Chinese investments because of certain geopolitical considerations.[62] For instance, foreign ownership of critical infrastructure, core technologies, or elements of the defence sector.[63]

Moreover, as already mentioned,[64] depoliticization of investment disputes also entails the (partial) empowerment of the investor in the international legal arena. Initially, the investor was subject to political opportunism, as the home state would not always escalate and challenge the host state—again, for political reasons—if the foreign investor felt aggrieved in its relations with the capital-importing state.[65] In ISDS, however, the investor takes centre stage: it can exercise certain procedural rights (whether those rights belong to them or were simply exercised in the name of the home state[66] is of far lesser importance here) to vindicate its substantial rights.

[59] Partial in the sense that ISDS must be provided for *via* different mechanisms (usually treaties). Unless they exist, there can be no judicialization of foreign investment disputes.

[60] *See* generally, Paulsson (1995).

[61] There is a number of treaties which limit the discretion of the host state when it comes to the establishment of a foreign investment by prohibiting discriminatory treatment when it comes to this phase: host states must treat potential foreign investors, when it comes to the pre-establishment phase, in the same way they would treat another foreign, or domestic investor, finding itself in like circumstances (basically, extending most-favoured-nation and national treatment to the pre-establishment phase). For instance, *see* Article II of the Agreement between the Government of Canada and the Government of Barbados for the Reciprocal Promotion and Protection of Investments (signed 29 May 1996, entered into force 17 January 1997). *See* also, Joubin-Bret (2008).

[62] For instance, *see* Lampo (2021), pp. 434–435.

[63] Bian (2021), pp. 56–54, 587.

[64] *Supra* n 15 and 18 and the accompanying text.

[65] Kriebaum (2019), pp. 27–28.

[66] Paparinskis (2013).

This is another major effect of depoliticization and the subsequent judicialization of investment disputes.

In this context, the complexity and nuances of depoliticization become clearer. This occurs to varying degrees and it is not always the same, depending on the angle one uses to look at the issue. Based on this complexity, the existing nuances, and the multitude of involved stakeholders, together with the nature of ISDS and investment disputes, we propose a different model to approach the depoliticization goal. One that looks at the differences and the potential of depoliticization depending on the realm in which it occurs: institutional/procedural and substantial. The suggested model assumes that only procedural depoliticization tends towards somewhat of a complete form of depoliticization. This is further explained in Part II. In terms of the substantive aspect of disputes, Part III will explain how depoliticization here is very difficult to achieve and also how identifying the exact scope of depoliticization here can be highly onerous.

3 The Elements of Procedural Depoliticization

Arbitral tribunals are recurrently posited with questions and issues relating to public policy measures adopted by States. Such public policy measures, *inter alia*, include regulating public services, economic and financial measures, and environmental measures.[67]

The first tool that is used to ensure that ISDS benefits from an independent and objective dispute settlement mechanism (thus preventing, for instance, the exercise of political preferences by arbitrators) is the set of rules ensuring the arbitrators' independence and impartiality.[68] Independence and impartiality are invariably two fundamental aspects of procedural integrity of any dispute resolution process.[69] The perception of bias of arbitrators in ISDS is directly linked with their independence and impartiality.[70] As ISDS disputes generally involve a political perspective, arbitrators appointed by disputing parties may end up in certain cases vigorously representing the interests of the party that appointed them in the first place.[71] This potential bias of arbitrators is often attributed to the vested interest of the arbitrators seeking repeat or future appointments.[72]

As argued by Gus van Harten, the tenets of arbitral independence and impartiality are particularly challenged when the perception is of the presence of inherent bias:

---

[67] Paparinskis (2012), pp. 271–289.

[68] Giorgetti et al. (2020), p. 441.

[69] Park (2010), pp.189–251; Sobota (2015), pp. 293–319.

[70] Giorgetti et al. (2020), p. 441.

[71] Puig and Strezhnev (2017), pp. 371–398. *See*, also, Langford and Behn (2018), pp.551–580.

[72] Langford and Behn (2018), pp. 551–580.

> The dependence of arbitrators on government and business bellies the claim that investment treaty arbitration removes sensitive disputes from the political realm and subjects them to the rule of law...The problem with this claim is that adjudication is neither independent nor impartial where the adjudicator is appointed by a political or corporate entity on a case-by-case basis. . .It is precisely because they are not appointed and assured tenure by the state that arbitrators are exposed to undue political pressure. There can be no rule of law without an independent judiciary.[73]

In light of the above, it is not surprising to note that States have been actively incorporating provisions in their investment treaties regarding the qualifications and experience of arbitrators, ethic rules and codes of conduct of arbitrators.[74] Consequently, given the significance of ensuring independence and impartiality in ISDS, the UNCITRAL Working Group III has been focusing on reform measures countering the connections between parties and arbitrators, double hatting, issue conflict, the inherent issues pertaining to appointment of arbitrators and the alleged systemic pro-investor or pro-investment bias.[75] More precisely, the Working Group III in its November 2018 report states:

> Independence and impartiality were described as key elements of any system of justice, including arbitration. The concerns relating to the possible lack of independence and impartiality of decision makers, or of the perception thereof, were said to be particularly acute in the field of ISDS, as ISDS cases usually involved public policy issues and involved a State. It was re-affirmed that, in order to be considered effective, the ISDS framework should not only ensure actual impartiality and independence of decision makers, but also the appearance thereof. Therefore, it was said that any reform in that respect should aim at addressing both actual and perceived lack of independence and impartiality.[76]

The process of appointing arbitrators by parties and the jurisdiction of the tribunal is often perceived as a window for political interference.[77] Moreover, the legitimacy of the entire process is called into question when the party-appointed arbitrators are seen as potentially exacerbating the political divide between the investor and the host state.[78]

---

[73] Van Harten (2008), p. 173.

[74] Korzun (2021), pp. 355–414.

[75] United Nations Commission on International Trade Law (2018) Ensuring independence and impartiality on the part of arbitrators and decision makers in ISDS Note by the Secretariat. A/CN.9/WG.III/WP.151, available at: http://undocs.org/en/A/CN.9/WG.III/WP.151 (last accessed: 8 February 2023).

[76] United Nations Commission on International Trade Law (2018) Report of the Working Group III (Investor-State Dispute Settlement Reform) on the Work of its Thirty/Sixth Session. UN Doc. A/CN.9/964, p. 67.

[77] Pauwelyn and Elsig (2013), pp. 463–4. See also, Bjorklund et al. (2019), available at: https://www.jus.uio.no/pluricourts/english/projects/leginvest/academic-forum/papers/papers/11-bjorklund-et-al-selection-and-appointment-isds-af-11-2019.pdf.

[78] Pauwelyn and Elsig (2013), pp. 445, 463. See also, Bjorklund et al. (2019), available at: https://www.jus.uio.no/pluricourts/english/projects/leginvest/academic-forum/papers/papers/11-bjorklund-et-al-selection-and-appointment-isds-af-11-2019.pdf.

The reform process currently being undertaken by the UNCITRAL Working Group III has been considering a range of options to address the issue of political interference via the arbitrator appointment process. The possibilities range from creating a list of arbitrators from one end to establishing a standing mechanism with a permanent adjudicatory body.[79] All options considered, the creation of the permanent investment court wherein arbitrators would be employed full time subject to strict ethical requirements appears to be a feasible option to counter the alleged biasness of party-appointed arbitrators.[80] This permanent investment court would ensure to a great extent breaking the link[81] between the parties and arbitrators which is the main criticism levelled against party-appointed arbitrators.[82]

From a procedural standpoint, politicization in the arbitrator appointment process can be countered through specific transparency measures such as advertisement of openings, public hearings, publication of candidates' resumes, promotion of direct applications by potential candidates and a robust screening mechanism of potential arbitrators.[83] Notably, the procedural aspects of investment arbitration proceedings include within its ambit rules concerning *inter alia*, jurisdiction, evidence, pleading requirements, execution of awards, costs and other related matters that ensure a roadway for enforcing rights of the parties involved therein. Additionally, an important facet of procedural depoliticization is procedural fairness which implies an objective and pre-formulated dispute resolution mechanism based on agreed standards that ensures predictability and fairness in the outcome of the dispute resolution mechanism.

The focus of this chapter is only on procedural fairness, of which the conduct of arbitrators, particularly the independence and impartiality thereof, forms the essence. As observed by one author, "*the ability of a State to have recourse to an impartial and independent judicial tribunal openly applying known legal rules in order to determine what the law is and so resolve its legal disputes with another State is fundamental to the existence of the international rule of law.*"[84]

More generally, the notion of independence in ISDS connotes the absence of any relationship (either based on power or influence) between the arbitrator and the disputing parties. Similarly, impartiality denotes the lack of pre-judgment of the arbitrator in relation to the case. [85]

---

[79] See Secretariat of the U.N. Comm'n on Int'l Trade Law, Working Group III, Possible Reform of Investor-State Dispute Settlement (ISDS): Selection and Appointment of ISDS Tribunal Members, Note by the Secretariat, 1 9–11, U.N. Doc. A/CN.9/WG.IIIWP.169 (July 31, 2019).

[80] Ibid.

[81] Schacherer (2018), p. 22.

[82] Bungenberg and Reinisch (2018), p. 17, Bjorklund (2021), p. 433; Lee (2021), p. 484.

[83] Kaufmann-Kohler and Potesta (2017), pp. 74–87.

[84] Watts (1993), p. 28.

[85] *Suez, Sociedad General de Aguas de Barcelona S.A. and InterAguas Servicios Integrales del Agua S.A. v The Argentine Republic* (Decision on a Second Proposal for the Disqualification of a Member of the Arbitral Tribunal, 22 October 2007) ICSID Case No. ARB/03/17, para. 28; *Suez, Sociedad General de Aguas de Barcelona, S.A. and Vivendi Universal, S.A. v Argentine Republic*

Currently, the ISDS regime comprises of disclosure requirements and challenge procedures governing the independence and impartiality of arbitrators.[86] The existing regime under the UNCITRAL Arbitration Rules[87] and the ICSID Convention do contemplate measures to ensure the independence and impartiality of arbitrators. The ICSID Convention provides that arbitrators shall be "*persons of high moral character*", possess "*recognized competence in the fields of law, commerce, industry or finance*" and are "*capable of being relied upon to exercise independent judgment*".[88] Arbitral institutions such as the International Chamber of Commerce (ICC), London Court of International Arbitration (LCIA) and Stockholm Chamber of Commerce (SCC) require arbitrators to maintain high standards of independence and impartiality.[89] However, systemic concerns remain prevalent, especially given the varied roles played by a handful of arbitrators.[90]

Against this backdrop, disclosure obligations envisaged under various Rules become pivotal. The ICSID Arbitration Rules mandate disclosure of any circumstance that might lead to questions being raised regarding the independence of the arbitrator.[91] Similarly, the UNCITRAL Arbitration Rules and the ICC Rules require

(Decision on the Proposal for the Disqualification of a Member of the Arbitral Tribunal, 22 October 2007) ICSID Case No. ARB/03/19, para. 29; *Tidewater Investment SRL and Tidewater Caribe, C.A. v Bolivarian Republic of Venezuela* (Decision on the Proposal for the Disqualification of a Member of the Arbitral Tribunal, 23 December 2010) ICSID Case No. ARB/10/5, para. 37; *ConocoPhillips Petrozuata B.V. ConocoPhillips Hamaca B.V. and ConocoPhillips Gulf of Paria B.V. v Bolivarian Republic of Venezuela* (Decision on the Proposal to Disqualify L. Yves Fortier, Q.C. Arbitrator, 27 February 2012) ICSID Case No. ARB/07/30, para 54; *Blue Bank International & Trust (Barbados) Ltd. V. Bolivarian Republic of Venezuela* (Decision on the Parties' Proposals to Disqualify a Majority of the Tribunal, 12 November 2013) ICSID Case No. ARB 12/20, para. 59; *Burlington Resources Inc. v Republic of Ecuador* (Decision on the Proposal for Disqualification of Professor Francisco Orrego Vicuña, 13 December 2013) ICSID Case No. ARB/08/5, para 66; *Abaclat and Others v Argentine Republic* (Decision on the Proposal to Disqualify a Majority of the Tribunal, 4 February 2014) ICSID Case No. ARB/07/5, para. 75.

[86] Giorgetti et al. (2020), p. 447.

[87] UNCITRAL Arbitration Rules, art 6(7), UNGA Res 65/22 (10 January 2011) UN Doc A/RES/65/22. Available at: https://uncitral.un.org/sites/uncitral.un.org/files/media-documents/uncitral/en/arb-rules-revised-2010-e.pdf *UNCITRAL Arbitration Rules).

[88] Article 14 and Article 40 of the ICSID Convention. *See* also, Giorgetti et al. (2020), pp. 441–474.

[89] International Chamber of Commerce Rules of Arbitration, (Jan. 1, 2021). Available at: https://iccwbo.org/dispute-resolution-services/arbitration/rules-of-arbitration/ ("ICC Arbitration Rules 2021"); London Court of International Arbitration, (Oct. 1, 2014). Available at: http://www.lcia.org/dispute_resolution_services/lcia-arbitration-rules-2014.aspx ("LCIA Arbitration Rules 2014"); Arbitration Rules of the Arbitration Institute of the Stockholm Chamber of Commerce, (Jan 1, 2023). Available at: https://sccarbitrationinstitute.se/sites/default/files/2023-01/scc_arbitration_rules_2023_eng.pdf ("SCC Arbitration Rules 2023").

[90] Dunoff and Giorgetti (2019), p. 279.

[91] Rule 19 of the ICSID, Rules of Procedure for Arbitration Proceedings (21 March 2022) (ICSID Rules).

disclosure of all circumstances that might give rise to justifiable doubts regarding the independence and impartiality of arbitrators.[92]

Additionally, soft law instruments such as the Guidelines on Conflicts of Interest in International Arbitration ("***IBA Guidelines***") also provide guidance with regard to the independence and impartiality of arbitrators. [93] The IBA Guidelines postulate non-binding general principles applicable to the independence and impartiality of arbitrators and provide guidance by way of prescribing specific situations and circumstances (Red, Orange and Green lists) that might result in the disqualification of arbitrators.[94]

The manifestation of the rule of law in asymmetrical ISDS is noteworthy at this juncture. The traditional understanding of the rule of law comprising of tenets such as (1) to be ruled by law and not by discretion; (2) to be equal before law and (3) to be governed by the jurisdiction of ordinary courts[95] were designed in the context of governing the actions and relationships of States. As international institutions increase in influence, it is imperative to understand and assess the significance of the rule of law within the ISDS regime, as dispute settlement mechanisms play a pivotal role. At an international level, the rule of law, for all purposes, formalizes the consensual character of law amongst States through treaties in the absence of an international authority. [96]

Notwithstanding the above, there have been three different meanings attributed to international rule of law: (1) international rule of law denotes the application of rule of law principles to relations between States and other subjects of international law, (2) international rule of law implies "*rule of international law*" thereby essentially implying the precedence of international norms over domestic law, and (3) international rule of law is nothing but a "*global rule of law*".[97]

In light of the above, evaluating the ISDS regime from the lens of an international rule of law aids in highlighting its shortcomings and possible measures that can be adopted to address the legitimacy crisis of ISDS. The issue of legitimacy plays a

---

[92] Article 11 of UNCITRAL Arbitration Rules (as adopted in 2013). Available at: https://uncitral.un.org/sites/uncitral.un.org/files/media-documents/uncitral/en/21-07996_expedited-arbitration-e-ebook.pdf. Article 11 of UNCITRAL Arbitration rules states that: When a person is approached in connection with his or her possible appointment as an arbitrator, he or she shall disclose any circumstances likely to give rise to justifiable doubts as to his or her impartiality or independence. An arbitrator, from the time of his or her appointment and throughout the arbitral proceedings, shall without delay disclose any such circumstances to the parties and the other arbitrators unless they have already been informed by him or her of these circumstances. See also, Article 11 of ICC Rules, available at: https://iccwbo.org/dispute-resolution/dispute-resolution-services/arbitration/rules-procedure/2021-arbitration-rules/#block-accordion-11.

[93] Council of the International Bar Association, "IBA Guidelines on Conflict of Interest in International Arbitration, 2014" ("IBA Guidelines"). Available at: https://www.ibanet.org/MediaHandler?id=e2fe5e72-eb14-4bba-b10d-d33dafee8918.

[94] Ibid.

[95] Beaulac (2007), p. 4.

[96] Pavel (2019), p. 332.

[97] Chesterman (2008), p. 331.

pivotal role in investment arbitration which has increasingly come under great scrutiny *inter alia*, on the grounds of appearance of bias,[98] increase in costs and length of arbitration proceedings, inconsistencies in decision making and interpretations of investment treaties by arbitral tribunals which invariably impacts the policy space of states to the benefit of foreign investors.[99] As noted by one author, the emergence of the legitimacy issue in ISDS can be understood as:

> a reaction to the metamorphosis of international arbitration from a dyadic dispute settlement mechanism into a stable institution of transnational governance. It contributes not only to settling disputes, but to stabilizing and generating normative expectations in transborder social relations and therefore exercises transnational authority that demands justification in order to be considered as legitimate. Finally, it is critical to note that the framework in which criticism and legitimacy concerns regarding international arbitration are formulated stems from a constitutional legal analysis. In fact, constitutional arguments set out the contours of the concept of legitimacy used by critics of international arbitration.[100]

More prudently, the compatibility of ISDS with the rule of law is often questioned in the context of (i) legal certainty, (ii) procedural fairness and (iii) transparency.[101]

The criticism leveled against the ISDS regime in the context of independence and impartiality of arbitrators is both systemic and individual, with concerns ranging from party appointment, multiple appointments, double-hatting, issue conflict and implicit pro-investor bias.[102] Party appointment of arbitrators is considered to be one of the major concerns by critics who observe that the practice constitutes a "*moral hazard*", is unsatisfactory, and problematic.[103] The problem, according to critics, is twofold: (i) parties tend to choose arbitrators who are sympathetic and of a similar view to the appointing party,[104] and (ii) party appointment of arbitrators results in creeping unconscious bias and cognitive bias thereby resulting in arbitrators advocating for reduced awards of damages or costs and inaccurate decisions and interpretations.[105]

However, it can be argued that given that each disputing party appoints its arbitrator, there is a counterbalance. Further, the professionalism and self-policing nature of arbitrators act as the most significant incentives for delivering an unbiased award.

Commentators arguing for the status quo of the independence and impartiality standards in ISDS state that the current procedural safeguards are sufficient in tackling any possible issue that might arise, and the practice of party appointment

[98] Van Harten (2010), p. 453.

[99] Brower et al. (2003), p. 415.

[100] Schill (2016), pp. 106–124.

[101] Reinisch (2016), pp. 291–308.

[102] Giorgetti et al. (2020), p. 447.

[103] Paulsson (2010), p. 339. *See*, also Paulsson (2009).

[104] Branson (2010), p. 367.

[105] Brekoulakis (2013), p. 553.

should not be wholly done away with for the lack of a better alternative.[106] More importantly, those commentators also argue that party autonomy forms an essential aspect of arbitration *per se* and any alterations to it might change the very fundamentals of ISDS.[107]

The issue of independence and impartiality has to be considered vis-à-vis the issue of arbitrators exercising their jurisdiction to assert public law implications in investment arbitration proceedings. In a domestic legal system, the presence of certain safeguards such as security of tenure and security of income ensures that the judiciary is independent and impartial at the same time.[108] However, the absence of security of tenure and security of payments project a real possibility of bias in investment arbitration. After all, perception of bias as compared to actual bias is inherently essential to ensure the legitimacy of any method of dispute resolution.[109] Consequently, the above discussion leads to an incisive analysis of the structural defects present in the ISDS mechanism that propagate such perception of bias that merit greater attention since "[n]ot only must justice be done; it must also be seen to be done".[110]

It is stated that concerns pertaining to perception of bias are manifested in ISDS in the form of party appointment, connections between arbitrators and parties, the issue of multiple appointments, double hatting, issue conflicts, and implicit pro-investor bias which are systemic concerns that are pivotal to the overall legitimacy of ISDS.[111]

For example, in ICSID arbitrations, the presiding arbitrator in a three-member tribunal in case of any conflict between the two appointed arbitrators is either appointed by the Chairman of the ICSID Administrative Council or by the ICSID Secretary General.[112] Notably, the ICSID Administrative Council is chaired by the President of the World Bank, who is nominated by the US Government and confirmed by the Bank's Board of Directors.[113] The present appointing authority is former under the secretary of the US Treasury for International Affairs, currently David Malpass.[114] Thus, the underlying implication emanating from the above is

[106] Giorgetti et al. (2020), p. 447.

[107] Ibid.

[108] Grant and Kieff (2022), p. 171.

[109] Behn et al. (2020), p. 240.

[110] *R v Sussex Justices*, Ex parte McCarthy [1924] 1 KB 256. Giorgetti et al. (2020), p. 445.

[111] Giorgetti et al. (2020), p. 445.

[112] Rule 18 of ICSID Arbitration Rules. Available at: https://icsid.worldbank.org/sites/default/files/Arbitration_Rules.pdf.

[113] Article 5 of the ICSID Convention states that "The President of the Bank shall be ex officio Chairman of the Administrative Council (hereinafter called the Chairman) but shall have no vote. During his absence or inability to act and during any vacancy in the office of President of the Bank, the person for the time being acting as President shall act as Chairman of the Administrative Council.". See also, Van Harten (2008), p. 170.

[114] World Bank Group (2023) About David R. Malpass. Available at https://president.worldbankgroup.org/en/president.

that arbitrators are dependent upon a handful of capital exporting countries for their appointment.[115] In spite of the integrity and high ethical standards set by some arbitrators, it has been suggested that repeated appointments tend to propagate the *idea* of bias irrespective of the *existence* of actual bias.[116]

In order to combat this alleged bias of arbitrators, the UNCITRAL Working Group III has formulated the Draft Code of Conduct, which in Article A11 (6) imposes a continuous duty of disclosure on arbitrators.[117] Article A11(2) enumerates a list of non-exhaustive matters that must be disclosed by the arbitrator while accepting the appointment.[118] The Draft Code of Conduct in Article A4 also addresses the issue of multiple appointments and double hatting by stipulating three different options that could be possibly adopted.[119] It is to be noted that Article A4 pertains to adjudicators only, who act as legal counsels and expert witnesses. Overall, the Draft Code of Conduct provides for broad standards of disclosures intending to enhance the transparency of the process and allow disputing parties to assess any potential conflict of interest.

Additional reforms currently being deliberated upon by the UNCITRAL Working Group III, such as the proposed Multilateral Investment Court (MIC),[120] could potentially tackle the issue of biased arbitrators and double hatting. As adjudicators in the MIC are appointed on a long-term tenure thereby preventing them from

---

[115] Puig (2016), p. 659.

[116] Van Harten (2008), p. 173.

[117] UNCITRAL Working Group III (Investor-State Dispute Settlement Reform) Forty-fourth session, Possible reform of investor-State dispute settlement (ISDS), Draft Codes of Conduct and Commentary A/CN.9/WG.III/WP.223. Available at: https://documents-dds-ny.un.org/doc/UNDOC/LTD/V22/183/01/PDF/V2218301.pdf?OpenElement.

[118] UNCITRAL Working Group III (Investor-State Dispute Settlement Reform) Forty-fourth session, Possible reform of investor-State dispute settlement (ISDS), Draft Codes of Conduct and Commentary A/CN.9/WG.III/WP.223. Available at: https://documents-dds-ny.un.org/doc/UNDOC/LTD/V22/183/01/PDF/V2218301.pdf?OpenElement. Article 10(2) of the Draft Code of Conduct states that: "*[T]he following information shall be included in the disclosure: (a) Any financial, business, professional, or personal relationship in the past five years with: (i) Any disputing party or an entity identified by a disputing party; (ii) The legal representative(s) of a disputing party in the IID proceeding; (iii) Other Arbitrators and expert witnesses in the IID proceeding; and (iv) [Any entity identified by a disputing party as having a direct or indirect interest in the outcome of the IID proceeding, including a third-party funder]; (b) Any financial or personal interest in: (i) The outcome of the IID proceeding; (ii) Any other IID proceeding involving the same measure(s); and (iii) Any other proceeding involving a disputing party or an entity identified by a disputing party; (c) All IID and related proceedings in which the Candidate or the Arbitrator is currently or has been involved in the past five years as an Arbitrator, a legal representative or an expert witness; and (d) Any appointment as an Arbitrator, a legal representative, or an expert witness by a disputing party or its legal representative(s) in an IID or any other proceeding in the past five years.*"

[119] Article 4 of the Draft Code of Conduct (*supra* n 121).

[120] UNCITRAL Secretariat, 'Appellate and Multilateral Court Mechanisms' (29 November 2019) UN Doc A/CN.9/WG.III/WP.185.

occupying multiple positions.[121] Further, appointing adjudicators on a long-term basis would eliminate the motivation of any biasness towards the appointing party, since permanent judges would not be dependent upon the parties for re-appointments. The establishment of the MIC would ensure a clear-cut demarcation between ICSID and other institutions, thereby directly countering the perception of bias that is often leveled against ISDS mechanisms.

The current trajectory of the reform process being undertaken by the UNCITRAL Working Group III makes it difficult to predict whether systemic issues pertaining to independence and impartiality will be successfully addressed. The Draft Code of Conduct is a bright start as it addresses various issues such as double hatting, and repeat appointments. However, there remains a lot to be desired in the reform process as the EU and its member states push for significant changes while other states opt for nuanced changes in the current existing mechanism of appointing arbitrators in ISDS.

The importance of pushing forward the procedural depoliticization endeavour to the highest extent possible becomes clearer when looking at the extent to which substantive depoliticization can occur. This is why the next Part of this article elaborates upon the impact of politicization when it comes to the substance of a dispute, demonstrating how complete substantive depoliticization has never occurred so far. And, while also looking at future prospects, the following sections explains why such a change (complete substantive depoliticization) is improbable in the future and also why it is even undesirable.

4 Why Complete Substantive Depoliticization Never Occurred and Is Not Even Desirable

It is counter-intuitive to approach the topic of (de)politicization of investment disputes in purely black-or-white terms. For instance, it is unproductive to ascertain as to whether there should be complete depoliticization or none at all. Otherwise, the existing nuances, owing to the nature of the dispute settlement system—including its history—in investment arbitration, are ignored. Or one cannot explain, if the politicization/depoliticization dynamic is seen exclusively as a choice between black-or-white alternatives, why even the ICSID Convention permits recourse to diplomatic protection when a losing respondent state fails to comply with an ICSID arbitral award.[122]

Instead, it is pivotal to understand that depoliticization (at least substantively), *per se*, is multifaceted in nature. Through this lens it is easier to suggest a different approach, namely that politicization is not necessarily an unwelcome development

[121] Giorgetti et al. (2020), p. 470.

[122] *Supra* n 39.

and/or feature of the system, as long as it is restricted by certain parameters, with different degrees of depoliticization existing.[123]

As aptly pointed out by one author, politicization has many layers to it:

> the investment arbitration process is in several aspects very much a political one. On the one hand, subject matters of disputes adjudicated by arbitral tribunals inevitably raise political questions. The evaluation of public policies by tribunals, such as the treatment of economic and financial crises, including sovereign debt restructuring, or those regarding environmental and health measures, lead to a certain degree of indirect control of state policies by the investment arbitration process. On the other hand, new forms of 'diplomatic' protection are employed in order to interfere with or influence investment arbitrations, such as, for instance negative votes concerning the renewal of international bank loans vis-à-vis a country involved in an investment dispute or the use of the WTO dispute settlement body to 'circumvent' investment arbitration.[124]

In the context of ISDS, which can be analogized to domestic administrative law in terms of structure and types of measures that are reviewed by arbitral tribunals,[125] a parallel may be drawn to domestic systems, such as the United Kingdom (UK).[126] There judicial review of administrative acts is limited in scope.[127] For example, it is a fundamental principle in UK administrative law that judicial review cannot touch upon the merits of an administrative decision.[128]

And while we do not advocate for a complete transposition of this system in ISDS (a system of international law, after all), there is evidence of some movement towards arbitral tribunal restraint when it comes to review of measures that contain a public policy element.[129] In other words, there is a conscious attempt to prevent arbitral tribunals from exceeding their ambit of their powers and indulging in reviewing decisions that should, finally, be settled by other bodies. Primarily the ones performing an executive function.

In domestic law (the UK, for example), this is perceived as a form of separation of powers.[130] It is generally accepted that the judiciary should not review measures that involve a public policy component. Otherwise, the separation of powers between the judiciary (in the present case, the arbitral tribunal) and other powers, such as the executive, or even the legislative in certain instances, would be blurred and the distinction between such powers would dissipate.[131]

---

[123] Kriebaum (2019), p. 38.

[124] Titi (2015), p. 265.

[125] Schill (2010), p. 4.

[126] Any parallels to domestic systems are made for illustrative, and explanatory, purposes. Otherwise, this article focuses exclusively on the aspects concerning the potential politicization of arbitral tribunals, and in particular politicization to an unjustified extent.

[127] Daly (2012), p. 269.

[128] Harris (2003), p. 654.

[129] Henckels (2015), pp. 130–133.

[130] Masterman (2011), pp. 113–114.

[131] Banfield and Flynn (2018), p. 141.

Arbitral tribunals review measures that can be seen to have a highly political element and can be best understood by reference to a few examples from ISDS jurisprudence – for instance, arbitrators reviewing measures taken by Argentina during the 2001 economic crisis.[132] Notably, the authority of arbitral tribunals to adjudicate sovereign acts can be attributed to the influence of neoliberal economic theory on the drafting of investment treaties (although only partially, since a complete impact would have also included liberalization when it came to establishment of foreign investment).[133] This is quite apparent in the earliest treaties that entered into force, as most States struck a bargain between sacrificing a portion of their policy space and attracting foreign investments.[134]

The political nature of investment treaty disputes often hinges on the issue of national sovereignty involving challenges to public acts[135] and often to the public regulatory actions[136] of host states. A cursory glance over the claims usually raised in ISDS fora highlights that the cases typically cluster around an array of government measures that are politically sensitive,[137] such as, *inter alia*, energy, environmental regulation, public procurement, communication services, corruption, hazardous waste disposal, preservation of cultural heritage and tobacco control.[138]

In other words, investor-state disputes, followed by their adjudication, occur in "*highly politicized contexts*",[139] which can be viewed as a challenge to the normal functioning of the political processes of host states.[140] This compromise of national sovereignty has led to much skepticism of the ISDS framework.[141] Arguably, the

---

[132] *CMS Gas Transmission Co. v. Argentine Republic*, ICSID Case No. ARB/01/8 (Decision on Objections to Jurisdiction of July 17, 2003); *Azurix Corp. v. Argentine Republic*, ICSID Case No. ARB/01/12 (Decision on Jurisdiction of Dec. 8, 2003); *Enron Corp. v. Argentine Republic*, ICSID Case No. ARB/01/3 (Decision on Jurisdiction (Main Claim) of Jan. 14, 2004); *Enron Corp. v. Argentine Republic*, ICSID Case No. ARB/01/3 (Decision on Jurisdiction (Ancillary Claim) of Aug. 2, 2004; *Siemens A.G. v. Argentine Republic*, ICSID Case No. ARB/02/8 (Decision on Jurisdiction of Aug. 3, 2004); *LG&E Energy Corp. v. Argentine Republic*, ICSID Case No. ARB/02/1 (Decision on Jurisdiction of Apr. 30), para. 20.

[133] Slobodian (2021), pp. 51–52. *See* also, Kentikelenis and Babb (2019), pp. 1745–1746. On the freedom of states to regulate admission of foreign investment, *see* Dolzer et al. (2022), p. 132.

[134] Spears (2010), p. 1041.

[135] Brower II (2009a), pp. 348–356.

[136] Zamir and Barker (2017), p. 210. *See* also, Born (2012), pp. 839–40 and Schill (2011), p. 895:

> The cases relating to the Argentine economic crisis, [and] also several NAFTA disputes in which investors challenged what the respondent state argued to be legitimate regulatory action to protect the public interest, such as the protection of public health, the environment, or labour standards, raised the concern about how much 'regulatory space' investment treaties left.

[137] Laird (2016), p. 108.

[138] Brower II (2017), p. 286.

[139] Brower (2009b), p. 183.

[140] Salacus (2007), p. 156. *See* also, Van Harten and Loughlin (2006), p. 146.

[141] Titi (2015), p. 261.

most well-known instance of politics being involved in ISDS is the economic and political crisis in Argentina in 2001 and the stream of cases emanating therefrom.[142]

The underlying allegations advanced by several Claimants were that Argentina had violated various substantive protections such as fair and equitable treatment, non-discrimination and the expropriation standard afforded to foreign investors under bilateral investment treaties (BITs).[143] In reply, Argentina, in addition to relying on an essential security interest clause in its BITs, also raised admissibility objections to the claims advanced against it. According to the respondent, the investors' claims raised against its economic measures infringed its sovereign right to legislate for public welfare.[144] Consequently, there were several awards delivered by tribunals hearing similar disputes arising out the economic measures adopted by Argentina which were annulled on grounds of manifest errors of law and failure of tribunals to apply the correct applicable law.[145]

Similarly, the politicization of the ISDS regime was recently highlighted in the case of *Philip Morris v. Uruguay*,[146] a dispute regarding packing requirements of tobacco products in Uruguay. At its core, Philip Morris International challenged the tobacco control measures concerning branding and warning levels of tobacco products introduced by the Government of Uruguay.[147] The Claimants argued that the challenged measures breached Respondent's obligations under a BIT entitling the Claimants to compensation under the relevant Treaty and international law.[148] *Per Contra*, Respondent averred that the challenged measures were in consonance with its international obligations of protecting public health.[149] Ultimately, the tribunal observed that Uruguay had complied with its national and international legal obligations for protecting public health and had not acted in bad faith and in a discriminatory manner.[150]

These examples demonstrate that the very nature of investment disputes rotates around a political axis. In other words, politics percolate through the very fabric of international investment law, when it comes to the substance of investment disputes. Failure to see this entails negative systemic consequences. For example, this is why simply arguing for complete substantive depoliticization, as already mentioned earlier,[151] risks challenging the very existence of international investment law. The paradox pins the depoliticization narrative and objectives against the nature of investment disputes.

---

[142] *Supra* n 132.

[143] Ibid.

[144] Ibid.

[145] Ibid.

[146] *Philip Morris Brands Sàrl* et al. *v. Oriental Republic of Uruguay*, ICSID Case No. ARB/10/7.

[147] Mohanty (2022), pp. 103–125.

[148] Ibid.

[149] Ibid.

[150] Ibid.

[151] *See supra* n 52.

It is in this context that this article suggests a demarcation between procedural and substantive depoliticization. To reach the desired aims, one does not need to make major adjustments when it comes to the substance of investment disputes. It only needs to ensure that the proper institutional framework and the proper procedures are in place.

Another way to examine the difference between procedural depoliticization and substantive depoliticization—and to explain the added benefit of tweaks made from the procedural angle—is to employ John Rawls's distinction between procedural and substantive justice (the latter referring to justice in terms of the outcome). Essentially, Rawls's argument posits that, in order to reach certain substantive outcomes, one must seek a fair procedure that leads to those desired outcomes. More precisely, he theorises that "*the essential thing is that there is an independent standard for deciding which outcome is just and a procedure guaranteed to lead to it*".[152]

There is clear flexibility in this approach. Firstly, the precise outcome must not be known before one, or more parties, enter a process. It is enough for two elements to exist. One is to be able to evaluate the outcome (again, unpredictable before the fact) in terms of justice. The second is to have a proper procedure in place that properly ensures that whatever outcome ensues, the result is just. In other words, the result itself is not important. What matters is whether one can characterise that result as just or not.

This brings about an added benefit to processes which tend to reach a high degree of complexity. To stick to the depoliticization example, while identifying a substantive outcome (in the present case, reaching a certain level of depoliticization, although not entirely clear what that level should be) occurs by necessity in this process, the exact outcome (with every detail set out—that precise level of depoliticization) must not necessarily be established from the beginning.

It is enough to enact a fair procedure and follow it to reach a beneficial outcome—this can be as abstract as justice for the claimant, as long as the procedure guides the decision-makers to a result that settles the dispute. In fact, if one thinks about the outcomes of investment arbitration proceedings (taking any dispute as an example can work in this case), the end result in the majority of cases is not the same with the one envisioned by either party. Neither do arbitrators know (and nor should they) what the end result will be. But they follow the procedure, nonetheless, trusting that the eventual award will bring an end to the dispute.

Of course, in Rawls's example, there is a clear, desirable, outcome—the equal division of a cake between certain persons.[153] This is as specific and detailed as possible. However, as already mentioned, procedural justice works equally well even if we cannot exactly pinpoint the precise desired substantive outcome. In fact, it might make more sense in this case, if the approximate parameters of the desired outcome are identified and demarcated. Or if there is a tool that can evaluate the substantive outcome in terms of justice – and lead it there (procedurally).

[152] Rawls (1999), p. 74.

[153] Ibid.

Applying this theory to the present example even further, the complexity of substantive (de)politicization prevents us from knowing exactly to what extent depoliticization is desirable without hindering the functioning of the ISDS mechanism. This is also similar to the proposition advanced by Rawls of a *quasi-pure procedural justice*.[154] In certain complex areas, it is impossible to pinpoint exactly when the result is just or not—so we assume that it is just as long as it conforms to certain parameters.[155] Thus, we allow a quasi-impersonal mechanism,[156] a predetermined procedure, to dictate the exact outcome, just like market forces in a market economy.[157]

Applying this principle, or mechanism, to ISDS leads to certain benefits which can certainly aid in avoiding undesirable outcomes. If complete substantive depoliticization is impossible and, in any case, unwanted, then the question arises: to what extent can substantive politicization be permitted in ISDS?

Realistically speaking, it is difficult to definitively answer the above raised query. And this is precisely why Rawls's theory is suitable here: we do not know the exact degree to which substantive depoliticization in ISDS is desirable. But we understand that with proper procedures in place, the outcome will be satisfactory. The complexity of ISDS, and of the factual matrixes underpinning investor-state disputes, prevent a clear answer about the degree to which substantive depoliticization should be achieved.

In some cases, the disputes themselves are highly politicized in their nature. In such scenarios, the pertinent question that needs to be addressed seems to be whether such disputes could be removed from the competence of a tribunal (either as a matter of jurisdiction or as a form of inadmissibility). If the above question is answered in the affirmative, then the subsequent question which merits attention is: what would be the consequences of preventing the tribunal's competence? Prohibiting tribunals from adjudicating such disputes could jeopardize foreign investments as foreign investors are left without any international (legal) form of protection.[158] There are no clear-cut answers, and forcing them may cause more harm than benefits. Our examination shows that ensuring proper mechanisms are in place to guarantee depoliticization, at least in its procedural form, will lead to beneficial outcomes.

---

[154] Idem, p. 176.

[155] Ibid, p. 176.

[156] Quasi-impersonal in the sense that procedures, and procedural guaranteed, are still applied/enforced by decision-makers, but they apply, in an abstract way, to all arbitral proceedings.

[157] Although Rawls himself argues that market forces should not be compared to procedures that are to lead to just outcomes (he is referring, more specifically, to legislative procedures that lead to just legislation), since the former seek efficiency, while the latter seek that just outcome that was mentioned earlier. *See* Rawls, p. 316.

[158] At least geared towards foreign investment as a discipline. This is not to say that other legal areas may partially overlap with international investment (law and) relations—thus, offering partial protection. For instance, the European Convention of Human Rights or European Union law may offer protection and remedy to breaches of applicable rules and principles—at least to an extent. *See* Giupponi (2017), pp. 141–151 and Moskvan (2022), pp. 9–12 and 14–15.

5 Conclusion

One of the central tenets of this chapter is that depoliticization should not be understood as a simple phenomenon. It is incongruous to assume that investment disputes can ever be fully depoliticized. To this end, the chapter attempted to explain the complexity of (de)politicization in the settlement of foreign investment disputes.

It also highlighted that there are many layers to depoliticization, and that the ideal way to approach this process is to make a distinction between procedural and substantive depoliticization. While the former can be considered to be a real example of complete depoliticization (or, at least, something resembling it), the latter is not. Further, it is not even desirable, in certain circumstances, to reach perfect substantive depoliticization – including for the functioning of the system, which by design is set up to deal with politically-charged disputes. As a result, we suggest an emphasis on procedural depoliticization, as a *systemic good*, that will also have consequences upon depoliticization in the substantive area.

References

Alter KJ et al (2019) Theorizing the judicialization of international relations. Int Stud Q 63(449): 453–458

Banfield A, Flynn G (2018) Activism or democracy? Judicial review of prerogative powers and executive action. Parliam Aff 68(135):141

Basedow JR (2022) Why de-judicialize? Explaining state preferences on judicialization in World Trade Organization dispute settlement body and investor-to-state dispute settlement reforms. Regul Gov 16:1362, 1374

Beaulac (2007) An Inquiry into the International Rule of Law. 14 EUI MWP. Available at http://hdl.handle.net/1814/6957, p 4

Behn D, et al (2020) Empirical perspectives on investment arbitration: what do we know? Does it matter?. J World Investment Trade 21(2–3):188, 240

Bian C (2021) Foreign direct investment screening and National Security: reducing regulatory hurdles to investors through induced reciprocity. J World Investment Trade 22:561, 587

Bjorklund A (2021) Arbitration, the World Trade Organization, and the creation of a multilateral investment court. Arbitr Int 37(2):433–447

Bjorklund A, et al (2019) Selection and Appointment of International Adjudicators: Structural Options for ISDS Reform. 14 Academic Forum on ISDS, available at https://www.jus.uio.no/pluricourts/english/projects/leginvest/academic-forum/papers/papers/11-bjorklund-et-al-selection-and-appointment-isds-af-11-2019.pdf

Bjorklund AK (2010) Article: symposium: arbitration and National Courts: conflict and cooperation: sovereign immunity as a barrier to the enforcement of investor-state arbitral awards: the re-politicization of international investment disputes. Am Rev Int Arbitr 21:211

Born G (2012) A new generation of international adjudication. Duke Law J 61:775–879

Boute A (2019) Economic statecraft and investment arbitration. Univ Pennsylvania J Int Law 40(2): 383, 398–415

Branson D (2010) Sympathetic Party-Appointed Arbitrators: Sophisticated Strangers and Governments Demand on Them. ICSID Rev 25:367–392

Brekoulakis S (2013) Systemic bias and the institution of international arbitration: a new approach to arbitral decision-making. J Int Disp Settlement 4:553–585

Broches A (1995) Settlement of investment disputes, address to the world conference on world peace through law. In: Broches A (ed) Selected essays: World Bank, ICSID, and other subjects of public and private international law. Martinus Nijhoff, p 163
Brower CH (2009a) Obstacles and pathways to consideration of the public interest in investment treaty disputes. In: Sauvant KP (ed) Yearbook on international investment law and policy 2008-2009. Oxford University Press, pp 348–356
Brower CH (2017) Politics, reason, and the trajectory of investor-state dispute settlement. Loyola Univ Chicago Law J 49:271, 286
Brower CN (2009b) The evolution of the international judiciary: denationalization through jurisdictional fragmentation. Proc Annual Meeting (Am Soc Int Law) 103:171, 183
Brower CN et al (2003) The coming crisis in the global adjudication system. Arbitr Int 19(4): 415–440
Bungenberg M, Reinisch A (2018) From bilateral arbitral tribunals and investment courts to a multilateral investment court. Springer, p 17
Chesterman S (2008) An international rule of law? Am J Comp Law 56(2):331–361
Cutler C (2018) The Judicialization of private transnational power and authority. Indiana J Glob Stud 25(1):61, 73–78
Daly P (2012) A theory of deference in administrative law. Basis, application and scope. Cambridge University Press, p 269
Dautaj Y (2021) Between Backlash and the re-emerging "Calvo Doctrine": investor state dispute settlement in an era of socialism, protectionism, and nationalism, Northwest J Int Law Bus 41(3):273, 288–293
Dolzer R et al (2022) Principles of international investment law, 3rd edn. Oxford University Press, p 2
Duanmu J (2014) State-owned MNCs and host country expropriation risk: the role of home state soft power and economic gunboat diplomacy. J Int Bus Stud 45:1044–1060
Dunoff J, Giorgetti C (2019) Introduction to the symposium: a focus on ethics in international courts and tribunals. AJIL Unbound 113:279–283
Giorgetti C et al (2020) Independence and impartiality of adjudicators in investment dispute settlement: assessing challenges and reform options. J World Investment Trade 21(2–3): 441–447
Giupponi BO (2017) Disentangling human rights and investors' rights in international adjudication: the legacy of the Yukos cases. Willamette J Int Law Disp Resol 24(2):127, 141–151
Graham L (2020) Strategic admissibility decisions in the european court of human rights. Int Comp Law Q 69(1):79–102
Grant T, Kieff FS (2022) Appointing arbitrators: tenure, public confidence, and a middle road for ISDS reform. Mich J Int Law 43(1):171–239
Guilfoyle D (2019) The rule of law and maritime security: understanding lawfare in the South China Sea. Int Aff 95(5):999–1017
Haljan D (2019) A public law view of the new generation FTAs. Neth Int Law Rev 66:237, 252–253
Harris BV (2003) Judicial review, justiciability and the prerogative of mercy. Cambridge Law J 62(3):631, 654
Henckels C (2015) Proportionality and deference in investor-state arbitration: balancing investment protection and regulatory autonomy (Cambridge Studies in International and Comparative Law). Cambridge University Press
Joubin-Bret A (2008) Admission and establishment in the context of investment protection. In: Reinisch A (ed) Standards of investment protection. Oxford University Press, p 10
Kaufmann-Kohler G, Potesta M (2017) The Composition of a Multilateral Investment Court and of an Appeal Mechanism for Investment Awards. CIDS Supplemental Report, pp 74–87
Kentikelenis A E and Babb S (2019) The making of neoliberal globalization: norm substitution and the politics of clandestine institutional change. Am J Sociol 124(6):1720, 1745–1746

Kleinheisterkamp J (2015) Investment treaty law and the fear for sovereignty. Mod L Rev 78:793–825

Korzun V (2021) The right to regulate in investor-state arbitration: slicing and dicing regulatory carve-outs. Vanderbilt Law Rev 50:355–414

Kozawa S (2002) Depoliticization of international dispute settlement. A comparison of the dispute settlement provisions of the WTO and the energy charter treaty. J World Investment Trade 3(5): 793–829

Kriebaum U (2019) Evaluating social benefits and costs of investment treaties: depoliticization of investment disputes. In: Gómez KF et al (eds) European yearbook of international economic law. Special Issue: international investment law and the law of armed conflict. Springer, pp 23–40

Laird IA (2016) TPP and ISDS: the challenge from Europe and the proposed TTIP investment court. Canada – United States Law J 40:106, 108

Lampo G (2021) Italy's exercise of foreign investment screening power against Chinese takeover. An assessment under international law. Italian Rev Int Comp Law 1:433–435

Landwehr C (2017) Depoliticization, repoliticization, and deliberative systems. In: Fawcett P et al (eds) Anti-politics, depoliticization, and governance. Oxford University Press, p 51

Langford M, Behn D (2018) Managing backlash: the evolving investment arbitrator? Eur J Int Law 29(2):551–580

Lee S (2021) ISDS reform: analysis on establishing a multilateral investment court system. Arbitr Int J Arbitr Mediat Disp Manage 87(4):484

Malintoppi L (2022) Article 27. In: Schill SW et al (eds) Schreuer's commentary on the ICSID convention. A commentary on the convention on the settlement of investment disputes between states and nationals of other states. Cambridge University Press, pp 649–650

Masterman R (2011) The separation of powers in the contemporary constitution. Judicial competence and independence in the United Kingdom. Cambridge University Press, pp 113–114

Mehranavar L, Johnson L (2022) Missing masters: causes, consequences and corrections for the states' disengagement from the investment treaty system. J Int Disp Settlement 13:264–308

Mohanty G (2022) Chapter 7: visualizing the role of international rule of law in "not-for-profit funding" in investment arbitration. In: Sooksripaisarnkit P, Prasad D (eds) Blurry boundaries of public and private international law. Springer, pp 103–125

Moskvan D (2022) Protection of foreign investments in an intra-EU context: not one BIT? Edward Elgar

Odumosu IT (2007) The law and politics of engaging resistance in investment dispute settlement. Penn State Int Law Rev 26:251, 271–272

Paparinskis M (2012) The limits of depoliticisation in contemporary investor-state arbitration. In: Crawford J, Nouwen S (eds) Select proceedings of the European Society of International law, vol 3. Hart Publishing, pp 271–289

Paparinskis M (2013) Investment treaty arbitration and the (new) law of state responsibility Eur J Int Law 24(2):617, 625–627

Park WW (2010) Arbitrator integrity. In: Waibel M et al (eds) The backlash against investment arbitration. Kluwer Law International, pp 189–251

Paulsson J (1995) Arbitration without privity. ICSID Rev – Foreign Investment Law J 10(2): 232–257

Paulsson J (2009) Are Unilateral Appointments Defensible?. Kluwer Arbitration Blog, 2 April 2009. Available at https://arbitrationblog.kluwerarbitration.com/2009/04/02/are-unilateral-appointments-defensible/

Paulsson J (2010) Moral hazard in international dispute resolution. ICSID Rev – Foreign Investment Law J 25(2):339–355

Pauwelyn J, Elsig M (2013) The politics of treaty interpretation: variations and explanations across international tribunals. In: Dunoff J, Pollack M (eds) Interdisciplinary perspectives on international law and international relations: the state of the art. Cambridge University Press, pp 463–464

Pavel C (2019) The international rule of law. Crit Rev Int Soc Pol Phil 23(3):332–351
Peters A (2016) Beyond human rights. The legal status of the individual in international law. Cambridge University Press, p 291
Philips A (2011) Saving civilization from empire: belligerency, pacifism and the two faces of civilization during the second opium war. Eur J Int Rel 18(1):5, 20
Puig S (2016) Blinding international justice. Virginia J Int Law 56:647, 659
Puig S, Strezhnev A (2017) Affiliation bias in arbitration: an experimental approach. J Legal Stud 46:371–398
Rawls J (1999) A theory of justice, Revised edn. Harvard University Press, p 74
Reinisch A (2016) The rule of law in international investment arbitration. In: Pazaratzis P et al (eds) Reconceptualising the rule of law in global governance, resources, investment and trade. Bloomsbury Publishing, pp 291–308
Reinisch A (2022) Article 54. In: Schill SW et al (eds) Schreuer's commentary on the ICSID Convention. A commentary on the convention on the settlement of investment disputes between states and nationals of other states. Cambridge University Press, pp 1498–1506
Salacus JW (2007) the treatification of international investment law. Law Bus Rev Am 13:155, 156
Schacherer S (2018) Independence and impartiality of arbitrators – a rule of law analysis. Res Collect Yong Pung How Sch Law 17:22
Schill SW (2010) International investment law and comparative public law – an introduction. In: Schill SW (ed) International investment law and comparative public law. Oxford University Press, p 4
Schill SW (2011) W(h)ither fragmentation? On the literature and sociology of international investment law. Eur J Int Law 22:875, 895
Schill SW (2016) Conceptions of legitimacy of international arbitration. Oxford University Press, pp 106–124
Shihata I (1986) Towards a greater depoliticization of investment disputes: the roles of ICSID and MIGA. ICSID Rev – Foreign Investment Law J 1(1):1–25
Slobodian Q (2018) Globalists: the end of empire and the birth of neoliberalism. Harvard University Press, pp 129–131
Slobodian Q (2021) The Backlash against neoliberal globalization from above: elite origins of the crisis of the new constitutionalism. Theory Cult Soc 38(6):51–52
Sobota LA (2015) Repeat arbitrator appointments in international investment disputes. In: Giorgetti C (ed) Challenges and recusals of judges and arbitrators in international courts and tribunals. Brill, pp 293–319
Spears SA (2010) The quest for policy space in a new generation of international investment agreements. J Int Econ Law 13(4):1037, 1041
Titi C (2015) Are investment tribunals adjudicating political disputes?: Some reflections on the repoliticization of investment disputes and (new) forms of diplomatic protection. J Int Arbitr 32(3):261–288
Ginsburg T (2013) Chapter 22: Political Constraints on International Courts. The Oxford Handbook of International Adjudication. https://global.oup.com/academic/product/the-oxford-handbook-of-international-adjudication-9780198748281?cc=pl&lang=en&#
Van Harten G (2008) Investment treaty arbitration and public law. Oxford University Press, p 173
Van Harten G (2010) Perceived bias in investment treaty arbitration. In: Waibel M, Kaushal A (eds) The Backlash against investment arbitration: perceptions and reality. Kluwer Law International, p 453
Van Harten G, Loughlin M (2006) Investment treaty arbitration as a species of global administrative law. Eur J Int Law 17:121, 146
Vicuña FO (2010) International dispute settlement in an evolving global society: constitutionalization, accessibility, privatization. Cambridge University Press, p 67

Voeten E (2022) Is the Public Backlash against globalization a Backlash against legalization and judicialization. Int Stud Rev 24(2):4–5, 14
Watts A (1993) The international rule of law. German Yearb Int Law 36(15):15, 28
Zamir N, Barker P (2017) The trans-pacific partnership agreement and states' right to regulate under international investment law. Denver J Int Law Policy 45:205, 210.

Gautam Mohanty is a PhD student at Kozminski University, Warsaw, Poland. He researches on the legitimacy crisis of investor-state dispute settlement and third-party funding. Prior to commencing his doctoral studies, Gautam was a practitioner of law enrolled as an advocate in India and an Assistant Professor (on leave) at Jindal Global Law School India (JGLS), India. He is also Fellow at JGLS Centre for Alternative Dispute Resolution (CADR).

Alexandros Bakos is a PhD candidate in international economic law at City, University of London. His research focuses on the protection international (economic) law offers foreign investors against the negative effects of economic sanctions, using a mixed legal and geopolitical methodology. Alexandros was a visiting lecturer in international investment law at Brunel University and is a graduate teaching assistant at City, University of London. Formerly, he worked as a researcher in international economic law at the British Institute of International and Comparative Law.

The OECD Good Regulatory Practices Toolbox and Brazil's Reform Through Transnational Lenses

Magali Favaretto Prieto Fernandes

Contents

Abstract Brazil has embraced institutional and legal reforms towards "good regulatory practices" (GRP) built on the OECD's "better regulation" agenda. New laws and decrees made Regulatory Impact Assessment (RIA) mandatory in all public administration's rulemaking, as well as stock reviews and "ex-post" evaluations. Following such steps, a regulatory oversight body is under scrutiny by policymakers. This paper assesses national regulatory reforms through international and transnational lenses. It primarily argues that nation-states make policy immersed in a dense web of networks, highlighting that it is not possible to understand domestic legal changes without assessing transnational legal processes. It further argues the importance of the OECD as a purveyor of ideas and a critical node in transnational regulatory governance. First, it unpacks the concept of GRP codified into the OECD recommendations and its construction through *data collection, checklists, and toolkits,* challenging its coherence and functions as a golden standard policy for "better regulation." Secondly, it unveils how these techniques are disseminated worldwide through mechanisms of soft governance, such as *peer review, persuasion, surveillance*, *comparison,* and *ranking*. Then, it turns to the case of Brazil, assessing how these tools and technical knowledge have been transmitted to this

---

M. F. P. Fernandes (✉)
Fundação Getúlio Vargas (FGV), São Paulo School of Law, Sao Paulo, Brazil

M. de Amstalden et al. (eds.), *International Economic Law*, Special Issue,
https://doi.org/10.1007/978-3-031-41996-6_2

specific institutional context. The case of Brazil sheds light on the effectiveness of policy and legal transfers through transnational processes involving peer pressure, social learning, the role of indicators, and cultural change.

1 Introduction

Brazil has embraced legal and institutional reforms in its regulatory system. Since 2015 Brazil has reoriented its rulemaking process towards the adoption of "good regulatory practices" (GRP) according to the "better regulation" agenda promoted by the OECD.[1] New laws and executive decrees from 2018 to 2021 made the employment of "ex-ante" Regulatory Impact Assessment (RIA) mandatory for all federal public administration's rulemaking.[2] Regulatory agencies and other national governmental bodies have been encouraged to conduct "ex-post" evaluations and manage stock reviews to reduce, simplify, and consolidate existing regulations. A new institution to oversee regulatory decision-making is under scrutiny by policymakers. A mixture of deregulation and re-regulation has taken the stage.

This chapter assesses Brazilian regulatory reforms through transnational lenses. It draws on the rationale that, although nation-states still make policy, they are immersed in a dense web of transnational networks and processes.[3]

Reforms started domestically almost 15 years earlier, but Brazil's formal request to accede to the OECD in 2017[4] catalyzed previous efforts, provided political support, and helped to overcome resistance. As a result, in 2020, Brazil adhered to two OECD recommendations on regulatory governance.[5] Although not legally binding, such instruments represent the political will of adherent countries.

Brazilian public law scholars have welcomed the recent reforms as a milestone in introducing GRP in Brazil since 2007.[6] Likewise, political scientists have considered

---

[1] OECD (2016), pp. 113–122 and Querbach and Arndt (2017), pp. 37–39.

[2] Law n° 13.874/19 (Economic Freedom Act - EFA) (Law n. 13,874, from 20 Sept 2019. Available at: http://www.planalto.gov.br/ccivil_03/_ato2019-2022/2019/lei/L13874.htm) set the framework for the regulatory environment: i) the institutionalization of RIA as mandatory for all proposals or amendments of normative acts edited by all entities of the federal public administration; and ii) the recognition of international standards. Both provisions were regulated by Decrees 10.411/2019 (Decree n. 10,411, from 30 Jun 2020, available at: https://www.gov.br/mdr/pt-br/assuntos/analise-de-impacto-regulatorio-air/D10411.pdf; and Decree n. 10,229, from 05 Feb 2020, available at: https://www.planalto.gov.br/ccivil_03/_ato2019-2022/2020/decreto/D10229.htm.

[3] Shaffer (2013), p. 2; Halliday and Shaffer (2015), pp. 3–6 and Mahon and McBride (2008), p. 3.

[4] Decree n. 9, 920/2019 established the Council for the Preparation and Monitoring of the Accession Process of the Federative Republic of Brazil to the Organization for Economic Cooperation and Development, available at: https://www2.camara.leg.br/legin/fed/decret/2019/decreto-9920-18-julho-2019-788847-norma-pe.html; for a timeline on Brazil's engagement with the OECD, see the OECD webpage, available at: https://www.oecd.org/latin-america/countries/brazil/.

[5] OECD (1995) and OECD (2012).

[6] Jordão and Cunha (2020), pp. 227–255.

a paradigmatic change in rulemaking and a key tool to maximize good governance, understood in the context of the diffusion and implementation of independent regulatory agencies (IRA),[7] which has led to a Latin American version of the Regulatory State.[8]

Brazil is not an exception to such a trend, neither among transition economies[9] nor within Latin American countries.[10] A recent Policy Brief from the Development Bank of Latin America highlighted the case of Brazil, arguing that state structural changes have been carried out through consensus-building, strategic leadership, capacity-building, and large-scale cultural change.[11]

The influence of the OECD's regulatory policy agenda on Brazil's reforms is unquestionable. However, from a domestic perspective, the OECD's model has usually been taken as an indisputable blueprint, a coherent and complete body of regulatory policy drawn from member countries' diverse—and "successful"—experiences. Hence, it is usually referred to as a "toolbox" that governments have at their disposal as highly technical knowledge to employ in the way it fits better in a continuous (*and never-ending*) learning process.[12]

This work unpacks the OECD's toolbox and challenges this conventional discourse by asking: How has the concept of GRP been developed and codified into the OECD recommendations and practices? Is this concept translated into a coherent and complete policy to drive reforms? Have been such concepts and practices effectively transmitted to the Brazilian institutional context?

The chapter is structured into three sections following this introduction. Section 2 examines the role of the OECD as a critical node in transnational regulatory governance and the construction of GRP through *data collection, checklists, and toolkits.* It provides an overview of this particular transnational norm[13] by showing

---

[7]Carvalho et al. (2020), pp. 1–9 and Holperin (2019), pp. 1116–1137.

[8]Levi-Faur and Jordana (2006), pp. 335–366 and Dubash and Morgan (2012), pp. 261–281.

[9]Ponciano and Derek (2016), pp. 1–145 and Jarvis (2017), pp. 1386–1416.

[10]Aquila et al. (2019), pp. 1–9 and Donadelli et al. (2020), pp. 255–266.

[11]Albuquerque and López Azumendi (2022), pp. 1–13.

[12]The term "toolbox" is usually referred in policy literature such as working papers and reports from the OECD and the World Bank. See OECD (2021a), pp. 25–27 and WORLD BANK GROUP (2010), pp. 16. The term is applied both to the European Commission policies and to the U.-S. policies and regulations. See, as examples, European Commission (2021) and Cai (2016), pp. 296;511. Academic literature also refers to "regulatory toolbox", either as a blueprint for regulatory governance or in a critical perspective. For some examples see Kjaer (2018), p. 14; Lodge and Kai (2012), pp. 18–25 and Queiroz-Cunha and Rodrigo (2012), p. 17. For the idea of a "never-ending" process, see particularly Pal (2008), as described better in Sect. 2.1 of this chapter.

[13]I employ here the term "transnational norm" as "a collection of legal norms and associated institutions within a given domain that order behavior across national jurisdictions". The related concept "transnational legal process" is "the process through which the transnational construction and conveyance of legal norms take place". Both terms are defined in Shaffer and Halliday's framework as a sociolegal approach and methodological conception, where they shift the focus from transnational law as a body of law or legal doctrine to processes of transnational legal ordering and the construction and migration of legal norms across borders, regardless of whether they address transnational activities or purely national ones.

contradictions inside the so-called "GRP's toolbox". Section 3 turns to the case of Brazil, illustrating how such tools and technical knowledge have been conveyed to a specific institutional context through mechanisms of soft governance,[14] alternating movements of resistance, skepticism, and full embracement. Section 4 concludes.

2 Unpacking the GRP's Toolbox and the OECD's Techniques of Soft Governance

This section focuses on the OECD and its role as a standard-setting institution and a knowledge producer in transnational regulatory governance through the construction of GRP.[15] In Halliday & Shaffer's framework for analyzing transnational legal processes and the dimensions and determinants of state change, one key factor to assess is the nature of the transnational norm being conveyed.[16] Breaking down this idea, it becomes necessary to understand the transnational legal norm's legitimacy, clarity, and coherence.[17] By unpacking what lies behind the construction of the "GRP toolbox," I challenge specifically its coherence, illustrating the complexities, tensions, and contradictions enmeshed in the apparent "neutral" concept of GRP. Then, I briefly explain how the OECD has developed and refined techniques of soft governance to transmit its transnational norm.

2.1 *Putting the Tools inside the Box*

This analysis is inspired by Leslie Pal's work, which delved into representative OECD documents on the concept of "governance."[18] I take the same steps to assess the primary documents that constitute the OECD transnational norm in regulatory governance, here named simply as the "GRP toolbox". Pal called "modernization under stress" the emulation and borrowing among nations that wish to move towards modernity.[19] His narratives provide a series of 'inversions without end,' as "the OECD moved from the particular to the universal, from models to modalities, and

[14]Marcussen (2004), pp. 103–128 and Pal (2012), pp. 63;96;121–156.

[15]Baldwin (2010), pp. 259–278; Jakobi (2012), pp. 2–26 and Lang (2019), pp. 8–22.

[16]Halliday and Shaffer (2015), pp. 11–15.

[17]Halliday and Shaffer (2015), p. 32.

[18]Pal (2008), pp. 60–76.

[19]Pal (2008), p. 61.

from reform to redemption".[20] The literary allegory used by Pal[21] resembles the Greek mythological figure of Sisyphus, who was forced to roll an immense boulder up a hill and then to roll down every time it neared the top, repeating this action for eternity. Not by chance, the World Bank named a cross-country survey on the implementation of regulatory reforms in developing countries "Giving Sisyphus a Helping Hand".[22]

Progressively, the OECD became a global advocate for the New Public Management (NPM) model.[23] Beginning in the 1990s, the OECD's Public Management Committee (PUMA)[24] has produced a whole body of regulatory policy reference documents, checklists, recommendations, and toolkits on the design and implementation of regulatory reforms. It has influenced member and non-member countries from different political and institutional backgrounds.[25] Over time, this agenda moved from a deregulation approach based on competition, market orientation, and reduction of administrative burdens to a broader concept of regulatory governance.[26] Countries have implemented the recommendations and requested periodic reviews of their efforts and results.[27] After the OECD's enlargement process in 2004, emerging economies, such as Brazil, also began to adhere to programs of regulatory reforms.

The OECD crafted the normative concept of GRP, which is generally understood today and highly accepted worldwide.[28] Notwithstanding its high level of adherence, scarce studies assess this whole body of work, especially examining the process of changing from deregulation to the broad meaning of regulatory governance and,

---

[20] Id., in Pal's (2008) own words, "*reform would be a project without end, since the reformation of one part of the system will inevitably perturb other parts, which will, in turn, have to be adjusted and reformed, ad infinitum. Inversions without end.*" (p. 78)

[21] See Cormac (1985), cited by Pal (2008).

[22] Ladegaard Peter and Kamkhaji (2018). This World Bank cross-country quantitative study mapped developing countries' regulatory reforms in 60 countries from 2001 to 2016 to understand which ones produced successful RIA systems despite adhering or not to the overall package of GRP. Brazil and Armenia were considered notable outliers for having put in place functional RIA systems with limited observations of "good practices".

[23] Pal (2008), p. 60. For a reference study on NPM, see Hood (2004).

[24] PUMA had a critical role in developing and disseminating New Public Management Reforms. In 2004 the name was changed to Public Governance Committee and in 2009 to Regulatory Policy Committee, which has acted as the central venue for the development and implementation of regulatory policy programs.

[25] Pal (2012), pp. 34–57.

[26] Jakobi (2012), pp. 9–10; Lang (2019), pp. 8–22.

[27] Jakobi (2012), pp. 14–17.

[28] The OECD does not define "Good Regulatory Practices" (GRP), but it does mention the expression in several documents. A vast academic and policy literature also refers to GRP. The idea of a normative concept comes from a compilation of the main OECD recommendations, guidelines, reports, country peer reviews and working papers on regulatory governance and reforms. The main OECD webpage referencing all these documents is available at: https://www.oecd.org/regreform/regulatory-policy/recommendations-guidelines.html.

more recently, to "agile regulatory governance".[29] Jakobi considers the regulatory policy of the OECD "*unclear at best and contradictory at worst*", despite presenting itself as "*systematically developed over time, declaring seemingly contradictions as different stages in the development*".[30] For Lodge and Wegrish, this agenda is based on contradictory views regarding regulation and contested assumptions underlying such tools.[31] As they remark, anyone would disagree with "high-quality regulation" instead of "low-quality regulation"; however, it is unclear what high quality *exactly* means.[32] Lang argued that the difficulty of grasping the whole regulatory policy developed by the OECD along almost 20 years "*goes to the heart of (his) understanding of regulatory policy as a technique of global regulatory 'un-governance.'*"[33]

The first Recommendation, proposed by PUMA and adopted by several countries, is a prosaic *Reference* Checklist[34] based on a questionnaire of ten questions in a problem-solving format to guide regulators in drafting new regulations on a rational basis.[35] The message in the Checklist is simple: there is a need to rationalize the process through which regulations are made. Despite this apparent simplicity, the context in which the Checklist was produced matters in understanding its underlying assumptions. Regulators from industrialized democracies were asked to report their "*successful governing responses to the diverse interests and values of modern societies.*"[36] Deregulation and market-driven approach were keywords in the resulting document. The United States deregulation movement in the '70 s mixed with the UK's Deregulation Unit in the '80 s. The following experiences of Canada, Australia, New Zealand, Japan, and European countries were added. While some responses emphasized economic analysis and cost reduction, others stressed "due process", and others focused on simplicity.[37] In the face of diverse experiences, the OECD's task was to find *key principles* that "*should be flexible enough to apply to regulatory decisions in all or most policy areas*" and "*to provide practical guidance*

---

[29] OECD (2021b).

[30] Jakobi (2012), p. 3.

[31] Lodge and Wegrich (2009), p. 151.

[32] Lodge and Wegrich (2009), p. 145.

[33] Lang (2019), p. 30. By 'un-governance,' Lang means that GRP embeds a set of *open-ended* organizational routines into regulatory decision-making, which may be associated with different political projects in diverse contexts. The constant ability to enact such rituals implies that GRP is not part of a broader rule-making project but rather a *contestability* project about *un-settling* market orders and un-making institutions.

[34] OECD (1995).

[35] The questions are: 1. Is the Problem Correctly Defined? 2. Is Government Action Justified? 3. Is Regulation the Best Form of Government Action? 4. Is there a Legal Basis for Regulation? 5. What is the Appropriate Level (or Levels) of Government for this Action? 6. Do the Benefits of Regulation Justify the Costs? 7. Is the Distribution of Effects across Society Transparent? 8. Is the Regulation Clear, Consistent, Comprehensible, and Accessible to Users? 9. Have All Interested Parties had the Opportunity to Present their Views? 10. How will Compliance be Achieved?

[36] OECD (1995), p. 8.

[37] OECD (1995), p. 9.

on the design of "high-quality regulations".[38] Such a construction demonstrates how transnational institutionalization of norms elevates one (or more) country's particular norms to the transnational status of universals.[39]

In 1997, the OECD complemented the Checklist with a contextual analysis of the reforms undertaken by members, presenting a more realistic view of the challenges and resistances faced by governments.[40] Again, the experiences were "distilled" to extract their essence and offer a "plan of action" to promote regulatory reforms,[41] presented as an "integrated package" of seven principles, although with very conflicting perspectives.

Baldwin and Sahlin-Anderson have described well such a conflict. Baldwin remarks that the rise of the "better regulation" agenda in the UK, for example, was a rhetorical device designed to give coherence between the deregulation agenda ("red tape"), "regulatory quality" developments, and a third dynamic related to "rational planning" tools, such as RIA and cost-benefit analysis (CBA).[42] Therefore, the language of 'better regulation' or 'high-quality regulation' was "an attempt to bridge these three related, but also conflicting dynamics".[43] Sahlin-Andersson refers to "*an amalgam of public choice theory, principal-agency theory, and transaction cost economics*", arguing that PUMA has edited out country-specific experience to produce generalizable conclusions, assembled as a reform agenda or policy package as if there was a common logic and common explanations to the reforms.[44]

In 2002, the Regulatory Committee released a new report[45] setting three pillars for high-quality regulation: (i) *regulatory reform,* related to individual regulations; (ii) *regulatory policy*, to optimize the whole context in which regulations are set and ensure only "high-quality regulations"; and (iii) *regulatory governance*, as the most ambitious concept. Various tools and one key institution were included inside the box: the systematic use of RIA as an empirical decision-making method, administrative simplification, diverse ways to increase transparency, public consultation, and improve accountability, and a key institution to oversee regulatory bodies close to the government, which most of the member states had already set at the

38 OECD (1995), p. 9.

39 Halliday (2012), p. 91.

40 OECD (1997), p. 2.

41 OECD (1997), p. 2.

42 Baldwin (2010), p. 4.

43 Baldwin (2010), p. 4.

44 Sahlin-Andersson (2000). National, international and transnational construction of new public management. Stockholm Centre for Organizational Research (SCORE) Working Paper 2000-4, cited by Mahon and McBride (2008), p. 11.

45 OECD (2002).

time.[46] The final message in this report was that governments should *permanently* pursue "regulatory governance" as a broad agenda.[47]

From 1998 to 2004, twenty member countries underwent peer review in their regulatory systems. New reports and guides were published, adding new layers to the debate while maintaining the seven principles from the 1997 Report.[48] In 2005, a famous study about better regulation discourse in the European Union provided a cautionary note.[49] According to Radaelli, although a community of discourse emerged around better regulation programmes and RIA across Europe, the political and bureaucratic context played a pivotal role in the emergence of significant divergence. In some cases, RIA had been imported into EU countries with largely unrealistic models of the policy process. In Radaelli's metaphor, "*the result ha [d] been new bottles with poor or no wine at all*".[50]

Notwithstanding, in 2008, the global financial crisis put pressure on the OECD Regulatory Policy Committee. The crisis exposed flaws in regulation, and effective regulation was part of the answer to regaining confidence from consumers and entrepreneurs. As countries emerged from the crisis, they were under intense pressure to strengthen their regulatory systems to avoid financial instability. On October 2010, participants in the international OECD Conference on "Regulatory Policy: Towards a New Policy Agenda" called for *new principles to redefine* the agenda for regulatory policy.[51] A further recommendation should provide "*a clearer dialogue with members and non-members about the policies, practices, and institutions needed for systemic improvements to regulatory quality*".[52]

In 2012, the OECD Council finally approved the new "*OECD Council Recommendation on Regulatory Policy and Governance*", heralding that "*in the shadow of the global financial crisis, the importance of sound regulatory frameworks has become more evident than ever*" and achieving good regulation is "*a demanding task and one that is never over*", in the words of Gary Banks, Chair of the Regulatory Policy Committee.[53] The Recommendation targeted developing a systemic governance framework that could deliver *ongoing* improvements to the quality of regulations. The twelve principles are the following: a "whole of government" approach at the highest political level (1st); transparency and participation in the regulatory process (2nd); mechanisms and institutions to provide oversight of regulatory

---

[46]The Office of Regulation Review in Australia, the Office of Regulatory Affairs in Canada, the Better Regulation Task Force (BRTF) in the UK, the United States Office of Information and Regulatory Affairs (OIRA); and the Japan's Administrative Reform Committee.

[47]OECD (2002), pp. 28–37.

[48]Regulatory Impact Assessment Inventory (2004); OECD Guiding Principles for Quality and Regulatory Performance (2005); Introductory Handbook for Undertaking RIA (2008); Determinants of Quality in Regulatory Impact Analysis (2009).

[49]Radaelli (2005).

[50]Radaelli (2005), p. 940.

[51]OECD (2010), pp. 22–26.

[52]OECD (2010), p. 28.

[53]OECD (2012), p. 2.

procedures (3rd); integration of RIA at early stages (4th); systematic stock reviews (5th); reports on the performance (6th); consistent policy for regulatory agencies (7th); effective systems to review the legality and procedural fairness of regulation (8th); risk-assessment and management to design and implement regulation (9th); regulatory coherence through coordination across supranational, national and sub-national levels (10th and 11th), and consideration to all relevant international standards (12th).[54]

The 2012 Recommendation is currently the critical legal reference for regulatory policy adopted worldwide as a benchmark and an almost uncontested blueprint for reforms in non-member countries. Yet, like many other countries, Brazil has struggled to complete these twelve principles and roll up the boulder to the top of the hill, in a Sisyphus' work.

In 2019, the advent of the pandemic required new adjustments, and a new Recommendation was published on October 2021.[55] It provided for the following adjustments: (i) to ensure that regulations are fit for the future; (ii) to enable the development of agile, adaptive, and future-proof regulation; (iii) to help innovators navigate the regulatory environment, and cooperation within and across jurisdictions; and (iv) to adapt enforcement activities to evolving needs.[56] Building on momentum from the pandemic and disruption of supply chains, this Recommendation brings new challenges to governments and regulators, resembling Pal's allegory of "*inversions without end*",[57] renewed at each crisis.

2.2 Exporting the Toolbox

The OECD recommendations on regulatory governance have been widely diffused in several countries and adopted in diverse institutional contexts.[58] To disseminate its policies, the OECD has developed and refined techniques of soft governance,

---

[54]OECD (2012), pp. 6–12.

[55]OECD (2021a).

[56]OECD (2021a).

[57]Pal (2008).

[58]The spread of policies, ideas, and institutions across different countries have been studied in international relations, public policy, comparative politics, sociology and other fields, with a terminological and conceptual diversity among scholars. Some studies focus on processes and others on outcomes. The most common denominations to explain these phenomena are "policy transfer", "policy diffusion" (Marsh and Sharman, 2009), "policy convergence" (Knill 2005), and "institutional isomorphism" (DiMaggio and Powell 1983). In this article, I employ "diffusion" as defined by Dobbin et al. (2007): "*international policy diffusion occurs when government policy decisions in a given country are systematically conditioned by prior choices made in other countries (sometimes mediated by the behavior of international organizations or private actors and organizations)*". For policy diffusion's analyses specifically involving the OECD Regulatory Policy, see De Francesco (2013) and Radaelli (2005) as primary references.

such as peer review, persuasion, surveillance, comparison, and ranking. I turn to elaborate on these techniques below.

Peer review is a practice, more than a concept, having no definition or procedure narrowly established.[59] The OECD is the IO that has primarily developed the technique of peer review, but it has never laid down a standardized mechanism. Each peer review has its procedure, and the level of procedural detail can vary widely according to the context.[60] The effectiveness of peer review relies on the persuasion exercised during the process, known as "peer pressure".[61] This process translates into recommendations, public scrutiny, comparison, and ranking among countries. Together, all such mechanisms may substantially impact domestic public opinion, national administrations, and policymakers. Constructivists argue that IOs do more than just manage relations among states. They help define the *identity of member states and their perceptions of self-interest.*[62] This approach to understanding the OECD suggests that there are reasons to see its work as much more significant than is recognized by rationalist theories.[63] More than a highly technical research organization and a think-thank based on "evidence-based" policies, the OECD's knowledge production shapes the identity of its member states and those aspiring to be members.[64] As Robert Wolfe argued, "*the most important thing that changes because of the OECD might be the thinking of the people – from technical officials to ministers – who attend its meetings or participate in its peer-review process.*"[65]

In practical terms, the OECD peer review often begins with a questionnaire formulated by the Secretariat, a sophisticated instrument with a vocabulary that conceptualizes the problem under analysis. The questionnaire usually covers macroeconomic issues and may raise critical political events, such as elections, and their influence on specific policies or plans to change laws and regulations. The Secretariat decides the review's focus, which topics should be covered, and the subsequent

[59] There is scarce literature on peer review, and the topic is often addressed marginally in the context of compliance. See generally Downs et al. (1996).

[60] Pagani (2002).

[61] Pagani (2002), p. 18.

[62] Porter and Webb (2008), p. 44. Constructivist approaches assert that significant aspects of international relations are shaped by ideational factors, historically and socially constructed. For relevant references on this approach, see Ruggie (1998) and Finnemore and Sikkink (2001). Porter and Webb provide a case study of the OECD work on corporate governance from a constructivist approach, presenting the organization as a space where intersubjective meanings emerge through social interactions of its member states, and identities are socially constructed.

[63] Rationalist theories of international institutions see them as efficient mechanisms for states to pursue their self-interests, on the basis of rational calculation of the material costs and benefits of membership. Rationalist models operate according to a "logic of consequences"—with international negotiations understood primarily as strategic interaction among actors seeking to maximize exogenous interests (March and Olsen 1998). Neo-liberal institutionalists also posit that international organizations assist states in achieving their ends (Hobson 2000).

[64] Porter and Webb (2008), pp. 43–59.

[65] Wolfe (2008), p. 41.

assessment phase. When the country under review answers the questionnaire, its government representatives must enter into the "mental framework" established by the Secretariat. They have to address specific economic and political variables as they were previously framed in the questions.[66]

After the answers are provided, the Secretariat conducts consultations with authorities, interest groups, civil society, and academics in the reviewed country. It may involve a visit by the OECD mission and meetings with ministries and domestic experts. Then, a report is prepared and shared with the government. In the final stage, members and the state discuss the draft report and then adopt it, in general, by consensus. The report's credibility is based on the reviewed state's involvement and the guarantee that it will endorse it and implement recommendations. However, "*the states' involvement should not go so far as to endanger the fairness and the objectivity of the review*" and "*should not be permitted to veto the adoption of the final report*".[67] Therefore, at the end of the process, participants are immersed in the same collective knowledge construction based on parameters that would barely be contested.

In addition, the report usually includes a comparison and ranking among countries. To make this comparison, the OECD identifies "appropriate" indicators to permit cross-national comparison and ranking, calling attention to "leaders" and "laggards".[68] In the case of regulatory policy, there are two systems of indicators: the Indicators of Product Market Regulation (PMR) and the Indicators of Regulatory Policy and Governance (iREG). PMR measures the country's regulatory barriers to competition, state involvement in the economy, the role of SOEs, and barriers to entry for domestic and foreign firms. [69] A key feature of the PMR database is that it captures the "*de jure*" policy settings. This means that the answers are not based on *subjective* assessments by market participants but on the laws in force in the country. iREG assesses regulatory policy practices according to the 2012 Recommendation, covering three principles: RIA, stakeholder engagement, and ex-post evaluation. In addition, it diagnoses successes and failures in specific regulatory policies and tools.[70]

The peer-review mechanism, accompanied by extensive and previous data collection through directed questionnaires, followed by surveillance, persuasion,

---

[66] Noaksson and Jacobsson (2003), pp. 25–31. The authors nicely describe the cycle of the peer review process, involving the joint efforts by the reviewed country, the examiners countries and the OECD Secretariat. The expression "mental framework" is referred by Rianne Mahon and Stephen McBride, when commenting on the OECD questionnaires and how the questions posed to the reviewed country direct their attention to a set of problem areas that the OECD finds interesting. (Mahon and McBride 2008, p. 9).

[67] Pagani (2002), p. 19.

[68] March and Olsen (1998), p. 961.

[69] Vitale et al. (2020). This publication analyses the 2018 edition of the OECD PMR indicators and database.

[70] The OECD Measuring Regulatory Performance programme is available at: www.oecd.org/gov/regulatory-policy/measuring-regulatory-performance.html.

comparison, and ranking, is at the heart of the OECD work. Technical knowledge and peer pressure are tools comparable to material power. Moreover, the creation and dissemination of complex indicators influence the terms in which problems are conceptualized and solutions imagined. As such, the OECD Regulatory Governance Indicators represent a quiet form of power translated into a governance technology.[71]

3 Brazil's Regulatory Reform

This section turns to Brazil's engagement with the OECD on regulatory reforms. It assesses domestic political struggles and legal changes and how they interrelate with international and transnational norms on regulatory governance. The assessment covers the period from 2000 to today, divided into three phases: (1) an early approach, when Brazil started as an observer at PUMA Committee, voluntarily submitting to a peer review in 2007, but was immersed in domestic controversies related to the proper role of regulatory agencies; (2) a period of government's skepticism towards the OECD, when the concepts of regulatory coherence and GRP entered in Brazil through bilateral channels, especially with the US and the UK, keeping the GRP agenda alive and mobilizing new actors; and (3) the last 6 years when the Brazilian government reoriented its political economy towards neoliberal policies, relying firmly on OECD indicators, and speeding up reforms.

This account shows how domestic political battles play a crucial role in reforms. But conversely, it also attempts to demonstrate how they are entangled in a web of transnational relations and processes influencing how states change. More importantly, it argues that self-perceptions of public officials and private actors involved in the process change according to the inter-relation they maintain with IOs, such as the OECD and networks of experts, in complex dynamics that lead to broad cultural changes.

3.1 Early Approach: Peer Review and Resistance (2000–2010)

In 2000, Brazil joined the PUMA Committee as an observer. At this time, PUMA was committed to assisting members in improving their public institutions' performance. PUMA's work was increasingly sought for innovative products, including popular policy briefs, practical handbooks, and toolkits on strengthening government capacity. The OECD Secretariat had just launched a "reinvention" of the program on public governance as a response to the Russian and Asian crises. This program identified "good governance" as the third element of its central

[71] Merry et al. (2015).

priority-setting approach. Member countries have accepted the responsibility to support governance reforms in countries *outside the OECD area*, bilaterally and through International Institutions.[72] According to the Revised Program of Work, "*the audience [was] there, and PUMA want[ed] to be heard and raise its voice to help governments stay the course in the reform of governance*".[73]

From a Brazilian domestic perspective, the importance of regulatory policy as a transversal theme across sectoral regulation was only "discovered" by public officials in 2005, during Lula da Silva's first administration (2003–2011).[74] The Chief of Staff of the Presidency had set up an Inter-ministerial Working Group (GTI) to evaluate the role of the regulatory agencies and the institutional arrangements created during Cardoso's privatization era.[75] The GTI's final report reaffirmed the agencies' model as essential for the success of private investments. Nevertheless, it defended that regulatory agencies were not eminently responsible for formulating sectoral policies and that such power should remain with Ministries, provided by "*a well-defined border between both*".[76] The GTI proposed a controversial bill sent to Congress called "General Law of the Regulatory Agencies" (PL 3,337/2004), which remained for 15 years in the Legislative.[77] It became clear that the Worker Party's government preferred strengthening presidential influence over the regulatory agencies.[78] This controversy somewhat hindered Brazil's regulatory quality reforms at the domestic level.

Despite such controversy over the amount of power given to the regulatory agencies, in 2007, the Chief of Staff of the Presidency launched the Program for Strengthening the Institutional Capacity for Regulatory Management (PRO-REG) with the Ministries of Finance, Planning, Budget, and Management.[79] The Inter-American Development Bank (IADB) financed the project, following the OECD Recommendations and Guidelines on Regulatory Policy. In March 2007, Brazil asked for a peer review with the OECD. In the same year, Brazil's relationship with the OECD had scaled to "enhanced engagement."[80] For the OECD, the Brazilian

[72] OECD (1998), p. 4.

[73] OECD (1998), p. 5.

[74] Interview with a representative from the Ministry of Economy. On file with author.

[75] Bresser-Pereira (2004), p. 173.

[76] Brazil, Casa Civil. Análise e avaliação do papel das agências reguladoras no atual arranjo institucional brasileiro: relatório do Grupo de Trabalho Interministerial. Editora República Federativa do Brasil, Casa Civil, 2003. Available at: http://www.nuca.ie.ufrj.br/furnas/fianibibliografia/camara2.pdf.

[77] Câmara dos Deputados, EMP 16/2004, PL 3,337/2004. Available at https://www.camara.leg.br/proposicoesWeb/fichadetramitacao?idProposicao=251367.

[78] Prado (2008), pp. 27–42.

[79] Presidential Decree n. 6,062, March 17th, 2007. Available at: http://www.planalto.gov.br/ccivil_03/_ato2007-2010/2007/decreto/d6062.htm.

[80] OECD (2007).

peer review would be the first for a country involved in the *Enhancement Engagement Strategy.*[81]

This new status of the relationship between Brazil and the OECD should not be understated to explain the peer review context and its importance in seedling the ground for the "better regulation" agenda promoted by the OECD. Since the 1990s, the OECD began to face pressures to include non-members in its work to oversee the "developing dialogue".[82] After 1994, the OECD expanded its membership to Mexico, South Korea, and East European countries. In 2006, the former Mexican foreign minister, Angel Gurría, took office as the new Secretary-General, declaring his aim to make the OECD a "globalization hub."[83] In June 2007, during the OECD Ministerial Conference held after the G8 Summit, enlargement and engagement with non-members became a contentious theme. From one side, leaders asked the Organization to act as a platform for dialogue with the major emerging economies of Brazil, China, India, Mexico, and South Africa. On the other side, according to Noboru's report, [84] only "like-minded" countries that shared the OECD's democratic political values and market-based economics could contribute to the OECD's voluntary consensus-building and socialization processes.

Moreover, this shared identity was indispensable for the functioning of the OECD's deliberative processes and peer review mechanisms. Therefore, a core dilemma was on the table: expanding membership to sustain the institution's relevance could undermine the shared identity. The Ministerial Council responded to this dilemma by inviting five countries[85] and initiating discussions for "enhanced engagement" with Brazil, China, India, Indonesia, and South Africa for possible future membership.[86]

For these reasons, the "enhanced engagement" with the OECD and the peer review on regulatory governance, both in 2007, represented a mechanism for the OECD to strengthen its relationship with Brazil, one of the emerging countries targeted for the necessary enlargement of the Organization to remain effective in a new geo-economic scenario.[87] This inter-relation between domestic struggles over regulatory reforms and the momentum of the OECD in the international scenario brings new light to the context of peer review. Although this mechanism is usually referred to for its importance to the reviewed country in terms of receiving an international endorsement for domestic reforms, it also reveals how processes that

[81] OECD (2008).

[82] Wolfe (2008), p. 32.

[83] Mahon and McBride (2008), p. 3.

[84] Noboru (2004).

[85] The five countries invited were Chile, Estonia, Israel, Russia, and Slovenia.

[86] Porter and Webb (2008).

[87] Mahbubani (2012).

produce and reinforce identity and knowledge can be located in transnational spaces.[88]

At the outset, the OECD peer review report highlighted that Brazil had entered a new phase of economic development "*with the need to strengthen the institutional foundations for a market-based economy.*"[89] Regarding the controversies over PL 3,337/04, the report was straightforward: "*The debates over a new bill on agencies discussed in Congress reflected the variety of views in the country. If Brazil wants to close the gap with the OECD countries, there is a need to ensure that agencies will be 'put to work,' fulfilling the mission for which they were created*".[90] Concerning the implementation of GRP's toolbox, recommendations were also clear: "*Brazil lacks a systematic use of regulatory quality tools*", and the "*diversity of experience offered by OECD countries provides a wide range of possible solutions that could be adapted to the Brazilian context*".[91]

After the peer review, from 2008 to 2010, PRO-REG produced more than a thousand pages of studies and reports. Three books were published,[92] and intense capacity-building training programs took place in Brazil.[93] Despite that, PRO-REG lost political support and slowed down after 3 years. In 2011, after Rousseff's election, the Brazilian government remained skeptical about seeking OECD membership.[94] Without direct governmental support, the regulatory program kept dormant, starting to run only with resources from the Federal Budget.[95]

The PL 3337/04 represented an endogen initiative, raising a controversial but fundamental debate over the power of the Executive on regulatory agencies. In contrast, PRO-REG was backed by an exogen influence. For some officials involved, the program lacked "substantive political support from the heart of the government" and had an overly "theoretical grip" besides being too focused on the regulatory agencies.[96]

In 2016, a week before Rousseff's impeachment, PRO-REG was strategically transferred to the Ministry of Planning, Budget, and Management and revitalized, as described in Sect. 3.3 below. However, between the down of PRO-REG and its

---

[88] Porter and Webb (2008), p. 58.

[89] OECD (2008), p. 11.

[90] OECD (2008), p. 13.

[91] OECD (2008), p. 15.

[92] For a thorough review of PRO-REG and the documents produced, see https://www.gov.br/casacivil/pt-br/assuntos/governanca/regulacao/sistema-regulatorio-brasileiro/historico-do-pro-reg.

[93] Brazil signed a Cooperation Agreement with the United Kingdom to carry out a project on "Better regulation." A course on "Regulation Theory and Practice" was held in July 2010, taught by professors Martin Lodge from the London School of Economics and Kai Wegrich from the Hertie School of Governance. National and foreign consultant experts were hired to study international experiences on RIA, oversight bodies, institutional designs, the development of databanks to support evidenced rulemaking, and ombudsman institutions for regulatory agencies.

[94] Sanchez (2008) and Davis (2016).

[95] Queiroz-Cunha and Rodrigo (2013), p. 8.

[96] Interview with a public official from the Ministry of Economy. On file with author.

recoup in 2016, different initiatives started taking place in Brazil connected to the "better regulation" agenda.

3.2 *Government's Skepticism and the Role of Bilateral Trade Relations with the US (2011–2015)*

From 2011 to 2015, while PRO-REG languished in the Civil House of Presidency, a separate and more diffuse initiative concerned with regulatory improvement mobilized public officials from the Ministry of Development, Industry and Foreign Trade (MDIC) and the Brazilian Foreign Trade Board (CAMEX). The view of this initiative as "separate" from PRO-REG was articulated in a short position document published by the Brazil-US Business Council (BUSBC), aiming to advance the Regulatory Coherence Agenda in Brazil through meaningful engagement from the private sector and civil society.[97]

During this period, new expressions such as "regulatory coherence", "regulatory cooperation," and "regulatory convergence" entered the lexicon of Brazilian foreign trade discourses, coming from the government's agenda backed by the private sector and the academy.[98] However, those expressions and initiatives did not seem predominately endogenous either. Instead, they reflected and reverberated a broader movement at the international level, which started to be disseminated in Brazil through bilateral commercial relations with the US, the EU, and the UK.[99]

'Regulatory Coherence', GRP, and 'Regulatory Cooperation' may be understood as dimensions of a broader phenomenon related to how domestic regulation

---

[97] Brazil-US Business Council (2014): Advancing the Regulatory Coherence Agenda in Brazil. Available online at https://www.brazilcouncil.org/wp-content/uploads/2015/11/021933_Brazil_RegCoherence_IN_final.pdf.

[98] Ministério do Desenvolvimento, Indústria e Comércio Exterior. Brasil e Estados Unidos anunciam novos acordos em convergência regulatória e patentes, 19/11/2015, http://www.comexresponde.gov.br/portalmdic/sitio/interna/noticia.php?area=5&noticia=14179; Casa Civil da Presidência da República, Coerência e Boas Práticas Regulatórias, Abril, 2015, available at: https://www.gov.br/casacivil/pt-br/assuntos/governanca/regulacao/eventos/2018/coerencia-regulatoria-sag-casa-civil-se-camex-einmetro/apresentacoes/apresentacaocoerenciaregulatoria_sag_06abr2018.pdf.

[99] International Trade Administration. US Brazil Commercial Dialogue Statement, March 2015, available at: https://www.trade.gov/brazil-us-brazil-commercial-dialogue-statement-march-2015; FGVEESP Centro de Estudos do Comércio Global e Investimento. Regulatory Coherence and Convergence. Presentation of the project supported by the Great Britain and Northern Ireland Embassy and funded through the Prosperity Fund. Available at: https://ccgi.fgv.br/en/regulatory-coherence-and-convergence; Thorstensen and Nogueira (orgs.) Coerência e Convergência Regulatória: Modelos Regulatórios de Parceiros do Brasil. EUA, EU, Canadá, Coréia do Sul, Japão, México, Acordos Regionais de Comércio de EUA e UE. Available at: https://ccgi.fgv.br/sites/ccgi.fgv.br/files/u5/Coerencia-Convergencia-Regulatoria-INMETRO2019_TN.pdf; http://camex.gov.br/images/Eventos/ConvRegulatoria/RELATORIO-FINAL-Vol-4%2D%2D-Sintese-e-Concluses.pdf.

intersects with the international trade regime. This relation gained prominence from the beginning of the millennium, with the failure of the Doha Round and the increasing distrust of the multilateral trading system. In this context, the political economy built around global supply chains pushed countries to align regulations through different instruments and institutions to minimize regulatory divergence and reduce transaction costs.[100] Among such tools were enhanced transparency and notifications commitments embedded in new preferential trade agreements (PTAs) and evidence-based regulatory processes supported by GRPs, with a special role for RIA. At this point, regulatory reforms in the transition and developing countries met with a new wave in trade relations characterized by the pressing need to reduce non-tariff barriers to trade, which means domestic regulations.

While Brazil was taking its peer review on regulatory governance and struggling with domestic concerns over the appropriate role of the newly established regulatory agencies, new PTAs were negotiated, including regulatory coherence and GRP clauses to tackle regulatory divergences and ease trade in goods and services. Both the Transatlantic Trade and Investment Partnership (TTIP) between the US and the EU[101] and the Transpacific Partnership (TPP), later signed as the Comprehensive and Progressive Agreement for Trans-Pacific Partnership (CPTPP) among eleven Asia Pacific countries,[102] had the first regulatory clauses and chapters. As political scientist scholars pointed out, there was a "regulatory turn" in international trade, through which the US and EU started exporting their rules by promoting their regulatory systems abroad.[103] Nevertheless, beyond treaty-based provisions in PTAs, the promotion of regulatory coherence, cooperation, and GRP took two other venues and channels of diffusion: plurilaterally, through the OECD work on regulatory governance, and bilaterally, through informal trade relations between the US and the EU and their trading partners, such as private commercial dialogues, pushing their regulatory systems over other countries.

---

[100] Hoekman and Sabel (2019), p. 217.

[101] In 2007, the Transatlantic Economic Forum (TEC) for regulatory cooperation and economic convergence was established between the United States and the European Union. In the TEC's founding document signed by U.S. President George Bush and German Chancellor Angela Merkel, both countries committed themselves to a robust regulatory cooperation agenda, promising "to remove unnecessary differences between their regulations to foster economic integration. Available at: http://ec.europa.eu/trade/policy/countries-and-regions/countries/united-states/.

[102] The TPP - Trans-Pacific Partnership was the result of an expansion of the Trans-Pacific Strategic Economic Partnership Agreement (TPSEP, also referred to as P4), between Brunei, Chile, New Zealand and Singapore in 2005. From 2008, other countries joined the discussion for a broader agreement: Australia, Canada, Japan, Malaysia, Mexico, Peru, the United States, and Vietnam. In January 2017, the United States withdrew from the TPP. On December 30, 2018, the CPTPP entered into force among the 11 remaining countries.

[103] Young (2015); Benvenisti (2015) and Laursen and Roederer-Rynning (2017). See also the critical academic project jointly coordinated by the Institute for International Law and Governance (IILJ), the New York University (NYU) Law School, and the National Graduate Institute for Policy Studies (GRIPS) in Tokyo on the TPP as a U.S. megaregulation and political ordering project (Kingsburry et al. 2019).

The 2012 OECD Recommendations, as mentioned in Sect. 2, already reflected such a conceptualization when it included its 10th to 12th principles on "*regulatory coherence through coordination across supranational, national and sub-national levels*" and "*consideration to all relevant international standards and potential effects of regulation outside jurisdictions*".[104] A year later, in 2013, the OECD published a report on "International Regulatory Cooperation" (IRC),[105] which was highly diffused to countries as a paradigm of a new step for regulatory coherence in the world of supply chains. The 2012 Recommendation became the blueprint for most regulatory clauses in the new PTAs and influenced regulatory reform programs and foreign trade policies worldwide. Also, US president Barack Obama issued Executive Order 13,609,[106] emphasizing IRC by establishing a working group led by the Office of Information and Regulatory Affairs (OIRA) to address "*unnecessary regulatory differences between the United States and its major trading partners across borders*". [107] As a result, pursuing regulatory coherence and GRP as an international trade policy became a priority objective of US domestic trade policy.[108]

Against this background, although Brazil had kept relatively isolated from the mega-regional agreements[109] and remained skeptical of seeking OECD's membership within the Enhanced Engagement program,[110] the regulatory coherence agenda in Brazil made its way through more informal trade channels. In March 2011, a visit of US President Obama to president Dilma Rousseff ignited trade talks between both countries, having regulatory coherence and cooperation issues as relevant topics.[111] During President Obama's visit, the US and Brazil concluded an Agreement on Trade and Economic Cooperation (ATEC),[112] creating a new bilateral trade dialogue designed to foster deeper cooperation on intellectual property rights, trade facilitation, and technical trade barriers.[113]

---

[104] OECD (2012).

[105] OECD (2013).

[106] Executive Order 13,609 (May 1, 2012), 77 FR 26413.

[107] The Office of Information and Regulatory Affairs (OIRA) is a U.S. sub-agency within the Office of Management and Budget (OMB), integrating the President's Executive Office. It was created in the Paperwork Reduction Act signed by President Carter in 1980 and was given the role of reviewing Regulatory Impact Analysis (RIA) for all major regulations by Executive Order 12291.

[108] Sunstein (2012).

[109] Trubek et al. (2017).

[110] Sanchez (2008) and Davis (2016).

[111] Under the Worker Party's administration, Brazilian foreign policy had prioritized relations with nontraditional partners in the developing world ("South-South" relations) and coalitions with Brazil-Russia-India-China- South Africa (BRICS) group and the India-Brazil-South Africa (IBSA) forum.

[112] Joint Statement on the Occasion of the Visit by President Barack Obama to Brazil (March 19, 2022). Available at: https://www.brazilcouncil.org/wp-content/uploads/2015/11/JointStatementObamaandRousseff-Mar192011.pdf.

[113] White House, Office of the Press Secretary, "Strengthening the U.S.-Brazil Economic Relationship," March 19, 2011.

Reflecting on such trade talks with the US in September 2011, the Brazilian Foreign Trade Board (CAMEX) formed an Inter-ministerial Technical Group on Trade Regulation to consolidate and improve domestic regulation related to foreign trade to harmonize, rationalize, and simplify it.[114] In August 2014, the BUSBC, Amcham-Brasil, and Brazil's National Confederation of Industry (CNI) organized a series of 'Regulatory Coherence Roundtables' to engage *"all relevant players to move forward with the regulatory coherence agenda in Brazil"*.[115] The event was supported from Brazil's side by MDIC and CAMEX and the US's side by the Department of Commerce (DoC) and the OIRA. The idea of regulatory coherence as a mechanism to simplify, rationalize and produce 'better regulation', not only related to trade but on a cross-sector basis, spread out to the Brazilian foreign trade agenda, to regulators, the private sector, and the academy.[116] In addition, regulatory coherence was raised as a top priority in the Trade Dialogue between MDIC and DoC,[117] an informal mechanism established to advance bilateral trade relations.[118]

Therefore, while the OECD's Regulatory Policy dialogue with the Chief of Staff of the Presidency weakened and the PRO-REG kept dormant, the GRP's agenda moved through different channels within the Brazilian bureaucracy, involving informal trade dialogues, Memorandum of Understandings (MoUs) between ministries of trade, regulatory agencies, and public and private bodies.[119] During this period of skepticism from the Brazilian government concerning a closer relationship with the OECD, bilateral trade relations and private sector engagement kept the GRP's agenda alive. The mechanisms of socialization and persuasion among trade officials and capacity-building with regulators continued. The GRP agenda would return fully in 2015 when the political economy was reoriented towards more neoliberal policies at the domestic level, and the foreign trade policy agenda began to prioritize Brazil's accession to the OECD.

---

[114] CAMEX Resolution 44/2011. Available at: http://www.camex.gov.br/resolucoes-camex-e-outros-normativos/58-resolucoes-da-camex/1000-resolucao-n-44-de-11-de-julho-de-2011.

[115] Brazil-US Business Council (2014).

[116] Ministério do Desenvolvimento, Indústria e Comércio Exterior. Brasil e Estados Unidos anunciam novos acordos em convergência regulatória e patentes, 19/11/2015, available at: http://www.comexresponde.gov.br/portalmdic/sitio/interna/noticia.php?area=5&noticia=14179; Casa Civil da Presidência da República, Coerência e Boas Práticas Regulatórias, Abril, 2015, available at: https://www.gov.br/casacivil/pt-br/assuntos/governanca/regulacao/eventos/2018/coerencia-regulatoria-sag-casa-civil-se-camex-e inmetro/apresentacoes/apresentacaocoerenciaregulatoria_sag_06abr2018.pdf.

[117] The Trade Dialogue was originally established in 2006 through a Letter of Intent to intensify the dialogue between the defense industries of the two countries and increase the trade flow in this sector. Available at: www.mdic.gov.br/index.php/component/content/article/61-noticias/1951-brasil-e-estados-unidos-assinam-carta-de-intencoes-para-intensificar-dialogo-na-industria-da-defesa.

[118] Brazilian Ministry of Economy, Industry, Foreign Trade, and Services. Available at: www.trade.gov/bcd/pdfs/moi-coherence-private-sector.pdf.

[119] For a full reference of these informal trade dialogues, see Sect. 3.3. of this chapter, especially notes 143–146.

3.3 Full Embracement with GRP and the Role of OECD Indicators (2015–2021)

In 2015, Brazil faced a sharp drop in GDP by 3,8%, and the economy returned to the level of 2011. The country entered one of its longest recessions and political turmoil following the impeachment process in 2016 and corruption scandals involving the Worker Party in the context of the Car Wash Operation.[120] In January 2015, Joaquim Levy, an engineer trained in economics from the University of Chicago, took over the Brazilian Ministry of Finance amid a severe financial crisis at the beginning of the second Rousseff mandate.[121] Levy proposed an ambitious fiscal adjustment plan and economic reform package, reorienting the Brazilian economy. This shift provoked friction with government members from the Worker Party, and most of the proposals ended up not being approved in a Congress increasingly hostile to Rousseff's government. After that, however, the economic gears would steadily change towards more liberal winds.

At this point, Brazil reapproximated to the OECD and signed a Framework Cooperation Agreement, which provided the legal basis for the relationship between Brazil and the Organization.[122] According to Levy, the agreement was "*part of a series of actions aimed at reviving economic growth and penetrating the international market*". [123] The signing of the agreement followed the launching of Brazil's Economic Summary 2015 by the OECD, concluding that Brazil should pursue "*convergence with advanced economies*", fiscal and monetary policies able to stabilize the public debt/GDP ratio and reduce inflation.[124] The Agreement led to a biennial work program for 2016–17, designed to support Brazil in advancing its reform agenda and informing public policies. The program's launching also reignited an Inter-Ministerial Working Group on the OECD led by the Ministry of

---

[120] Sanchez-Badin and Badin (2019).

[121] Levy has experience in left and right-wing governments. He is a former secretary of the National Treasury of Lula da Silva's government (2003), a former finance minister of the Dilma Rousseff government (2015), and a former president of BNDES of the Bolsonaro government (2018). Interview to BBCNews Brasil. Available at: https://www.bbc.com/portuguese/brasil-50677801.

[122] OECD. Signing of cooperation agreement between the OECD and Brazil. Available at: https://www.oecd.org/brazil/signing-of-cooperation-agreement-between-oecd-and-brazil.html. Despite the signing of the agreement happened in 2015, only in 2019, under the Bolsonaro's administration, the Decree 10,109, of November 7, promulgated the Cooperation Agreement between Brazil and the OECD.

[123] The event of signature was attended by Joaquim Levy, Minister of Finance; Mauro Vieira, Minister of Foreign Affairs; and Angel Gurría, Secretary-General of the OECD; besides several representatives from Fundação Getúlio Vargas. (FGV). Available at: https://portal.fgv.br/en/news/fgv-participates-signing-protocol-between-brazilian-government-and-oecd.

[124] OECD (2015), p. 28.

Foreign Affairs, which had been created in 2007 as a mechanism of steering and monitoring cooperation with the Organization.[125]

The new Ministry of Foreign Affairs, Mauro Vieira, conveniently dubbed the new orientation a "diplomacy of results" and a reconciliation with Brazil's middle-power status.[126] During Rousseff's previous mandate, she had decided to pull Brazil out from global initiatives. However, Rousseff did not give up on the diplomatic ambitions of a rising Brazil, such as the BRICS, and kept working alongside its emerging partners to launch, in the same year, 2015, the New Development Bank. and even becoming the only Latin America country to join the China-led Asian Infrastructure Investment Bank (AIIB).[127]

Between Rousseff's impeachment in 2016 and the election of President Bolsonaro in 2018, despite heated debates about Brazil's orientations, the interim government of Michel Temer boosted the relationship between Brazil and the OECD. It accelerated formal adherence to several OECD legal documents.[128] As Trubek, Morosini, and Sanchez-Badin pointed out, despite "grand debates" and rhetoric between "developmentalists" from one side and "opening-ists" from the other, *Brazil pragmatically and quietly experimented with new directions in trade policies and international insertion strategies* during this period.[129] Three directions are relevant for our purposes: (i) Brazil's formal request to accede to the OECD in 2017; (ii) the beginning of Brazil's bilateral trade negotiations with Mexico, Colombia, and Chile, outside of the Mercosur framework; and *iii*) exploratory relations with the US.

The political decision to legalize the relationship with the OECD in 2015, and the formal request in 2017, united scattered efforts and separated agendas toward GRP in Brazil. Regulatory reform attempts during the PRO-REG heyday met with experimentations by Brazilian diplomats and trade officials in negotiating agreements involving GRP with Mexico, Colombia, and Chile. These three negotiations involved non-binding commitments to adopt regulatory coherence and GRP in rulemaking.[130] More importantly, two different bureaucracies in Brazil that did not have much in common and usually were understood as pursuing quite diverse objectives started to maintain closer relations and seek common goals: regulators

[125] OECD, The OECD and Brazil, March 2018. Available at: https://www.oecd.org/brazil/Active-with-Brazil.pdf.

[126] See Casarões (2020), pp. 89–90 and Cervo e Lessa (2014), pp. 133–151.

[127] China Daily. 2015. Brazil Sole Nation in LatAm to Join AIIB, 7 April. Available at: http://www.chinadaily.com.cn/cndy/2015-04/07/content_20012806.html.

[128] OECD Legal Instruments. Available at: https://legalinstruments.oecd.org/en/instruments?mode=advanced&adherentIds=27&yearFrom=2015&yearTo=2018.

[129] Trubek et al. (2017), pp. 651–656.

[130] Ministério das Relações Exteriores, "Negociação Brasil-México para ampliação e aprofundamento do ACE-53-Troca de Lista de Pedidos Recíprocos (2015); available at: http://perma.cc/FA3K-B4AK; Ministério das Relações Exteriores, "República da Colômbia"; available at: http://perma.cc/CD7P-WDX5; Ministério das Relações Exteriores, "República do Chile"; available at: http://perma.cc/P9J4-8XUG.

and trade officials. The mobilizations made by CAMEX and MDIC between 2011–2014, supported by the private sector (CNI and BUSBC), encountered now fertile soil within the heart of the government, represented by the Chief of Staff of the Presidency, explicitly reoriented to the OECD accession process. In 2016, a week before Rousseff's impeachment, PRO-REG was transferred to the Ministry of Planning, Budget, and Management and revitalized.

Two Brazilian officials responsible for negotiations with Mexico commented that *"in 2015, "when we started negotiations, Mexico arrived with a "TPP-style" proposal for supervision, good practices... then a bomb dropped, nobody knew what it was. The Itamaraty did not know, the MDIC did not know".*[131] Regarding the new approach from Chief of Staff officials, they reported, "*...as soon as [they] went to the Chief of Staff, we went there, in the first week, and said: look, we have these plans, these ideas, we have negotiations with Mexico already, in which we saw that it was necessary to establish a mechanism or procedure for the coordination and supervision of foreign trade regulation, and we wanted to have this support and partnership from the Chief of Staff (...) CAMEX can be this mechanism or a partnership with the Chief of Staff for coordinating foreign trade."*[132]

A leading reformer currently working on the front line of the OECD accession process reaffirmed the year 2016 as an inflection point:

> In Brazil, the topic has been addressed for at least fourteen years. (...)Closely linked to cultural aspects, the regulatory improvement agenda takes time to be understood, learned, and effectively implemented. (...) The processes of specialization and agencification in the public sector have generated advantages but also challenges. One of these challenges was the fragmentation of the public sector into silos that did not communicate. (...) Discussions continued for a long time, mostly erratically, depending on the period, but with a relatively low degree of institutionalization and governance. As of 2016, there was a turning point, with new actions following up on those adopted by PRO-REG. (Free Translation)[133]

Two laws and one federal decree materialized such actions: Law 13.334/2016 on the investment partnership program for the strengthening and interaction between the state and the private sector and the regulatory role of the state;[134] Law 13.726/2018 for the de-bureaucratization and efficiency of the state;[135] and Federal Decree 9.203/2017, which established an Interministerial Governance Committee to advise the

[131] Interviews with a trade official and a diplomat. Interviews on file with author. "Itamaraty" refers to the Brazilian Ministry of Foreign Relations. The origin of the name is due to a tribute to the palace that belonged to the Barão do Itamaraty located in the city of Rio de Janeiro, and which served as the first headquarters of the Ministry of Foreign Affairs of the country between 1898 and 1970.

[132] Interviews with a trade official and a diplomat. Interviews on file with author.

[133] Albuquerque and López Azumendi (2022), pp. 10–11.

[134] Presidência da República, Secretaria-Geral, Subchefia para Assuntos Jurídicos. Available at: https://legislacao.presidencia.gov.br/atos/?tipo=LEI&numero=13334&ano=2016&ato=cf9ITW650dZpWT5b4.

[135] Ministério da Justiça e Segurança Pública, Conselho Nacional de Arquivos. Available at: https://www.gov.br/conarq/pt-br/legislacao-arquivistica/leis-e-decretos-leis/lei-no-13-726-de-8-de-outubro-de-2018.

policy and governance of the federal public administration.[136] One of the critical actions was the creation of a Chief of Analysis and Monitoring of Governmental Policies of the Chief of Staff of the Presidency (SAG/CC). Such a body took over the strategic leadership to coordinate discussions within a technical group integrated by the Ministries of Finance and Planning, all the regulatory agencies, and INMETRO.[137] This group became an essential locus for technical debate, information exchange, consensus building, and joint elaboration of documents.

The third thread mentioned by Trubek et al. was the scaling up of bilateral exploratory trade relations between Brazil and the US. In 2015, MDIC and CAMEX signed two Memorandum of Understanding (MoU) with DoC and Commerce's International Trade Administration (ITA). The first concerned Joint Cooperation on Regulatory Coherence and Meaningful Engagement with the Private Sector,[138] and the second addressed Standards and Conformity Assessment.[139] Brazil has maintained a pragmatic and dynamic relationship with the US on trade relations since 2006, based on MoUs as umbrella agreements for several other sectorial cooperation.[140] The inclusion of GRP as a transversal theme and a top priority in this bilateral trade agenda catalyzed future actions related to regulatory reforms in Brazil. After these MoUs were signed, several high-level meetings and Joint Commercial Dialogues between Brazil and the US concerning GRP would dominate the international trade agenda.[141] A culmination of such arrangements was the signature, in 2020, already in Bolsonaro's administration, of the Protocol on Trade Rules and Transparency, containing wide-scope and binding provisions on GRP.[142] The Protocol was the first subsequent agreement to use the GRP framework established in the USMCA between the US, Mexico, and Canada.[143] The joint

[136] Presidência da República, Secretaria-Geral, Subchefia para Assuntos Jurídicos. Available at: http://www.planalto.gov.br/ccivil_03/_ato2015-2018/2017/decreto/d9203.html.

[137] INMETRO is the Brazilian regulatory body for quality and safety product regulation.

[138] Memorandum of Intent on Joint Cooperation on Regulatory Coherence and Meaningful Engagement with the Private Sector. Available at: https://legacy.trade.gov/bcd/pdfs/moi-coherence-private-sector.pdf.

[139] US Department of Commerce and Brazil Ministry of development, Industry and Foreign Trade, "Joint Statement of the 13th edition of the Brazil-US Commercial Dialogue" (Brasília, Nov. 19, 2015). Available at: http://perma.cc/E792-V58D.

[140] Trubek et al. (2017), p. 668.

[141] For a full reference of US-Brazil Commercial Dialogues, see: https://www.trade.gov/brazil-us-commercial-dialogue.

[142] Ministério das Relações Exteriores. Protocol to the Agreement on Trade and Economic Cooperation Between the Government of the Federative Republic of Brazil and the Government of the United States of America Relating to Trade Rules and Transparency. Available at: https://www.gov.br/mre/en/contact-us/press-area/press-releases/protocol-to-the-agreement-on-trade-and-economic-cooperation-between-the-government-of-the-federative-republic-of-brazil-and-the-government-of-the-united-states-of-america-relating-to-trade-rules-and-transparency.

[143] The Protocol was signed during the Coronavirus health crisis. On May 21, 2020 the governments issued a joint statement highlighting the commitment to reduce trade barriers and to increase bilateral trade and investment. Topics were trade facilitation, regulatory practices, technical

statement on the new Protocol stated that it "*complemented Brazil's domestic reforms to improve competitiveness and opportunities for innovation, including the Regulatory Agencies Law, the Economic Freedom Law, and its succeeding presidential Decrees*".[144]

After Bolsonaro's election in 2018, the steps taken during Temer's interim administration, closer to the OECD, gained full traction. Brazil thoroughly embraced the GRP's international agenda, made accession to the OECD a foreign policy priority, and approved several laws and executive decrees, as described below. In addition, regulatory agencies and other national government bodies were encouraged to manage stock reviews to reduce existing regulations.[145]

The Regulatory Agencies' Bill (PL 3337/2004), stuck in Congress for 15 years, was finally approved as Law 13,848/19.[146] At this time, the Brazilian regulatory agencies had already implemented RIA in their rulemaking process on an *ad hoc* basis. However, to be in line with the OECD's best practices, it was necessary to make it mandatory. The law's approval resulted from a consensus between the Chief of Staff of the Presidency, regulatory agencies, and the Ministries of Finance around an essential text. According to two officials in charge of the reforms in the new government, "*it was basic, but after just over 20 years of the creation of the first agencies and after 15 years of debate on the same topic, the basics become revolutionary and urgent*".[147]

---

regulations, standards and conformity assessment procedures, intellectual property, and digital trade. The Protocol was negotiated entirely virtual during lockdowns, with great efforts from private sector entities in both countries. Available at: https://ustr.gov/about-us/policy-offices/press-office/press-releases/2020/april/brazil-us-joint-statement-enhancement-bilateral-economic-and-trade-partnership. There was an underlying pressure to conclude this agreement before the presidential elections in the U.S on November 3, 2020. The goal was to take advantage of the narrow "political window" opened by the synergy between presidents Trump and Bolsonaro because only an agreement that did not include tariffs could be negotiated without the US Congress' approval and the MERCOSUR's consent. US Congress' approval was highly unlikely, given robust and explicit opposition by the Democrats to pursuing any type of trade agreement or expanded economic partnership with Brazil's President Jair Bolsonaro.

[144] Brazil. Ministério das Relações Exteriores. [19 Oct 2020] Available at: https://www.gov.br/mre/en/contact-us/press-area/press-releases/joint-press-release-united-states-and-brazil-sign-new-protocol-on-trade-rules-and-transparency.

[145] Brasil. Casa Civil. Gestão do Estoque Regulatório: Iniciativas das Agências Reguladoras Federais. Maio 2018. Available at: https://www.gov.br/casacivil/pt-br/assuntos/governanca/regulacao/apresentacao-regulacao-pasta/acesse-aqui/gestao-estoque-regulatorio/gestao-estoque-regulatorio-iniciativas-das-agencias-reguladoras-federais. Decree No. 10.139/19 stated the obligation to review and consolidate all normative acts lower than a decree in the federal administration. Presidência da República, Secretaria-Geral, Subchefia para Assuntos Jurídicos. Decreto N 9,203/2017. Available at: http://www.planalto.gov.br/ccivil_03/_ato2015-2018/2017/decreto/d9203.html.

[146] Brasil. Presidência da República, Secretaria-Geral, Subchefia para Assuntos Jurídicos. Lei N 13.848/2019. Available at: http://www.planalto.gov.br/ccivil_03/_ato2019-2022/2019/lei/l13848.htm.

[147] Albuquerque and Guaranys (2018), PL das Agências Reguladoras: quando o básico é revolucionário e urgente. Jota, 28/08/2018. Available at: https://www.jota.info/tributos-e-empresas/regulacao/pl-das-agencias-reguladoras-quando-o-basico-e-revolucionario-e-urgente-28082018 (free translation).

Despite all that, the primary law that set the stage to anchor all the subsequent reforms was the Economic Freedom Act (EFA), Law n° 13.874/19.[148] EFA is a controversial law resulting from a provisional measure sent by President Bolsonaro to Congress on April 30, 2019.[149] The reasons underpinning the proposal stated that a "Declaration of Economic Freedom" was urgent to "*change the reality of Brazil as an emergence*", representing "*the rights of the Brazilians against an irrationally controlling State*".[150] In addition, the document departed from the assumption that "*the Brazilian entrepreneur, in contrast to the rest of the developed and emerging world, did not feel safe to produce, generate employment and income*".[151] Yet, according to the provisional measure's reasoning, Brazil ranked 150th in the Heritage Foundation/Wall Street Journal Economic Freedom ranking, 144th in the Fraser Institute ranking, and 123rd in the Cato Institute ranking. Such a lousy performance was supposedly the leading cause of more than 12 million unemployed, economic stagnation, and the lack of real income growth, *urging* precise action from the government.[152]

In 2019, Bolsonaro's government reorganized several institutions, merging five former ministries (finance, planning, labor, industry, foreign trade and services, and social security) into the Ministry of Economy (ME), headed by Paulo Guedes, a Chicago-trained economist.[153] The new ME and their secretariats started to rely heavily on indicators, attempting to improve Brazil's figures on such indexes. One such indicator was the OECD's PMR.[154] Several speeches and official presentations from the ME's representatives usually started with Brazil's shameful performance on the OECD PMR index as a "laggard" country compared with the OECD

[148] Presidência da República, Secretaria-Geral, Subchefia para Assuntos Jurídicos. Lei N 13.874/2019. Available at: http://www.planalto.gov.br/ccivil_03/_ato2019-2022/2019/lei/L13874.htm.

[149] Congresso Nacional. Medida Provisória N 881/2019 (Liberdade Econômica). Available at: https://www.congressonacional.leg.br/materias/medidas-provisorias/-/mpv/136531.

[150] The document with the reasons for the proposal was electronically signed by Marcelo Pacheco dos Guaranys, Sergio Fernando Moro, and Renato de Lima França. EMI n° 00083/2019 ME AGU MJSP, Brasília, 11 de Abril de 2019. Available at: https://www.planalto.gov.br/ccivil_03/_ato2019-2022/2019/Exm/Exm-MP-881-19.pdf.

[151] EMI n° 00083/2019 ME AGU MJSP, p. 2.

[152] EMI n° 00083/2019 ME AGU MJSP, p. 1.

[153] The result was the creation of seven special secretariats and the National Treasury Attorney's Office, coordinated and supported by the Executive Secretariat. Each ME special secretariat has between one and four secretariats or equivalent units. The ministry had approximately 42,000 civil servants, a payroll of R$2 billion (Brazilian real) per month, and more than 1300 buildings. See Brasil – Ministério da Economia: Análise das funções principais e seus macroprocessos operacionais Macroprocessos operacionais de benchmarking com experiências do Canadá, da Espanha, dos Estados Unidos, da França, do México, do Peru e do Reino Unido. Available at: https://publications.iadb.org/publications/portuguese/document/Brasil-Ministerio-da-Economia-Analise-das-funces-principais-e-seus-macroprocessos-operacionais-Macroprocessos-operacionais-de-benchmarking-com-experincias-do-Canada-da-Espanha-dos-Estados-Unidos-da-Franca-do-Mexico-do-Peru-e-do-Reino-Unido.pdf.

[154] See supra note 69.

average.[155] Therefore, the passing of the provisional measure would symbolize a "landmark legislation on regulatory policy", changing historical statutes reflecting "anti-business legal doctrines" by proclaiming the principles of "*in dubio pro libertatem*", the legal vulnerability of citizens and companies, and the economic freedom as a *right before the state.*[156]

The provisional measure was converted into law by Congress only 5 months later, on September 2019.[157] The Law (EFA) set two relevant provisions regarding the regulatory environment in Brazil: (i) the institutionalization of RIA for *all* proposals or amendments of normative acts edited by *all entities of the federal public administration*; and (ii) the recognition of international standards by expressly stating the rights of every person to develop, execute, operate or commercialize new types of products and services when the infra-legal rules become outdated due to internationally consolidated technological development. Both provisions were later regulated in detail by two decrees.[158]

Additionally, a Council for the Monitoring and Evaluation of Public Policies (CMAP) was established as a collegiate body comprised of the Ministry of Economy, the Chief of Staff of the Presidency, and the Office of the Comptroller General (CGU). Later, the Secretary for Competition Advocacy and Competitiveness (SEAE) within the Ministry of Economy was informally appointed to lead regulatory activities in Brazil. However, it still lacks a formal specific mandate.[159]

After these changes in law, in 2020, Brazil formally adhered to the two main OECD recommendations on regulatory governance: (i) the 1995 Recommendation of the Council on Improving the Quality of Government Regulation (1995) and (ii) the 2012 Recommendation of the Council on Regulatory Policy and Governance. In 2021–2022 the country was submitted to a new peer review to listen to the OECD about the work performed domestically. The new report, published in June 2022,

---

155 An example of such presentations may be found at: https://events.iadb.org/events/handler/geteventdocument.ashx?AFCF784DCD0CBF43BE2C6862BF334401 8BA7DAC5632DC23F96E18F163AE4759CB4A62D8098D5AA588F0E2825B52F233ADF4C0BA8E245E6BD8AE0D1A0B986D2FDE23A6575964F078E. Geanluca Lorenzon was the head of the Secretary of Advocacy for Competition and Competitiveness of the Ministry of Economy (SEAE). He was one of the formulators of the Economic Freedom Provisional Measure, and first occupied the directorate of debureaucratization of the Ministry of Economy. Before working to the Ministry of Economy, Lorenzon was a consultant at McKinsey and director of the Mises Institute in Brazil.

156 EMI n° 00083/2019 ME AGU MJSP, p. 6–7. Available at: https://www.planalto.gov.br/ccivil_03/_ato2019-2022/2019/Exm/Exm-MP-881-19.pdf.

157 Câmara dos Deputados. MPV 881/2019. Available at: https://www.camara.leg.br/proposicoesWeb/fichadetramitacao?idProposicao=2199763.

158 Respectively, Decree 10.411/20 and Decree 10.229/20. Decree 10.411/2020 also regulated an embryo of ex-post evaluation, specifying that public entities of the federal government shall conduct an evaluation of regulatory outcomes (called ARR - Análise de Resultado Regulatório). Such obligations came into force in October 2022.

159 SEAE's roles and responsibilities are established in Article 119 of Decree 9,745/2019, which defines the structure of the Ministry of Economy. However, the decree does not specify an explicit mandate to promote and oversee the regulatory policy.

comprised two parts.[160] First, a comprehensive assessment based on the PMR Indicators. The information used to evaluate Brazil's PMR was collected through a questionnaire sent to national authorities in 2018, including over 1000 questions on economy-wide or industry-specific regulatory provisions.[161] The overall result of this assessment was that *Brazil's PMR indicator values often compare markedly unfavorably with the OECD average.*[162] They also compared *unfavorably with the average PMR values for Latin American OECD economies*. For the OECD, recent reforms *may pave the way for more substantial changes that could bring Brazil in line with OECD economies.*[163] In other words, Brazil seems "on the right track" from the OECD's perspective, yet still quite far from being in line with the PMR Indicators.

In the second part of the review, the OECD's overall conclusion was that, *despite Brazil having introduced several initiatives to foster the development of high-quality regulations, these efforts are not part of a long-term strategy with explicitly defined goals.*[164] For the OECD's experts, the introduction of legal instruments is *not underpinned by a single, high-level policy statement, such as a law that covers all the regulatory policy's tools, institutions, and instruments.*[165] This means that Brazil *lacks an integrated, comprehensive policy framework that supports the design and adoption of a whole-of-government program on better regulation.*[166] For the OECD experts, Brazil has gradually introduced tools such as RIA, *ex-post* evaluation, and administrative simplification. However, the challenge is to embed such tools in the rulemaking culture. The challenge most often quoted during the fact-finding mission was the need to change the culture of most public officials.

Another interesting finding in the report was that several Brazilian stakeholders mentioned that the obligation for carrying out due public consultation in RIAs would not derive from national laws but from Brazil's commitments set out in the Protocol on GRP signed with the US.[167] Such a finding reveals how an international commitment may act as a *harder* instrument to constrain domestic policies in the absence of a national statute or regulation. Moreover, it confirms what has been said in the joint statement about the Protocol that it complemented Brazil's regulatory reform. Such bilateral trade relations with the US concerning GRP demonstrate how different channels may mobilize domestic actors around the same agenda and trigger other mechanisms of "best practices" transmission. Frequently, other channels come into operation when a track becomes blocked or slows down the transmission flow. In this case, Brazil's commitment before the US with binding GRP clauses may

[160] OECD (2022).

[161] OECD (2022), p. 5.

[162] OECD (2022), p. 31.

[163] OECD (2022), p. 31.

[164] OECD (2022), p. 69.

[165] OECD (2022), p. 69.

[166] OECD (2022), pp. 43;70;80.

[167] OECD (2022), p. 72.

function as a crucial instrument for implementing GRP's rules, institutions, and practices.

4 Concluding Remarks

The case of Brazil's engagement with the OECD on regulatory reforms illustrates the interrelation between domestic political struggles, legal changes, and transnational norms and processes on regulatory governance. Although governments with different political orientations determine diverse interactions, in any case, national policymaking is immersed in a web of transnational networks that shapes state and cultural changes. As sharply pointed out by Lang about the features of the GRP, as a set of *open-ended* organizational routines in regulatory decision-making, such routines may be associated with different political projects and transmitted to diverse contexts.[168]

By unpacking the GRP's toolbox, this chapter demonstrated the OECD's role as a knowledge producer and the contradictions enmeshed in the apparent "neutral" and "complete" concept of GRP as "high-quality regulation". It further explained how the OECD has developed and refined techniques of soft governance to transmit its transnational norm, relying primarily on persuasion, peer pressure, and cultural change. Indicators, public scrutiny, comparison, and ranking among countries complete the transmission mechanisms, representing subtle forms of material power. In this process, the state's identity and public officials' self-perceptions are carefully molded in collective knowledge construction based on parameters of modernity. Extensive data collection and directed questionnaires force national policymakers to conceptualize the problems into a pre-defined framework.

In the case of Brazil, three particular moments and types of interaction were identified. First, during Brazil's early approach to the OECD, enhanced engagement and the first regulatory peer review were fundamental in seedling the ground for the "better regulation" agenda. If Brazil was reticent towards the OECD, the OECD was eager to include Brazil in its socialization processes, together with other transition economies. But Brazil was still struggling over the proper role of its new regulatory agencies. For these reasons, the program was seen as a more exogenous initiative, running slowly. After that, in Rousseff's mandate, while the government remained skeptical of seeking OECD membership, the regulatory coherence and GRP's agenda made their way through bilateral trade relations, moving different actors within the Brazilian bureaucracy and engaging the private sector.

After a turning point in 2015, with the reorientation of the political economy towards more liberal winds, Brazil reapproximated to the OECD and started to follow "*convergence with advanced economies*".[169] Brazil's formal request to

[168] Lang (2019), p. 24.

[169] OECD (2015), p. 28.

accede to the OECD in 2017, bilateral negotiations with Latin American countries outside the Mercosur framework, and exploratory commercial relations with the US put the GRP's agenda in motion again. With Bolsonaro's election in 2018, this agenda was thoroughly embraced. A symbolic provisional measure of economic freedom was converted into law and made RIA mandatory for all federal regulations.[170] The new Ministry of Economy, which merged five former ministries, started to rely heavily on indicators, including the OECD's PMR. However, despite all such initiatives, the OECD second peer review concluded that Brazil still lacks a long-term strategy and a *comprehensive policy framework that supports adopting a whole-of-government program on better regulation.*[171] The challenge ahead is *to change the culture.*

Besides the OECD recommendations, a binding Protocol on GRP signed with the US triggered a different set of mechanisms for "best practices" transmission, which requires further research on the role of the international trade regime in developing regulatory reforms in transition and development economies.

All such reasons highlight the importance of understanding the OECD as a purveyor of ideas and a relevant node in transnational regulatory governance. The case of Brazil sheds light on the effectiveness of policy and legal transfers through transnational processes involving peer pressure, social learning, the role of indicators, and cultural change. National policymakers, trade officials, and diplomats, immersed in bilateral, plurilateral, and transnational networks, operate as conveyors of state change within transnational legal processes.

References

Albuquerque K, López Azumendi S (2022) Estados ágeis na América Latina: a coordenação dentro do setor público como fator chave das estratégias de melhoria regulatória e o caso do Brasil. Available at: http://cafscioteca.azurewebsites.net/handle/123456789/1876

Aquila G et al (2019) Quantitative regulatory impact analysis: experience of regulatory agencies in Brazil. Util Policy 59:100931. https://doi.org/10.1016/j.jup.2019.100931

Baldwin R (2010) Better regulation: the search and the struggle. In: Baldwin R, Cave M, Lodge M (eds) The Oxford handbook on regulation. Oxford University Press, pp 259–278

Benvenisti E (2015) Democracy Captured: The Mega-Regional Agreements and the Future of Global Public Law. Global Trust Working Paper Series 08/2015. https://doi.org/10.2139/ssrn.2646882

Brazil-US Business Council (2014) Advancing the Regulatory Coherence Agenda in Brazil. Available at: https://www.brazilcouncil.org/wp-content/uploads/2015/11/021933_Brazil_RegCoherence_IN_final.pdf

Bresser-Pereira LC (2004) Democracy and public management reform. Oxford University Press, Oxford

[170] Presidência da República, Secretaria-Geral, Subchefia para Assuntos Jurídicos. Lei N 13.874/2019. Available at: http://www.planalto.gov.br/ccivil_03/_ato2019-2022/2019/lei/L13874.htm.

[171] OECD (2022), pp. 43;70;80.

Cai PXF (2016) Regulatory coherence and standardization mechanisms in the trans-Pacific partnership. Br J Am Leg Stud 5(2):505–538
Carvalho B et al (2020) Better utility regulation through RIA? Merits and implications based on the Brazilian case. Util Policy 64:101023. https://doi.org/10.1016/j.jup.2020.101023
Casarões G (2020) Leaving the club without slamming the door: Brazil's return to middle-power status. In: Esteves P et al (eds) Status and the rise of Brazil: global ambitions, humanitarian engagement and international challenges. Palgrave Macmillan, Switzerland, pp 89–110
Cervo AL, Lessa AC (2014) O declínio: inserção internacional do Brasil (2011–2014). Revista Brasileira de Política Internacional 57(2):133–151
Cormac M (1985) Blood Meridian or the evening redness in the west. Random House
Davis CL (2016) More than Just a Rich Country Club: Membership Conditionality and Institutional Reform in the OECD. Princeton University Working Paper. Available at: https://scholar.harvard.edu/sites/scholar.harvard.edu/files/cldavis/files/davis2016b.pdf
De Francesco F (2013) Transnational policy innovation: the OECD and the diffusion of regulatory impact analysis. ECPR Press, Colchester
DiMaggio PJ, Powell WW (1983) The iron cage revisited: institutional isomorphism and collective rationality in organizational fields. Am Soc Rev 48:147–160
Dobbin F et al (2007) The global diffusion of public policies: social construction, coercion, competition, or learning? Annu Rev Sociol 33:449–472
Donadelli et al (2020) 'Post-NPM' by force or fiat? A comparison of administrative reform trajectories in Brazil and Mexico. Public Admin Dev 40(5):255–266
Downs GW et al (1996) Is the good news about compliance good news about co-operation? Int Organ 50(3):379–406
Dubash N, Morgan B (2012) Understanding the rise of the regulatory state of the south. Regul Gov 6(3):261–281
European Commission (2021) 'Better Regulation' Toolbox. https://commission.europa.eu/system/files/2022-07/br_toolbox_-_june_2022-chapter_1.pdf
Finnemore M, Sikkink K (2001) Taking stock: the constructivist research program in international relations and comparative politics. Annu Rev Polit Sci 4(1):391–416
Halliday T (2012) Architects of the state: international organizations and the reconstruction of states in East Asia. Law Soc Inq 37(2):265–296
Halliday T, Shaffer G (eds) (2015) Transnational legal orders. Cambridge University Press, New York
Hobson JM (2000) The state and international relations. Cambridge University Press, Cambridge
Hoekman B, Sabel C (2019) In a world of value chains: what space for regulatory coherence and cooperation in trade agreements? In: Kingsbury B et al (eds) Megaregulation contested. Oxford University Press, Oxford, pp 217–239
Holperin M (2019) Diffusion and adaptation of the regulatory agency model in Brazil. Rev Adm Pública 53(6):1116–1137
Hood C (2004) The art of the state: culture, rhetoric, and public management. Oxford University Press, Oxford
Jakobi T (2012) Regulating regulation? The regulatory policy of the OECD. Paper presented at the ECPR Standing Group on Regulation and Governance Conference, University of Exeter, Exeter, 27 June 2012. Available at: https://regulation.upf.edu/exeter-12-papers/Paper%20263%20-%20Jakobi%202012%20-%20Regulating%20Regulation.pdf
Jarvis D (2017) The OECD and the reconfiguration of the state in emerging economies: manufacturing 'regulatory capacity'. Dev Chang 48(6):1386–1416
Jordão E, Cunha LF (2020) Revisão do estoque regulatório: a tendência de foco na análise de impacto regulatório retrospectiva. In Revista de Direito Administrativo & Constitucional, Belo Horizonte 80:227–255
Kingsburry et al (2019) (org.) Megaregulation contested: global economic ordering after TPP. Oxford University Press

Kjaer PF (2018) Facilitating transfers: regulatory governance frameworks as 'rites of passage'. Contemp Polit 24(5):507–523. https://doi.org/10.1080/13569775.2018.1452105
Knill C (2005) Introduction to cross-national policy convergence: concepts, approaches, and explanatory factors. Eur Public Policy 12:764074
Ladegaard Peter L, Kamkhaji J (2018) Giving Sisyphus a helping hand. Pathways for Sustainable RIA Systems in Developing Countries. World Bank Group. Available at: https://documents.worldbank.org/en/publication/documents-reports/documentdetail/691961521463875777/giving-sisyphus-a-helping-hand-pathways-for-sustainable-ria-systems-in-developing-countries
Lang A (2019) Keeping the rules in play: the OECD's regulatory policy initiatives. Paper presented at the Interdisciplinary Workshop on the Theme of 'Global Un-Governance', University of Edinburgh, Scotland, 23–24 May 2019. Available at: https://www.law.ed.ac.uk/news-events/events/interdisciplinary-workshop-theme-global-un-governance
Laursen F, Roederer-Rynning C (2017) Introduction: the new EU FTAs as contentious market regulation. J Eur Integr 39(7):763–779
Levi-Faur D, Jordana J (2006) Toward a Latin American regulatory state? The diffusion of autonomous regulatory agencies across countries and sectors. Int J Public Adm 29(4–6): 335–366
Lodge M, Kai W (2012) Managing regulation: regulatory analysis, politics, and policy. Palgrave Macmillan, Basingstoke
Lodge M, Wegrich K (2009) High-quality regulation: its popularity, tools, and future. Public Money Manage 29(3):145–152
Mahbubani K (2012) The OECD a classic sunset organisation. Global Policy 3(1):117–118
Mahon R, McBride S (eds) (2008) The OECD and transnational governance. UBC Press, Vancouver
March JG, Olsen JP (1998) The institutional dynamics of international political orders. Int Organ 52(4):943–969
Marcussen M (2004) OECD governance through soft law. In: Mörth U (ed) Soft law in governance and regulation: an interdisciplinary analysis. Elgar, Cheltenham, pp 103–128
Marsh MD, Sharman JC (2009) Policy diffusion and policy transfer. Policy Stud 30(3):269–288
Merry SE, Davis K, Kingsbury B (2015) The quiet power of indicators: measuring governance, corruption, and rule of law. Cambridge University Press, New York
Noaksson N, Jacobsson K (2003) The production of ideas and expert knowledge in OECD. The OECD jobs strategy in contrast with the EU employment strategy. SCORE, Stockholm (Stockholms centrum för forskning om offentlig sektor). Available at: http://www.score.su.se/polopoly_fs/1.26554.1320939796!/20037.pdf
Noboru S (2004) Report by the Chair of the Heads of Delegation Working Group on the Enlargement Strategy and Outreach: A Strategy for Enlargement and Outreach OECD, 13 May 2004. Available at: https://www.oecd.org/global-relations/globalrelationsstrategy/37434513.pdf
OECD (1995) Recommendation of the Council on Improving the Quality of Government Regulation, OECD/LEGAL/0278. Available at: https://legalinstruments.oecd.org/en/instruments/OECD-LEGAL-0278
OECD (1997) The OECD Report on Regulatory Reform Synthesis. Available at: https://www.oecd.org/gov/regulatory-policy/2391768.pdf
OECD (1998) PUMA (98)12, Public Management Service: Public Management Committee: Revised Programme of Work 1999–2000. Presented at 18th Session of the Committee, Château de la Muette, Paris, 28–29 October 1998. Available at: https://www.oecd.org/officialdocuments/publicdisplaydocumentpdf/?cote=PUMA(98)12&docLanguage=En
OECD (2002) Regulatory Policies in OECD Countries: From Interventionism to Regulatory Governance. Available at: https://www.oecd-ilibrary.org/governance/regulatory-policies-in-oecd-countries_9789264177437-en
OECD (2007) OECD Council Resolution on Enlargement and Enhanced Engagement. Available at: https://www.oecd.org/brazil/oecdcouncilresolutiononenlargementandenhancedengagement.htm

OECD (2008) OECD Reviews of Regulatory Reform: Brazil 2008: Strengthening Governance for Growth, OECD Reviews of Regulatory Reform. OECD Publishing, Paris

OECD (2010) Regulatory Policy at the Crossroads: Towards a New Policy Agenda. Regulatory Policy Conference Paris, OECD Conference Centre, 28–29 October 2010. Available at: https://www.oecd.org/governance/regulatorypolicy/oecdregulatorypolicyconference2010.htm

OECD (2012) Recommendation of the Council on Regulatory Policy and Governance, OECD/LEGAL/0390. Available at: https://legalinstruments.oecd.org/en/instruments/OECD-LEGAL-0390

OECD (2013) International regulatory co-operation: addressing global challenges. OECD Publishing, Paris

OECD (2015), OECD economic surveys: Brazil 2015. OECD Publishing, Paris. Available at: https://doi.org/10.1787/eco_surveys-bra-2015-en

OECD (2016) OECD Indicators of Regulatory Policy and Governance (iREG) for Latin America 2016. In: Government at a Glance: Latin America and the Caribbean 2017. OECD Publishing, Paris

OECD (2021a) Recommendation of the Council for Agile Regulatory Governance to Harness Innovation. OECD/LEGAL/0464. Available at: https://legalinstruments.oecd.org/en/instruments/OECD-LEGAL-0464

OECD (2021b) Davidson P., Kauffmann C., de Liedekerke M.-G. How laws and regulations affect competitiveness: The role for regulatory impact assessment, OECD Regulatory Policy Working Papers No. 15, 2021. Available at: https://doi.org/10.1787/7c11f5d5-en

OECD (2022) Regulatory Reform in Brazil, OECD Reviews of Regulatory Reform. OECD Publishing, Paris

Pagani F (2002) Peer review as a tool for co-operation and change. Afr Secur Rev 11(4):15–24

Pal L (2008) Inversions without end: the OECD and global public management reform. In: Mahon R, McBride S (eds) The OECD and transnational governance. UBC Press, Vancouver

Pal L (2012) Frontiers of governance: the OECD and global public management reform. Palgrave Macmillan

Ponciano I, Derek G (2016) The Development of Regulatory Management Systems in East Asia. Deconstruction, Insights, and Fostering ASEAN's Quiet Revolution. Economic Research Institute for ASEAN and East Asia. Available at: https://www.eria.org/publications/the-development-of-regulatory-management-systems-in-east-asia-deconstruction-insights-and-fostering-aseans-quiet-revolution/

Porter T, Webb M (2008) Role of the OECD in the orchestration of global knowledge networks. In: Mahon R, McBride S (eds) The OECD and transnational governance. UBC Press, Vancouver, pp 43–59

Prado MM (2008) O contrato e o plano de gestão no projeto de Lei n. 3.337/04: controle desejável e justificado ou influência política indevida? Revista de Direito Público da Economia – RDPE 22: 115–119

Queiroz-Cunha B, Rodrigo D (2012) Regulatory Governance in Brazil. Paper presented at the 4th Biennial ECPR Standing Group for Regulatory Governance Conference, University of Exeter, 27–29 June 2012. Available at: http://clone.osservatorioair.it/wp-content/uploads/2013/10/OsservAIR_QueirozCunha-Rodrigo_RegulatoryGovernanceBrazil_P4-2013.pdf

Queiroz-Cunha B, Rodrigo D (2013) Assessing Regulatory Governance and Patterns of Regulatory Reform in Brazil. Osservatorio sull'Analisi di Impatto della Regolazione. Available at: http://clone.osservatorioair.it/wp-content/uploads/2013/10/OsservAIR_QueirozCunha-Rodrigo_RegulatoryGovernanceBrazil_P4-2013.pdf

Querbach T, Arndt C (2017) Regulatory policy in Latin America: An analysis of the state of play, OECD Regulatory Policy Working Papers, No. 7, OECD Publishing, Paris, Available at: https://doi.org/10.1787/2cb29d8c-en

Radaelli CM (2005) Diffusion without convergence: how political context shapes the adoption of regulatory impact assessment. J Eur Publ Policy 12(5):924–943

Ruggie JG (1998) What makes the world hang together? Neo-utilitarianism and the social constructivist challenge. Int Organ 52(4):855–885
Sanchez MR (2008) O Brasil e a OCDE: uma aproximação "pelas bordas", Textos Cindes. Available at: http://perma.cc/JU9N-4X3F
Sanchez-Badin MR, Badin A (2019) Anticorruption in Brazil: from transnational legal order to disorder. AJIL Unbound 113:326–330
Shaffer G (ed) (2013) Transnational legal ordering and state change. Cambridge University Press, Cambridge
Sunstein C (2012) The White House vs. Red Tape: A new executive order will help harmonize U.S. regulations with foreign ones, reducing costly redundancies while preserving public safety. Wall Street Journal, 5/1/2012. Available at: https://www.wsj.com/articles/SB10001424052702304811304577369934135888006
Trubek DM et al. (2017) Brazil in the shadow of mega-regional trade and investment standards: beyond the grand debate, pragmatic responses. In: Kingsbury B et al (eds) Megaregulation contested. Oxford University Press, Oxford, pp. 650–678
Vitale C et al (2020) The 2018 edition of the OECD PMR indicators and database: Methodological improvements and policy insights, OECD Economics Department Working Papers, No. 1604, OECD Publishing, Paris. Available at: https://doi.org/10.1787/2cfb622f-en
Wolfe R (2008) From reconstructing Europe to constructing globalization: the OECD in historical perspective. In: Mahon R, McBride S (eds) The OECD and transnational governance. UBC Press, Vancouver, pp 25–42
World Bank Group (2010) Better Regulation for Growth: Regulatory Governance in Developing Countries. Available at: http://regulatoryreform.com/wp-content/uploads/2014/11/Regulatory-Governance-Jacobs-Ladegaard-2010.pdf.
Young AR (2015) Liberalizing trade, not exporting rules: the limits to regulatory co-ordination in the EU's 'new generation' preferential trade agreements. J Eur Publ Policy 22(9):1253–1275

Magali Favaretto Prieto Fernandes is a Ph.D. Candidate in Law & Development from Fundação Getúlio Vargas São Paulo Law School, Brazil; LL.M. in International Business Law from American University, Washington College of Law, Washington, DC.; and LL.B. in Law and Social Sciences from University of São Paulo Faculty of Law, Brazil. Legal Researcher at the Center for Global Trade and Investment Studies (CCGI), Fundação Getúlio Vargas School of Economics, a WTO Chair Program and the Global Law and Development Center, Fundação Getúlio Vargas São Paulo Law School. Granted with the Mário Henrique Simonsen Scholarship and the Postgraduate Support Program for Private Education Institutions from the Coordination of Superior Level Improvement (CAPES-PROSUP).

The Role of Multilateral Institutions in the Perpetuation of Climate Breakdown and Vulnerability

Sean Madden

Contents

Abstract Within the stated purview of the United Nations (UN), International Monetary Fund (IMF), World Bank (WB), and related Multilateral Institutions (MLI) is the facilitation of sustainable development and economic growth, purportedly leading to reductions in global poverty and inequalities. These goals permeate supranational institutions of global governance; their centrality emphasised through agreements such as the Sustainable Development Goals (SDG) and propagated through instruments including Structural Adjustment Programmes (SAP).

This chapter argues, however, that these goals are inherently contradictory, bordering on nonsensical, and that the effect of IMF and WB policy towards the Third World is, contrary to stated aims, the perpetuation of vulnerability for some of the world's most impoverished people, and the exacerbation of anthropogenic climate breakdown.

Third World Debt is inexorably entwined with the colonial encounter, and subsequent centuries of extraction and exploitation legitimised through globalisation. When the IMF and WB mandate SAP in exchange for loans proffered in order to service this debt, Third World states embark upon extensive trade liberalisation, and the privatisation of natural resources and land. The subsequent extractive

S. Madden (✉)
Birmingham Law School, University of Birmingham, Birmingham, UK
e-mail: SXM1611@student.bham.ac.uk

M. de Amstalden et al. (eds.), *International Economic Law*, Special Issue,
https://doi.org/10.1007/978-3-031-41996-6_3

activity of Transnational Corporations (TNC) and foreign states serves to propagate the cycle of exploitation and environmental depredation, whilst enabling wealthier states to both materially gain from the activity, and offset their Nationally Determined Contributions (NDCs) under the Paris Agreement (PA). This activity is not only sanctioned, but encouraged through a neoliberal policy platform that prioritises economic growth and Western conceptions of development and sustainability above all else.

Consequently, Third World peoples, rather than experiencing alleviation from the cycle of debt locked in since the colonial encounter, are rendered further impoverished, bereft, and dependent, severely impeding their ability to mitigate or adapt to the effects of climate breakdown.

1 Introduction

The stated purview of the World Bank (WB), International Monetary Fund (IMF), United Nations (UN), and other Multilateral Institutions (MLI) is a reduction in poverty and inequalities, and the encouragement of sustainable development and economic growth. These goals permeate supranational institutions of global governance, and their importance is emphasised through agreements such as the Sustainable Development Goals (SDG), and instruments including Structural Adjustment Programmes (SAP).

When considered alongside the activities encouraged and legitimised through the epistemologies and praxis of these institutions, however, it can be argued that these aims are contradictory, and may in fact result in the exacerbation of inequality and anthropogenic climate breakdown (hereon in: ACC, or climate breakdown), and consequently, the perpetuation of vulnerability for some of the world's most impoverished peoples.

Significant scholarship has articulated the inexorable connection between the colonial encounter and Third World debt,[1] and subsequent centuries of extraction and exploitation legitimised through globalisation; indeed, postcolonial theory itself posits a continuity between the exploitation of the imperial past, and contemporary neoliberal globalisation.[2] When the IMF and WB mandate SAP in exchange for loans proffered in order to service this debt, the sale and privatisation of resources and access to land within the boundaries of the state invariably follows.[3] The subsequent extractive activity of Transnational Corporations (TNC) and foreign states may then propagate the cycle of exploitation and environmental depredation, whilst allowing former colonial states and other powers of the Global North to simultaneously profit and offset Greenhouse Gas (GHG) emissions. This activity

[1] Penet and Zendejas (2021), p. 7.

[2] Mishra and Hodge (2005), p. 388 and D'Souza (2022), p. 20.

[3] Summers and Pritchett (1993), p. 383 and Pfeiffer and Chapman (2010), p. 150.

appears not only to be sanctioned, but encouraged through a neoliberal policy platform that prioritises economic growth and Western conceptions of development and sustainability above all else.

Consequently, Third World[4] peoples, rather than experiencing alleviation from the cycle of debt locked in since the colonial encounter, are rendered further impoverished and dependent, severely impeding their ability to mitigate or adapt to the effects of climate breakdown exacerbated by MLI policy.

This chapter contends that SAP aggravate climate breakdown and environmental depredation through the encouragement of extractive activity and industrial production in order to stimulate economic growth. It further argues that vulnerable Third World communities, the recipients of aid and associated SAP, bear the brunt of this devastation by virtue of their sustained impoverishment, and inability to mitigate or adapt to their effects.

I begin by describing how the inception of MLI occurred as a direct result of a system of international law that precipitated and entrenched impoverishment and environmental depredation—particularly amongst Third World peoples—and how this has inexorably led these institutions to emerge as propagators of impoverishment, explaining how this poverty is an aggravating factor in climate vulnerability. After describing the emergence of SAP from this context, I then briefly outline and rebuff the arguments in favour of the policy, as presented by the IMF and WB. I then elaborate upon their ramifications for inequality and the environment, before presenting the example of Madagascar. Here, I detail how the imposition of SAP has proved detrimental to the environment, to GHG emissions, and subsistence, and how the consequences are intensified by worsening levels of impoverishment and inequality also propagated by MLI.

Whilst this chapter analyses the impacts of MLI upon the climate and the world's most vulnerable populations, in-depth analysis of WB and IMF macroeconomic policy is beyond its remit. Instead, the intention is to provide an overview of these organisations' structures and practices, positing that their activities are borne of ideological underpinnings. My aim is to articulate how this is emergent of the existing system of international law, and describe the implications of their agenda and practice.

[4] *I choose this nomenclature as I feel it better reflects the (post)colonial dynamic, and disavows Western conceptions of 'development'. More detail can be found at:* Pahuja (2011), p. 261.

2 Origins of the MLI and Roots in Extractivism

The institutions of international law and finance that predominate twenty-first century global discourse are possessed of origins rooted firmly in the colonial encounter.[5] This expansion of European empires across Africa, Asia, and the Americas was an inescapably extractivist and exploitative endeavour,[6] with subjugation of indigenous peoples acting to facilitate the removal of resources.[7] Indeed, it arguably served to solidify a relationship that had begun to emerge prior to formal colonial incursion.[8]

As such, it is possible to articulate how the nascent colonial desire for resource extraction, that sculpted initial forays into the Third World and precipitated environmental depredation, also influenced the creation of global institutions and structures of power. Albeit with markedly-changed rhetoric, the goal of utilising land and resource as capital in order to accumulate wealth is one which demonstrably persists into the modern era.

During the 16th Century, European states operated in explicit concord in order to minimise warfare within and between empires, establishing a regime of international law that facilitated their incursion into the Third World, notionally in order to engage in trade and exchange with local populations. This new regime, however, explicitly and deliberately failed to recognise the sovereignty of Third World peoples, deeming them to lack the 'civilisation' necessary to engage as equal parties in treaty and contract negotiations.[9]

There are distinct parallels to be drawn between Western perceptions and treatment of indigenous and subaltern communities, and of the natural environment. Both were viewed as expendable and disposable resources through which the continued growth of civilisation could be assured and maintained; both were merely elements of dominion over nature, bequeathed by God,[10] under the control of, generally, White, European males.[11]

Natural philosophers of the era were clear in their disdain for conceptions of stewardship that emphasised environmental protection, and the interconnection between humanity and the planet. Robert Boyle was unequivocal in his intent to rid indigenous Third World peoples of views that emphasised the importance of

---

[5]Chimni (2004), p. 30, Pahuja (2011), p. 3, Anghie (2005), pp. 115–195, Hickel et al. (2021), pp. 1030–1047.

[6]Girvan (2014), pp. 49–61, Greco (2020), pp. 511–521.

[7]Leurs (2019), p. 96.

[8]Omeji (2017), p. 3.

[9]Anghie (2005), pp. 13–31.

[10]Bacon (1620), aph. 59.

[11]The intersection of gender, race, the natural environment, and colonialism is one which bares deeper investigation in itself. Examples of previous discussion of some of these elements range from: Westlake (1894), p. 143, and Fanon (1961), p. 47, to Charlesworth (2016), pp. 137–144, Maguire and Jessup (2021), pp. 105–126.

coexistence and interconnection with nature, which he considered 'ridiculous',[12] and Francis Bacon wrote of 'subduing' and 'conquering nature'.[13]

The view that the natural world and its non-European inhabitants represented a resource to be plundered and controlled pervaded geopolitical discourse of the era and was clearly reflected in the work of early international legal scholars. De Vitoria, in articulating a rationale for the novel concept of international law and *Just War*, was manifestly influenced by Eurocentric conceptions of statehood.[14] Since the inception of modern international law, state sovereignty has been a 'foundational'[15] concept. Its importance as a tool through which rights and legal personality could be instilled—or withheld—was axiomatic to De Vitoria's worldview. In articulating a theory of natural law by which all peoples are bound and entitled through possession of reason, capacity, and polity, a point of coalescence between the cultural and societal structures of European and non-European civilisations was created.[16] It conferred upon inhabitants of the Third World the ability to engage in trade and to participate in treaty negotiations with European powers and jurisdiction over territory, provided their organisational structures conformed to European notions of statehood.[17]

What followed from the provision of limited rights for non-Europeans under this conception of international law, however, was the concomitant right of European powers to encroach upon their territory. In construction of what has been described as the 'sovereignty doctrine'[18]—or the set of customs and values through which imperial powers decided which polities should have sovereignty bestowed upon them—European values and customs were elevated, and the cultures and polities of the Third World considered inferior, and subordinated. The narrative of uncivility and backwardness that the dichotomy between European and non-European peoples engendered was used to justify an imbalance in the enjoyment of rights and legal personality, and legitimise incursion and exploitation.

This body of law, in effect, legitimised not only conquest, but the extraction and consumption of natural resources to which the European imperial powers had no prior claim, through its relegation of indigenous communities to partially-sovereign peoples with concomitantly fewer rights.[19] In order to achieve this, the primacy of European civilisation was asserted, universalising its values and proclaiming them as antidote to the backwardness of native and indigenous cultures;[20] the label of

[12]Quoted in Shiva (2016), p. 127.

[13]Ibid.

[14]Anghie (2005), p. 14.

[15]Shrinkhal (2021), p. 71.

[16]De Vitoria (1532), 3.1 sections 3-5.

[17]Ibid.

[18]Anghie (2005), p. 16.

[19]Anghie (2005), p. 15.

[20]German Prince Otto Von Bismarck, quoted in Mutua (2001), p. 847.

savagery bestowed in order to justify withholding rights.[21] Through this, they were able to justify the subjugation inherent within initial treaties and trade agreements forced upon Third World cultures. Such agreements conferred partial-sovereignty upon indigenous peoples, thus allowing them to engage in the transfer of land and resource to the control of conquering imperial powers.[22]

What is crucial is to recognise that the very inception of modern international law, governing the relationships between European and non-European states, is emergent of a desire to legitimise European extractivism; to homogenise and universalise, juxtaposing two interrelated kinds of dominance Shiva very aptly describes as "monocultures of the mind and of the land".[23]

The system of international law that consequently emerged from this dynamic of subjugation was intrinsically linked to European epistemologies and praxis, elevating the continent's values above those of colonised peoples.[24] In withholding sovereignty, and with it, rights to land and resource, the regime of international law imposed by European empires considered native land, in essence, *terra nullius*.[25] This thereby rendered it a legitimate target for sequestration, extraction and exploitation.

Wealth accumulation enabled through this exploitation catalysed the Industrial Revolution in Europe. From the period of colonial expansion in the mid-16th century, annual global carbon emissions rose steadily, emanating predominantly in the UK as mechanisation and enhanced production techniques fuelled economic growth, facilitated by fossil fuel extraction and emissions associated with transnational trade and distribution. The explosion of GHG emissions that accompanied this period of frenzied extraction and production meant that between 1750 and 2020, average global carbon emissions per capita increased from 0.01 to almost 4.5 tonnes, with the overwhelming majority of this increase related to the activity of European states leading up to the twentieth century,[26] or from a total of around 4 billion tonnes globally, to 36 billion.[27] For colonial states of the Global North, the average level of emission had exceeded 13 tonnes per capita by the early twenty-first century.[28]

Concurrently, states whose land, resource, and populations were exploited were doubly impacted. Firstly, they were unable to avail themselves of the produce of this

---

[21] *See generally*, Mutua (2001).

[22] Anghie (2006), p. 745.

[23] Shiva (2016), p. 127.

[24] Anghie (2005), p. 14.

[25] Rigney (2021), p. 125.

[26] Global Carbon Project, *Global Carbon Budget* 2021, available at: https://www.globalcarbonproject.org/carbonbudget/index.htm.

[27] Rebecca Lindsey, '*Climate Change: Atmospheric Carbon Dioxide*', (Climate.gov, 23 June 2022), available at: www.climate.gov/news-features/understanding-climate/climate-change-atmospheric-carbon-dioxide.

[28] *Ibid.*

activity, suffering impoverishment, displacement, and malnourishment.[29] Secondly, with the acceleration of the Industrial Revolution, and the preponderance of global trade resulting in a precipitous rise in emissions from production at the expense of Third World states, those still-impoverished peoples have become further imperilled in the face of burgeoning environmental crises.[30]

In 1884, the Berlin Conference[31] sought to consolidate the material interests of European powers in a manner considered equitable to all but those inhabiting the states under consideration, enabling the 'Scramble for Africa'.[32]

It is throughout this era—of colonial expansion, of subjugation, and extraction—that the plunder and exploitation of resources across Africa entrenched the 'under-development' imperial powers claimed to be seeking to arrest, and thus the structural insufficiencies and inequalities that allow the continent's continual subjugation.[33] It can then be considered the beginning of the vicious cycle of a developmentalism that continues to enforce exploitation of resources, and so is in itself environmentally depredatory, and damaging to communities.[34] In this context, it is both very telling, and no coincidence, that the recipients of loans through SAP are former colonial states, weighted with debt precipitated as a consequence of centuries of imperial exploitation and asset-stripping.[35]

The *de jure* end of colonialism and the 'long nineteenth century'[36]—an interconnected period of history asserted to have begun with the French revolution in 1789 and ended with the start of World War I (WWI) in 1914, and the associated geopolitical upheaval it entailed—precipitated the advent of the League of Nations. It has also been associated with the nascence of an individualistic and transnational economic trajectory that would culminate in the advent of neoliberalism.[37] In the aftermath of WWI, its founders sought to 'promote international cooperation, and to achieve international peace and security'[38] through the establishment of an organisation predicated on the ideal that serving the collective socioeconomic interest could help avoid war. What became clear, however, is that the organisation was built on predominantly European political and bureaucratic norms, and emphasised the primacy of European epistemologies of polity and power.[39] Echoing the legacy of empire, embedded within the aims of this alliance was the supremacy of European

---

[29] de Waal (2018), p. 188.

[30] Parks and Roberts (2006), p. 335.

[31] *See*, Craven (2015), p. 31.

[32] *The common, informal phrase, describing the period between approximately 1885 and 1914, during which European powers competed for Africa's territory and resources.*

[33] Rodney (1972), p. 143.

[34] Sachs (1992), p. 24.

[35] Rodney (1972), p. 14.

[36] Hobsbawm (1987), p. 6.

[37] Moreton (2007), p. 103.

[38] Covenant of the League of Nations (1919), Preamble, p. 72.

[39] Dykmann (2015), p. 721.

socio-political and economic norms, and the civilisation of backward states considered unworthy of or unable to sustain independent self-governance. This was made manifest through inception of the system of Mandates and Protectorates that would prove central to the operation of the League. However, such a reformation only served to entrench existing power dynamics and their associated extractive and exploitative relationships. Into the twentieth century, mandated territories—often brutally forged in the aftermath of the Berlin Conference, and distributed with the end of the 'Age of Empire'[40] after WWI—were utilised as a source of materials and labour to enable the unimpeded economic growth of former colonial powers, under the guise of encouraging civilisation. The desire of European powers to cement the "welfare and even the existence of our great population"[41] through exploitation of their former charges, their land, and their resources remained strong.

As the League was reconstituted after World War II with ratification of the UN Charter, the Bretton Woods Institutions (BWI) were established as the supranational economic arbiters of global governance. In contrast to the UN, the decision-making processes of the IMF and WB operate through use of a quota system, privileging states possessed of a higher GDP with greater leverage over policy creation. In choosing to place such emphasis on economic considerations, the hierarchy of concerns is abundantly clear—as is the place of traditionally-European, free market economic ideology: The virtually unimpeachable power vested in these institutions provides supreme representation of the 'transcendence'[42] of the economic above all other concerns—social, political, and environmental.

3 The Inception of Structural Adjustment and Foundations in Neoliberalism Extractivism

SAP were devised by the WB in 1980, in the wake of the 1979 oil shock, ostensibly as a means to prevent large and obstructive deficits proliferating within states of the Global South.[43] As the 1980s progressed, the IMF expanded their own loan programmes to include Structural Adjustment, with both organisations now committed to the dual policy objectives of reducing deficits and facilitating economic growth,[44] to be achieved by tying the provision of development loans to specific conditionalities related to domestic legislative reform. They entailed the enactment of free-market, neoliberal economic policy within the recipient state, in the form of

[40] Hobsbawm (1987), p. 4.

[41] Joseph Chamberlain, quoted in Woolf (1920), p. 7.

[42] Pahuja (2011), p. 98.

[43] Easterly (2005), p. 3.

[44] *Ibid.*

trade liberalisation, privatisation of state assets and reduced government spending, currency stabilisation and devaluation, and deregulation.[45]

Although these programmes are, *prima facie*, levied at the request of an aid recipient state, the extent to which they exercise complete autonomy in embarking upon such reform is a matter of significant debate. It is arguable that the requirement to undertake drastic structural changes in order to facilitate the ingress of foreign capital—and, conversely, the hostility of the WB, IMF and capital-exporting wealthy nations to any form of protectionism–[46] represents a form of coercion.[47] This perspective is lent significant weight with consideration of the fact that the targets of these programmes are often post-colonial states carrying significant and historic structural debt,[48] as a result of an imperial extractivism that left Third World peoples bereft of income and assets,[49] and also visited significant damage upon socioeconomic and political infrastructure that hampered restorative attempts.[50]

As such, it has been variously argued that the purpose of SAP was not only to address acute financial need, but to fundamentally alter the economic underpinnings of the state in line with the globalised, neoliberal, and Western conception of economic development perpetually espoused by MLI, with the provision of necessary funds used as incentive.[51] In accordance with this orthodox economic ideology, the logic of SAP is that income can be generated through boosted exports and slashed public spending, and that these monies can also be utilised to service existing debts.[52]

Within this dynamic, economic growth, industrial development, and global trade are lauded as solutions to poverty, but evidence suggests that when SAP encourage privatisation and trade liberalisation in countries already fraught with iniquity, fragility, and debt, there are catastrophic consequences for the environment[53] and for vulnerable people.[54]

When this vulnerability is juxtaposed alongside the prevailing regime of international law enforced by MLI and crafted by wealthier, often former colonial powers, we can begin to see how the power of these institutions may be sufficient to enforce the neoliberal economic agenda, inclusive of privatisation and trade liberalisation, upon aid-recipient states, codifying the legitimacy of foreign capital incursion, and reducing the purview of the state. Whilst it is possible to construe these legislative changes as the autonomous decisions of a sovereign state, their direct coincidence

---

[45] Clapp and Dauvergne (2005), p. 200.

[46] International Monetary Fund (2022), p. 23.

[47] Wigger (2019), p. 359; Muralidharan (1992), p. 30.

[48] Rudin and Sanders (2019), p. 170; McMichael (1998), p. 98.

[49] Bernards (2022), p. 23.

[50] *Ibid.*

[51] Peet (2003), p. 62.

[52] Shandra et al. (2011), p. 210.

[53] *Ibid.*

[54] Oberdabernig (2010), p. 20; Thomson et al. (2017), p. 14, *inter alia.*

with the imposition of SAP and the necessity of such reforms as conditionality for the provision of financial support arguably introduces an element of coercion, manifest with the asymmetric power relationship between indebted state and MLI,[55] potentially taking advantage of Third World vulnerability,[56] and encouraging the state to enact legislation it otherwise may not.

The paradox of such involvement in the domestic sphere is that Third World governments are often receptive to, or even eager to execute, legislative reform in order to attract the investment perceived as a necessity in order to service debt and build infrastructure.[57] Where this becomes particularly problematic, however, is not necessarily in the arena of economic growth or increased trade, but in how it impacts upon vulnerable populations, and how such intervention lends itself to environmental depredation. It is a dynamic redolent of the quintessence of colonial extractivism: the continued enmeshment of Western socioeconomic epistemology within states of the Third World in order to legitimise use of resources and land, under the auspices of development, as it was once under the pretence of building civilisation.

The conceit of the WB and IMF is that their interventional programmes enable the creation of economic growth, and, in archetypal neoliberal fashion, that this is the primary means through which impoverishment will be alleviated and sustainability ensured. It is regrettable, therefore, that evidence of the effects of these interventions does not support the claims, and that the ghosts of international law's past are present in the modern day international institution—maintaining that actions are undertaken in the interests of disadvantaged or impoverished peoples, whilst effectively ensuring the continued enrichment of western corporations, and the perpetuation of hemispherical imbalance.

Whilst this chapter will argue that such activity is indeed antithetical to sustainability and the reduction of global inequality, and in actuality merely represents the continuation of the extractive and environmentally-depredatory colonial dynamic, this is not to suggest that environmental and human consequences of these actions remain unconsidered and unaddressed by institutions of global governance. As the following section discusses, these organisations have devoted extensive resource to demonstrating their commitment to environmental safeguarding and the amelioration of climate breakdown.

4 Rhetoric and Reality

At their creation, the IMF and WB were tasked with coordinating matters of international finance and managing global monetary policy in the post-war, and post-Eurocentric era. The initial remit of the Bank was to 'assist in the reconstruction

[55] Babb (2013), p. 278.

[56] Simmons et al. (2008), p. 14.

[57] Riofrancos (2020), p. 4.

and development of territories',[58] 'promote private foreign investment[59]'. For the IMF, the aim was promotion of 'international monetary cooperation', the facilitation of 'the expansion and balanced growth of international trade[60]', and promotion of 'exchange stability...making the general resources of the Fund temporarily available to [members] under adequate safeguards.'[61] Whilst the IMF's mandate was to provide short-term funding in order to address acute financial need, the Bank's purview was focused on longer-term provision for larger development projects.[62]

A consistent refrain of the IMF and WB is that the purpose of SAP centres around poverty reduction, as well as on economic development, within the world's most impoverished states. The primary arm through which this is to be achieved is lending through the Poverty Reduction and Growth Facility—formerly the Enhanced Structural Adjustment Facility, and before that, simply the Structural Adjustment Facility. Instruments including the Extended and Standby Credit Facilities provide payments of various lengths to poorer states, notionally in attempts to build state capacity, and reduce poverty levels in line with state aims.[63]

The IMF argue that their "global reach [and] institutional experience" enables them to provide capacity development across a number of intersectional issues, including climate change, corruption, gender equality, and income inequality "within its areas of expertise", especially within impoverished and Third World states.[64]

Even with reference to the most recent global events, rhetoric continues to emphasise the centrality of both poverty alleviation, and action to address climate breakdown. With language focused on its rapid adaptation and preparation for climate challenges,[65] they state that:

> Policymakers across the globe are rightly focused on fighting the COVID-19 crisis. But the climate change crisis remains, as does the need for decisive policy action to address it. Indeed, current policy decisions to facilitate recovery from the crisis may shape the world's climate for decades. This calls for fiscal policymakers to "green" their response to the crisis. The IMF has rapidly scaled up its work on climate. Climate-related issues and policies are being more systematically integrated into surveillance, and various policy papers and books have been published on energy subsidies, carbon pricing, natural disaster clauses in state-contingent debt instruments, and the impact of climate change on macroeconomic and financial stability.[66]

---

[58] International Bank of Reconstruction and Development (1944), Article I (i).

[59] *ibid* Article I (ii).

[60] International Monetary Fund (1944), Article I (ii).

[61] *ibid* Article I (iii).

[62] Anghie (2005), p. 219.

[63] World Bank Group (2001), p. 84.

[64] International Monetary Fund (2021), p. 37.

[65] *Ibid*, p. 38.

[66] *Ibid*, p. 18.

It is also argued that these facilities help to engender good economic practice, and help the recipient state in their efforts towards achieving the Sustainable Development Goals.[67]

The WB has suggested that the involvement of FDI within an aid-recipient state could contribute significantly to economic growth and poverty alleviation,[68] and their literature argues that, whilst impacts of their SAP are hard to generalise, they are likely to have had a net positive effect on environmental protection.[69] In addition, almost two-thirds of SAP agreements contain a general section reassuring an absence of environmental effects emergent of the provision of loans.[70]

Such statements are lent support by adherents to MLI operations, who contend that, in the privatisation of land and resource, SAP actively encourage more stringent environmental protections as a means of safeguarding a valuable commodity and assigning it a true market value as 'natural capital'.[71] Also, they posit that environmental pressures are alleviated through reduced reliance upon agricultural practices, with emphasis shifted to industry and services.[72]

Of concern is that the poverty reduction solutions posited and implemented by MLI are "generally rooted in neoliberal economic theory",[73] and focus on commodification and marketisation of natural resources in order to grow an economy out of impoverishment; a position difficult to reconcile with environmental sustainability in its current guise,[74] and associated with widening equality gaps and growing impoverishment.[75]

The founding documents of both the IMF and WB, however, point to an overarching purpose that puts them more in line with globalised, free-market capitalist principles espoused by wealthier, former colonial powers. The Articles of Agreement assert that the purpose of the IMF is to promote monetary cooperation and stability, and encourage the expansion of global trade, thus increasing income and employment.[76] Similarly, albeit with less opacity as regards its intention, the International Bank for Reconstruction and Development (as was) asserted its purpose as capital investment for purposes of development, and to promote and supplement private foreign investment into developing economies.[77]

---

[67] Towe (2022), p. 46.

[68] Gonzalez-Gonzalez et al. (2021), p. 4.

[69] World Bank Group (1994), p. 14.

[70] World Bank Group (2001), p. 61.

[71] Glover (1995).

[72] Fischer (1996), pp. 247–251.

[73] Shandra et al. (2011), p. 211.

[74] Adelman (2018), p. 16.

[75] Stiglitz (2016), p. 134.

[76] *Supra* note 60, Article I (i).

[77] *Supra* note 58.

Whilst MLI present themselves as "neutral, and apolitical",[78] and rhetoric has evolved in the intervening decades, there is little doubt that focus has remained solidly upon the promotion of growth and liberalisation of trade in order to facilitate the proliferation of global capital that has continued to enrich TNC and wealthier states at the expense of Third World peoples.

With clear commitment to free market principles, the primacy of private capital, and their role in stimulating growth and poverty alleviation, Anghie has asserted that "it is hardly possible to dispute that these institutions are intensely political institutions, notwithstanding their attempts to suggest otherwise",[79] and that cemented within these politics is a commitment to extractivism and economic growth more-than reminiscent of imperial encroachment within the colonial state.

It would appear then, *prima facie*, that MLI have devoted considerable effort and resource to evidence the positive impacts that their policy agenda has had on recipient states. However, these statements should be treated with acute scepticism. Worthy of consideration are the metrics of success utilised by these institutions and their backers and members across wealthier, former colonial powers in the Global North.

Further, information regarding the impacts of SAP upon the natural environment is nebulous at best. In stark contrast to the line taken by MLI, much research has evidenced the negative impacts of such programmes upon living standards, poverty levels, and population health.[80]

A multitude of evidence suggests that the commodification of natural resources, and concomitant emphasis on trade liberalisation alongside the encouragement of extractive industry may have in fact exacerbated deforestation and environmental breakdown, whilst associated privatisation and shrinkage within the public sector limits the capacity of the state to address the loss of woodland and associated environmental costs.[81] Further, numerous scholars have cast doubt on the validity of claims regarding the positive effects of FDI on environmental stewardship, land management, and pollution.[82]

Should this in fact be the case, the ramifications for increased vulnerability in the face of loss and damage from climate breakdown are manifest. It is difficult to escape the conclusion that it is a nexus of issues compounded in the Third World, if not entirely created, by the imposition of SAP. The direct impact this has on the environment and on population vulnerability, whilst assertions to the contrary are made across MLI, really is worthy of consideration: the global organisations and institutions self-imbued with the authority to coordinate the struggle against anthropogenic climate change are in fact perpetuating it.

---

[78] Anghie (2005), p. 221.

[79] *Ibid.*

[80] Jolly (1991), Easterly (2001), Hickel (2016).

[81] Goldman (2005), McMichael (2004), Barbosa (2001), Peet (2003).

[82] De Schutter (2009), Borras Jr et al. (2011), Anseeuw et al. (2012).

5 Structural Adjustment and Inequality

Despite assertions by some scholars that SAP mechanisms of operation are associated with the furtherance of economic growth[83] data has demonstrated significant impact upon income distribution and, subsequently, inequality.[84] The benefits of such growth are, in fact, felt exclusively by those at the higher end of income distribution, and existing inequalities are amplified.[85] It is sometimes compounded by increased economic volatility precipitated by FDI.[86] This is more likely to be the case within Third World states,[87] engendering greater impacts upon poorer communities.[88]

Stabilisation techniques have been shown to reduce the possibility of inflation,[89] however, some scholars suggest that higher interest rates demonstrably benefit wealthy creditors—frequently foreign investors—at the expense of those who are indebted, invariably the poorest in society, and so only furthering inequality.[90] These effects are intensified by borrowing restrictions imposed with the goal of curtailing levels of external debt, which often lead states to cut spending on social programmes that disproportionately benefit poorer citizens, and felt most acutely in heavily-indebted Third World states already vulnerable to crises.[91] That privatisation occurs in conjunction with limitations placed upon borrowing incurs further curtailment of government expenditure. The ramifications of these cutbacks are wide-reaching, and further impact upon socioeconomic programmes designed to provide assistance to those in the most need.[92] Resultantly, there is strong correlation within states between the imposition of SAP and a higher Gini index, associated with greater inequality.[93]

In part, this increased inequality results from a growing income share amongst those who already possess the most, as limits to additional external debt increase the value of existing bonds.[94] The subsequent increase in capital returns has the effect of further enticing external investors,[95] in line with the stated goals of the IMF.

The effects of these programmes on people living within loan-dependent states are stark. Levels of inequality increased in three quarters of Third World societies

[83] Henry (2007), pp. 887–935.

[84] Kentikelenis et al. (2016), pp. 534–582, Stubbs and Kentikelenis (2018), and Woods (2006).

[85] Roine et al. (2009), pp. 974–988.

[86] Mensah and Mensah (2021), p. 10.

[87] Gnangnon (2021), p. 125.

[88] De Haan and Sturm (2017).

[89] Dreher and Walter (2010).

[90] Forster et al. (2018), p. 7.

[91] Wibbels (2006).

[92] Abah and Naankiel (2016), p. 4, Forster et al. (2020), p. 7.

[93] Garuda (2000).

[94] Forster et al. (2018), p. 86.

[95] *Ibid*, p. 89.

between 1990 and 2013,[96] coinciding with the imposition of SAP—a fact variously and consistently highlighted in the literature.[97] That the IMF and WB are able to exert such influence, and mandate such sweeping structural reforms,[98] is due to the global reach of their lending policy, and that IMF membership encompasses almost every state on Earth.[99] It is a level of control that presents MLI with vast capacity to force the implementation of policy with significant potential to affect not only the economic but also physical environment of any particular state.

The notion that SAP themselves facilitate debt repayment, rather than perpetuating the cycle of Third World indebtedness, is at best contentious, but one which is essential to the maintenance of orthodox neoliberal globalisation. It has been evidenced[100] that despite the debt servicing made possible through the provision of loans, external debt liability, crucially, has increased amongst multiple Third World states, with data provided by the WB itself demonstrating how funds proffered by MLI act as a contributing factor.[101] As consequence of this, the need to attract external capital, and to offer land and resources to external agents, is compounded. When the likely impacts upon the natural environment are considered, these effects are more acutely observable.

Imperial extractivism left Third World peoples bereft of income and assets,[102] and visited significant damage upon socioeconomic and political infrastructure that hampered restorative attempts.[103] It is bitter irony that, having fostered enduring impoverishment, former colonial powers, through MLI, are now enabled to take advantage of such vulnerability to enforce another extractive and damaging ideology.

6 Structural Adjustment and Environmental Depredation

Whilst it can be argued that FDI has stimulated benefits for the host state, particularly with regards to the establishment of necessary infrastructural improvements[104] and growing export sectors, the increased level of impoverishment associated with the inequality often engendered by investment of this kind contributes substantially to the inability of vulnerable populations to safeguard themselves against the effects of climate breakdown.

---

[96] UNDP (2013), p. 3.

[97] Kentikelenis (2017), pp. 296–305; Oberdabernig (2013), pp. 113–142.

[98] Copelovitch (2010).

[99] Woods (2006).

[100] Aluko and Arowolo (2010), p. 120.

[101] World Bank Group (2022).

[102] Bernards (2022), p. 23.

[103] *Ibid.*

[104] Onjala (2018), p. 711.

The imposition of SAP and subsequent ingress of foreign capital has invariably led to the proliferation of extractive activity, furthering environmental depredation in the pursuit of economic growth. Additionally, the privatisations and borrowing restrictions imposed through SAP diminish the ability of the state to engage in mitigation and adaptation techniques in order to address the climate crisis.[105]

The importance of the state in tackling climate breakdown is widely acknowledged,[106] even within MLI such as the UN, with Nationally Determined Contributions playing a significant role in mitigation efforts outlined through the Paris Agreement.[107] State intervention is considered a necessity to facilitate transition to low carbon and sustainable infrastructure, either in terms of agenda-setting through legislation,[108] or directly financing necessary projects, infrastructure, and innovation.[109] The state's willingness to relinquish power to the private sector, and to investors from foreign states or TNC makes it extremely difficult to achieve these goals as primacy is granted to the activities of the investor, and attempts to foster economic development. As the government of the recipient state unilaterally decides to liberalise and privatise, the populace are denied agency whilst inequality proliferates. Especially detrimental is the ability of wealthier states and TNC to offset GHG emissions produced within the recipient state, increasing the likelihood of Third World peoples' suffering, whilst profits are exported.

Whilst literature exploring the direct environmental impacts of SAP has been produced since their inception,[110] findings have been rebuffed, to an extent, by the WB, which displays ambivalence at best, describing evidence as 'inconclusive',[111] and dependent upon regional factors.[112] This however contrasts with research conducted by the IMF, which appears to delineate a connection between SAP and environmental degradation.[113]

It is also possible that research conducted by the WB has failed to consider the enduring implications of activity stimulated by SAP. Deforestation represents a clear example of such an omission. The WB itself recognises that the increased production of cash crops for export within Third World states likely increases incidence deforestation and use of pesticides,[114] but along with other MLI, asserts its impacts are offset through tree planting initiatives,[115] agreements such as Reducing

[105] Shandra et al. (2016), p. 6.

[106] Tosun and Peters (2020), p. 4 and Mazzucato (2015), pp. 121–178.

[107] UNFCCC (2015), Article IV (ii).

[108] Mazzucato and Ryan-Collins (2022), p. 345.

[109] Mazzucato (2015), p. 153.

[110] Panayotou and Hupe (1996), p. 56; Kentikelenis et al. (2016), p. 6.

[111] Gueorguieva and Bolt (2003), p. 26.

[112] *Ibid*, p. 29.

[113] Fischer (1996).

[114] Gueorguieva and Bolt (2003), p. 5.

[115] UNEP (2008).

Emissions through Deforestation and Degradation (REDD+),[116] or other solutions limited in efficacy. The displaced effects, however, whilst not necessarily immediately tangible, are ultimately both incredibly damaging and not easily remediable.

Amongst the largest contributors to GHG emissions, and thus to climate breakdown, through both the release of sequestered carbon and the fact forest is frequently cleared through burning,[117] deforestation is also associated with soil degradation and desertification in the long-term.[118] Whilst communities in post-colonial states have long utilised land for subsistence, deforestation on a massive scale has occurred in tandem with the expansion of export crops and livestock, particularly amongst former colonial states in Sub-Saharan Africa and Latin America.[119] It is also widely linked with increases in mining activity.[120] This huge increase in export capacity has been systematically and actively encouraged through SAP, by the IMF and WB, as a means to ensure economic growth. Levels of deforestation have increased substantially since the inception of SAP in the 1980s, as the amount of produce for export rapidly increased also.[121]

Alongside this, reduction in state capacity limits governments' ability to provide support for those displaced by environmental depredation, or rendered under or unemployed by increased extractive activity through incursion by TNC. The confluence of difficult circumstances enabled by this activity arguably precipitates a vicious cycle of environmental destruction, as displaced or impoverished persons are forced to clear more woodland in order to subsist.[122] Such desperation may also lead to the abandonment of traditional, conservational methods of land cultivation in favour of fast production, wreaking further damage upon the natural world. Relatedly, the confluence of impoverishment and climactic effects is evident in the propensity for societies living under SAP to use a higher volume of solid fuels in household heating, thereby contributing to deforestation, to detrimental health impacts, and to pollution and climate breakdown through emission of GHG.[123]

Compounding the imbalance between recipient states and TNC, and serving to ensconce damaging activity, investors are insulated from changes in domestic law that facilitate environmental protection through the ability to avail themselves of Investor-State Dispute Settlements (ISDS) and arbitration, regulated by MLI in the form of the UN Conference on Trade and Development (UNCTAD).[124] Further, SAP-mandated reforms can serve to actively weaken environmental laws, and to cement impoverishment through failure to address structural causes of inequality,

---

[116] 4/CP.15, UNFCCC (2009).

[117] UN SDG (2022), p. 56.

[118] Austin (2010), p. 511.

[119] UN (n. 117), p. 56.

[120] Morley et al. (2022), p. 8; Gonzalez-Gonzalez et al. (2021), p. 16.

[121] Rudel et al. (2009), p. 1396.

[122] Hosonuma et al. (2012), p. 8.

[123] Austin and McCarthy (2016), p. 177.

[124] Nunnenkamp (2017), p. 851.

and by rendering employment insecure and deregulated.[125] Such a dynamic only serves to reinforce the role played by MLI in maintenance of the existing international socioeconomic order, as the interests of capital, and focus on development, subsume domestic considerations within the post-colonial state.

In the following, penultimate, section, I present an example of a post-colonial state, structurally and materially-impoverished following exploitation by European imperial powers, and illustrate how acceptance of development loans in order to alleviate this impoverishment has served to accentuate vulnerability to climate breakdown—itself exacerbated by neoliberal, growth-driven MLI policy—whilst little to nothing in the arena of poverty reduction is accomplished.

7 From Colony to Coercion? The Case of Madagascar

In Madagascar, the consequences of this coercion are increasingly evident. In the 1980s, Anglo-Australian mining corporation Rio Tinto discovered deposits of the mineral ilmenite in Port Dauphin, Taolagnaro. The mineral is highly-valued as a source of titanium dioxide, and the company had established a 6000 hectare mineral sand mine in conjunction with Madagascar's government by 2008. With Rio Tinto owning the rights to 80% of the mine, and the state the remaining 20%, this partnership was named QIT Madagascar Minerals (QMM). The operation is responsible for the extraction of around 750,000 tonnes of ilmenite from the coastal sands annually. This is refined, and shipped globally, to be used in the production of numerous household goods.

The rallying of numerous organisations against the establishment of the mine[126] led to the creation of QMM's Biodiversity Committee, and a pledge to leave a Net Positive Impact (NPI) on the environment. Within a decade, the corporation had reneged on this promise, disturbing forests and failing to compensate for environmental loss and damage. In order to mine Ilmenite, all plant life must be removed from the site of extraction.[127] With the Rio Tinto operation located within an area of littoral forest, there has been significant deforestation of older woodland, resulting in the release of CO2 sequestered for centuries. Concomitantly, the chemical processes utilised and generated by the sector have resulted in the release of lead, uranium, and other volatile compounds into land and water courses, polluting soil and waterways, with clear implications for aquatic life and subsistence farming. This damage has also significantly stunted the capacity of each to sequester CO2 and other GHG, compounding issues of both pollution and deforestation.

One thousand kilometres away, just west of the Andasibe-Mantadia National Park, the Ambatovy mine extracts nickel and cobalt in the country's largest mining

125 Reinsberg et al. (2019), pp. 1224–1225.

126 World Rainforest Movement (2016), Friends of the Earth (2017).

127 Gerety (2019).

operation. Established by a Canadian multinational company—backed by the WB and IMF—In 2007, the site is now owned by a consortium of Japanese and Korean corporations. In contrast to Rio Tinto, the site has attracted plaudits for its efforts to offset the deforestation engendered by its operation—an increasingly common practice within climate mechanisms and environmentally depredatory industries. Yet this offsetting fails to account for the loss of biodiversity and its role in ecosystem regulation, and the dramatically reduced capacity of new forest to sequester GHG in comparison to older and ancient woodland.

The Rio Tinto and Ambatovy operations are emblematic of the extractive and damaging activity, predominantly undertaken by externally-incorporated TNC, that dominates the Madagascan landscape, and whose environmental impacts are cumulative, and compounded by the production, transportation, and distribution of extracted materials. The combined emissions of extraction, refinement, and export of produce amounts to a substantial increase in the state's GHG.

The scale of this incursion was facilitated through the imposition of several SAP throughout the 1980s and 1990s, and the subsequent intrusion of MLI into Madagascan law. In exchange for development loans, the WB encouraged the adoption of law that facilitated the ingress of FDI. One such law became statute in 1999, and paved the way for foreign mining corporations to begin operations, whilst diminishing the role of the state.[128] In 2021, the effects were compounded by legislation rolling back law introduced in 2006, and reducing the land rights of peasantry and subsistence farmers, allowing the state to exercise compulsory purchase in order to redistribute amongst foreign investors.[129] Each of these monumental changes had the effect of reducing the efficacy of the public sector in favour of the economic demands of TNC, whilst increasing the vulnerability of some of the world's most impoverished people, struggling under threat of climate breakdown and unsustainable extractivist practices.

These incursions within the Madagascan domestic legal sphere are emblematic of reforms to African mining laws effectively mandated by MLI since the mass imposition of SAP in the 1980s and 1990s. A common theme of these reforms is the strengthened position of the private sector with regards access to land and resource, whilst the authority and capacity of the state is weakened.[130] On these broad terms, it is not difficult to draw parallels between SAP, and the nascence of international law, wherein power was maintained and proliferated by European states and quasi-autonomous corporations, such as the East India Company. A functional apathy towards environmental concerns appears to be another shared characteristic.

The island still reels from the impact of colonialism, having only gained independence in 1961. It is considered an economically impoverished state,[131] with

---

[128] *Law 99-022.*

[129] *Law 2021-016.*

[130] Campbell (2009).

[131] World Bank Group (2009).

two-thirds of the rural population living below the poverty line.[132] Remaining significantly indebted as a result of colonial exploitation, it typifies the manner in which wealthy states are still able to exert pressure upon their former charges despite the *de jure* end of the colonial relationship. This pressure to accept draconian economic and political conditionality in order to receive necessary financial aid acts as the driving force the encroachment of companies, such as Rio Tinto, into the sphere of the nation state, and so encourages the environmental depredation associated with such investment. It is a bitter irony, then, that only does a net contribution to climate breakdown often emerge from the imposition of SAP, but, as with Madagascar, the proliferation of impoverishment and inequality continues unabated. Here, MLI fail on both counts: first, in their inability to reduce levels of poverty, and second, in engendering the environmental damage that will only serve to increase vulnerability of the world's poorest, both within the host state, and globally.

8 Conclusions

Poverty reduction and the fostering of climate resilience are, purportedly, at the heart of the programmes undertaken by institutions of global governance such as the IMF and WB. In this chapter, I have demonstrated that these aims, however seemingly laudable, are inherently contradictory—and in fact border on nonsensical—when considered alongside the activities encouraged and legitimised by these institutions. The result of, in particular, SAP, is in fact the exacerbation of environmental depredation, anthropogenic climate breakdown, and inequality. Consequently, this entrenches the perpetuation of vulnerability for some of the world's most impoverished peoples.

There can be no doubt that, in tandem, the IMF and WB operate a steadying hand on global public financial governance. Whether this oversight amounts to a wholly positive influence, with a stabilising effect, however, is highly doubtful. From their inception, these institutions clearly represented an ideologically-motivated undertaking; emergent of a regime of international law crafted during the colonial encounter, and so analogous with extractivism. The notional neutrality of these institutions belies a commitment to free-market neoliberalism that prioritises economic growth above all else, viewing it as a panacea for poverty relief; the 'rising tide' which 'lifts all boats'.[133]

The inequality intensified by SAP is itself a source of climate injustice and precarity; vulnerability is amplified by the fact that the policy agenda encourages environmentally-depredatory activity, and exposes people to conditions that worsen their living environment, as well as leaving them vulnerable to the effects of climate breakdown. Despite myriad recent overtures towards sustainability and climate

[132] Sarrasin (2006), p. 14.

[133] *A phrase often attributed to President John F. Kennedy – possibly erroneously.*

consciousness, environmental considerations have remained secondary whilst neoliberal growth—borne of FDI, privatisation, and a diminished public sector—is allotted primacy in the quest for poverty alleviation. An interesting and necessary extension to this chapter should involve an exploration of the ambivalence and complicity of UN institutions in perpetuating this relationship.

Such focus on driving wealth accumulation which predominantly favours wealthier states and corporations is, in itself, more than reminiscent of the earliest colonial encounters. The case of Madagascar is demonstrative of the manner in which wealthier states, possessed of greater power and agency within the IMF and WB, are enabled to enforce economic policy favourable to themselves, whilst the nomenclature of development remains the overarching narrative. This whilst, substantively, significant elements of the asymmetric power relations that typified the colonial encounter remain.

Whilst this dynamic persists, the conflict that arises between the alleviation of impoverishment and environmental protection, and neoliberal conceptions of development centred on limitless growth, will provoke accusations of contradiction, and possibly hypocrisy, within institutions of global governance. Resultantly, efforts to promptly and equitably address climate breakdown will likely continue to flounder, and it is the most vulnerable communities of the Third World who will suffer most at the hands of Western intransigence.

References

Abah D, Naankiel PW (2016) Structural adjustment programme in Nigeria and its implication on socio-economic development, 1980–1995. Cal Hist J 6(2):1–16

Adelman S (2018) The sustainable development goals, anthropocentrism and neoliberalism. In: French D, Kotze LJ (eds) The sustainable development goals: law, theory, and implementation. Edward Elgar, pp 15–41

Aluko F, Arowolo D (2010) Foreign aid, the Third World's debt crisis and the implication for economic development: The Nigerian experience. Afr J Pol Sci Intl Rel 4(4):120–127

Anghie A (2005) Imperialism, sovereignty, and the making of international law. Cambridge University Press, Cambridge

Anghie A (2006) The evolution of international law: colonial and postcolonial realities. Third World Qtly 27(5):739–753

Anseeuw W, Boche M, Breu T, Giger M, Lay J, Messerli P, Nolte K (2012) Transnational land deals for agriculture in the global south: analytical report based on the land matrix database. The Land Matrix Partnership. Available at: https://www.almendron.com/tribuna/wp-content/uploads/2015/06/analytical-report.pdf

Austin KF (2010) Soybean exports and deforestation from a world systems perspective: a cross-national investigation of comparative disadvantage. Soc Qtly 3:511–536

Austin KF, McCarthy K (2016) Choking on structural adjustment: dependency and exposure to indoor air pollution in developing countries. Wld J Soc Sci Res 3(2):161–184

Babb S (2013) The Washington consensus as transnational policy paradigm: its origins, trajectory and likely successor. Rev Intl Pol Econ 20(2):268–297

Bacon F (1620) Novum Organon

Barbosa LC (2001) The Brazilian Amazon rainforest: global ecopolitics, development, and democracy. University of American Press, New York, NY

Bernards N (2022) A critical history of poverty finance: colonial roots and neoliberal failures. Pluto Press, London
Borras Jr SM, Hall R, Scoones I, White B, Wolford W (2011) Towards a better understanding of global land grabbing: an editorial introduction. J Peas Stud 38(2):209:216
Campbell B (2009) Mining in Africa: regulation and development. Pluto Press
Charlesworth H (2016) Gender and international law. In: Steans J, Tepe D (eds) Handbook on gender in world politics. Edward Elgar, pp 137–144
Chimni BS (2004) International institutions today: an imperial global state in the making. Euro J Intl Law 15(1):1–37
Clapp J, Dauvergne P (2005) Paths to a green world: the political economy of the global environment. In: Benatar S, Brock G (eds) Global health: ethical challenges. Cambridge University Press, Cambridge
Copelovitch M (2010) The international monetary fund in the global economy: banks, bonds, and bailouts. Cambridge University Press, Cambridge
Craven M (2015) Between law and history: the Berlin Conference of 1884-1885 and the logic of free trade. London Rev Intl Law 3(1)
D'Souza R (2022) a radical turn in international law and development? Corporations, capitalist states and imperial governance. J Dev Stud 43(1):20–38
De Haan J, Sturm JE (2017) Finance and income inequality: a review and new evidence. Euro J Pol Econ 50:171–195
De Schutter O (2009) Large-scale land acquisitions and leases: a set of core principles and measures to address the human rights challenge'. Briefing note. Office of the High Commissioner for Human Rights. Available at: http://www.csa-be.org/IMG/pdf_SRRTFlarge-scalelandacquisitions9_6_09.pdf
De Vitoria F (1532) De Indis
De Waal A (2018) The end of famine? Prospects for the elimination of mass starvation by political action. Pol Geo 62(1):184–195
Dreher A, Walter S (2010) Does the IMF Help or Hurt? The effect of IMF programs on the likelihood and outcome of currency crises. World Dev 38(1):1–18
Dykmann K (2015) How international was the secretariat of the League of Nations? Intl His Rev 37(4):721–744
Easterly W (2001) The lost decades: developing countries' stagnation in spite of policy reform 1980–1998. J Econ Growth 6(2):135–157
Easterly W (2005) 'What did structural adjustment adjust? The association of policies and growth with repeated IMF and World Bank adjustment loans. J Dev Econ 76(1):1–22
Fanon F (1961) The wretched of the earth, Revised edn. Penguin, London
Fischer S (1996) What is reasonable to expect of the International Monetary Fund on the Environment? In: Gandhi VP (ed) Macroeconomics and the Environment. International Monetary Fund, Washington D.C
Forster T, Kentikelenis AE, Reinsberg B, Stubbs TH, King LP (2018) How structural adjustment programs affect inequality: a disaggregated analysis of IMF conditionality, 1980–2014. Soc Sci Res 80:83–113
Forster T, Kentikelenis AE, Stubbs TH, King LP (2020) Globalization and health equity: The impact of structural adjustment programs on developing countries. Soc Sci Med 267:1–9
Friends of the Earth (2017) New Tricks: Biodiversity offsetting an mining, available at: https://policy.friendsoftheearth.uk/insight/new-tricks-biodiversity-offsetting-and-mining
Garuda G (2000) The distributional effects of IMF programs: a cross-country analysis. World Dev 28(6):1031–1051
Gerety RM, 'The Ecologists and the Mine' (Scientific American, 1 July 2019), Available at: https://www.scientificamerican.com/article/the-ecologists-and-the-mine/
Girvan N (2014) Extractive imperialism in historical perspective. In: Petras J, Veltmeyer H (eds) Extractive imperialism in the Americas. Brill, pp 49–61

Global Carbon Budget (2021) Global Carbon Project. Available at: https://www.globalcarbonproject.org/carbonbudget/index.htm.
Glover D (1995) Structural adjustment and the environment. J Intl Dev 7:285–289
Gnangnon SK (2021) Effect of volatility of foreign direct investment inflows on corporate income tax revenue volatility. App Econ An 29(86):124–151
Goldman M (2005) Imperial nature: The World Bank and struggles for social justice in the era of globalization. Yale University Press, New Haven, CT
Gonzalez-Gonzalez A, Clerici N, Quesada B (2021) Growing mining contribution to Colombian deforestation. Environ Res Lett 16(6):064046
Greco E (2020) Africa, extractivism, and the crisis this time. Rev Afr Pol Econ 47(166):511–521
Gueorguieva A, Bolt K (2003) A critical review of the literature on structural adjustment and the environment. World Bank Environment Department General Papers, Washington D.C. 2003. At: https://openknowledge.worldbank.org/entities/publication/3313af17-04ea-55d2-b874-b95590bb6096
Henry PB (2007) Capital account liberalization: theory, evidence, and speculation. J Econ Lit 45(4): 887–935
Hickel J (2016) The true extent of global poverty and hunger: Questioning the good news narrative of the Millennium Development Goals. Third Wld Qtly 37(5):749–767
Hickel J, Sullivan D, Zoomkawala H (2021) Plunder in the post-colonial era: quantifying drain from the global south through unequal exchange, 1960–2018. New Pol Econ 26(6):1030–1047
Hobsbawm E (1987) The Age of Empire: 1875-1914. Weidenfeld and Nicolson, London
Hosonuma N, Herold M, De Sy V, De Fries RS, Brockhaus M, Verchot L, Angelsen A, Romijn E (2012) An assessment of deforestation and forest degradation drivers in developing countries. Environ Res Lett 7:044009
International Bank of Reconstruction and Development (1944) Articles of Agreement. United Nations Monetary and Financial Conference. Bretton Woods, N.H. At: https://thedocs.worldbank.org/en/doc/722361541184234501-0330022018/original/IBRDArticlesOfAgreementEnglish.pdf
IMF (1944) Articles of Agreement. United Nations Monetary and Financial Conference. Bretton Woods, N.H. At: https://www.imf.org/external/pubs/ft/aa/pdf/aa.pdf
IMF (2021) Annual Report: Build Forward Better. Washington DC. At: https://www.imf.org/external/pubs/ft/ar/2021/eng/downloads/imf-annual-report-2021.pdf
IMF (2022) G-20 Report on Strong, Sustainable, Balanced, and Inclusive Growth, Washington D.C. At: https://www.imf.org/external/np/g20/pdf/2022/111322.pdf
Jolly R (1991) Adjustment with a human face. World Dev 19(12):1807–1821
Kentikelenis AE (2017) Structural adjustment and health: a conceptual framework and evidence on pathways. Soc Sci Med 187(2):296–305
Kentikelenis AE, Stubbs TH, King LP (2016) IMF conditionality and development policy space, 1985–2014. Rev Intl Pol Econ 23(4):534–582
League of Nations (1919) Covenant of the League of Nations, Preamble 28 April 1919
Leurs K (2019) Migration infrastructures. In: Smets K, Leurs K, Georgiou M, Witteborn S, Gajjala R (eds) The SAGE handbook of media and migration. Sage, pp 91–102
Lindsey R (2022) Climate Change: Atmospheric Carbon Dioxide. Climate.gov, 23 June 2022. At: www.climate.gov/news-features/understanding-climate/climate-change-atmospheric-carbon-dioxide
Maguire R, Jessup B (2021) Gender, race and environmental law: a feminist critique. In: Vijeyarasa R (ed) International women's rights law and gender equality. Routledge, London, pp 105–126
Mazzucato M (2015) The entrepreneurial state: debunking public vs private sector myths. Perseus Books, New York
Mazzucato M, Ryan-Collins J (2022) Putting value creation back into "public value": from market fixing to market-shaping. J Eco Pol Ref 25(4):345–360
McMichael P (1998) Global food politics. Mon Rev NY 50(3):97-111
McMichael P (2004) Development and social change: a global perspective. Pine Forge Press

Mensah I, Mensah EK (2021) The impact of inward FDI on output growth volatility: a country-sector analysis. Res In Glob 3:1–15
Mishra V, Hodge B (2005) What was postcolonialism? New Lit His 36:375–402
Moreton BE (2007) The soul of neoliberalism. Soc Text 92 25(3):103–124
Morley J, Buchanan G, Mitchard ETA, Keane A (2022) Quasi-experimental analysis of new mining developments as a driver of deforestation in Zambia'. Nature SR 12(18252):1–12
Muralidharan S (1992) Structural adjustment and the state: from consent to coercion. Soc Sci 20(1–2):29–46
Mutua M (2001) Savages, Victims, and Saviors: The Metaphor of Human Rights. Harv Intl LJ 42(1):201–245
Nunnenkamp P (2017) Biased arbitrators and tribunal decisions against developing countries: stylized facts on investor-state dispute settlement. J Intl Dev 29(6):851–854
Oberdabernig DA (2010) The effects of structural adjustment programs on poverty and income distribution. Seminar given 9 March 2010 at Vienna Institute for International Economic Studies. Available at: https://citeseerx.ist.psu.edu/document?repid=rep1&type=pdf&doi=c76c3fac72314481a0c41cb8f562ecdd0949567d
Oberdabernig DA (2013) Revisiting the effects of IMF programs on poverty and inequality. World Dev 46:113–142
Omeji K (2017) Extractive economies and conflicts in the global south: re-engaging rentier theory and politics. In: Omeji K (ed) Extractive economies and conflicts in the global south. Routledge, pp 1–26
Onjala J (2018) China's development loans and the threat of debt crisis in Kenya. Dev Pol Rev 36(2):710–728
Pahuja S (2011) Decolonising international law: development, economic growth and the politics of universality. Cambridge University Press, Cambridge
Panayotou T, Hupe K (1996) Environmental impacts of structural adjustment programs: synthesis and recommendations'. In: Munasinghe M (ed.) Environmental impacts of macroeconomic and sectoral policies. Intl Soc Eco Econ/United Nations Environmental Programme/World Bank, Washington DC, pp 55–101
Parks B, Roberts JT (2006) A climate of injustice: global inequality, north-south politics, and climate policy. MIT Press, Cambridge, MA
Peet R (2003) The unholy trinity: The International Monetary Fund, World Bank, and World Trade Organization. Zed Books, London
Penet P, Zendejas F (2021) Sovereign debt diplomacies: rethinking sovereign debt from colonial empires to hegemony. Oxford University Press, Oxford
Pfeiffer J, Chapman R (2010) Anthropological perspectives on structural adjustment and public health. Annu Rev Anthropol 39:149–165
Reinsberg B, Stubbs TH, Kentikelenis AE, King LP (2019) The world system and the hollowing out of state capacity: how structural adjustment programs affect bureaucratic quality in developing countries. Am J Soc 124(4):1222–1257
Rigney S (2021) On hearing well and being well heard: indigenous international law at the league of nations. TWAIL Rev 2:122–153
Riofrancos T (2020) Resource radicals: from petro-nationalism to post-extractivism in Ecuador. Duke University Press, Durham
Rodney W (1972) How Europe Underdeveloped Africa. Bogle-L'Ouverture, London
Roine J, Vlachos J, Waldenström D (2009) The long-run determinants of inequality: what can we learn from top income data? J Pub Econ 93(7-8):974–988
Rudel TK, Defries R, Asner GP, Laurence WF (2009) Changing drivers of deforestation and new opportunities for conservation. Cons Bio 23(6):1396–1405
Rudin J, Sanders D (2019) Debt, structural adjustment, and health. In: Benatar S, Brock G (eds) Global health: ethical challenges. Cambridge University Press, Cambridge
Sachs W (1992) Environment. In: Sachs W (ed) The development dictionary; A guide to knowledge as power. Zed Books, pp 24–38

Sarrasin B (2006) The mining industry and the regulatory framework in Madagascar: some developmental and environmental issues. J Clean Prod 14(3-4):388–396
Shandra JM, Shircliff E, London B (2011) The international monetary fund, World Bank, and structural adjustment: a cross-national analysis of forest loss. Soc Sci Res 40:210–225
Shandra JM, Rademacher H, Coburn C (2016) The World Bank and organized hypocrisy? A cross-national analysis of structural adjustment and forest loss. Env Soc 2(2):192–207
Shiva V (2016) Who really feeds the world? Bloomsbury Publishing, London
Shrinkhal R (2021) "Indigenous sovereignty" and right to self-determination in international law: a critical appraisal. Alternatives 17(1):71–82
Simmons B, Dobbin F, Garrett G (2008) Introduction: the diffusion of liberalization. In: Simmons B, Frank Dobbin F, Garrett G (eds) The global diffusion of markets and democracy. Cambridge University Press, Cambridge, pp 1–63
Stiglitz JE (2016) Inequality and economic growth. In: Mazzucato M, Jacobs M (eds) Rethinking capitalism, Wiley-Blackwell, pp 134–155
Stubbs TH, Kentikelenis A (2018) Conditionality and sovereign debt: an overview of human rights implications. In: Bantekas I, Lumina C (eds) Sovereign debt and human rights. Oxford University Press, Oxford, pp 359–380
Summers LH, Pritchett LH (1993) The structural-adjustment debate. Am Econ Rev 83(2):383–389
Thomson M, Kentikelenis AE, Stubbs TH (2017) Structural adjustment programmes adversely affect vulnerable populations: a systematic-narrative review of their effect on child and maternal health. Pub Health Rev 38(3):1–18
Tosun J, Peters BG (2020) The politics of climate change: domestic and international responses to a global challenge. Intl Pol Sci Rev 42(1):3–15
Towe C (2022) The IMF and Capacity Development— Prioritization and Allocation. Background Paper BP/22-02/07. Independent Evaluation Office of the IMF
UN SDG (2022) Annual Report 2022. United Nations New York, NY. At: https://unstats.un.org/sdgs/report/2022/The-Sustainable-Development-Goals-Report-2022.pdf
UNDP (2013) Humanity Divided: Confronting Inequality in Developing Countries (New York). At: https://www.undp.org/sites/g/files/zskgke326/files/publications/HumanityDivided_Full-Report.pdf
UNEP (2008) Plant For the Planet: Billion Tree Campaign, (United Nations 2008) At: https://wedocs.unep.org/bitstream/handle/20.500.11822/7661/-Plant%20for%20the%20Planet_%20%20The%20Billion%20Tree%20Campaign-2008810.pdf?sequence=5&isAllowed=y
UNFCCC (2009) Report of the Conference of the Parties on its fifteenth session, held in Copenhagen from 7 to 19 December 2009. At: https://unfccc.int/resource/docs/2009/cop15/eng/11a01.pdf
UNFCCC (2015) Paris Agreement. At: https://unfccc.int/sites/default/files/english_paris_agreement.pdf
Westlake J (1894) Chapters on the principles of international law. Cambridge University Press, Cambridge
Wibbels E (2006) Dependency Revisited: International Markets, Business Cycles, and Social Spending in the Developing World. IO, 60(2):433–468
Wigger A (2019) The new EU industrial policy: authoritarian neoliberal structural adjustment and the case for alternatives. Globalizations 16(3):353–369
Woods N (2006) The globalizers: The IMF, The World Bank, and their borrowers. Cornell University Press, New York
Woolf L (1920) Empire and commerce in Africa. Routledge
World Bank Group (1994) Adjustment in Africa: Reforms, Results, and the Road Ahead. Washington D.C. at: https://documents1.worldbank.org/curated/en/219981468192845881/pdf/multi-page.pdf
World Bank Group (2001) Adjustment Lending Retrospective: Final Report, Operations Policy, and Country Services (World Bank, Washington D.C. 2001) at: https://documents1.worldbank.org/curated/en/363591468313755270/pdf/446660WP0BOX0334096B01PUBLIC1.pdf

World Bank Group (2009) Madagascar – Economic Update: 2009 and Beyond. Washington D.C. At: http://web.worldbank.org/archive/website01330/WEB/IMAGES/ECOUP021.PDF
World Bank Group (2022) International Debt Statistics. Washington D.C. At: https://www.worldbank.org/en/programs/debt-statistics/ids
World Rainforest Movement (2016). Available at: https://www.wrm.org.uy//wp-content/uploads/2016/06/Article_Rio_Tinto_in_Madagascar.pdf

Sean Madden is a PhD Candidate at Birmingham Law School, University of Birmingham, UK. He previously received a Master of Laws in International Development Law and Human Rights from the University of Warwick, UK. His research interests lie in international law, human rights, environmental law, food security, and (Post)colonialism.

A TWAIL Approach to Reforming the International Investment Regime

Olufunmilola Olabode

Contents

Abstract In recent times, foreign investors have challenged a broad range of government measures that impact negatively on their investments through the Investor-State Dispute Settlement (ISDS) mechanism. Certain controversial investor-state disputes have led to allegations that the International Investment Regime (IIR) is another model of a modern-day manifestation of imperialism. These manifestations can be seen, for instance, in the regime's sole focus on investor protection, its lack of responsiveness to the impact of investor activity on the local communities and the environment of the developing host states, and the categorization of some public policies as treaty violations.

The last couple of years have witnessed a global debate on the need to address the imbalance embedded in the IIR. New international investment treaties and policies are currently being introduced and implemented globally. How then do developing countries wish to address this bias in IIR? The important questions to ask are, what type of foreign investment protection rules would best suit the interests of developing countries? Most importantly, in what ways can developing countries avoid the consequences of the earlier signed treaties? What is the most effective way to approach the reform? These questions are of great importance because presently, the world is witnessing a power-bases shift in the investment regime, the developing

O. Olabode (✉)
Olabisi Onabanjo University, Ago-Iwoye, Nigeria

M. de Amstalden et al. (eds.), *International Economic Law*, Special Issue,
https://doi.org/10.1007/978-3-031-41996-6_4

states are becoming capital-exporting states, and unlike during the twentieth century, they are now able to influence the development of a balanced IIR.

This paper employs the Third World Approaches to International Law (TWAIL) as a tool in analysing the IIR and its impact on the developmental needs of third world countries. The main contention in the paper is that the Bilateral Investment Treaties (BITs) and the ISDS system were originally designed to favour foreign investors who are mostly from developed countries thereby creating a bias against developing countries in the IIR.

Therefore, it is suggested that, rather than using a piecemeal approach, the key to ensuring consistency and addressing the deficiencies in the IIR is through more harmonised efforts by policy makers at the regional and continental levels to actualise developing countries' desire for a balanced investment regime. The MERCOSUR State Parties' Protocol on Investment Cooperation and Facilitation and The African Union's African Continental Free Trade Area (AfCFTA) provide the right opportunity for developing countries to address the bias in the IIR and they also serve as good templates for other developing countries to adopt at the regional or continental levels.

1 Introduction

There is no gainsaying the fact that the International Investment Regime (IIR) was introduced to provide legal protection against the abuse of power and egregious behaviour of governments. In fact, when entering into Bilateral Investment Treaties (BIT) arrangements, host states recognised that concessions had to be made for the sake of economic development in their countries. However, the problem is that there are concerns that the current IIR may have diminished the overall welfare of developing countries in particular. There have been several conflicts between obligations of host states to protect foreign investments and their other international and domestic law obligations. As a result of these conflicts, foreign investors have challenged a wide range of government measures that impact negatively on their investment through the Investor-State Dispute Settlement (ISDS) mechanism. For instance, more than 40 cases were instituted against the government of Argentina due to emergency measures taken to deal with the economic and financial crisis of 2001.[1] Other instances include claims that arose due to legislative reforms in the

[1]Reed (2009), Scorecard of Investment Treaty Cases Against Argentina since 2001, Kluwer Arbitration Blog, 2 March 2009, available at: http://arbitrationblog.kluwerarbitration.com/2009/03/02/scorecard-of-investment-treaty-cases-against-argentina-since-2001/.

[2]UNCTAD' May 2017 IIA Issues Note on Investor-State Dispute Settlement: Review of Developments in 2016, available at: https://unctad.org/system/files/official-document/diaepcb2017d1_en.pdf.

[3]Philip Morris Brands Sarl, Philip Morris Products S.A. and Abal Hermanos S.A. v. Oriental Republic of Uruguay, ICSID Case No. ARB/10/7, available at: https://www.italaw.com/cases/460.

renewable energy sector,[2] or the right to regulate to protect public health under the Fair and Equitable Treatment (FET) and indirect expropriation clauses.[3] In sum, investment treaties have become "an open invitation to unhappy investors, tempted to complain that a financial and business failure was due to improper regulation, misguided macroeconomic policy or discriminatory treatment by the host government and delighted by the opportunity to threaten the national government with a tedious, expensive arbitration".[4]

One of the main points in this chapter is that the IIR provides reasons to suspect regime bias as described by Gathii based on its neoliberal agenda of foreign investment protection; its disregard for the host states' environmental or sustainable development goals, the need for the protection of health and safety, labour rights; and the way the regime eludes developing countries' effective participation in its dispute settlement process.[5]

How then can developing countries address this bias in IIR? The regime is at a watershed moment and a lot of changes are going on globally. The important questions to ask are, what type of foreign investment protection rules would best suit the interests of developing countries? Most importantly, in what ways can developing countries avoid the consequences of the earlier treaties of the 1990s and early 2000s? What is the most effective way to approach the reform? These questions are of great importance because presently, the world is witnessing power-bases shift in the investment regime, the developing states are becoming capital-exporting states, and unlike during the twentieth century, they are now in a position to influence the development of a balanced international investment regime. These circumstances present developing countries with an opportunity to reform the IIR and transform it in such a way that they are no longer just rule takers but effective rule makers.

This chapter is structured into three main sections. The first section will discuss briefly the evolution of the IIR and the controversy surrounding the regime between the developed and developing countries. The next section focuses on the recent efforts made by some developing countries at the national and bilateral levels to address the inequities in the IIR. The third section discusses the need for harmonized efforts by developing countries at the regional and continental levels in reforming the IIR.

Finally, this chapter argues that the piecemeal approach adopted at the national and bilateral levels will not tackle all the defects in the system. It is therefore recommended that developing countries have a better chance at reforming the IIR by implementing new investment policies through harmonized efforts at the regional and continental levels. The MERCOSUR State Parties' Protocol on Investment Cooperation and Facilitation and The African Union's African Continental Free Trade Area (AfCFTA) serve as good examples for other developing countries to adopt at the regional or continental levels.

---

[4]Peterson (2001), p. 13.

[5]Gathii (2008), pp. 261–264.

2 Controversy in the IIR from a TWAIL Perspective

IIR has generated significant controversy in recent years.[6] In fact, the issue of controversy in the regime can be traced to as far back as the middle of the twentieth century when formerly colonized states gained their independence.[7] During this period, decolonized states from Africa, Asia and Latin America, based on their mutual ideological views started questioning the provisions of international rules regulating foreign investment.[8]

The controversy between colonisers and formerly colonised states centred mainly on the type of rules regulating foreign investment such as the minimum standard of treatment, settlement of disputes, the standards of compensation and national treatment.[9] Developing countries' grievances with the international investment regime primarily lie in the fact that those rules emanated from Europe and were therefore imposed on them without giving them any other option than to accept the rules. The exclusion of developing countries from the design of the international investment framework was affirmed in a 2015 European Commission Concept Paper on international investment law where it was claimed that "international investment rules were invented in Europe".[10]

To buttress this point further, as far back as 1758, Vattel advocated for a special standard of treatment for Europeans investing abroad, a treatment superior to that given to the domestic investors based on the fear that certain domestic legal systems might not offer adequate protection to the foreigners.[11]

To the newly independent states, the rules governing foreign investments have their foundation in the 'colonial encounter'[12] and it has evolved into a system that protected only the interests of the western countries.[13]

Throughout the nineteenth century and over the years, the developing countries have, with a united voice rejected all proposals from developed countries for multilateral investment treaties.[14] A major bone of contention was that the provisions of these draft treaties demanded that foreign investors be treated in

[6] See e.g. a recent public statement on the international investment regime supported by numerous academics with expertise relating to international law, investment law, arbitration and regulation, Van Harten et al. (2010), Public Statement on the International Investment Regime, Osgoode School of Law, available at: http://www.osgoode.yorku.ca/public_statement.

[7] Sornarajah (2010), p. 1.

[8] Ibid., Newcombe and Paradell (2009), p. 26.

[9] Sornarajah (2010), p. 1.

[10] European Commission (2015) Concept Paper, Investment in TTIP and beyond–the path for reform Enhancing the right to regulate and moving from current ad-hoc arbitration towards an Investment Court, available at: https://ec.europa.eu/commission/presscorner/detail/en/IP_15_5651.

[11] Sornarajah (2010), p. 19.

[12] Anghie (2005), pp. 6–7.

[13] Miles (2012). p. 2.

[14] Ibid.

accordance with the minimum standard of treatment provided for by international law.[15] Developing countries wanted foreign investors to receive the same treatment as their nationals while the developed countries demanded that foreign investors be treated in accordance with the minimum standard principle of international law.[16] The developed and developing countries also failed to reach a consensus on the applicable laws when settling disputes and the compensation to be paid. The provisions of the draft conventions required the disputes to be settled in the host state courts by applying the host state law, however, developed countries did not sign the draft conventions on the ground that the provisions were far behind the position of the law at the time as they failed to recognize the minimum standard principle.[17]

As for the developed countries, the hostility of developing countries toward foreign investment caused them to strengthen their efforts to provide legal protection for foreign investment through international investment agreements. These agreements, although relatively few, were focused on providing increased protection for foreign investment against political risk.

The desire for self-determination in the post-colonial era made developing countries to constantly pursue a different vision of international investment principles from that of developed countries.[18] Although, a multilateral framework for investment principles could, arguably, result in a more transparent and predictable investment regime than the current patchwork of bilateral obligations, the era witnessed several failed attempts by the world community, especially the UN and OECD, to form a comprehensive multilateral investment agreement. This was largely due to the difficulty in reaching a consensus between developed and developing countries. Developing countries always wanted to protect their sovereignty and natural resources while developed nations wanted maximum protection of their investments abroad.

The scale of hostilities towards a multilateral treaty on foreign investment rules has over the years made it difficult for developed and developing countries to reach a consensus at the global level.[19]

As newly emergent states, the desire of developing countries for a reformed international law that takes into account their socio-economic interests led to the formation of the Third World Approaches to International Law (TWAIL).[20] This approach emerged as an analytical tool which sought to assess the validity and the claim of universality of international law's relation with developing countries.[21]

---

[15] Dodge (2006), p. 3; Newcombe and Paradell (2009), p. 20.

[16] Newcombe and Paradell (2009), p. 16.

[17] Ibid.

[18] Poulsen (2010a, b), p. 107.

[19] Ibid.

[20] Badaru (2008), p. 380.

[21] Ibid.

This chapter draws on the theoretical perspective of TWAIL in order to analyse the IIR.[22] In particular, the chapter adopts TWAIL as a lens through which the bias or the inequities in the investment regime is revealed. TWAIL's main claim is that "international law disadvantages countries that were subjected to colonialism and benefits narrow elites, based especially in the West."[23] According to Okafor, TWAIL is a

> movement within the discipline of international legal studies . . . viewed as a broad dialectic . . . of opposition to the generally unequal, unfair, and unjust character of an international legal regime that all-too often . . . helps subject the Third World to domination, subordination, and serious disadvantage.[24]

To Professor Gathii, TWAIL is a tool for critical examination of international law.[25] Gathii's definition is very apt for this paper as TWAIL is being used as a lens to critically assess the international investment law regime from developing countries' viewpoint.

TWAIL is different from the conventional theoretical framework in the sense that there is no generally accepted approach amongst its scholars, they are all however united in their opposition to the politics of empire and attuning international law to the plight of developing countries.[26]

TWAIL jurists illustrate the manner in which development of foreign investment law has excluded the active participation of developing countries and how developed countries have always tailored the rules to suit their interests. Due to the recent rise in claims brought against developed host countries in Investor State Dispute Settlement (ISDS) cases, they are once again significantly engaging in the re-development of foreign investment law.[27]

While recognising the need to continue to encourage the inflow of foreign direct investment (FDI) to developing countries, research carried out reveals that the current IIR is biased towards the "economically powerful investors" from developed countries.[28] As at the early 80s, the main objective for signing BITs was to create a favourable and conducive environment for foreign investment however, the rise in investor-state disputes has brought to light the unanticipated downside of these

[22] The TWAIL perspective is approached on its own terms, that is, it is used as a basis for review and not subjected to close scrutiny for its claims and assumptions.

[23] Van Harten (2011), p. 3.

[24] Okafor (2005), p 176.

[25] Gathii (2011), p. 27.

[26] Eslava and Pahuja (2011), p. 104.

[27] Alvarez (2009), pp. 943–975.

[28] UNCTAD's World Investment Report: Reforming International Investment Governance (2015), pp. 112–114. Available at http://unctad.org/en/PublicationsLibrary/wir2015_en.pdf. Many scholars have written in great details on the structural bias in favour of the investors in the international investment regime. Insert further references about named scholars. See Odumosu (2007), pp. 251–287; Hippolyte (2019), pp. 34–52.

treaties which is their one-sided approach and their exclusive emphasis on the rights and privileges of foreign investors without addressing their corresponding duties.

Furthermore, the International Investment Agreements (IIAs) and arbitral decisions did not give due considerations to economic development and other public policy objectives that are relevant to developing countries.[29] This is partly due to the fact that many of these IIAs were entered into by desperate developing countries with developed countries as a means of attracting FDI.[30] Therefore,, those agreements were negotiated between parties of unequal bargaining power.[31] The developed countries that wanted to invest in developing countries mostly used BIT templates designed by them during the negotiations of the investment agreements, with many of the treaty standard clauses being non-negotiable.[32] Tienhaara likened this with non-negotiable standard form contracts, except according to her, "while standard form contracts are to be read in the powerless consumer's favour, BITs are not interpreted in the 'less-powerful' developing country's favour".[33]

For instance, a review carried out by the United Nations Economic Commission for Africa (UNECA) on BITs in Africa, revealed that a number of these agreements were negotiated and signed without taking into consideration the complexities of socio-economic challenges as well as national development policies and strategies of African countries.[34]

Furthermore, after reviewing the IIAs signed in the post-apartheid era, the South African government concluded that the government "had no history of negotiating IIAs and the risks posed by such treaties were not fully appreciated at that time. [...] As a result the Executive entered into agreements that were heavily stacked in favour of investors without the necessary safeguards to preserve flexibility in a number of critical policy areas".[35]

Regarding the dispute settlement system, (ISDS), recent research shows that claims under BITs are overwhelmingly directed against developing countries, with

[29]Investment Treaties in a state of Flux: Strategies and Opportunities for Developing Countries. Meeting Report of the 9th Annual Forum of Developing Country Investment Negotiators held in Brazil in 2015, available at: https://www.iisd.org/system/files/meterial/IISD%209th%20Annual%20Forum%20Meeting%20Report%20English.pdf. pp. 1–28.

[30]Tienhaara (2009), p. 48.

[31]Ibid.

[32]Ibid, p. 14.

[33]Ibid.

[34]United Nations Economic Commission for Africa (2016) Investment Policies and Bilateral Investment Treaties in Africa: Implications for Regional Integration, available at https://archive.uneca.org/sites/default/files/PublicationFiles/eng_investment_landscaping_study.pdf, pp. 1–46.

[35]Republic of South Africa 2009: IIA Policy Framework Review, Government Position Paper, Pretoria, June 2009. As cited by Fritz (2015), pp. 7–9, available at: https://www.tni.org/files/download/iias_report_feb_2015.pdf.

very few filed against developed countries.[36] In a study carried out by Gallagher and Shresthra in 2011, the average claim brought by investors from the United States against host developed countries was about 150 million USD, while the average claim against host developing countries was about 451 million USD.[37] The amounts claimed by investors in 2016 alone ranged from $10 million[38] to $16.5 billion.[39] A damage of $2 billion was awarded against Egypt in 2018.[40] According to the 2022 UNCTAD IIA Issues Note, as in previous years, the majority of new cases were brought against developing countries.[41] The South African government in expressing its lack of confidence in the international arbitration system alleged that the decisions of these arbitral tribunals are heavily influenced by private firms and multinational corporations.[42] As stated, studies carried out reveal that some arbitrators have business connections with foreign investors and that international investment arbitration is no longer cost effective because of undue delays.[43] And to worsen the issue, there is no appellate mechanism and as argued, this prevents host states from fully seeking redress. The international arbitration system is not equipped to deal with domestic policy issues in the disputes therefore, the arbitrators are likely to render decisions which would 'upset the delicate balance that the Investment Act seeks to achieve'.[44]

At the international level, the United Nations Conference on Trade and Development (UNCTAD) acknowledges huge flaws in the ISDS. In one of their reports, it was noted that concerns with the current ISDS system relate, among other things, to a perceived deficit of legitimacy and transparency; contradictions between arbitral awards; difficulties in correcting erroneous arbitral decisions; questions about the independence and impartiality of arbitrators, and concerns relating to the costs and time of arbitral procedures".[45]

---

[36] UNCTAD's IIA Issues Note, No 1: (2022) Facts on Investor-State Arbitration in 2021: With a Special Focus on Tax-Related ISDS Cases, available at:https://unctad.org/system/files/official-document/diaepcbinf2022d4_en.pdf, p. 2.

[37] Gallagher and Shresthra (2011), p. 927.

[38] Grot and Others v. Moldova and Görkem Insaat v. Turkmenistan (ICSID Case No. ARB/16/30), available at: https://www.italaw.com/cases/6338.

[39] Cosigo Resources, Ltd., Cosigo Resources Sucursal Colombia, Tobie Mining and Energy, Inc. v. Republic of Colombia, available at: https://www.italaw.com/cases/3961.

[40] See the case of Union Fenosa Gas, S.A v Arab Republic of Egypt. ICSID case No ARB/14/4, available at: https://www.italaw.com/cases/2456.

[41] UNCTAD's IIA Issues Note, *supra* note 36 p. 2.

[42] Mossallam (2015), pp. 7–10.

[43] Ibid.

[44] Ibid.

[45] Reform of Investor-state Dispute Settlement: In Search of a Roadmap. UNCTAD IIA Issues Note Report No, 2 June 2013, available at: http://unctad.org/en/PublicationsLibrary/webdiaepcb2013d4_en.pdf. See also Eaton (2013), Multiple Countries Reject Investor States. Available at: http://www.sierraclub.ca/en/main-page/multiple-countries-reject-investor-state-2013-update.

Furthermore, investor-state arbitration developed in response to the need to better protect foreign investors and their investments. This protection was achieved by establishing International Centre for Settlement of Investment Disputes (ICSID) to provide a more effective and depoliticised forum for the resolution of investor-State disputes. Simultaneously, developed States drafted and concluded BITs mostly with developing countries which later offered arbitration under ICSID and are seemingly skewed in favour of investors. However, the prominence of ICSID as the preferred forum for ISDS and the proliferation of BITs as well as investment tribunal practice, have not been favourable to developing host countries who have had to defend a relatively high percentage of ICSID arbitrations. According to the July 2022 UNCTAD IIA Issues Note, as at the end of 2021, the total number of ISDS cases have risen to 1190, and about 65% of these cases were brought against developing countries.[46]

While developing countries signed several BITs at the height of their pursuit of FDI, they had little if any input in their drafting or the subsequent development of investment arbitration. The consequence of the imbalance of negotiating power became even more problematic in the past two decades, as investors have increasingly used BITs not as a shield as was expected, but instead as a sword by employing the treaty standards as tools in challenging host states' regulatory measures.[47]

Developing countries have always viewed the ISDS system with suspicion. This may be because the ISDS system evolved based on the assumption that their domestic legal systems and legal processes are weak and, as such, their courts are unable to deliver fair judgments.[48]

Their dissatisfaction with the system is aggravated due to the fact that these developing host countries "tend to find themselves strangers in their own cases when arbitrating in Europe or North America".[49] They often appear before arbitrators who are usually from developed countries in matters administered by international dispute settlement institutions in which they have limited or no representation at all.[50] For instance, Kidane observed that "frustration with the imposition of external substantive standards has been exacerbated by the lack of African representation in the decision-making process".[51] This was revealed in the most recent publicly available statistics of the World Bank's ICSID. While cases against developing countries constituted more than 60% of the total caseload, only about 21% of arbitrators, conciliators and ad hoc Committee Members appointed in ICSID and

[46] UNCTAD's IIA Issues Note, *supra* note 36, p. 2.

[47] Ibid, p. 54.

[48] Kidane (2018), p. 5.

[49] Ibid.

[50] Ibid.

[51] For a discussion and statistical analysis of ICSID cases involving African states, see generally Kidane (2014), p. 35.

Additional Facility held cases were from developing countries.[52] Furthermore, it is no surprise that developing countries have expressed their dissatisfaction and frustration with the ISDS system given the fact that the arbitrators are from developed countries who may not really appreciate the plight of the developing countries. According to Kidane, although many developing countries did not appreciate the consequences of their choices as at when they signed the BITs, they now dread being called upon to defend claims of expropriation, denial of fair and equitable treatment, discrimination and such other violations of treaty standards before "all-Western tribunals".

More generally, it is often alleged that many Investor-State Arbitration awards display little coherence in the tribunals' reasoning and interpretation of similar concepts.[53] In particular, the approach taken by arbitrators to the concept of fair and equitable treatment or the concept of indirect expropriation is by no means uniform and often difficult to reconcile with earlier awards. Observers have also expressed concerns about the intellectual independence of arbitrators, particularly those who have acted as counsel in some cases and as arbitrators in others.[54] There have been calls for this practice to stop or, at least, for the adoption of codes of conduct to regulate the selection and actions of arbitrators.[55] There have been many calls, too, for greater transparency of the dispute resolution process, both as to the selection of arbitrators and with respect to the conduct of proceedings and the publication of awards.[56]

Many developing countries, after a long "honeymoon" with foreign investors, have been re-considering the pros and cons of the ISDS mechanism and have become more cautious in their negotiations of BITs and IIAs in general. While some are calling for a reform of the system either in form of creating an appeal mechanism, others are advocating for a complete change in form of replacing the present system with an international investment court.

The next section discusses some major changes that some developing countries have introduced to address the shortcomings of the ISDS system.

[52]The ICSID Caseload- Statistics (The ICSID Caseload-Statistics 2022), available at: https://icsid.worldbank.org/sites/default/files/publications/The_ICSID_Caseload_Statistics_2022-2_ENG.pdf.

[53]De Mestral (2017), The Impact of Investor-state Arbitration on Developing Countries, available at: https://www.cigionline.org/articles/impact-investor-state-arbitration-developing-countries/.

[54]Ibid.

[55]Ibid.

[56]Ibid.

3 Efforts Being Made at Reforming the IIR

The South African government's view about the existing investment agreements and investment arbitration sums up the general view about the investment regime, at least from the perspective of developing countries. The government stated that:

> Unequal and exploitative investment agreements, which prohibit the very policies developing countries need to fight poverty, is no way to put trade and investment at the service of sustainable development. Existing international investment agreements are based on a 50-year-old model that remains focused on the interests of investors from developed countries. Major issues of concern for developing countries that are vital from the perspective of sustainable development are not being addressed in the current negotiating processes.[57]

It goes on to point out that:

> Host states may put certain policies in place that seek to promote and enhance human rights interest. Examples of such intervention may include . . .policy measures designed to promote the right to food, the right to health or the right to water. These measures may be challenged through international [investment] arbitration.[58]

In fact, it is generally agreed that the regime is in a watershed moment as developing host states are beginning to realise the impact of the treaties signed in the 1990s and early 2000s on their economy. A lot of debates are going on globally on how to address the concerns about the investment regime. Indeed, this period could be the perfect opportunity needed by developing countries to address their grievances against the international investment regime.[59] As far back as 2003, Howard Mann noted that the investment regime was at a crossroad and that it could either "crystallize as a new form of colonialism or evolve into a new field of global cooperation on development".[60] It is hoped that the developing countries would take active steps in ensuring that the investment regime is reformed into a field of global cooperation on development.

Before the 1990s, investment rules seemed legitimate and acceptable to major capital-exporting countries, until investor-state arbitration cases were instituted against them.[61] Since then, it became a global concern that the investment rules are biased in favour of investors' interests, and now, economically powerful states are increasingly adopting formerly untenable "Third World" arguments against the

---

[57] Republic of South Africa Department of Trade and Industry, Bilateral investment treaty policy framework review, Government position paper (June 2009), available at: http://www.thedti.gov.za/ads/bi-lateral_policy.pdf, p. 46.

[58] Ibid.

[59] Perrone (2015), pp. 12–14.

[60] Mann (2003), p. 247.

[61] Odumosu (2007), pp. 251, 256.

investment regime.[62] These earlier rejected arguments, including concerns about the interference with regulatory sovereignty of developing host states, have gained prominence and acceptance globally.[63] Host states, from both developed and developing countries are now intensifying their efforts to ensure that the IIR respects their policy space It is impossible to overstate the importance of a BIT as it guarantees standards of protections for investors however, it is important to note that investor protection is only a means to advance public welfare and not an end in itself. There is need for a reformed IIR which recognises that developing host States have a fundamental right to regulate on behalf of the public welfare and this right must not be subordinated to the interests of foreign investors where this right is exercised in good faith and for a legitimate purpose. It is therefore recommended that new BITs need be negotiated with clear analysis, taking into consideration the national development strategies and changing socio-economic development of the developing countries.

In the last couple of years, there have been more calls by developing countries for a new international investment policy framework. The first challenge policymakers in developing countries face is simply to get the contents of IIAs right. New treaty templates should be drafted in a way that takes into account their experience with ISDS cases. This is important as these cases reveal how investment treaties have been used by foreign investors successfully or not, to challenge the executive, legislative or judicial actions of host states.

Furthermore, the treaty templates should reflect national policy priorities enshrined in the body of national investment-related laws and regulations. Alongside the need to increase the capacity of their bureaucracies, developing countries must develop strategies to avoid investor–state arbitration by implementing alternative methods of dispute resolution.

The backlash against the IIR has generated some major reactions from stakeholders and the debate and policy review in developing countries is taking many forms.

As rightly noted by Gazzini,[64] dissatisfaction with traditional BITs has generated four main types of reaction:

(a) reluctance to ratify BITs. (in Africa, only 25 BITs, including 3 between African countries have entered into force since 2012;[65]

[62] See the OECD's Government perspectives on investor-state dispute settlement: a progress report. Freedom of Investment Roundtable held on14 December 2012, available at: https://www.oecd.org/daf/inv/investment-policy/ISDSprogressreport.pdf, p. 83.

[63] Alvarez and Park (2003), pp. 368–371.

[64] Gazzini (2017) Nigeria and Morocco Move Towards a "New Generation" of Bilateral Investment Treaties, available at: https://www.ejiltalk.org/nigeria-and-morocco-move-towards-a-new-generation-of-bilateral-investment-treaties/.

[65] Ibid.

(b) conclusion of facilitation agreements, which radically downgrade the substantive protection standards found in traditional BITs and do not provide for arbitration[66] (see for example, treaty between Brazil and Mozambique);
(c) termination of BITs and adoption of investment legislation (see South Africa Protection of Investment Act, 2015[67]) and;
(d) introduction of new models of BITs that aim to strike a better balance between the private and public interests at stake.[68] India's 2015 Model BIT and the 2016 BIT concluded, but not in force yet, between Morocco and Nigeria.

The 2021 World Investment Report records that all IIAs concluded in 2020 contain reform-oriented provisions aimed at preserving regulatory space and promoting sustainable investment. In particular, they focus on preservation of regulatory space, investment dispute settlement reform, more sustainable development-oriented provisions, and investment promotion and facilitation.[69]

The 2022 World Investment Report records four substantive IIAS concluded in 2021 which feature provisions that mainly preserve regulatory space while also ensuring the protection of investments.[70] The IIAs also made clarifications on the Fair and Equitable Treatment (FET) standard and the scope of indirect expropriation.[71] Three of the IIAs contain general exceptions for the protection of human, animal or plant life or health while two IIAs incorporated provisions on the promotion of corporate social responsibility standards.[72]

Brazil's response to the criticisms of the current regime was to deviate totally from the adversarial approach of the BITs and to adopt a cooperative approach, focusing on the elements of mutual benefit to foreign investors and states.[73] The Brazilian government in an attempt to avoid the deficiencies of traditional BITs decided to adopt a model that aims to promote investment, and not just protect it.[74] With that in mind, a governmental team led by the Ministries of Finance (MF), Foreign Relations (MRE) and Industry and Foreign Trade (MDIC), in consultations with other institutions and private sector coalitions, developed the Cooperation and

---

[66] Ibid.

[67] The Protection of Investment Act is available at: https://investmentpolicy.unctad.org/investment-laws/laws/157/south-africa-investment-act.

[68] Gazzini (2017), *supra* note 64.

[69] The UNCTAD World Investment Report (2021): Investing in Sustainable Recovery, available at: https://unctad.org/system/files/official-document/wir2021_en.pdf, p. 131.

[70] UNCTAD World Investment Report (2022): International Tax Reforms and Sustainable Investment, available at: https://unctad.org/system/files/official-document/wir2022_en.pdf, p. 86.

[71] Ibid. p. 86.

[72] Ibid. p. 86.

[73] Martins (2017), Brazil's Cooperation and Facilitation Investment Agreements (CFIA) and Recent Developments, available at: https://www.iisd.org/itn/2017/06/12/brazils-cooperation-facilitation-investment-agreements-cfia-recent-developments-jose-henrique-vieira-martins/.

[74] Ibid.

Facilitation of Investments Agreements (CFIA) model.[75] These new agreements focus on investment promotion more than protection, and on dispute prevention more than resolution.[76] All CIFAs concluded include innovative preambular language, a best-efforts obligation on corporate social responsibility (CSR), and safeguards to restrict transfers. The provision on CSR for investors surely addresses the issue of imbalance in the investment regime as it will ensure investors take active steps in contributing to the sustainable development of the host states in one way or the other.

India's approach is to renegotiate existing BITs around the substantive protections in its 2015 Model BIT while retaining arbitration as the means of ISDS.[77] With this new model BIT, India intends to increase its policy space, while at the same time reduce its risk of exposure of receiving claims by foreign investors. With the absence of protections such as Most Favored Nation, Fair and Equitable Treatment and the specific exclusion of claims based on taxation or provision of non-commercial services by the State in this new model, it is evident that India is seeking to reduce exposure to future investment claims by limiting protections afforded to foreign investors considering recent experiences.

In 2007, South Africa undertook a thorough review of its BITs with a view of assessing their impact on both the economic growth of the country and its regulatory powers. The result of the review was published in June 2009 by the DTI in a position paper titled the Bilateral Investment Treaty Policy Framework Review.[78] The review highlighted the one-sided nature of the protection provided to foreign investors by first-generation BITs and exhibited suspicion regarding investment arbitration. The overall conclusion reached was that the system had opened the doors "for narrow commercial interests to subject matters of vital national interest to unpredictable international arbitration that may constitute direct challenges to legitimate, constitutional and democratic policy-making".[79] It was therefore recommended, among other things, that South Africa review its practices with a view to developing a model BIT which would be in line with its development needs; that the need for investor certainty should not compromise South Africa's own legitimate interests; and that further domestic legislative intervention could be brought to ensure that a proper balance is achieved.[80]

[75] Ibid.

[76] Ibid.

[77] Chaudhary, India's Bilateral Investment Treaties: Once BITten 57 times More Shy (2016). Available at: http://www.hindustantimes.com/analysis/india-s-bilateral-investment-treaties-once-bitten-57-timesmore-shy/story-2d0VyByBuCC55TYz0zDzNK.html.

[78] South Africa Department of Trade and Industry, Bilateral Investment Policy Framework Review, General Notice 961, Government Gazette 32386 (7 July 2009); available at: https://www.gov.za/sites/default/files/gcis_document/201409/32386961.pdf.

[79] Carim (2013), p. 1.

[80] Department of Trade and Industry Bilateral Investment Treaty Policy Framework Review (2009), p. 56.

It has been suggested that the cause of the review was due to the challenge of the Black Economic Empowerment (BEE) policy by foreign investors in the 2007 Foresti case.[81] In that case,[82] the investors challenged South Africa's Mineral and Petroleum Resources Development Act, which required foreign-owned mining companies to divest a percentage of their equity to historically disadvantaged South Africans at fair market value to encourage greater ownership of mining industry assets by these individuals. The investors maintained that the legislation breached BIT provisions on expropriation, fair and equitable treatment, and national treatment.

The case raised concerns in South Africa over whether the protections the BITs provided hindered the South African government's ability to redress the negative economic and social effects of apartheid through legislation.

As a response to the ruling in that case, the Department of Trade and Industry in 2010 indicated its intention to codify its BITs into a single piece of legislation and review the BITs to which South Africa was a party.[83] Subsequently, in the face of foreign criticism, the government terminated its BITs with European countries such as Denmark, Spain, Germany, Belgium, Luxembourg, Switzerland and the Netherlands.[84] The cancellation of BITs was a clear signal that South Africa was on a firm path to change the investment regime.

In 2015, the Protection of Investment Act 22 of 2015 was enacted and it came into force in July 2018. Some of the concerns which led to this Act are stated in the preamble. They include the need to secure "a balance of rights and obligations of investors to increase investment in the Republic" and "the government's right to regulate in the public interest in accordance with the law."[85]

After South Africa terminated its BITs with EU countries, it also took steps to implement subsequent treaties that addressed the limitations of the traditional investment treaties and engage in a more region- and continent-driven approach. To this end, a South African Development Community Model BIT was created with the specific goal of developing a comprehensive approach from which South African Development Community Member States can choose to use all or some of the model provisions as a basis for developing their own specific model investment treaty or as a guide through any given investment treaty negotiation.[86]

---

[81] Farish (2016), Protection of Investments Act -A balancing Act between policies and investments, available at: https://www.derebus.org.za/protection-investments-act-balancing-act-policies-investments/.

[82] *Piero Foresti, Laura de Carli and others v. Republic of South Africa* (ICSID Case No. ARB(AF)/07/1), available at: https://www.italaw.com/cases/446.

[83] Qumba (2016), p. 48.

[84] Ibid.

[85] The Act is available at: https://www.thedti.gov.za/gazzettes/39514.pdf.

[86] SADC Model Bilateral Investment Treaty Template, available at: www.iisd.org/itn/wp-content/uploads/2012/10/SADC-Model-BIT-Template-Final.pdf.

Although the South African Model BIT maintains some of the common features of IIAs, such as expropriation and FET standards, it also adds some clauses that seek to remedy the inadequacies of the old treaties, such as, among others:

a. requiring foreign investors or their investments to comply with environmental and social assessment screening criteria and prior to the establishment of their investment;
b. making foreign investors subject to civil actions for liability in the judicial process of their home state for acts, decisions or omissions made in the home state in relation to investment where these acts, decisions or omissions lead to significant damage, injury and loss of life in the host state;
c. reserving the right of a state party to grant preferential treatment in accordance with domestic legislation to any qualifying enterprise, to achieve national or sub-national regional development goals; and
d. proposing comprehensive reforms to the ISDS mechanism.

The 2016 Morocco-Nigeria BIT which is yet to come into force has been described as one of the most innovative and balanced BITs ever concluded.[87] The BIT provides some innovative approaches to the balance of rights and obligations as between investors and the respective host States. In particular, Articles 13, 14 and 15 of the BIT ensure that each contracting party reserves the right to adopt, maintain or enforce any measure to ensure that investment activities in its territory is undertaken in a manner that is sensitive to environmental and social concerns. Unlike traditional investment treaties, the new model imposes additional obligations on investors and as aptly noted, it appears to address, to a certain extent, the criticism that the old BITs were too heavily geared towards protecting investor interests.[88] Furthermore, the BIT imposes environmental obligations on investors and provides for the recognition and enforcement of high levels of labour and human rights protection appropriate to each contracting party's economic and social situation.

An analysis of these new generation of treaties shows that they depart greatly from the traditional treaties. This is evident from the content of these new investment instruments, which except for Brazil, show that they respond to the inequities of the ISDS claims as these new trends shift the focus of their purpose away from the sole protection of foreign investors and their investments to accommodating each countries' local needs. Furthermore, the fact that these new treaties or investment policies place emphasis on each country's specific needs affirms the fact that they are homegrown investment treaties.

[87] Gazzini (2017), *supra* note 64, p. 3. See also Leon et al. (2017), Is the recently signed Morocco-Nigeria BIT a step towards a more balanced form of intra-African investor protection? available at: https://hsfnotes.com/arbitration/2017/05/23/is-the-recently-signed-morocco-nigeria-bit-a-step-towards-a-more-balanced-form-of-intra-african-investor-protection/.

[88] Leon et al. (2017), also *supra* note 87.

This approach is apparent not only in the inclusion of specific provisions aimed at balancing out the rights and obligations of host States and investors but also in the limitation of coverage or omission of certain investment protection provisions.

4 The Need for a Harmonised Effort in Reforming the Investment Regime

The new approaches adopted by the above stated countries are laudable, however it is contended that a plethora of new investment treaties and policies at the national and bilateral levels would only make the investment regime more complex, rather, it is submitted that a harmonised approach by the developing countries at the regional and continental levels would bring about a systematic and coherent investment framework.

In order to address the allegation of bias in the IIR, this chapter adds a voice to the widening choir recommending that the developing countries need to depart from the traditional investment policy framework and design more of their own model of investment treaties, devoid of western influence.[89] They need to learn from the shortcomings and deficiencies of traditional BITs that were imposed on them as a result of their economic weakness and negotiate a new all-inclusive investment policy framework that not only promotes and protects foreign investment but that which safeguards the host states' right to regulate and also enhances sustainable development. There is no doubt that the promotion and protection of investment is an important factor in the investment regime, however, these rights are not absolute. The duty to promote and protect foreign investment should be weighed against a variety of non- investment concern matters, such as environmental protection, health and safety regulations, protection of human rights and labour, and wealth redistribution through taxation.

Also, these new treaties would need to consider the different socio - economic conditions of developing host states. To do this, the regulatory freedom of the host states to pursue measures for welfare or legitimate public policy purposes must not be compromised. In addition, these treaty templates should reflect national policy priorities enshrined in the body of national investment-related laws and regulations of the host states while also ensuring that they strike the right balance between the interests of investors and the public interest.

As stated earlier, one major contributing factor to an unequal investment regime was the desperation of the individual developing countries to attract more foreign investments than their neighbouring countries. They were so desperate that they waived their developmental needs for robust investment protection clauses in order

[89] See generally Gathii (2008); Hippolyte (2019), pp. 72–125; Adeleke (2016), p. 48; Odumosu (2007), pp. 251–287; Gazzini (2017), *supra* note 64.

to attract the investors to their countries. Hence, as individual countries, they lacked the economic power to negotiate for a balanced investment treaty.

To reform the dispute settlement system, a more pragmatic approach to alleviate developing countries concerns about the investment regime is to enhance their participation in the system. One way to do this is if the institutions for dispute settlement such as ICSID encourage the appointment of more arbitrators from developing countries. Also, the establishment of dispute settlement centers in developing countries should be encouraged. This would pave the way for a more constructive engagement of developing countries in the international investment regime Also, establishing more dispute settlement centres in developing countries will bring the dispute settlement system closer to the local people thereby encouraging their participation through many ways, one of which is through the amicus curia briefing. It will also prevent the domination of the developed countries, as the lack of participation of developing countries right from the inception is part of what has enabled the developed countries to be so powerful.

Therefore, it is recommended that a balanced, all-inclusive investment framework may be more achievable through regional and continental efforts given the fact that some developing countries have stronger economies and louder voices in the global world than others. To the TWAIL jurists, a legitimate international regime is one which considers the needs of developing countries, values their contributions while also ensuring their equal participation with the developed countries. Therefore, it is suggested that developing countries need to rise through their regions in order to meaningfully engage in shaping the international investment regime according to their priorities.

5 Conclusion

An analysis of the new treaty models being introduced by developing countries signify that they have once again attempted to attune the international investment regime to also serve their interests albeit mostly at the national and bilateral levels. The policy makers in these countries have introduced some important novelties meant to rebalance the rights and obligations of the various stakeholders as well as to safeguard host States' policy space. Evident that these new approaches are a response to the inequities of the ISDS claims as the new trends shift the focus of their purpose away from sole protection of foreign investors and their investments to also accommodating each country's local needs.

To answer the question whether the new treaties and policies depart from the traditional ones, the answer is yes. These new treaties and policies are home grown, without western influence in that they not only include specific provisions aimed at balancing out the rights and obligations of host states and investors but also in the limitation of coverage or omission of certain investment provisions.

The contents of their new investment treaties have been brought more in line with the evolution of international law, especially with regard to the protection of the environment, social and human rights, transparency, corruption, public scrutiny, economic development, and corporate social responsibility.

However, it is argued that in order to avoid the consequences of the traditional international investment regime, a legitimate and effective system is one which not only addresses the bias, it is one which also bring uniformity to a fragmentized structure caused by the plethora of BITs. What the system needs is for developing countries to reach a consensus on a model of investment treaties that would then be adopted at the national or bilateral levels.

Furthermore, all the new approaches adopted by these developing countries are laudable, however it is argued that a plethora of new investment treaties and policies at the national and bilateral levels will only add to the complexity of the system.

It is suggested that a balanced, all-inclusive investment framework may be more achievable through harmonised efforts at the regional and continental levels given the fact that some developing countries have stronger economies and louder voices in the global world than others.

To this end, this section discusses the MERCOSUR Protocol on Investment Cooperation and Facilitation and the African Continental Free Trade Area (AfCFTA) as these two different agreements adopted at the regional and continental level serve as good models of harmonized efforts in reforming the IIR.

5.1 The Mercosur Protocol on Investment Cooperation and Facilitation[90]

In April 2017, the States Parties of the MERCOSUR (Argentina, Brazil, Paraguay, and Uruguay) signed the Protocol on Investment Cooperation and Facilitation ("MERCOSUR Protocol"). The Protocol is fashioned after the Brazilian model of Agreement on Cooperation and Facilitation of Investments (the ACFI), which stands out for departing from the traditional design of BITs, particularly, by excluding the possibility of the ISDS mechanism.[91]

The emergence of the MERCOSUR Protocol is significant in the IIR, as it represents a step towards the regionalization of the Brazilian model. It reflects the attempt to include in a single document, the realities of four countries with important political, economic and investment policy differences, as expressed by the varying paths taken by Argentina and Brazil in the investment area.[92]

[90] Perez Aznar and Choer Moraes (2017) The MERCOSUR Protocol on Investment Cooperation and Facilitation: regionalizing an innovative approach to investment agreements, available at: https://www.ejiltalk.org/the-mercosur-protocol-on-investment-cooperation-and-facilitation-regionalizing-an-innovative-approach-to-investment-agreements/.

[91] Ibid.

[92] Ibid.

The aim of the MERCOSUR Protocol on Investment Cooperation and Facilitation is to develop and adopt an instrument that would "promote a transparent, agile, positive environment for investment in member countries". It recognizes "the fundamental role of investment in promoting sustainable development, economic growth, poverty reduction, job creation, expanding production capacity, and human development.[93]

Furthermore, the Protocol provides a strategic institutional legal framework to encourage reciprocal investment and afford the necessary predictability to attract extra-regional investors.

The MERCOSUR Protocol excludes the standards of "fair and equitable treatment", "full protection and security" and the protection against indirect expropriation.[94] The MERCUSOR protocol aims at striking a balance between the rights and duties of foreign investors and the right of States to make regulations on environmental, labor, health and safety policies.[95]

One of the major components of the Protocol is that it focuses specifically on conflict prevention. The Protocol establishes a National Focal Point or Ombudsman, whose main responsibilities consist in providing support to foreign investors locally.[96]

With regards to settlement of disputes, the procedures set out therein include direct State-to-State negotiations,[97] intervention by the MERCOSUR's (diplomatic level) Common Market Group[98] and 'ad hoc' State-to-State arbitration.[99] The Protocol also provides for a permanent review procedure[100] as well as a procedure for claims submitted by (natural and legal) private persons.[101]

This innovative dispute prevention and resolution system reflects the Member States' commitment as a bloc to introduce a harmonized legal framework that would lead to a significant increase in intra-regional investment.

As aptly stated by Takene, the conclusion of the Protocol indicates Mercosur member states' willingness to revive their economic and trade agenda with a new vision of the bloc's integration process, strongly focused on their economic growth and sustainable development.

---

[93] Ibid.

[94] See Article 6.6 of the Intra MERCOSUR Cooperation and Facilitation Investment Protocol (2017) (hereafter referred to as The Protocol), available at: https://investmentpolicy.unctad.org/international-investment-agreements/treaties/treaties-with-investment-provisions/3772/intra-mercosur-cooperation-and-facilitation-investment-protocol-2017-.

[95] See also Article 13 of the Protocol for duties of foreign investors.

[96] Ibid.

[97] Article 4 of the Protocol.

[98] Articles 6–9 of the Protocol.

[99] Articles 9–16 of the protocol.

[100] Articles 17–22 of the Protocol.

[101] Articles 39–44 of the Protocol.

A mechanism that reduces investment uncertainty within the region is an essential prerequisite for expanding trade flows and taking full advantage of the wider MERCOSUR market.

5.2 The African Continental Free Trade Area (AfCFTA)

Africa is also a good model through its adoption of a continent-wide investment treaty model under the auspices of the African Union. The African Continental Free Trade Area (AfCFTA) could provide a legal basis to rewrite the rules in a way that better integrates the interests of African nations while also providing a fair and balanced investment regime for foreign investors and host states.

The ongoing negotiation of the Phase II protocols of the African Continental Free Trade Area (AfCFTA) seeks to facilitate, promote and protect intra-Africa investors and investments. It will also encourage investors and investments from outside Africa. The extent to which the AfCFTA will attract investment depends on how its commitments and legal instruments will be implemented, and how it creates a balance between investment protection and the developmental needs of Africa.

The AfCFTA does not exclusively focus on trade in goods, it also covers a broader spectrum of issues critical to FDI strategies and activities including trade in services, competition policy, intellectual property rights, investment and dispute settlement. Such an approach allows for greater policy coherence within the AfCFTA.

The AfCFTA protocol on investment should endeavour to address barriers to investment entry in Africa, reduce time and costs of investment approvals, enhance transparency, improve efficiency, and promote investment-related cooperation and coordination across the continent, and also address the imbalance between investment protection and the developmental needs of Africa. Investors should have direct access to effective dispute settlement mechanisms and access to remedies when their rights are violated by the host governments rather than placing reliance on their home governments to initiate dispute settlement proceedings on their behalf.

The Phase II protocol of the AfCFTA, if properly negotiated, could contribute to attracting more investment into Africa. However, the end goal is not to attract more investment into Africa, but to attract quality investment that will contribute to the sustainable development needs of the continent. Investment can help the continent to address challenges of youth unemployment, skills development, industrialisation, women empowerment and infrastructure development. The current regime has done little in addressing these challenges and it is hoped that a continental coordination of investment policies will achieve what a fragmentized system could not.

The AfCFTA protocol on Investment can lead to enhanced cooperation and coordination of investment policy at the continental level. Governments will need to reform their investment policies to harness the investment benefits into the host economies. Most countries lack cohesive, synergised and coordinated strategies to harness investments in the growth sectors. Domestic investment policies should harmonise regulatory and institutional frameworks for investment and strengthen the linkages between foreign and domestic investors, among other things.

The recent moves adopted by developing countries indicate a good start of a significant change in the international investment regime. The tide has turned in the investment regime against "powerful foreign investors" and it is obvious that there is a deliberate shift away from just focusing on the promotion and protection of foreign investments, active steps are being taken to ensure that the system also accommodates non-investment concerns of the public. Third world countries have changed from being mere observers and rule takers in the international investment regime to fully fledged rule makers and active participants in the system.

References

Adeleke F (2016) Human rights and international investment arbitration. South Afr J Human Rights 32:48

Alvarez GA, Park W (2003) The new face of investment arbitration: NAFTA Chapter 11. Yale J Int Law 28:365

Alvarez JE (2009) Contemporary foreign investment law: 'An Empire of Law' or the law of empire? Alabama Law Rev 60:943

Anghie A (2005) Imperialism, sovereignty and the making of international law. Cambridge University Press, Cambridge

Badaru OA (2008) Examining the utility of third world approaches to international law for international human rights. Int Commun Law Rev 10:379

Carim X (2013) Lessons from South Africa's BITs review. Vale Columbia center on Sustainable International Investment

De Mestral (2017) The Impact of investor-state arbitration on developing countries. Available at: https://www.cigionline.org/articles/impact-investor-state-arbitration-developing-countries/

Dodge W (2006) Investor-State Dispute Settlement between Developed Countries: Reflections on the Australia-United States Free Trade Agreement. Vanderbilt J Int Law 39:1

Eaton JM (2013) Multiple Countries Reject Investor States. Available at: http://www.sierraclub.ca/en/main-page/multiple-countries-reject-investor-state-2013-update

Eslava L, Pahuja S (2011) Between resistance and reform: TWAIL and the universality of international law. Trade, Law Dev 3(1):103

EU Commission Concept Paper, Investment in TTIP and beyond–the path for reform Enhancing the right to regulate and moving from current ad-hoc arbitration towards an Investment Court. http://trade.ec.europa.eu/doclib/docs/2015/may/tradoc_153408.PDF

Farish (2016) Protection of Investments Act -A balancing Act between Policies and Investments. Available at: https://www.derebus.org.za/protection-investments-act-balancing-act-policies-investments/

Fritz T (2015) International Investment Agreements Under Scrutiny Bilateral Investment Treaties, EU Investment Policy and International Development. Available at: https://www.tni.org/files/download/iias_report_feb_2015.pdf

Gallagher KP, Shresthra E (2011) Investment treaty arbitration and developing countries: a reappraisal. J World Invest Trade 12:927

Gathii JT (2008) In: Falk R, Stevens J, Rajagopal B (eds) Third World Approaches to International Economic Governance in International Law and the Third World: Reshaping Justice. Routledge, Abington

Gathii JT (2011) TWAIL: a brief history of its origins, its decentralized network, and a tentative bibliography. Trade, Law Dev 3(1):27

Gazzini T (2017), Nigeria and Morocco Move Towards a "New Generation" of Bilateral Investment Treaties, blog post of the Journal of European Journal of International Law. Available at: https://www.ejiltalk.org/nigeria-and-morocco-move-towards-a-new-generation-of-bilateral-investment-treaties/

Hippolyte A (2019) Foreign investment law and developing countries. In: Krajewski M, Hoffman R (eds) Research Handbook on Foreign Direct Investment. Edward Elgar, Cheltenham, pp 72–125

Kidane W (2014) The China–Africa factor in the ICSID legitimacy debate. Univ Pennsylvania J Int Law 559, 561–562

Kidane W (2018) Alternatives to Investor-State Dispute Settlement: An African Perspective. Available at: https://www.africaportal.org/publications/alternatives-investor-state-dispute-settlement-african-perspective/

Mann H (2003) International investment agreements: building the new colonialism? Am Soc Int Law Proc 97:247

Miles K (2012) Imperialism, Eurocentrism and International Investment Law: Whereto from here for Asia? Available at: http://asiansil-jp.org/wp/wp-content/uploads/2012/07/kate_miles.pdf

Mossallam M (2015) Process Matters: South Africa's Experience Exiting its BITs. GEG Working Paper 2015/97. Available at: http://www.globaleconomicgovernance.org/sites/geg/files/GEG%20WP_97%20Process%20matters%20%20South%20Africas%20experience%20exiting%20its%20BITs%20Mohammad%20Mossallam.pdf

Newcombe A, Paradell L (2009) Law and practice of investment treaties: standards of treatment. Kluwer Law International, Alphen aan Den Rijn

Odumosu IT (2007) The law and politics of engaging resistance in investment dispute settlement. Penn State Int Law Rev 26:251–287

Okafor OC (2005) Newness, imperialism, and international legal reform in our time: a TWAIL perspective. Osgoode Hall Law J 43(171):174

Pal Chaudhary P (2016) India's Bilateral Investment Treaties: Once BITten 57 times More Shy. http://www.hindustantimes.com/analysis/india-s-bilateral-investment-treaties-once-bitten-57-timesmore-shy/story-2d0VyByBuCC55TYz0zDzNK.html

Perez Aznar F, Choer Moraes H (2017) The MERCOSUR Protocol on Investment Cooperation and Facilitation: regionalizing an innovative approach to investment agreements. Available at: https://www.ejiltalk.org/the-mercosur-protocol-on-investment-cooperation-and-facilitation-regionalizing-an-innovative-approach-to-investment-agreements/

Perrone NM (2015) The international investment regime at a crossroad: should we be rethinking foreign investment governance? Investment Treaty News. https://www.iisd.org/itn/en/2015/02/19/the-international-investment-regime-at-a-crossroad-should-we-be-rethinking-foreign-investment-governance/ and https://www.iisd.org/system/files/publications/iisd-itn-february-2015-en.pdf

Peterson LE (2001) Challenges under bilateral investment treaties give weight to calls for multilateral rules. World Trade Agenda. Available at: http://www.iisd.org/pdf/200 1/trade law commentary.pdf

Poulsen L (2010a) The importance of BITs for foreign direct investment and political risk insurance: revisiting the evidence. In: Sauvant K (ed) Yearbook on Foreign Investment Law and Policy 2009/2010. Oxford University Press, Oxford

Poulsen LS (2010b) The significance of South-South BITs for the international investment regime: a quantitative analysis. Northwest J Int Law Bus. https://scholarlycommons.law.northwestern.edu/cgi/viewcontent.cgi?article=1702&context=njilb

Qumba MF (2016) Balancing the Protection of Foreign Direct Investment and the Right to Regulate for Public Benefit in South Africa. LLM Dissertation. Available at: http://repository.up.ac.za/bitstream/handle/2263/58740/Qumba_Balancing_2016.pdf?sequence=1&isAllowed=y

Reed L (2009) Scorecard of Investment Treaty Cases Against Argentina since 2001. Kluwer Arbitration Blog of 2nd March 2009. Available at: http://arbitrationblog.kluwerarbitration.com/2009/03/02/scorecard-of-investment-treaty-cases-against-argentina-since-2001/

Republic of South Africa 2009: IIA Policy Framework Review, Government Position Paper, Pretoria, June 2009. As cited in T. Fritz, International Investment Agreements Under Scrutiny Bilateral Investment Treaties, EU Investment Policy and International Development. Available at: http://www.s2bnetwork.org/wp-content/uploads/2015/03/IIAs-report-Feb-2015-2.pdf

Republic of South Africa Department of Trade and Industry, "Bilateral investment treaty policy framework review, Government position paper (June 2009). Available at: http://www.thedti.gov.za/ads/bi-lateral_policy.pdf

Sornarajah M (2010) The international law on foreign investment, 3rd ed., Cambridge University Press, Cambridge

The ICSID Caseload-Statistics (2022). Available at: https://icsid.worldbank.org/sites/default/files/publications/The_ICSID_Caseload_Statistics_2022-2_ENG.pdf

The OECD's Government perspectives on investor-state dispute settlement: a progress report. Freedom of Investment Roundtable held on 14 December 2012. Report. Available at https://www.oecd.org/daf/inv/investment-policy/ISDSprogressreport.pdf

The UNCTAD World Investment Report 2021: Investing in Sustainable Recovery. Available at: https://unctad.org/system/files/official-document/wir2021_en.pdf

Tienhaara K (2009) The expropriation of environmental governance: protecting foreign investors at the expense of public policy. Cambridge University Press, Cambridge

UNCTAD World Investment Report 2022: International Tax Reforms and Sustainable Investment at p. 86. Available at https://unctad.org/system/files/official-document/wir2022_en.pdf

UNCTAD' May 2017 IIA Issues Note on Investor-State Dispute Settlement: Review of Developments in 2016. Available at: http://investmentpolicyhub.unctad.org/Upload/Documents/diaepcb2017d1_en.pdf

UNCTAD's IIA Issues Note, No 1, July 2022: Facts on Investor-State Arbitration in 2021: With a Special Focus on Tax-Related ISDS Case. Available at: https://unctad.org/system/files/official-document/diaepcbinf2022d4_en.pdf

UNCTAD's IIA Issues Note, No 1, July 2022: Facts on Investor-State Arbitration in 2021: With a Special Focus on Tax-Related ISDS Cases. Available at https://unctad.org/system/files/official-document/diaepcbinf2022d4_en.pdf

UNCTAD's World Investment Report: Reforming International Investment Governance (2015). Available at http://unctad.org/en/PublicationsLibrary/wir2015_en.pdf

United Nations Economic Commission for Africa (2016) Investment Policies and Bilateral Investment Treaties in Africa: Implications for Regional Integration pp 1–46. https://archive.uneca.org/sites/default/files/PublicationFiles/eng_investment_landscaping_study.pdf

Van Harten G (2011) TWAIL and the Dabhol Arbitration Comparative Research in Law & Political Economy. Research Paper No.19/2011 http://digitalcommons.osgoode.yorku.ca/clpe/5

Van Harten G et al (2010) Public statement on the international investment regime. Osgoode School of Law, available at http://www.osgoode.yorku.ca/public_statement

Olufunmilola Olabode is currently a lecturer in the Faculty of Law at Olabisi Onabanjo University, Nigeria. She obtained her LL. B degree in 2007 from Obafemi Awolowo University, Ile-Ife, Nigeria, and she became a qualified legal practitioner in Nigeria in 2008. In addition, she obtained an LL.M degree in Commercial Law from University College Dublin in 2013 and a PhD degree in Law from the same school in 2020. Her research interest is in the field of International Investment Law with a particular focus on how it affects developing countries. She was a State Counsel in the Ogun State Ministry of Justice, Nigeria with about 15 years' experience in civil litigations, contract, and legal drafting in Nigeria.

Part II
Technology and Innovation in International Economic Law

3D Printing, Valuation, and Service Inputs: Looking to the Future Rather Than the Past to Design Rules of Origin for Advanced Manufactured Products

Diana Elizabeth Wade

Contents

Abstract The use of digital technology in manufacturing has resulted in services becoming key inputs in global value chains (GVCs). Increasingly complex GVCs, however, complicate determining a good's origin through the rules of origin provisions in trade agreements. Once we consider a service, like the digital files used in 3D printing, as a crucial input of a tangible product, should the origin of that service play a role in determining the origin of the 3D printed good? If the 3D file is the input with the highest economic value, and economic value is a basis for origin determination, then the origin of the printed good may be determined by the origin of the 3D file design service.

This chapter examines how the origin of a service could be factored into the ad valorem approach for determining the origin of 3D printed good. If, as some scholars suggest, the greatest value of a 3D printed good lies in the design of the 3D file, then

The author thanks Prof. Chen Zhu and Prof. Bryan Mercurio for their comments of the version of this chapter presented at the 11th Postgraduate and Early Career Professionals conference organized by SIEL, the faculty and administration of the Ph.D School at Bocconi University for their support and funding of my research, the convenors of the PEPA/SIEL and the editors of the EYIEL, and Catalina Royero-Avila, Marcus Gustafsson and the other participants of the conference for their thoughts and insights.

D. E. Wade (✉)
Department of Legal Studies, Università Commerciale Luigi Bocconi, Milano, Italy
e-mail: diana.wade@bocconialumni.it

M. de Amstalden et al. (eds.), *International Economic Law*, Special Issue,
https://doi.org/10.1007/978-3-031-41996-6_5

we must take two steps before incorporating the value of the file into the ad valorem analysis: (1) assign a quantifiable value to the file, and (2) identify the origin of that file. While the trade law literature has not explored in depth the value of a digital input, the valuation of intellectual property rights provides some starting points for understanding how to place a value on the 3D file. Yet, 3D files are not considered by all industry participants to be an asset that must be exclusive to one owner, and this could impact a 3D file's value. Firms could also take advantage of references to "substantive business operations" in GATS and national or regional legislation to strategically locate the origin of the file in a particular country and thus benefit under a preferential trade agreement when trading the printed good. Finally, as determining the origin of digital transmissions is a complex process, designing and linking rules of origin for digital services to rules of origin for goods adds to the complications already inherent in determining the origin of goods produced through GVCs.

Keywords Rules of origin · Origin · 3D printing · 3D · Advanced manufacturing · Additive manufacturing · IP · Intellectual property · Valuation · Free trade agreements · FTA · Trade · Innovation · Customs · Services · Digital · European Union · EU · GATS · Agreement on Rules of Origin · GATT · Design · Tariffs

1 Introduction

The 1980s set the stage for international trade and manufacturing in the first decades of the twenty-first Century. In 1984, Charles W. Hull filed a US patent application for an "Apparatus for production of three-dimensional objects by stereolithography."[1] This patent covers the basic technology of 3D printing, and Hull would found 3D Systems, one of the first companies to commercialize 3D printing machines.[2] In 1986 members of the GATT met in Punta del Este, Uruguay for talks on trade policy issues.[3] Over the years, negotiations led to the formation of the World Trade Organization (WTO).[4] Across the globe, the manufacturing of goods shifted from centralized production to diverse facilities; in other words, the decade witnessed the rise of global value chains (GVCs).[5] Finally, trade analysts noticed certain activity by national policymakers—extensive use of rules of origin to regulate trade in imported goods.[6] Over 30 years later, the WTO and GVCs have been instrumental to the progress of international trade, and 3D printing offers new

---

[1] Hull (1984) Apparatus for production of three-dimensional objects by stereolithography. US Patent 4, 575,330, filed 8 August 1984, issued 11 March 1986.

[2] Tuomi et al. (2017), p. 2.

[3] World Trade Organization (WTO) (2023b) The Uruguay Round.

[4] WTO (2023a) The Uruguay Round.

[5] Mavroidis (2016), p. 233.

[6] Vermulst and Waer (1990), pp. 55–57.

potential for manufacturing goods and shortening GVCs. All this can be linked together by rules of origin (RoO), but doing so brings to light some important challenges to the legal framework for international trade in this era of digital trade.

Today, some trade experts highlight the importance of the "servicification" of manufacturing and the role of services as key inputs in GVCs.[7] With regard to RoO, if a service, like the digital file downloaded into a 3D printing machine, is a crucial input of a tangible product, should the origin determination of a good be linked to the origin determination of a service? Exploring this question takes up the thread of Duy Dinh's and also Dylan Geraets, Colleen Carroll, and Arnoud R. Willems's work on RoO.[8] Dinh examines RoO for services in connection with digital inputs for goods and Geraets, Carroll, and Willems explore whether R&D and design could be origin conferring inputs.

It is important to clarify that this chapter focuses on preferential RoO. There are two types of rules: non-preferential RoO and preferential RoO. They both assign a country or territory (e.g. the EU) to a product, but for different objectives. Non-preferential RoO are used in connection with non-preferential trade policy instruments relating to anti-dumping and countervailing duties or MFN tariffs, while preferential RoO are applied to determine which goods qualify for preferential tariff treatment under reciprocal preferential trade agreements (PTAs) or for non-reciprocal preferential treatment under Generalized System of Preference programs (GSPs).[9] PTAs can be bilateral, or involve multiple partners, like the USMCA[10] or CETA.[11] For example, under CETA, the preferential rules are used to determine if a good is a Canadian product. If so, it is applied a preferential tariff rate when imported into the EU.

Additive manufacturing, the industrial term for 3D printing, was chosen as the lens through which to examine preferential RoO, because of the changes it may bring about in the production and trade in goods. If the value of a 3D printed good derives from a file that instructs a 3D printer to print "ink" (metal or plastic) in layers, what role should this digital input have in determining the origin of 3D printed good? Reports for the Swedish National Board of Trade and the World Economic Forum on 3D printing question how to apply RoO to goods made through advanced manufacturing techniques, such as 3D printing, which require less human involvement and more digital and automated processing.[12]

---

7 Peng (2020), pp. 699–726; Dinh (2020), pp. 5–6, 66–67.

8 Dinh (2020), pp. 5–6, 66–67; Geraets et al. (2015), pp. 287–305.

9 Van den Bossche and Zdouc (2019), p. 458. One goal of preferential RoO is to prevent trade deflection. Inama (2022), p. 291.

10 Agreement between the United States of America, the United Mexican States, and Canada (USMCA) (entered into force 1 July 2020) ch 4 (Rules of Origin).

11 Comprehensive and Economic Trade Agreement (CETA) (signed 30 October 2016, some provisions entered into force on 21 September 2017) Protocol on Rules of Origin and Origin Procedure.

12 National Board of Trade – Sweden (2016), pp. 27–28. Fan et al. (2020), pp. 14–15.

This chapter examines the inclusion of service inputs to the RoO analysis to understand how this addition could support the adoption of innovative manufacturing techniques, such as 3D printing. On the one hand, retaining RoO that grant origin based on labour costs and processing could act as a disincentive to manufacturing goods with digital-based processing techniques. A producer who invested in a digitally-skilled workforce and 3D printers, could find, when trading the 3D printed goods, that due to reduced labour and overhead costs, the goods have the origin of the more costly third-country ink, and thus do not qualify for preferential tariff treatment. As 3D printing is being adopted in both developed and developing countries,[13] a RoO regime focused on traditional manufacturing could have a global impact on trade once 3D printed goods are produced and shipped regularly.

The *ad valorem* criterion for determining origin may allow for the inclusion of the service input as part of a RoO analysis. If the greatest value of a 3D printed good lies in the design of the 3D file (the 3D file input), then we must take two steps before incorporating the design service into the *ad valorem* origin determination: (1) assign a quantifiable value to the 3D file input, and (2) identify the origin of the 3D file input. While the trade law literature has not explored in depth the valuation of the 3D file input, the intellectual property law field provides some starting points for understanding how to place a value on the 3D file. However, this chapter also proposes that we should consider some technical implications (at a general level) resulting from the addition of a service input, suggesting that new rules should be designed with care.

Finally, this analysis proceeds on the basis of a few assumptions. First, that the WTO Moratorium on customs duties on electronic transmissions persists,[14] and thus, there are no tariffs or taxes on digital transmissions of 3D files. Second, there are no restrictions to the transmission of digital files between states.[15] While both issues are in reality more complicated, the focus of this chapter is determining the origin of the printed 3D product. The next part of this chapter looks at the fundamentals of rules of origin in connection with identifying the origin of a 3D printed good. Part III examines finding a value of a digital input in order to incorporate the digital input into the *ad valorem* analysis for determining the origin of a good. In Part IV, whether the geographic origin of the file should be the legal seat of the service supplier is considered and as well as the potential shift of origin from one country to another. The influence of a RoO system for advanced manufactured goods on trade, development, and manufacturing is explored in Part V. Finally, Part VI offers a conclusion and some thoughts on how to approach designing RoO for an era of digital trade.

---

[13] See e.g., GE.com (2018); Ministry of Electronics and Information Technology (2022), pp. 3, 5.

[14] Ministerial Decision, 'Work Programme on Electronic Commerce,' 17 June 2022, WT/MIN(22)/32, WT/L/1143.

[15] However, Hector Torres points out that technological methods for identifying origin of digital flows could raise barriers to the cross-border transfers of digital services and goods. Torres H (2023) Advocates for friendshoring have not reckoned with digital trade. Financial Times, 26 Jan 2023. Available at: https://www.ft.com/content/04d9c265-b4cd-4cd5-ab83-593fd37d8790.

2 A Brief Introduction to Rules of Origin and the Connection to 3D Printing

Preferential RoO are brought under the framework of the WTO through Annex II to the Agreement on Rules of Origin, The Common Declaration with Regard to Preferential Rules of Origin.[16] Preferential RoO are "those laws, regulations and administrative determinations of general application applied by any Member to determine whether goods qualify to the granting of tariff preferences going beyond the application of paragraph 1 of Article I of GATT 1994 [most-favored-nation treatment]."[17] The Declaration requires that criteria for qualifying for preferential tariff treatment are clearly defined along with transparency and reporting obligations.[18] However, there is no provision curtailing discrimination or the use of preferential RoO to create restrictive or distortive effects on international trade.[19]

Generally and broadly, the starting point for determining the origin of a good is to ask: (1) was the good wholly obtained or produced in a given territory?; (2) if not, where did the last substantial transformation to the good take place?[20] The first step requires that all of the inputs of an assembled product be wholly grown, produced, or manufactured in the territory for the good to qualify for preferential tariff treatment under the PTA.[21]

If the product is not wholly obtained or produced in one territory, three criteria are applied separately or conjointly to determine the territory in which the substantial transformation occurred. The 1973 Kyoto Convention was one of the first multilateral instruments to divide "substantial transformation" into three criteria: the Change of Tariff Heading (CTH), Manufacturing or Processing Operations, and the Ad Valorem Percentage Rule.[22] RoO in PTAs generally follow the parameters of the Kyoto Convention, but they are more detailed in the requirements of each criterion. As Hiroshi Imagawa and Edwin Vermulst state, none of these tests are "perfect" and there is no "'one size fits all' rule for the origin determination of thousands of products" and this "may also explain why rules of origin tend to be so complicated"[23] for traders and customs officials.

---

[16] Agreement on Rules of Origin (AOR) (15 April 1994) LT/UR/A-1A/7, Annex II, The Common Declaration with Regards to Preferential Rules of Origin. For more on the AOR, see Van den Bossche and Zdouc (2019), pp. 457–458 and Matsushita et al. (2017), pp. 237–238.

[17] AOR, Annex II, art 1.

[18] Puccio (2014), pp. 173, 192.

[19] This distinguishes the Declaration from the provisions on non-preferential rules of origin established by Article 2 of the Agreement on Rules of Origin. Puccio (2014) p. 199. Imagawa and Vermulst (2005), p. 612.

[20] Imagawa and Vermulst (2005), p. 604.

[21] van de Heetkamp and Tusveld (2011), p. 83.

[22] Inama (2022), pp. 6–8.

[23] Imagawa and Vermulst (2005), p. 609.

Under the CTH criterion, a finished product undergoes sufficient manufacturing or processing if it falls into a tariff heading different to the heading of the materials or inputs.[24] PTAs will specify which tariff classification system is applied, but most likely it will be the Harmonized System [HS] Nomenclature as most WTO Members are also contracting parties of the HS Convention, administered by the World Customs Organization.[25]

A second method for determining origin is the specific manufacturing or processing operations test, or a "technical test."[26] Under this criterion, a transformation to the materials must occur, but it does not require a change of tariff heading or subheading to occur for the transformation to qualify the good for preferential origin status.[27]

Finally, the *ad valorem* criterion. This chapter focuses on this criterion as it would be challenging to apply the other criteria when considering the 3D file as in input, for example, whether the 3D file undergoes a change of tariff heading or is subject to a technical test.[28] Using the 1973 Kyoto Convention as the foundational example of the *ad valorem* criterion, one must consider "the extent of the manufacturing or processing undergone in a country, by reference to the value thereby added to the goods. When this added value equals or exceeds a specified percentage, the goods acquire origin in the country where the manufacturing or processing was carried out."[29] Value generally derives from the cost of labour, manufacturing overhead, and materials—it does not derive from investments based on predictions of the good's success in the market or consumer perceptions of the product.[30]

Trade instruments set out the parameters for determining the *ad valorem* percentage. In many EU PTAs, there is a list of products, and for each, a specific percentage of required local value creation.[31] In US trade agreements, a formula is included for calculating the percentage of regional value content.[32] Further, RoO chapters will specify how to cumulate the value created when inputs are assembled into the final

---

[24] International Convention on the Simplification and Harmonization of Customs Procedures (Kyoto Convention 1973, signed 18 May 1973, entered into Force 24 September 1974) Annex D.1 (A).

[25] Van den Bossche (2008), p. 430; World Customs Organization (WCO) (2023) What is the Harmonized System (HS)? Available at: http://www.wcoomd.org/en/topics/nomenclature/overview/what-is-the-harmonized-system.aspx.

[26] Imagawa and Vermulst (2005), p. 608.

[27] While the Revised Kyoto Convention (entered into force in 2006) no longer includes this substantial transformation criterion, EU instruments and the USMCA include rules on manufacturing and processing operations. See Inama (2022), p. 9.

[28] For further discussion on using the CTH and technical test criteria to determine the origin of 3D printed parts, including the role of the 3D file in the origin analysis, see Wade DE (2022) Chapter 4, parts II and III.

[29] Inama (2022), pp. 7–8.

[30] Geraets et al. (2015), p. 288.

[31] Inama (2022), p. 293.

[32] Inama (2022), pp. 416–418.

product. This is just a very high-level view of the *ad valorem* criterion to provide an introduction to rules of origin analysis, and this chapter does not delve into issues of cumulation[33] or the links of RoO to the Customs Valuation Agreement of the WTO.

A critique of the *ad valorem* criterion is that it can discourage efficient manufacturing processes and innovation.[34] To qualify for preferential status, expensive domestic materials and labour-intensive, but not necessarily effective, methods may be used to raise the costs expended in the territory to process a good.[35] Or, traders may purchase foreign inputs or use more efficient methods, and trade under MFN rates.[36] In 1990, Edwin Vermulst and Paul Waer noted that "A producer will presumably aim its research and development efforts particularly at finding means of making the technically complex (and therefore initially most expensive) processes more cost-efficient. . .A test which focuses on value added rather than on the nature of the production process discourages such rationalization techniques."[37] Twenty-six years later, Petros Mavroidis confirmed that while, "[t]he 'value added' method is clear" it "could act as a disincentive to use the 'cheapest source of supply.'"[38] Studies by economists and trade scholars also suggest that the *ad valorem* criterion discourages the use of efficient sourcing or production of inputs.[39] As 3D printing reduces human involvement in manufacturing, it provides a testing-ground to examine how to design *ad valorem* rules to be more responsive to changes in manufacturing and be more encouraging of innovation.

3D printing could reconfigure the location where value is created and change the origin of the good. 3D printing promises to reduce labour and direct overhead costs linked to the operation of machinery.[40] However, as the costs of ink will likely be high, the value of materials could be more influential in determining where the value of the good is created.[41] The reshoring of manufacturing by 3D printing without adopting or increasing the domestic or regional production of ink may result in the production of printed goods having an origin that is tied to the origin of the ink rather than where the good is printed. For example, the metals aluminum, magnesium, and titanium are critical material for ink; while the EU is a producer of aluminum, Russia, China, Kazakhstan, the US, and Brazil are producers of titanium or

[33] The prime example is the Pan-Euro-Mediterranean Convention on Preferential Rules of Origin, which has 23 contracting parties, see: Inama (2022), pp. 296–299. See also European Commission (2022) The Pan-Euro-Mediterranean cumulation and the PEM Convention.

[34] Vermulst and Waer (1990), p. 95; Mavroidis (2016), p. 222.

[35] Imagawa and Vermulst (2005), p. 607.

[36] Vermulst and Waer (1990), p. 95.

[37] Vermulst and Waer (1990), p. 95.

[38] Mavroidis (2016), p. 224.

[39] See, e.g., Erasmus et al. (2006), pp. 288–289; also Estevadeordal et al. (2009); Conconi et al. (2018).

[40] Mims (2023), B4. This 3-D Printing fish-gutting machine contains the secret of a future, less-globalized economy.

[41] National Board of Trade (2016), p. 27.

magnesium.[42] While a good may be designed and printed in the EU, if the ink is the element with the highest value, the good may have non-EU origin.

However, analysts examining 3D printing suggest that the greatest value in a 3D printed good may not lie in the printing process, but with the file.[43] If it is true that most value comes from the design of the 3D file input, we must understand how to include the 3D file input in the RoO analysis through the *ad valorem* criterion. The next Part examines the first step, the valuation of the 3D file.

3 IP Valuation: Forward Looking Analysis of an Intangible Asset's Potential to Create Value

An IP right (IPR) is an intangible asset that can be given a monetary value. IPRs include copyright, patents, trademarks, and designs. While researchers are exploring the IPRs associated with a 3D file,[44] there are some general aspects about IPRs that allow us to perceive the 3D file as an asset with a monetary value. According to the World Intellectual Property Office, "The value of an IP asset essentially comes from the right the owner of that asset has to exclude competitors from using it. For an IP asset to have a quantifiable value it should: generate a measurable amount of economic benefits to its owner/user; and enhance the value of other assets with which it is associated."[45] Such value derives from direct exploitation of the IP right in connection with a product (a trademark on a piece of clothing) or selling or licensing the IPR to a third party.[46] Under the income-method of valuation, the present value of an IP asset can be calculated by estimating the income the use of that asset is expected to generate.[47]

IP valuation is not a perfect paragon of the type of value quantified for meeting the *ad valorem* criterion, which looks back at the percentage of value created in the territory though processing materials, labour costs, and overhead costs. However, if the design of a 3D file is to be a potentially origin conferring input, we may need to

[42] Regarding the impact of the source of raw materials for the 3D printing industry in the EU see, Opinion of the European Economic and Social Committee, 'Living tomorrow. 3D printing — a tool to empower the European economy' (own-initiative opinion) (2015/C 332/05) C 332/36, 8 October 2015, section 3.2.3–3.2.5; Duchêne et al. (2016), p. 21; Kretz and Van de Velde (2021), p. 20.

[43] Fan et al. (2020), p. 14; Osborn (2019), p. 17; Neeraj (2018), p. s126; Nordberg and Schovsbo (2017), p. 281; Gebhardt et al. (2019), pp. 71–72.

[44] Fan et al. (2020), pp. 16–18; Antikainen and Jongsma (2017), pp. 257–274; Nordberg and Schovsbo (2017), pp. 275–302.

[45] World Intellectual Property Office (2023) Valuing intellectual property assets. Available at: https://www.wipo.int/sme/en/ip-valuation.html.

[46] World Intellectual Property Office (2023) Valuing intellectual property assets.

[47] World Intellectual Property Office (2023) valuing intellectual property assets. Other methods include calculating the price paid to transfer ownership a similar IP right, and, less frequently used, the cost to develop a similar or identical IPR. See: Sharma and Kumar (2021), pp. 599–602.

think beyond the methods of calculating value in current RoO analysis. Although the income-method looks to the future, the process itself requires calculations and formulas to arrive at the net present value of the asset.[48] The goal of this chapter is not to provide a detailed technical response, but to highlight the possibility of IP valuation as an option and to identify the ways in which that valuation method will need to be critically assessed by technical experts. Finally, a business, as a part of its overall risk management and planning strategy, may perform an IP valuation analysis for its IPR portfolio,[49] which could include the IPRs associated with the 3D file design. Thus, the owner of the 3D file input may already have such information available to use for a RoO analysis.

If the 3D file input is the most valuable aspect of 3D printing, we need to understand in what way the file has value. Designing a 3D file using CAD (computer-aided design) programs may be less labour intensive than using a 3D scanner to create a 3D file of an existing object.[50] In their article on the impact of 3D printing on EU design law, Ana Nordberg and Jens Schovsbo state that "creating a CAD file can be as easy as taking a picture and using an app on a mobile phone."[51] However, the user must still clean up the file or fill in missing information, which requires skill and effort.[52] Looking at this from a labour-costs perspective, if a highly-paid General Electric engineer designs a file for a part of a plane engine, the value of the file could be equivalent to how much the engineer was paid. On the other hand, a designer at a SME, who is paid a fraction of a GE engineer's wages, could design a 3D file for an innovative and profitable product. Is this file worth less because this designer is paid less?

A 3D file can be integrated within the production chain of a product or sold or licensed to a third party who then downloads the file and prints the good. According to Lucas Osborn, once 3D printing becomes widespread, "digital objects will have almost as much value as tangible objects, and in some ways will embody more value...owning the digital file is in many ways as good as owning the tangible object. In one important way, it is better: one can print as many copies of the tangible object as desired."[53] Perhaps this is the value trade analysts are thinking of when referencing the value of a 3D file, such as RS Neeraj who states: "a major proportion of the value of 3D manufactured goods will be captured in designing and generating the CAD file which is the electronic blue print of the final manufactured product."[54] It seems that value of the 3D file input results from being the set of instructions to print multiple goods.[55]

[48] Sharma and Kumar (2021), pp. 601–602.

[49] McCollough (2017), p. 9.

[50] Antikainen and Jongsma (2017), pp. 260–261.

[51] Nordberg and Schovsbo (2017), p. 298.

[52] Antikainen and Jongsma (2017), p. 261; Osborn (2019), p. 37.

[53] Osborn (2019), p. 17.

[54] Neeraj (2018), p. s126.

[55] Nordberg and Schovsbo (2017), p. 281.

In their article, "Reconciling Rules of Origin and Global Value Chains: The Case for Reform," Geraets, Carroll, and Willems argue that RoO for goods should incorporate services as service inputs contribute significantly more value to the final product. They use the Apple iPhone 4 as an example, citing studies by Kraemer, Linden, and Dedrick which calculated that the manufacturing of the phone in China adds only 1.8% to the final value of the phone, and most of the value resides in designing the software and user interface.[56] Geraets, Carroll, and Willems argue that design, R&D, marketing, and transport should be considered value-adding steps in the production process [instead of including costs of such services in the direct overhead costs], as the "value added at these steps generally exceeds the value of the production or assembly activities."[57] A new approach to RoO is needed "in which the value added during these stages of the production process is taken into account in the origin determination."[58] They propose adding language in PTAs, such as a good is originating where "more than 50% of the final value of the good, as determined by the customs value, has been added in the territory of one of the parties, taking into account the following stages of the production process: research and development, artwork, design, intellectual property, manufacturing, marketing..."[59] Though the authors do not reference 3D printing, we could apply their analysis to the 3D file input: if the value of the design of the 3D file is greater than the value created by the production and post-processing of the good or the value of the "ink", then the authors' proposed language would allow the value of the 3D file input to play a key role in determining the origin of the 3D printed good.

However, such an approach means accepting that the origin of a good may change. Geraets, Carroll, and Willems, using the example of a Nike T-shirt,[60] point out that if design and marketing are taken into account, then custom duties would be determined on the location of the design of the T-shirt, the US, rather than the location of manufacturing, Bangladesh.[61] Regarding 3D printing, the dental aligner industry is based on a global services and manufacturing production chain.

---

[56] Geraets et al. (2015), p. 295; Dedrick et al. (2010), p. 81. A study by Gary Gereffi and Joonkoo Lee found that for the iPhone 4, which had a final factory price of $194.04, in terms of value added, $80.05 was created in South Korea, which supplied the display panels and memory chips, and only $6.54 of value came from assembly in China. Thus, in terms of the iPhone 4, the largest portion of the US trade deficit "incurred not with China, but via indirect exports from Korea and other high-value component suppliers." See: Gereffi and Lee (2012), p. 27. 3D printing is not currently applied with much frequency in electronics, due to technical restraints; see: Osborn (2019), p. 23.

[57] Geraets et al. (2015), pp. 299–300.

[58] Geraets et al. (2015), pp. 299–300.

[59] Geraets et al. (2015), p. 301. The authors acknowledge that this would mean interpreting the CVA to provide for services in the determination of customs value.

[60] Geraets et al. (2015), p. 302.

[61] Geraets et al. (2015), p. 302. See also: Inama (2022), pp. 30–32 for an example of meeting (and not meeting) the percentage requirements in the EU, US, and other territories for a sneaker and the iPhone.

Align (owner of the Invasalign brand) is headquartered in the US.[62] Scans of a patient's teeth created by an orthodontist in the US are sent to Pakistan and transformed into a series of digital models, and these files are sent to Mexico where they are printed into plastic models.[63] If we assign the most value to the design of the 3D file, the origin of the printed aligners could be Pakistan. Whether a good printed in Mexico originates in Mexico or Pakistan could have implications on tariff treatment of the final good, the business and fiscal strategy of the manufacturers and importers of the good, and the service suppliers, who choose to distribute R&D, design and manufacturing in different countries.[64]

It is important to note that additive manufacturing creates multiple "value shops" such as consultancy, engineering, and R&D services in addition to the workshops in which the good is printed.[65] As Bernard Hoekman and Douglas Nelson point out, when constructing "a global production structure, an essential part of such a strategy is to apply proprietary technology (product, process and managerial) to a corporate strategy involving a complex mix of exporting, direct investment and arm's length contracting (here as part of the overall production process, not the final exchange of a product)."[66] While firms "still have an interest in traditional trade policy disciplines," they are more interested in a trade environment "with good protection of property rights, reliable communication, and consistent, market-conforming regulatory environments."[67] Firms may choose to locate the production of the 3D file design in territories based on IPR protection, a decent telecommunications infrastructure, and a cost-efficient labour market for designers.

Identifying the origin based on the value of the 3D file input may be complicated if the file is licensed to an outside firm or distributed to subsidiaries. IPR owners generally grant an exclusive licence or a license with limitations to manufacturers not only to keep watch over use of the IPR, but also to monitor risks of product liability claims that could arise from use of the product incorporating the IPR.[68] For the automotive, aerospace, and medical products industries, IPR owners may continue to control which additive manufacturers use 3D files by granting licenses which indemnify against or limit liability for defective products.[69] It would be

[62] US Customs and Boarder Protection, Ruling Letter, *Re: Country of Origin Marking of Orthodontic 'Aligners'* (1 March 2001) HQ 562012, MAR-05 RR:CR:SM 562012 BLS.

[63] US Customs and Boarder Protection (2001) US Customs ruled that under the CTH criterion, the aligners originated in Mexico because they were printed there (and thus could qualify for NAFTA preferential marking treatment).

[64] Soprano (2019), p. 103.

[65] Miroudot and Cadestin (2017), p. 28.

[66] Hoekman and Nelson (2018), p. 5.

[67] Hoekman and Nelson (2018), p. 5.

[68] Weinmann (2005), p. 1394; Dreier (2000), A question of liability: Who's to blame when products developed by licensees cause unforeseen...? Reprinted from New Jersey LJ (3 Apr 2000). Available at: https://norrismclaughlin.com/articles/category/a-question-of-liability-whos-to-blame-when-products-developed-by-licensees-cause-unforeseen.

[69] Nieß and Wende (2017), pp. 128–129.

possible, given a close relationship between the IPR owner and the manufacturer, to determine the income value of the 3D file, because the IP right owner could receive accounting reports from the manufacturers of the goods printed and sold.

Yet, 3D files are not considered by all industry participants to be an asset that must be exclusive to one owner. For products aimed at individual consumers, the 3D printing industry is one of knowledge-sharing and file-sharing.[70] Platforms such as Thingiverse provide downloadable 3D files that can be modified, reshared, and printed by various users.[71] Individuals wishing to customize a certain product can modify the file, go to a 3D printing shop, select or provide their own materials, and print the good.[72] Under a value-created method (looking at expended costs), if the number of licensees, 3D design-modifiers, and printed goods is constantly changing, it may be challenging to determine the precise costs of the design and transmission of a 3D file, and thus, the value for the purposes of customs duties.[73] On the other hand, an income IP valuation-like method could take the data to predict the value to be created by sharing, modifying, and transmitting the 3D file to printers. This approach may be more in line with the entrepreneurial and sharing-culture ethos and the manufacturing strategies that underpin the production of goods in a digital international marketplace. Rewarding the risks and creativity that drive innovation with preferential tariff treatment based on the origin of the service (the 3D file design) may require allowing value to be assessed on future economic returns rather than on costs expended in the territory of origin.

While IP valuation gives us a starting point, the challenges discussed suggest that determining a quantifiable value of the 3D file input is complex. A new RoO regime would require the option of combining an income value for services inputs with the costs-expended value for tangible inputs. We would need to identify which IPRs of the 3D file would be the basis of the valuation, along with any other intangible assets, and would have to update this process as technology changes.[74] Finally, there are greater questions of whether we should quantify creativity, such as determining that one application of 3D file design is more valuable than another, which could

[70] Nordberg and Schovsbo (2017), pp. 300–301.

[71] Flores Ituarte et al. (2017), p. 43.

[72] Flores Ituarte et al. (2017), p. 53. Due to the plasticity of 3D files, some IP legal practitioners are beginning to advise IP rights owners to develop IP enforcement strategies that take advantage of these aspects of additive manufacturing, not only to protect IP rights, but also to protect public safety; see: Ferrill and Yoches (2013); Pierce (2015).

[73] See generally: Sotelo and Sundareswaran (2020) Would a digital border tax slow down adoption of 3D printing? 8 Jan 2020. Available at: https://www.weforum.org/agenda/2020/01/would-a-digital-border-tax-slow-down-adoption-of-3d-printing/.

Dinh (2020), pp. 158–161.

[74] Sharma and Kumar (2021), pp. 611–612. Further, a limitation is that the income-method relies on obtaining the necessary information about the asset, projected cash flow, and the rate of discounting (p. 606).

possibly have implications on future investment or the level of interest in innovation.[75]

Is the design of a 3D file a service that merits a role as an origin-conferring input? Why do we not confer such a role on blueprints? As mentioned above, Neeraj designates a CAD file as "the electronic blue print of the final [3D printed] manufactured product."[76] Blueprints for houses and goods are designed using CAD technology.[77] As Sam Fleuter notes, an additional service must be rendered by a human in order for the good to materialize from a blueprint.[78] For 3D printing, the CAD design is the first step.[79] Then the file is converted into a STL (standard triangle language) format, and then the layers to be printed are calculated.[80] The 3D file can then be downloaded remotely into the printing machine, and the manufacturing can be initiated with the click of a computer mouse, which may be the only human interaction during the printing process.[81]

In his book on rules of origin for services, Dinh identifies the designer of a CAD file as a service provider.[82] Designing is a type of service regulated under GATS. Services are defined as including "any service in any sector except services supplied in the exercise of governmental authority."[83] The WTO categorizes the design of

---

[75] Townley et al. (2019), pp. 12, 25–26.

[76] Neeraj (2018), p. s126.

[77] Fleuter (2016), p.168.

[78] Fleuter (2016), p. 168. CAD files are also used for CNC manufacturing. However, CNC manufacturing requires humans to set up the machine and the tools prior to processing; this incurs labour costs of production as it takes time; see: Flores Ituarte et al. (2017), p. 36.

[79] Fleuter (2016), p. 168.

[80] Tuomi et al. (2017), p. 5.

[81] Fleuter (2016), p. 168; Gebhardt et al. (2019), pp. 28–29. As processing done by humans is greatly reduced in 3D printing, an additional element to consider for designing RoO for advanced manufacturing is what constitutes sufficient processing in a territory to qualify for preferential tariff treatment; seeWade (2022) Chapter 4, Part A, section ii; Fan et al. (2020), pp. 14–15. See also, Dinh (2022), pp. 412–413 on incorporating intangible inputs into the analysis of meeting territoriality requirements in RoO chapters.

[82] Dinh (2020), pp. 20. In *US -Measures Affecting Trade in Large Civil Aircraft*, a dispute under the SCM Agreement, the WTO's Apellate Body found that "it may be difficult to separate goods from services, for instance, where services are an input or processing step in the production of goods." Appellate Body Report, *United States – Measures Affecting Trade in Large Civil Aircraft (Second Complaint)*, WT/DS353/AB/R (12 March 2012, adopted 23 March 2012), para. 619, fn. 1295. However, "'[g]oods' are tangible items. They are often contrasted against 'services', which are intangible...As opposed to goods, typical features of services include their immaterial, invisible, intangible, and non-storable, and transitory nature." [para. 619 fn. 1295]. As 3D files are intangible and immaterial when transmitted electronically, they could be considered services. On the other hand, they are not transitory in nature. As many digital products can be stored and used multiple times, it could be questioned whether digital products should be categorized as services, but this is also a debate that extends beyond the remit of this chapter.

[83] GATS General Agreement on Trade in Services (GATS)(15 April 1994) LT/UR/A-1B/S/1 art I (3)(b).

architectural and engineering blueprints as a service.[84] The Swedish National Board of Trade stated in its report on 3D printing that "3DP can involve a number of different services activities, including. . .designing and engineering computer-aided design (CAD) files. . ." and "[t]hese activities are regulated under the [GATS]."[85]

The next step is to determine whether GATS applies to digital services. Ines Willemyns argues that GATS "remains the relevant framework for digital services," although none of the legal provisions "expressly regulate digital services."[86] As GATS is technologically neutral, "some of the GATS' general obligations apply to digital services, regardless of their specific classification."[87] She concludes that "truly new services are rare, if they exist at all. Most digital services are services that have existed for many years, but can now be supplied in a different way, through the internet, boiling down to the transmission and processing of data."[88] Thus, general provisions such as determining the origin of a service could apply to digitally enabled or digitally transmitted services, like the design of 3D files.[89] When considered in this light, the creation and transmission of a 3D file for printing a tangible item could be a service regulated by GATS, and thus the origin provisions of GATS could apply to 3D files.

4 Here, There, and Everywhere: Finding the Origin of a 3D File

If most of the value of a good results from the service input, and origin is based on value, we come to the question of how to identify an origin for the service input. Rules for determining the origin of services do exist; one just has to know where to find them. While there is no WTO instrument like the Agreement on Rules of Origin for services, scholars have identified several provisions in the GATS that serve an origin identifying function.[90] Even though measures for services are generally applied behind the border,[91] there may still be some preferential treatment to foreign service suppliers under a PTA. In that case, Americo Beviglia Zampetti and Pierre Sauvé point out "the need to determine the origin of services and of service providers arises as soon as an international agreement providing for differential treatment between parties and non-parties is entered into."[92]

[84] WTO (2023a) Architectural and Engineering Services.
[85] National Board of Trade (2016), p. 24.
[86] Willemyns (2019), pp. 72–73.
[87] Willemyns (2019), p. 63.
[88] Willemyns (2019), pp. 79–80.
[89] Willemyns does not discuss 3D printing or rules of origin in her article.
[90] Mavroidis (2020b), p. 300.
[91] Guzman and Pauwelyn (2012), p. 594.
[92] Zampetti and Sauvé (2006), p. 118.

Zampetti and Sauvé,[93] as well as Dinh,[94] find that determining the origin of a service under the GATS requires a reading of the definitions in Article XXVIII with the four modes of supply indicated in Article I:2. The key definitions in Article XXVIII are "service of another Member", "service supplier", and "juridical person of another Member." A "juridical person of another Member" is one that is "constituted or otherwise organized under the law of that other Member, and is engaged in substantive business operations in the territory of that Member or any other Member."[95] How would this translate to 3D printing? The cross-border transmission of the 3D file is a service, supplied by a service supplier, who could be a company or an individual. If the file is sent to a printing facility and printed, that facility is providing a service by means of a commercial presence.

Origin is based on the mode of the service. Mode 1 services are supplied "from the territory of one Member into the territory of any other Member."[96] Mode 2 services are supplied "in the territory of one Member to the service consumer of any other Member."[97] According to Zampetti and Sauvé, for Mode 1 and 2 services, "the territory from which a service is supplied to the consumer confers origin...even if such a territory is that of the last (and potentially less significant) stage in a multicountry production process or that from which the service is only retailed."[98] In his examination of rules of origin for services, Mavroidis proposes that Article XXVIII GATS, by listing the definitions of a natural person of another Member and a juridical person, reproduces "the most frequently encountered bases for attributing origin in the realm of services (namely, nationality and seat of incorporation)."[99] Therefore, for services related to 3D printing, it will be necessary to identify the Mode for the service to identify its origin. According to Dinh, "[o]nce 3DP becomes mainstream, it may be the case that the provision of services via Mode 1 will become more crucial, and the need to identify the origin of services supplied via this Mode will increase."[100] However, this means identifying a specific geographical location from which that service was provided.

Services are created through GVCs, and this complicates assigning origin to a service.[101] Regarding Zampetti and Sauvé's work on the four modes of supply, Mavroidis finds that their "opinion has a lot of merit, even though, precisely because of the emergence of GVCs, defining origin in mode 1 might often prove to be a quixotic test because a service might be sent from country A but might have

[93]Zampetti and Sauvé (2006), pp. 140–142.

[94]Dinh (2020), p. 36.

[95]GATS art I:2(a).

[96]GATS art I:2(a).

[97]GATS art I:2(b).

[98]Zampetti and Sauvé (2006), pp. 140–141.

[99]Mavroidis (2020b), pp. 300–301.

[100]Dinh (2020), p. 110.

[101]Baldwin (2011), p. 15.

benefited from inputs in C and D."[102] It may be challenging to trace drafts of 3D files transmitted among office branches or among contractors in different countries and also to identity the costs expended at each stage.

A rules of origin regime based on the legal origin of the service provider may be feasible. Under the GATS, preferential treatment for services applies to service suppliers that have substantive business operations in the territory of the PTA.[103] On the one hand, claiming that a file originated from the legal seat of a company does not entirely acknowledge the global design of the file. On the other hand, firms may have strategic reasons for being legally based in one country and assigning design work to branches or contractors in a different country. Further, there are domestic and regional regulations and cases on business establishment and substantive business operations that can be consulted if questions arise as to the location of the legal owner of the 3D file.[104]

What happens when the 3D file is the input with the most value (i.e. greater than the value of labour, materials, and direct overhead costs to print the good). First, under a supplier regime, we are not interested in pinpointing at which point in the service-production chain the most value is created. We find the legal owner of the file, which has the right to distribute the file or license. The legal seat of this owner is then the origin of the file. As the file is a component of the printed good, the origin of the printed good shifts from the location of the printing facility to the location of the legal seat of the supplier of the 3D file, which could be in another territory.

This suggests that origin could be strategically designated in certain territories. Geraets, Carroll, and Willems note that if R&D and other services are factored into RoO, then "it is likely that more products would be found to originate in one of the developed economies (EU, USA, Japan)", with implications on customs duties for both home country and third countries.[105] Shifting the origin conferring value from traditional manufacturing inputs to service inputs could result in shifting the origin of a good to territories that have significant and strong service sectors, especially in the fields of R&D and digital design.

The decision of a multinational company to locate design and R&D services in different countries is motivated not only by the available workforce, but also by economic and fiscal benefits.[106] Firms may establish legal seats or head operating offices in territories with favorable tax or legal environments.[107] As a result, firms may claim the headquarter territory as the origin of the printed product, using the origin of the service input as the basis for origin, though the good is printed in

[102] Mavroidis (2020b), p. 301.

[103] GATS art V(6); also Latrille (2016), p. 446.

[104] Mavroidis (2020b), p. 301; Barnard and Snell (2020), pp. 471, 475–477.

[105] Geraets et al. (2015), pp. 301–302.

[106] Soprano (2019), p. 103.

[107] Mavroidis (2020a), pp. 78–79.

another territory.[108] There could be other strategic options. On the one hand, a company developing a 3D file, which outsources the final design of the file in another country, may wish to "retain" origin of the file by claiming that the outsourced design work does not contribute to the income-producing value of the file. On the other hand, a company may want the 3D file to originate in the country in which the outsourced design occurs. It could claim that significant income-producing value was created in the outsourced country and a subsidiary or entity is the owner of the file, and thus "obtain" origin for that file in that country. As further modification or downloading of the 3D file into printers may implicate use of IP licenses, firms may also need to reconcile the origin of the file with the territory in which it prefers to be taxed on revenues deriving from use of IP rights and assets connected to 3D files.[109]

A RoO regime incorporating the service input could impact whether 3D printed goods qualify for EU origin. In 2015, the European Economic and Social Committee was concerned that there was not a significant level of 3D file design capability in the EU and that innovative firms were being acquired by non-EU companies.[110] Six years later the report on 3D printing for the Commission's Executive Agency for SMEs noted that training and skill acquisition continues to be a challenge for adopting 3D printing manufacturing in the EU.[111] In this case, given the high value of a 3D file input from a third-country, a good, even if printed in the EU, would not qualify as an EU originating product. On the other hand, if the 3D file input incorporates design and other types of services, then a company having a headquarter in Ireland or Luxembourg could argue that this headquarter country is the origin of the 3D file input due to corporate structure, the location of certain personnel, communication patterns, the ownership of any IPR, and the ownership of the 3D file.[112]

For example, a company is seeking preferential tariff rates under CETA, though some of the design on a 3D file is done in Pakistan. The 3D file design service is the input with the most value of the final printed product. The company claims the designer in the third country (Pakistan) is only temporarily hired to work on the

---

[108] Headquarter economies with a high share of in-house services are Luxembourg, Switzerland, Germany, and the Netherlands; see Miroudot and Cadestin (2017), p. 19; also Barnard and Snell (2020), p. 438.

[109] For example, Google transferred its intellectual property holdings from Ireland to the US after closing its "double Irish" tax loophole subsequent to changes in the US tax law implemented by the Trump Administration; see generally Waters (2020). Delegates at the Virtual Working Group on the Future of Customs under the WCO's Permanent Technical Committee 3D found printing raises questions rules of origin, valuation, and VAT revenue, and whether digital blueprints should be taxable items; see WCO and WTO (2022), pp. 96, 98.

[110] Opinion of the European Economic and Social Committee. Living tomorrow. 3D printing — a tool to empower the European economy' (own-initiative opinion) 8 October 2015 (2015/C 332/05) C 332/36, para 3.2.6. 21.

[111] Kretz and Van de Velde (2021), pp. 20–21.

[112] See, e.g., Council Directive 2000/31/EC of 8 June 2000 (Directive on Electronic Commerce), recital 19.

design of the file; the "actual pursuit of economic activity" is conducted in headquarters in Ireland, where the company engages in substantive business operations. Even if the good is printed in a different third country, the company could benefit under CETA preferential rates when exporting the final printed good to Canada (provided the company can demonstrate that it has an effective and continuous link with Ireland).[113] As a result, not only will importers need to verify the source of the "ink" and quantify the labour hours and direct overhead expenditures for printing the good, they will need to provide evidence that the service inputs (representing the most value of the final good) do in fact originate in Ireland on the basis that the service supplier engages in substantive business operations there.[114] Yet, this would require provisions in RoO chapters on how to include proof of origin of the service when submitting certificates or declarations of origin with the final, tangible, good; and, in the EU, cooperation among the national customs offices on the interpretation of such documentation regarding origin of service inputs.[115] This could further complicate for traders the already complex process of qualifying goods for preferential tariff treatment.

[113] European Parliament, Answer given by Ms. Malmström on behalf of the European Commission (14 November 2018) E-004978/2018. Available at: https://www.europarl.europa.eu/doceo/document/E-8-2018-004978-ASW_EN.html. "The term 'substantive business operations' is a well-known concept used in Articles V(6) and XXVIII(m) of the World Trade Organisation (WTO) General Agreement on Trade in Services... The Commission considers, as is also stated in the context of the Commission Declaration on the meaning of the term 'substantial business activities' in Article 8.1 of the Comprehensive Economic Trade Agreement (CETA), that a corporation established in the territory of our trading partner could benefit from the agreement only where it can establish that it has substantive business activities in the foreign territory having an effective and continuous link with the trading partners' economy, in the sense of establishment as applied under the EU Treaty."

[114] Firms operating in the EU market would need to consider whether they are providing a service covered by the Directive on Electronic Commerce and Services Directive, whether they are providing services regulated by another EU or national instrument. See: Case C-434/15, *Asociación Profesional Élite Taxi v. Uber Systems Spain SL* [2017] ECLI:EU:C:2017:364, finding that the Uber app -a digital service- formed an integral part of an overall service, transport, and could not be classified as an information society service, thus bringing the service out of the scope of the Services Directive and potentially subject to national regulations, paras. 40 and 50. While 3D printing files are not transport services, they can be used to produce medical products; see Duchêne et al. (2016), pp. 52–54, 61–64. Healthcare services are also excluded from the Services Directive; see Services Directive, Directive 2006/123/EC, preamble 22. A 3D file design company that transmits files to 3D printers in a medical facility and controls the number of copies of goods printed, could potentially be providing a medical service, and thus, design of the 3D file could be subject to Union and national health regulations.

[115] Mavroidis (2016), p. 215; van de Heetkamp and Tusveld (2011), p. 160; European Commission (2023) EU Customs strategy. Available at: https://ec.europa.eu/taxation_customs/customs-4/eu-customs-strategy_en?.

5 International Trade Implications

This chapter takes proposals to include the value of the service input in the origin determination of the final good a few steps further into some general technical and legal implications of designing new preferential RoO. Complications arise when including service inputs: the GATS Schedules of Commitments and GATT Schedules of Concessions, the Common Declaration with Regards to Preferential Rules of Origin, and the GATS provisions relating to origin of a service were not negotiated for a hybrid system.[116] Further, while the transmission of the 3D file may not be subject to any tariffs, the final good's tariff rate would be determined by a service input that must be electronically transmitted, bringing into question how potentially conflicting provisions could be read together against customs duties on electronic transmissions and rules of origin within the same preferential trade instrument.[117] A mixed rules of origin regime, however, is not impossible. If the adoption of additive manufacturing grows significantly, industry lobbyists, customs officials, and customs organizations may begin to pressure policymakers and lawmakers to negotiate and design new rules. Further, the technical provisions of preferential rules of origin are in continuous change from one instrument to another, so the modification or inclusion of rules is not unusual in drafting RoO chapters in trade instruments.[118]

Adding the service input to the origin analysis could potentially reward investment in R&D and digital services development. However, designing a RoO regime for R&D, design services, and other intangible inputs, could remove preferential RoO from its functional purpose, which is to identify goods qualifying for preferential rates for customs purposes, and may also be out-of-sync with production processes. Should the iPhone, because the design and development is done in California, have US origin status when the majority of the phone is manufactured and assembled elsewhere? Would this indeed improve manufacturing, trade, and the spending power of consumers if such an approach is adopted universally for all goods with significant R&D and design expenditures? This may not incentivize producers in developed countries to reshore manufacturing with innovative techniques like additive manufacturing, because they can use relatively cheap labour in a foreign market and still qualify for developed country origin because of the R&D and design of the file is local. Furthermore, it may not improve services trade between developed and developing countries. Importing a bundle of intangible inputs (know-how, R&D, IPRs, designs) with developed country origin may mean that the final good (which is not to be traded back to the country providing the service inputs) does not qualify for preferential tariff rates for the regional trade agreements that the developing country seeks to trade under.

This chapter makes a more narrow proposal, which is to focus on designing RoO for advanced manufacturing techniques. While the United States and the EU look to

[116] Suavé (2019), pp. 360–362; Fleuter (2016), pp. 155–156.

[117] See Wade (2022) Chapter 5, Part III.

[118] See Inama and Crivelli (2019), p. 146.

3D printing as a means to reshore manufacturing,[119] 3D printers are being imported into developing countries.[120] This suggests that countries currently benefiting from preferential rates in regional trade agreements (due to the high value of local raw materials or the high value of human processing of inputs) could shift to 3D printing. Adopting innovative manufacturing techniques could have positive effects, such as leading to the acquisition of digital skills, the transfer of know-how, and perhaps better working conditions. A preferential RoO regime that is aligned with how both service and processing inputs are applied in advanced manufacturing could preserve manufacturing in territories where such manufacturing takes place and also help to support innovation in manufacturing by allowing traders of advanced manufacture goods to trade under preferential rates.

By looking at the valuation of the service input and the identification of origin of the service provider, we can see that the implications of adding a service input to the analysis needs to be thought through carefully. A producer in a developing country that downloads a file input that originates from a developed country (based on the legal seat of the supplier) could be penalized by having to pay developed country tariff rates or third country rates if trading within a regional trade bloc. This could become a burden, and the producer may revert back to the traditional, labour intensive means of production in order to trade under preferential rates. Adding an additional service input to the origin analysis would require new obligations for customs offices to monitor the cross-border movement of intangible inputs, especially when cumulation of service inputs and tangible inputs across PTA members has to be factored into their analysis.[121] The process of trying to certify that a good qualifies for preferential tariff treatment because of a 3D file input's value could be so complicated that the producer could decide to retain its current manufacturing methods.

However, as the current *ad valorem* approach penalizes innovation and the adoption of efficient labour methods, we should think about how to identify the origin of a good as production shifts from manual to more digital and automated forms of manufacturing. It is an opportunity to design rules that promote development and technological advancement. Though printing goods in a developing country may accelerate the adoption of advanced technologies and know-how, granting preferential tariff treatment based on the service input could allow goods manufactured in third-countries to enter into and then circulate within a PTA territory at a lower rate along with regionally manufactured goods. Thus, some balancing may be required to ensure that RoO for advanced manufactured goods do not create trade distortion, for example, the exchange of commitments to open up

[119] Opinion of the European Economic and Social Committee. Living tomorrow. 3D printing — a tool to empower the European economy' (own-initiative opinion) 8 October 2015 (2015/C 332/05) C 332/36; The White House (2011) President Obama launches advanced manufacturing partnership, 4 June 2011. Available at: https://obamawhitehouse.archives.gov/the-press-office/2011/06/24/president-obama-launches-advanced-manufacturing-partnership.

[120] Andrenelli and López González (2021), p. 21.

[121] WCO and WTO (2022), pp. 98–99.

a particular industry to foreign imports or to adopt social or environmental standards (though RoO chapters are not necessarily the best place for such provisions).[122] On the other hand, the designers of the rules, policymakers, and technical experts in trade offices should avoid falling back into familiar patterns: rules that in practice favor domestic industries or traditional manufacturing so that goods made with innovative production methods like 3D printing do not meet the origin qualifications. Further, traders and customs officials will need to work together to identify which country is the origin and thus the applicable tariff rate and this requires investment in technical assistance at the national level and in international organizations.

6 Conclusion

IP valuation provides a starting point for considering how to integrate service inputs into the origin analysis of a good. With IP valuation, we can assess the value of an intangible asset in a forward-looking manner rather than looking backward at the value of materials and labour and direct overhead costs expended, as required for the *ad valorem* approach for origin determination. The dynamics of the 3D file—the abilities to print an unknown quantity of goods and to modify the file—suggests that if the 3D file is to be included as an input, the numerical value assigned to the input should be assessed as value creation rather than value created.

This chapter examines 3D printing, because although in use, it is not yet a widespread form of manufacturing, and so we can still apply the exercise of "what if" without venturing too far off into the hypothetical. Yet, examining RoO and 3D printing technology also leads to the greater question of the steps the trade community could take to meet the needs of traders and customs officials as production and trade adapt to changes in technology. In fact, Mavroidis finds that 3D printing is one topic that the WTO should begin to explore now rather than after it has become a mainstream form of manufacturing.[123] We could question whether a plurilateral instrument on RoO for advanced manufacturing is feasible.[124] However, existing negotiating, trade assistance, and research resources at the WTO and the World Customs Organization could be applied to assist states in developing rules of origin in PTAs for advanced manufactured goods that would not be too complex and that could be updated as technological methods of production change.[125]

Even if the trade community and lawmakers do not embrace a combined goods and services regime, we should still consider how to allocate more weight to

[122] Hoekman and Nelson (2018), pp. 12–14; Erasmus et al. (2006), pp. 267–268; Hoekman and Kostecki (2009), pp. 585–586; Wade (2022) Chapter 5, Part IV(A)(i).

[123] Mavroidis (2020b), pp. 242–243.

[124] See Wade (2022) Chapter 5, Part IV.

[125] See Wade (2022) Chapter 5, Part V.

innovation and R&D in the origin determination process. Researchers at the World Economic Forum suggest applying a VAT or sales tax rather than custom duties to 3D files.[126] Dinh calls for designing an integrated RoO regime over the long term and in the short term, clarifying GATS definitions such as service supplier and ownership, as well as ensuring the compliance of PTAs with GATS requirements.[127] Finally, instead of isolating R&D and IP as independent origin-conferring inputs, the rules could be designed so that they more clearly state that R&D and service-design work can be incorporated into either labour costs or direct overheads.[128] Perhaps the costs for R&D and design could be included in the tally of expended costs differently to labour, overhead, and materials costs (for example, adding an additional 10% of the costs of design and R&D to the total cost of the final good) to counterbalance or even exceed the reduced labour costs from innovative production methods, and thus still obtain enough value-creation within the territory to qualify for preferential tariff treatment. Whatever the situation, the rules must be clear and there should be guidance from customs offices so that traders, great and small, can benefit from both the application of digital technology in production and trade under preferential tariff rates where this is appropriate.

References

Agreement between the United States of America, the United Mexican States, and Canada (USMCA) 30 November 2018 and 10 December 2019, in force 1 July 2020

Agreement on Rules of Origin (AOR) (15 April 1994) LT/UR/A-1A/7

Andrenelli A, López González J (2021) 3D printing and international trade: What is the evidence to date? In: OECD Trade Policy Paper, No. 256. Available at: https://www.oecd.org/publications/3d-printing-and-international-trade-0de14497-en.htm

Antikainen M, Jongsma D (2017) The art of CAD: copyrightability of digital design files. In: Ballardini RM, Norrgård M, Partanen J (eds) 3D printing, intellectual property and innovation: insights from law and technology. WoltersKluwer, Alphen aan den Rijn, pp 257–274

ASEAN Trade in Goods Agreement (ATIGA) 26 February 2009, in force 17 May 2010

Baldwin R (2011) 21st Century regionalism: Filling the gap between 21st Century trade and 20th Century trade rules. In: Policy Insight (Centre for Economic Policy Research). Available at: https://ideas.repec.org/p/zbw/wtowps/ersd201108.html

Barnard C, Snell J (2020) Free movement of legal persons and the provision of services. In: Barnard C, Peers S (eds) European Union law, 3rd edn. Oxford University Press, Oxford, pp 438–478

Case C-434/15, Asociación Profesional Élite Taxi v. Uber Systems Spain SL [2017] ECLI:EU:C:2017:364

[126] Sotelo and Sundareswaran (2020), Would a digital border tax slow down adoption of 3D printing? 8 Jan 2020. Available at: https://www.weforum.org/agenda/2020/01/would-a-digital-border-tax-slow-down-adoption-of-3d-printing.

[127] Dinh (2020), pp. 158–161.

[128] See ASEAN Trade in Goods Agreement (ATIGA) (entered into force 17 May 2010) ch 3 art 29(1) and 29 (2)(d).

Comprehensive and Economic Trade Agreement (CETA) 30 October 2016, some provisions entered into force on 21 September 2017, OJ L 11/23 (2017)
Conconi P, García-Santana M, Puccio L, Venturini R (2018) From final goods to inputs: The protectionist effect of rules of origin. Am Econ Rev 108:2335–2365
Council Directive 2000/31/EC of 8 June 2000 (Directive on Electronic Commerce) OJ L 178/1 (2000)
Council Directive 2006/123/EC of the European Parliament and the Council of 12 December 2006 on services in the internal market (Services Directive) [2006] OJ L376/36.
Dedrick J, Kraemer KL, Linden G (2010) Who profits from innovation in global value chains?: A study of the iPod and notebook PCs. Indus Corp Change 19:81–116
den Bossche V, Zdouc W (2019) The law and policy of the World Trade Organization: text, cases and materials, 4th edn. Cambridge University Press, Cambridge
Dinh D (2020) Rules of origin for services: from the early days of GATS to the era of servicification. Edward Elgar, Cheltenham
Dinh KD (2022) Revisiting the principle of territoriality in preferential rules of origin: are territoriality requirements obsolete? Legal Issue Econ Integr 49(4):399–414
Dreier WA (2000) A question of liability: Who's to blame when products developed by licensees cause unforeseen...? Reprinted from New Jersey LJ (3 Apr 2000). Available at: https://norrismclaughlin.com/articles/category/a-question-of-liability-whos-to-blame-when-products-developed-by-licensees-cause-unforeseen
Duchêne V et al (2016) Identifying current and future application areas, existing industrial value chains and missing competences in the EU, in the area of additive manufacturing (3D printing) Final Report for the Commission Executive Agency for Small & Medium-Sized Enterprises. Publications Office European Union. Available at: https://data.europa.eu/doi/10.2826/72202
Erasmus H, Flatters F, Kirk R (2006) Rules of origin as tools of development? Some lessons from SADC. In: Cadot O, Estevadeordal A, Suwa-Eisenmann A, Verdier T (eds) The origin of goods: rules of origin in regional trade agreements. Oxford University Press, Oxford, pp 259–293
Estevadeordal A, Harris J, Suominen K (2009) Multilateralising preferential rules of origin around the world. In: IDB Working Paper Series, #IDB-WP-I37. Available at: https://publications.iadb.org/publications/english/document/Multilateralising-Preferential-Rules-of-Origin-around-the-World.pdf
European Commission (2022) The Pan-Euro-Mediterranean cumulation and the PEM Convention'. Available at: https://taxation-customs.ec.europa.eu/customs-4/international-affairs/pan-euro-mediterranean-cumulation-and-pem-convention_en
European Commission (2023) EU customs strategy Available at: https://ec.europa.eu/taxation_customs/customs-4/eu-customs-strategy_en?
European Parliament, Answer given by Ms. Malmström on behalf of the European Commission (14 November 2018) E-004978/2018. Available at: https://www.europarl.europa.eu/doceo/document/E-8-2018-004978-ASW_EN.html
Fan Z, Sotelo J, Sundareswaran V. (2020) 3D printing: A guide for decision-makers. World Economic Forum – White Paper, January 2020. Available at: http://www3.weforum.org/docs/WEF_Impacts_3D_Printing_on_Trade_Supply_Chains_Toolkit.pdf
Ferrill E, Yoches ER (2013) IP law and 3D printing: Designers can work around lack of cover, September 2013. Available at: https://www.wired.com/insights/2013/09/ip-law-and-3d-printing-designers-can-work-around-lack-of-cover/
Fleuter S (2016) The role of digital products under the WTO: a new framework for GATT and GATS classification. Chicago J Int Law 17:153–177
Flores Ituarte I, Khajavi SH, Salmi M (2017). Current and future business models for 3D printing applications. In: Ballardini RM, Norrgård M, Partanen J (eds) 3D printing, intellectual property and innovation: insights from law and technology. WoltersKluwer, Alphen aan den Rijn, pp 33–61

GE.com (2018) GE Nigeria launches e-learning portal at Lagos Garage Week 2018, 7 December 2018. Available at: https://www.ge.com/news/press-releases/ge-nigeria-launches-e-learning-portal-lagos-garage-week-2018

Gebhardt A, Kessler J, Thurn L (2019) 3D printing: understanding additive manufacturing, 2nd edn. Hanser, Munich

General Agreement on Trade in Services (GATS)(15 April 1994) LT/UR/A-1B/S/1

Geraets D, Carroll C, Willems AR (2015) Reconciling rules of origin and global value chains: the case for reform. J Int Econ Law 18:287–305

Gereffi G, Lee J (2012) Why the world suddenly cares about global supply chains. J Supply Chain Management 48:24–32

Guzman AT, Pauwelyn JHB (2012) International trade law, 2nd edn. WoltersKluwer, New York

Hoekman B, Kostecki MM (2009) The political economy of the world trading system: the WTO and beyond, 3rd edn. Oxford University Press, Oxford

Hoekman B, Nelson D (2018) 21st Century trade agreements and the owl of Minerva. EUI Working Papers, RSCAS 2018/04. Available at: https://cadmus.eui.eu/bitstream/handle/1814/50964/RSCAS_2018_04.pdf?sequence=1&isAllowed=y

Hull CW (1984) Apparatus for production of three-dimensional objects by stereolithography. US Patent 4, 575,330, 8 August 1984

Imagawa H, Vermulst E (2005) The agreement on rules of origin. In: Macrory PRJ, Appleton EA, Plummer MG (eds) World Trade Organization: legal, economic and political analysis. Springer, New York, pp 601–678

Inama S (2022) Rules of origin in international trade, 2nd edn. Cambridge University Press, Cambridge

Inama S, Crivelli P (2019) Convergence on the calculation methodology for drafting rules of origin in FTAS using the Ad Valorem criterion. Global Trade Customs J 14:146–153

International Convention on the Simplification and Harmonization of Customs Procedures (Kyoto Convention 1973, signed 18 May 1973, entered into Force 24 September 1974) (UNTS vol. 950, p. 269)

Kretz D, Van de Velde E (2021) Advanced technologies for industry - Product watch: 3D printing of hybrid components, Report for the Commission Executive Agency for Small & Medium-sized Enterprises. Publications Office European Union, 14 September 2021. Available at: https://data.europa.eu/doi/10.2826/581451

Latrille P (2016) Services rules in regional trade agreements: how diverse or creative are they compared to the multilateral rules. In: Acharya A (ed) Regional trade agreements and the multilateral trading system. Cambridge University Press, Cambridge, pp 421–493

Matsushita M, Schoenbaum TJ, Mavroidis PC, Hahn M (2017) The World Trade Organization: law, practice, and policy, 3rd edn., Oxford University Press, Oxford

Mavroidis PC (2016) The regulation of international trade, vol 1. MIT Press, Cambridge (Massachusetts)

Mavroidis PC (2020a) And you put the load right on me: digital taxes, tax discrimination, and trade in services. Trade Law Dev 12:75–108

Mavroidis PC (2020b) The regulation of international trade, vol 3. MIT Press, Cambridge (Massachusetts)

McCollough J (2017) The basics in valuation of intellectual property assets. Federal Lawyer 64 (Aug):7–10

Mims C (2023) This 3-D Printing fish-gutting machine contains the secret of a future, less-globalized economy. Wall Street Journal, 14 January 2023, B4. Available at: https://www.wsj.com/articles/3-d-printing-iceland-fish-supply-chains-desktop-metal-11673642250

Ministerial Decision, 'Work Programme on Electronic Commerce' WT/MIN(22)/32 WT/L/1143, 17 June 2022

Ministry of Electronics and Information Technology (2022) National strategy for additive manufacturing. [24 February 2022) Available at: https://www.meity.gov.in/content/national-strategy-additive-manufacturing

Miroudot S, Cadestin C (2017) Services in global value chains: from inputs to value-creating activities. OECD Trade Policy Papers No. 197. Available at: https://www.oecd-ilibrary.org/trade/services-in-global-value-chains_465f0d8b-en

National Board of Trade – Sweden (2016) Trade regulation in a 3D printed world: A primer. Kommerskollegium 2016: 1. Available at: https://unctad.org/system/files/non-official-document/dtl_eweek2016_Kommerskollegium_en.pdf

Neeraj RS (2018) Trade rules for the digital economy: charting new waters at the WTO. World Trade Rev 18(2 Supp):s121–s141

Nieß V, Wende S (2017) Intellectual property and product liability challenges in three-dimensional printing. IEEE Consumer Electr Mag 6:128–163

Nordberg A, Schovsbo J (2017) EU design law and 3D printing: finding the right balance in a new E-ecosystem. In: Ballardini RM, Norrgård M, Partanen J (eds) 3D printing, intellectual property and innovation: Insights from law and technology. WoltersKluwer, Alphen aan den Rijn, pp 275–302

Opinion of the European Economic and Social Committee. Living tomorrow. 3D printing — a tool to empower the European economy' (own-initiative opinion) 8 October 2015 (2015/C 332/05) C 332/36

Osborn LS (2019) 3D printing and intellectual property. Cambridge University Press, Cambridge

Peng S (2020) A new trade regime for the servitization of manufacturing: rethinking the goods-services dichotomy. J World Trade 54:699–726

Pierce JE (2015) IP strategies for the rise of 3D printing, 14 April 2015. Available at: https://www.venable.com/insights/publications/2015/04/ip-strategies-for-the-rise-of-3d-printing

Puccio L (2014) 20 years after Marrakesh: reconsidering the effects of preferential rules of origin and anti-circumvention rules on trade in inputs and global production networks. Eur Yearb Int Econ Law 2014:173–200

Sharma D, Kumar A (2021) Methods for intellectual property valuation. In: Calboli I, Montagnani ML (eds) Handbook on intellectual property research. Oxford University Press, Oxford, pp 597–612

Soprano S (2019) Brexit and the EU-UK free trade agreement: dos and don'ts when drafting rules of origin. J Int Trade Law Policy 18:96–107

Sotelo J, Sundareswaran V (2020) Would a digital border tax slow down adoption of 3D printing? 8 Jan 2020. Available at: https://www.weforum.org/agenda/2020/01/would-a-digital-border-tax-slow-down-adoption-of-3d-printing/

Suavé P (2019) To fuse, not to fuse, or simply confuse? Assessing the case for normative convergence between goods and services trade law. J Int Econ Law 22:355–371

The White House (2011) President Obama launches advanced manufacturing partnership, 4 June 2011. Available at: https://obamawhitehouse.archives.gov/the-press-office/2011/06/24/president-obama-launches-advanced-manufacturing-partnership

Torres H (2023) Advocates for friendshoring have not reckoned with digital trade. Financial Times, 26 Jan 2023. Available at: https://www.ft.com/content/04d9c265-b4cd-4cd5-ab83-593fd37d8790

Townley B, Roscoe P, Searle N (2019) Creating economy: enterprise, intellectual property, and the valuation of goods. Oxford University Press, Oxford

Tuomi J, Chekurov S, Partanen J (2017) 3D printing history, principles and technologies. In: Ballardini RM, Norrgård M, Partanen J (eds) 3D printing, intellectual property and innovation: insights from law and technology. WoltersKluwer, Alphen aan den Rijn, pp 1–31

United States – Measures Affecting Trade in Large Civil Aircraft (Second Complaint), Appellate Body Report (12 March 2012, adopted 23 March 2012) WT/DS353/AB/R

US Customs and Boarder Protection, Ruling Letter, *Re: Country of Origin Marking of Orthodontic 'Aligners'* (1 March 2001) HQ 562012, MAR-05 RR:CR:SM 562012 BLS

Van de Heetkamp A, Tusveld R (2011) Origin management: rules of origin in free trade agreements. Springer, Berlin

Van den Bossche P (2008) The law and policy of the World Trade Organization: text, cases and materials, 2nd edn. Cambridge University Press, Cambridge

Vermulst EA, Waer P (1990) European Community rules of origin as commercial policy instruments? J World Trade 24:55–99

Wade DE (2022) Regulation of trade in 3D printed goods and WTO modernization: an opportunity for new preferential rules of origin. Dissertation, Università Commerciale Luigi Bocconi. Available upon request at: infobiblio@unibocconi.it

Waters R (2020) Google to end use of 'double Irish' as tax loophole set to close. Financial Times, 1 January 2020. Available at: https://www.ft.com/content/991f11ae-2c51-11ea-bc77-65e4aa615551

Weinmann C (2005) Trademark licensors and product liability claims - a European perspective. Trademark Reporter 95(6):1394–1414

Willemyns I (2019) GATS classification of digital services – Does "the cloud" have a silver Lining? J World Trade 53:59–82

World Customs Organization (WCO) (2023) What is the Harmonized System (HS)? Available at: http://www.wcoomd.org/en/topics/nomenclature/overview/what-is-the-harmonized-system.aspx

World Customs Organization (WCO) and World Trade Organization (WTO) (2022) WCO/WTO study report on disruptive technologies. Available at: https://www.wto.org/english/res_e/booksp_e/wco-wto_e.pdf

World Intellectual Property Office (2023) Valuing intellectual property assets. Available at: https://www.wipo.int/sme/en/ip-valuation.html

World Trade Organization (WTO) (2023a) Architectural and engineering services. Available at: https://www.wto.org/english/tratop_e/serv_e/architecture_e/architecture_e.htm

World Trade Organization (WTO) (2023b) The Uruguay Round. Available at: https://www.wto.org/english/thewto_e/whatis_e/tif_e/fact5_e.htm

Zampetti AB, Sauvé P (2006) Rules of origin for services: economic and legal considerations. In: Cadot O, Estevadeordal A, Suwa-Eisenmann A, Verdier T (eds) The origin of goods: rules of origin in regional trade agreements. Oxford University Press, Oxford, pp 114–146

Diana Elizabeth Wade Ph.D, holds a JD from the Gould School of Law, University of Southern California and has obtained degrees from Columbia University (B.A., Barnard College; M.A., School of the Arts). In 2022, she successfully defended her Ph.D dissertation before the faculty of the International and European Law Doctorate Program at Bocconi University in Milan, Italy. Her research focuses on international trade law, technology, and manufacturing. Prior to attending to Bocconi University, she worked as a bar-qualified lawyer at an intellectual property firm in Southern California. She is currently the Global Manager of Deloitte's Global Chief Legal Officer Program, which explores the interconnections of law, business, and innovation. She also is a lecturer for Bocconi University's LLM in Law of Internet Technology. She has published articles in Recherches sémiotiques/Semiotic Inquiry, Southern California Law Review, and The Italian Yearbook of International Law.

Challenges and Possibilities for Classifying Digital Cultural Products in the WTO: A Case Study of Video Games

Siqi Zhao

Abstract Digital cultural industries are economically and culturally significant. The treatment of digital cultural products under WTO law is a highly complex issue. This article explores the challenges and possibilities of classifying digital cultural products under WTO law, focusing on video games as a case study. This article conducts an in-depth legal analysis of three types of digital video games and the related classification issues that arise under WTO law. Specific difficulties and possibilities for classifying different types of digital video games are unveiled, reflecting the challenges and potential solutions. This chapter concludes with normative suggestions for advancing the WTO negotiations regarding the classification issue of digital cultural products.

Keywords WTO · Digital trade · Culture and trade · Goods and services classification · GATT · GATS · Video games

1 Introduction

1.1 What Are Digital Cultural Products?

The law of the World Trade Organization (WTO) regulates WTO Members' rights and obligations related to trade in goods and services, among others. This pertains to all kinds of goods and services, including digital cultural products (including digital cultural goods and digital cultural services). From both an economic and cultural standpoint, trade in digital cultural products is highly relevant today. However, under WTO law, there is still considerable uncertainty regarding the normative rules on trade in digital cultural products. The definition of digital cultural products

S. Zhao (✉)
KU Leuven, Leuven, Belgium
e-mail: siqi.zhao@kuleuven.be

M. de Amstalden et al. (eds.), *International Economic Law*, Special Issue,
https://doi.org/10.1007/978-3-031-41996-6_6

is unclear under WTO law.[1] However, a definition of cultural goods and services is provided by Article 4 of the UNESCO 2005 Convention on the Protection and Promotion of the Diversity of Cultural Expressions.[2] This paper primarily adopts the definition adopted by the UNESCO Convention and focuses on digital cultural goods and services. Article 4 of the UNESCO Convention provides that 'cultural goods and services refer to those goods and services, which at the time they are considered as a specific attribute, use or purpose, embody or convey cultural expressions, irrespective of the commercial value they may have'. Based on this definition, digital cultural products refer to the cultural goods and services which are digitally enabled, i.e., cultural goods digitally delivered and cultural services digitally encoded or digitally transmitted.[3]

1.2 Why Is Classifying Digital Cultural Products Relevant?

This chapter examines why classification of digital cultural products is relevant under WTO law from two perspectives. First, it is important to clarify the classification of goods and services because it is closely related to the application of WTO rules. Second, the treatment of digital cultural products has a significant impact on the WTO's negotiation of digital trade rules.

1.2.1 Classification Issue in WTO Law

The classification issue of goods and services under WTO law is a technical issue for the application of specific WTO rules. Classification is especially relevant for the application of the General Agreements on Trade in Services[4] because WTO Members have National Treatment (NT) and market access obligations in the service sectors whereby they have committed to liberalising.[5] Therefore, it is vital that

[1]There is no coherent use of terminology on this issue. For instance, the commonly used terms include cultural goods and services, creative goods and services, cultural and creative goods and services, cultural products, cultural (and creative) industries, creative economy, etc. At the WTO, there is no definition of cultural goods and services. Negotiations and debates are often limited to a certain specific category of goods or services. For instance, film and audiovisual services. For the scope of audiovisual services, see GATT Secretariat, Service Sector Classification List, GATT Doc. MTN.GNS/W/120 (July 10, 1991) [hereinafter Service Sector Classification List].

[2]UNESCO 2005 Convention on the Protection and Promotion of the Diversity of Cultural Expressions, Oct. 20, 2005, 2440 U.N.T.S. 311.

[3]See Burri and Weber (2012), p. 37.

[4]General Agreement on Trade in Service, Apr. 15, 1994, 1869 U.N.T.S. 185 [hereinafter GATS].

[5]GATS art. XVI; art. XVII.

schedules are 'clear, precise and based on a common format and terminology'.[6] The classification system of service sectors is the description basis of the service schedules. Arguably, a clear classification system may reduce the likelihood of trade disputes. In the history of WTO dispute settlements, there have been a number of disputes involving the classification issue of certain goods or services (as to whether a certain product is a good or a service, or which sector a certain service belongs to), such as the *China – Publications and Audiovisual Products,*[7] *Canada – Periodicals,*[8] and *US – Gambling.*[9] Moreover, a clear and well-accepted classification framework is consistent with the 'transparency' and 'progressive liberalisation' requirements inscribed in the Preamble to the GATS.[10] A precise classification system provides WTO Members with a clear and coherent framework for negotiating and committing to liberalisation in various service sectors.[11]

As will be discussed in the subsequent sections, the classification issue under WTO law includes two levels. Firstly, there is no clear guidance for separating goods from services. The common understanding of the classification of goods and services is based on their characteristics. Goods are tangible while services are intangible.[12] Secondly, the current service classification system is facing challenges. The current GATS service classification system is based on the 1991 Services Sectoral Classification List created by the Secretariat, MTN.GNS/W/120 (W/120).[13] All the service sectors (where possible) included in the W/120 are annotated with the corresponding 1991 Provisional Central Product Classification (the CPC Provisional) number.[14] WTO Members are allowed to use their own sub-sectoral classification or definitions, provided that they achieve concordance with the CPC or give a sufficiently detailed description to avoid uncertainty as to the scope of the commitment.[15] The

---

[6]Council for Trade in Services, Guidelines for the Scheduling of Specific Commitments under the General Agreement on Trade in Services (GATS), para 22, WTO Doc. S/L/92 (Mar. 23, 2001).

[7]Appellate Body Report, China - Measures Affecting Trading Rights and Distribution Services for Certain Publications and Audiovisual Entertainment Products, para 373–380, WTO Doc. WT/DS363/AB/R (adopted Dec. 21, 2009) [hereinafter China – Publications and Audiovisual Products AB Report].

[8]Appellate Body Report, Canada - Certain Measures Concerning Periodicals, pp. 4–5, WTO Doc. WT/DS31/AB/R (adopted Jun. 30, 1997) [hereinafter Canada – Periodicals AB Report].

[9]Appellate Body Report, US – Measures Affecting the Cross-Border Supply of Gambling and Betting Services, para 180-195, WTO Doc. WT/DS285/AB/R (adopted Aug. 20, 2007) [hereinafter US - Gambling AB Report].

[10]US – Gambling AB Report para 188. Zhang (2015) p. 3.

[11]See Zhang (2015) p. 2.

[12]For a critical analysis of the goods-services dichotomy under the current WTO law, see Peng (2020); Voon (2007).

[13]GATT Secretariat, Services Sectoral Classification List, Note by the Secretariat, WTO Doc. MTN.GNS/W/120 (July 10, 1991).

[14]The CPC is a classification structure for goods and services prepared by the United Nation. It serves as an international standard for all kinds of statistical purposes.

[15]Council for Trade in Services, Guidelines for the Scheduling of Specific Commitments under the General Agreement on Trade in Services (GATS), para 24, WTO Doc. S/L/92, (Mar. 23, 2001).

W/120 was adopted in 1991 and has never been updated, whereas the CPC has been updated four times since the 1991 CPC Provisional.[16] Evolving forms of services and supply modes (such as the Internet of Things [IoT], 3D printing, and social media platforms) challenge the current WTO service classification system.[17]

1.2.2 Digital Cultural Products Under WTO Law

The treatment of digital cultural products involves complicated legal issues under WTO law, which adds another facet of complexity to the digital trade rules that are still under negotiation in the WTO.[18]

The rationale for focusing on digital cultural products and relevant trade rules is two-fold, which are trade development and cultural protection. First, the cultural element is an important driving force of states' digital strategy, significantly affecting the digital trade rule-making process. For instance, to protect cultural diversity, the European Union (EU) proposed keeping cultural and audiovisual issues outside of the WTO e-commerce negotiations.[19] Such a proposal practically carves a significant portion of the digital market out of the negotiation coverage. It preserves substantial autonomy for the EU and its Member States to regulate their digital and cultural markets. On the contrary, the United States (US) aims to liberalise trade in digital cultural goods and services through inscribing related trade liberalisation commitments in Regional Trade Agreements (RTAs).[20] Second, despite a few big economies keeping (seemingly) uncompromisable positions on the digital cultural trade issue, culture is still largely neglected in the digital trade rule-making discussion,[21] especially from the perspective of promoting cultural diversity, inclusive digital trade, and sustainable digital trade for all countries. The digital divide[22] is

[16] See the website of UNSD-CPC: Economic statistics: Classifications > Economic statistics > CPC, https://unstats.un.org/unsd/classifications/Econ/cpc.

[17] For academic discussion on the service classification issue, see, among others, Wunsch-Vincent (2006a); Burri and Weber (2012); Willemyns (2021).

[18] For a systematic overview of the legal issue involved in the treatment of digital cultural goods and services, see e.g., Burri-Nenova (2008).

[19] Joint Statement on Electronic Commerce - EU Proposal for WTO Disciplines and Commitments Relating to Electronic Commerce - Communication from the European Union, WTO Doc. INF/ECOM/22 (Apr. 26 2019), p. 1. It is important to stress that the EU has persistently adopted this audiovisual exception approach since the Uruguay Negotiations. The EU does not undertake liberalisation commitments in the audiovisual service sector.

[20] Gagné (2019), p. 620; Gagné (2011), p. 1283.

[21] Ochai (2022), p. 91.

[22] The definition of 'digital divide' varies in different contexts. OECD provides one definition of 'digital divide' as 'the gap between individuals, households, businesses and geographic areas at different socio-economic levels with regard both to their opportunities to access information and communication technologies (ICTs) and to their use of the Internet for a wide variety of activities'. See OECE (2001) Understanding the digital divide. OECE publication, Paris, p. 5. See also, WTO (2018), p. 7.

becoming increasingly apparent in the global digital market, and its implications for cultural trade and cultural diversity protection have not attracted enough attention. Against such a divided digital market landscape, developing digital trade rules without sufficiently considering cultural diversity could worsen existing inequalities in artistic expression capacity. The digital divide could deepen the cultural divide among states and eventually diminish cultural diversity.[23]

Trade in digital cultural products is fundamentally different from traditional cultural goods and services trade in three aspects, which have important implications for WTO law.

To begin with, the internet provides practically limitless market space for cultural products.[24] Nowadays, consumers visit websites such as Amazon, Spotify, or Netflix to search for the content they are interested in. The limited availability of books, movies, and TV programmes in bookstores, cinemas, and TV broadcasts is no longer an issue for people who have access to the abovementioned online platforms. Therefore, the policy measures which function by affecting the quantity of the available goods and services, such as reserving 'shelf space', 'screen quota', and 'golden hour' for books, movies, and TV series respectively, lost much of their gravity in the digital market. Therefore, this type of measure should be re-examined to respond to the evolving market mechanism.

Furthermore, the impacts of digitalisation go beyond its bigness and are important in lowering the cost for content producers. The increasing availability of digital devices and the extremely low cost of online distribution provide opportunities for independent content creators without strong financial support. The online environment seems to offer an equal and inclusive platform for all countries, individuals, and cultures. Nevertheless, in reality, the big companies (e.g., Netflix or Spotify) are acting quickly to occupy the market,[25] which raises new challenges in regulating these digital cultural giants. The low-cost digital cultural market must overcome the digital divide and provide digital opportunities for all.

Last but not least, digital technology spurs new forms of digital cultural products, and new ways of producing, supplying, and consuming them. A critical impact of digitalisation is the rising convergence of different types of goods and services. For instance, WeChat and Instagram are both social network platforms that also provide live-streaming services, which could be categorised as a type of cultural service, too. At the same time, for instance, WeChat also functions as an online shopping website, an advertisement service provider, and a financial service provider. Another example is non-fungible tokens (NFTs), which challenge the traditional way of purchasing and consuming art and possibly lead to a blockchain-driven revolution in the art

[23] For an analysis regarding how inequality in cultural production and cultural consumption shapes representations and negatively impacts cultural diversity, see Brook et al. (2020).

[24] Burri-Nenova (2008), p. 38.

[25] See e.g., Choudhury SR (2020) Netflix bets big on Asia as it sees 'significant potential' in these markets, CNBC (in press), https://www.cnbc.com/2020/11/09/netflix-nflx-its-strategy-in-asian-markets-like-india-indonesia.html.

market.[26] In this light, digital markets and cultural markets are both intertwined and developing extremely fast. As a result, new forms of digital cultural products call for updated international trade rules to respond to recent developments.

1.2.3 Research Question and Research Method

As briefly discussed in the above sections, the treatment of digital cultural products under WTO law is a highly complex and multi-layered issue. This chapter focuses on the classification issue of digital cultural products. The main research question underlying this chapter is: What are the challenges and possibilities for classifying digital cultural products under WTO law? Because the scope of digital cultural products is wide and dynamic, the present chapter adopts a case study method to unveil the legal challenges and possibilities with the specific example of classifying video games.

The video game industry is a dynamic and fast-growing industry sector, which was estimated to be worth US dollar (USD) 178.73 billion in 2021, increased by 14.4% from 2020.[27] In terms of revenue, the video game industry solely is bigger than all other entertainment industries combined. For example, in 2018, global box office revenue was USD 41.7 billion, whereas video games generated USD 151.2 billion.[28] The digitalisation rate doubled (from around 40% to 80%) in the video game industry from 2010 to 2018.[29] Cloud gaming is becoming an increasingly applicable proposition.[30] Needless to say, nowadays, almost all video games can be downloaded from the internet.[31] Despite the importance of the digital video game industry, it is difficult to categorise the related goods and services under the current

[26] NFT is 'an irreplaceable unit of data that's verified on the blockchain. In an art context, this may point to either a real-life or purely digital piece, and has been touted as a solution to a perpetual challenge in that traditional scene: proof of provenance'. See Yip J (2022) How are NFTs disrupting the art market? Beeple's Everydays and CrytoPunk collectibles made millions at auction while Bored Ape Yacht Club drew celebs including Justin Bieber and Snoop Dogg. South China Morning Post. (in press), https://www.scmp.com/magazines/style/news-trends/article/3176887/how-are-nfts-disrupting-art-market-beeples-everydays; Small Z (2022) Madonna and Beeple collaborate on NFT project. The New York Times. (in press), https://www.nytimes.com/2022/05/09/arts/design/madonna-beeple-nft-videos.html. Hoffman C (2021) How NFTs might play a role in international trade. Trade Financial Global. (in press), https://www.tradefinanceglobal.com/posts/how-nfts-might-play-a-role-in-international-trade/ (last accessed 7 April 2023).

[27] Video Game Industry Statistics, Trends and Data In 2022 | WePC, https://www.wepc.com/news/video-game-statistics/.

[28] Top Video Game Industry Statistics (2022) | Fortunly, https://fortunly.com/statistics/video-game-industry-statistics/.

[29] CISAC (2015), Cultural times: the first global map of cultural and creative industries. UNESCO Pulibcation, Paris. p. 89.

[30] CISAC (2015), Cultural times: the first global map of cultural and creative industries. UNESCO Pulibcation, Paris. p. 92.

[31] OECD (2005), p. 9.

WTO regime. There is even no consensus on whether digital video games are goods or services.[32] Because of the diverse business models of video games and the fast-evolving digital technologies, classifying video games becomes increasingly challenging.

The structure of the subsequent analysis is as follows: Section II conducts an in-depth legal analysis of three types of digital-related video games and the related classification issues under WTO law. In an attempt to classify digital video game, two major challenges for classifying digital cultural products are identified and discussed. Section III draws the threads together and concludes with suggestions to update the classification system for digital cultural products, especially for digital video games.

2 Classifying Digital Cultural Products: A Case Study of Digital Video Games

2.1 Digitally Ordered Video Games in Tangible Carriers

It is relatively straightforward to classify the video games in tangible carriers which are ordered through the internet. There is little doubt that the video games stored in tangible carriers should be considered as goods and subject to the General Agreement on Tariffs and Trade.[33] The latest version of the CPC (CPC Version 2.1)[34] provides a classification method for video game goods. Firstly, video game consoles (38,581)[35] and software cartridges for video game consoles (38,582) fall within the scope of video games of a kind used with a television receiver (3858), which is one sub-category of the category of games and toy (385). Secondly, Packaged computer game software (47,822), including packaged software present on physical media of magnetic nature and optical nature, falls within the scope of packaged application software (4782), which is one sub-category of the category of packaged software (478). In other words, video game goods include video game consoles (such as Microsoft Xbox, Sony PlayStation, and Nintendo Switch) and video game software in cartridges, magnetic disks, Compact Discs (CDs), and Digital Video Discs (DVDs).

---

[32] Steiner (2009), p. 17.

[33] General Agreement on Tariffs and Trade, Apr. 15, 1994, 867 U.N.T.S. 190 [hereinafter GATT]; Fleuter (2016), p. 158.

[34] Central Product Classification Version 2.1, Series M: Miscellaneous Statistical Papers, No. 77 Ver. 2.1, New York: United Nations. ST/ESA/STAT/SER.M/77/VER.2.1, (2015), https://unstats.un.org/unsd/classifications/Family/Detail/1074.

[35] The numbers refer to the classification code from the CPC Version 2.1.

2.2 Video Game Software

It is a less simple task to classify the video game software which is downloadable from the internet (84,342).[36] In the context of the WTO, there is no clear-cut classification of a video game software. The first question that begs an answer is whether this type of video game is a good or a service? There is no official way of classifying goods and services in WTO law. The common understanding is that goods are tangible, whereas services are intangible.[37] Following this characteristic-based approach, video games downloaded from the internet should be categorised as services. However, this classification method is artificial to a certain extent, as video games with identical contents and functions might be subject to different trade rules and different levels of trade liberalisation merely because of the different ways of storage and delivery.

Current WTO digital trade rules negotiations have achieved little guidance regarding this classification question. The only substantial consensus reached regarding e-commerce is that Members will continue their current practice of not imposing customs duties on electronic transmissions, adopted at the Second Ministerial Conference in May 1998.[38] In September 1998, The WTO General Council adopted the Work Programme on Electronic Commerce and mandated four WTO bodies to explore the relationship between existing WTO agreements and e-commerce.[39] In this Work Programme, one broad definition of 'electronic commerce' is given: 'exclusively for the purposes of the work programme, and without prejudice to its outcome, the term 'electronic commerce' is understood to mean the production, distribution, marketing, sale or delivery of goods and services by electronic means'.[40] Based on this definition, it is impossible to answer whether video game software is a good or a service though it is clear that video game software falls within the scope of 'electronic commerce'.

[36]For the video game software, I refer to the video game application software which can be downloaded and stored on a local device for later execution (in this case, execution means playing the game on a device). Under the CPC Version 2.1, this type of video game is under the category of telecommunication, broadcasting and information supply services (84) – online content (843) – software downloads (8434) - application software downloads (84342). The CPC Version 2.1 describes the 84342 sub category as 'electronic files containing application software that can be downloaded and stored on a local device for later execution/installation'.

[37]Peng (2020), p. 700.

[38]World Trade Organization, Ministerial Conference Declaration on Global Electronic Commerce, WTO Doc. WT/MIN(98)/DEC/2, (May 25, 1998).

[39]General Council, Work Programme on Electronic Commerce, WTO Doc. WT/L/274 (Sep. 30, 1998).

[40]General Council, Work Programme on Electronic Commerce, WTO Doc. WT/L/274 (Sep. 30, 1998).

2.2.1 Challenge 1: Digital Products in the Dichotomic 'Good or Service' Regime

The difficulty of categorising video game software as good or service reveals a major challenge facing the dichotomic 'good or service' WTO regime in the digital age. The 'good or service' classification issue has sparked a heated debate in academia. Scholars have analysed the existing problems and proposed suggestions with regard to classifying digital products as goods or services, or both, or neither. In this sub-section, I firstly conduct a systematic literature review of the existing research. Secondly, I provide an analysis of the 'good or service' classification issue based on two scenarios. The innovative aspect of this analysis is that it unfolds the classification issue in two scenarios and provides a comprehensive analysis combining the current knowledge from WTO case-law, academic research, and developments from the RTAs.

Existing Research on the 'Good or Service' Classification Issue

The current academic research on the 'good or service' classification issue can be grouped into three routes according to their proposed solutions. The first proposal is to break down the 'good or service' dichotomy. Peng points out that the integration of goods and services (exemplified by 3D printing, IoT, and artificial intelligence) leads to increased complexity and convergence of the domestic regulatory framework.[41] Peng argues for an overhaul of international trade rules to address goods and services in a generic and neutral manner.[42] Voon's proposal is limited to the audiovisual sector where she calls for a harmonisation of the treatment of audiovisual products under the GATT and the GATS.[43] Her suggestion has a coverage limitation but gives a more specific explanation on how to break down the 'good or service' dichotomy exactly.[44] As the authors suggested themselves, the proposal of breaking down the GATT and the GATS regimes is 'utopian'.[45] Besides, another problem with the first proposal lies in its reasoning. The convergence of domestic trade regulations does not necessarily require the convergence of international trade rules because they are built on different legislation (or negotiation) mechanisms and serve different objectives. WTO law pursues multiple objectives among which promoting progressive trade liberalisation is an important one. It is unneglectable that trade in goods and trade in services face significantly different levels of liberalisation and different forms of restrictions. Therefore, it appears that it will

---

[41] Peng (2020), p. 705.

[42] Peng (2020), p. 724.

[43] Voon (2007), pp. 31–32.

[44] Voon (2007), pp. 31–32.

[45] Voon (2007), pp. 31–32; Peng (2020), p. 724.

be extremely difficult to harmonise the GATT and the GATS regimes at this moment.

The second proposal argues that the current 'good or service' regime is adaptable to the digital challenges and does not need an overhaul. Sauvé argues that fusing trade rules for goods and services is neither necessary nor feasible because of the structural and normative distinctions between the GATT and the GATS.[46] Chander dives into the case of IoT. He argues that IoT devices comprise both goods and services, and any regulation thereof thus should be subject to both the GATT and the GATS regimes.[47] This proposal rightly points out the adaptability of the WTO regime when services are embedded in goods and the practical difficulty of conducting a WTO overhaul. The problem is that it does not address the case when the carriers of goods transform from physical forms to non-physical forms, namely electronic forms. As this chapter will demonstrate in the following section, the scenario where goods transform into electronic 'service-like' products is a real challenge for WTO law.

The third proposal puts forward the need for a new category of service supply to address the challenge of 'servicification'.[48] Cernat, Kutlina-Dimitrova, and Antimiani proposed a 'mode 5' of service supply to reflect the services which are embedded in the production process of a manufacturing good.[49] For example, the software installed in the manufacturing goods and sold 'in boxes' should be considered as the 'mode 5 service'.[50] Farrokhnia and Richards believe that neither the GATT nor the GATS is comprehensive enough to cover digital products, and a new category for digital products is needed.[51] The 'mode 5 services' is proposed to specifically address the servicification trend. The authors' arguments are mainly based on the customs valuation and trade liberalisation considerations.[52] However, defining 'mode 5 services' might be a tricky process. For instance, if designing and engineering can be considered as services embedded in car manufacturing, what about assembling and delivering? Is there a risk that all manufacturing processes can be broken down into different stages of services?

These distinct suggestions expand our understanding and imagination in addressing the 'good or service' dichotomy. In the meantime, the wide divergence of these suggestions reveals the complexity of the problems. Comprehensive and

---

[46] Sauvé (2019), p. 371. It is worth noting that Sauvé argues that a more holistic negotiating framework that embraces the reality of the goods-services nexus is needed. Nevertheless, there is no specific explanation with regard to how a holistic negotiating framework shall be structured and achieved.

[47] Chander (2019), p. 9.

[48] Cernat and Kutlina-Dimitrova define 'servicification' as 'manufacturing firms purchasing, producing and selling more and more services to their customers (both domestically and abroad) at all stages along the value chain'. See Cernat and Kutlina-Dimitrova (2014), p. 1115.

[49] Cernat and Kutlina-Dimitrova (2014), pp. 1123–1124; Antimiani and Cernat (2018), pp. 80–82.

[50] Cernat and Kutlina-Dimitrova (2014), p. 1110.

[51] Farrokhnia and Richards (2016), p. 793.

[52] Antimiani and Cernat (2018), pp. 67, 74.

systematic research on the WTO classification issue is still lacking. No holistic understanding of the issue has emerged yet. The following analysis aims to stand on the shoulders of giants and continues to explore the goods and services classification issue.

Two Challenging Scenarios Related to Digital Products

The challenges brought by digital products in the dichotomic 'good or service' regime can be detailed into two scenarios.

The first scenario is when there is a digital service embedded in a certain good. To be specific, challenges arise when 'a measure involves a service relating to a particular good or a service supplied in conjunction with a particular good'.[53] It is common to have certain services and goods combined in digital products. For instance, a smart speaker is a typical internet-based good with integrated services. It is a loudspeaker and voice command device with an integrated virtual assistant.[54] When you purchase an Amazon's smart speaker, you will also receive the integrated virtual assistant service called 'Alexa', which can recognise and respond to voices. When you ask your Amazon smart speaker 'Will it rain tomorrow?', it will automatically search this question online and answer. A domestic measure that has an impact on the trade in smart speakers unavoidably has an impact on the trade in the integrated service, too.

The challenge mainly lies in the dispute over the applicability of the GATT or the GATS in such a scenario. For instance, in the *China – Publications and Audiovisual Products* dispute, the good and service involved are the hard-copy cinematographic film and the service of providing the content of the film, namely, the commercial licensing, distribution, and projection of the intangible content of the film.[55] In this case, the related services are supplied in conjunction with the good (film). The measure under dispute is one provision of the Film Regulation of China. China argued that the Film Regulation only regulates film-associated services. Therefore, the Film Regulation should not be subject to China's good-related WTO obligations. The Appellate Body (AB) was not convinced that the Film Regulation only regulates services.[56] The AB found that the Film Regulation regulates both goods and related services, and emphasised that 'a measure could be simultaneously subject to the

[53] Appellate Body Report, Appellate Body - European Communities - Regime for the Importation, Sale and Distribution of Bananas, WT/DS27/AB/R (adopted Sep. 9, 1997), para 221, [hereinafter EC – Banana III AB Report].

[54] Smart speaker - Wikipedia, https://en.wikipedia.org/wiki/Smart_speaker (last accessed 25 October 2022); Pyne H (2020) What is a smart speaker and how do they work? Radio Times. (in press) https://www.radiotimes.com/technology/what-is-a-smart-speaker/.

[55] China – Publications and Audiovisual Products AB Report, para 191.

[56] China – Publications and Audiovisual Products AB Report, para 193.

GATT and the GATS obligations', citing the reasonings from the *Canada – Periodicals* and *EC – Bananas III* AB Reports.[57]

Through three WTO dispute rulings, the AB established a consistent understanding regarding the relationship between the GATT and the GATS and the applicability of the GATT and/or the GATS. The first issue clarified by the AB is that the relationship between the GATT and the GATS is not mutually exclusive.[58] Obligations of the GATT and the GATS can co-exist, and one does not override another.[59] The second issue was clarified through the *Canada – Periodical* and the *EC – Banana III* rulings. The AB provided more guidance on how to identify whether a measure is good-related or service-related, that is, how to identify whether the GATT applies, or the GATS applies. The AB ruling in *Canada – Periodical* provides that the applicability of the GATT and/or the GATS depends on the entities (e.g., good producers, distributors, and service providers) who are affected/regulated by the measures at issue.[60] If the measure at issue has been directed at good providers, good-related obligations apply. If the measure at issue has been directed at service providers, service-related obligations apply. If good providers and service providers are directed at the same time, two regimes apply simultaneously.

These rulings are specifically meaningful when there are digital products involved in the disputes. First, it has been established through the method of evolutionary interpretation that the GATS applies to electronically delivered services.[61] Second, because of the co-applicability of the GATT and the GATS, when a domestic trade measure affects trade in a digital product that combines goods and services, there is little doubt that the GATT and the GATS can co-apply. There is no need to fuse the classification or conduct a reclassification.

The second scenario whereby digital products challenge the 'good or service' dichotomy is when there is a transformation from goods to 'service-like' intangible products.[62] The video game software mentioned above is a typical example of this type of digital product. The challenge that arises from this scenario is that the same content consumed would be classified differently when its carrier changes from tangible, physical forms to intangible, internet-based forms. Consequently, different trade obligations would apply to the same content.[63]

WTO case-law does not provide guidance with regard to this kind of scenario. In the *China – Publications and Audiovisual Products* AB Report, the AB made it clear

---

[57] China – Publications and Audiovisual Products AB Report, para 193.

[58] EC - Banana III AB Report, para 220.

[59] Canada – Periodical AB Report, page 19.

[60] Canada – Periodical AB Report, page 19.

[61] US – Gambling AB Report. China – Publications and Audiovisual Products AB Report, paras 396 – 397. Wunsch-Vincent (2006b), pp. 321–322.

[62] It would be inaccurate to say it's a transformation from goods to services because that way it is already assumed that the transformed product is a service. Then there is no meaning in discussing how to classify the product at issue.

[63] Wunsch-Vincent (2006a), p. 46.

that the coverage of 'sound recording distribution services' extends to the distribution of sound recordings in non-physical form, notably through electronic means.[64] This only means that when a certain defined service in the Member's service schedule has an electronic form, the committed liberalisation obligation shall extend to the electronic form of this service. However, there is no answer on the relationship between the importation of the hard-copy sound recording goods and the electronically distributed of these recordings.[65] This ruling does not provide guidance in understanding the relationship between a physical good and its related services in electronic forms. Therefore, there is no answer for whether an electronically delivered, non-physical, 'service-like' form of a good is a good or service.

Without guidance from the WTO case-law, is there useful inspiration from existing scholarly research? First, can a neutral and harmonised trade regime for goods and services help? In a utopian world, yes. However, the structural distinction and liberalisation divergence between the GATT and the GATS is almost impossible to be torn down in reality. The negotiation of digital trade rules already indicated the difficulty of fusing the GATT and GATS rules. Under the Work Programme on Electronic Commerce,[66] the definition of electronic commerce includes both goods and services. It shows a generic and inclusive tendency. However, the EU has already reiterated that in the electronic commerce negotiations, the EU and its Member States will not enter into commitments on audiovisual services. This disclaimer shows that WTO Members can always exclude certain sectors from a harmonised trade regime, leaving the trade regime unharmonised because of the incompleteness. Second, the proposal of not fusing GATT and GATS seems to be more feasible and appropriate. As analysed before, in the scenario where services are integrated or embedded in goods, the current WTO regime is applicable. If the current dichotomic GATT and GATS regime remains, the real thorny question that needs a solution is how to classify the 'service-like', electronically delivered products. Third, the proposal of the 'mode 5 service' does not seem to be helpful in classifying digital products. As the authors claim, 'the coverage of mode 5 reflects a production service which is an inseparable part of the production process of a manufacturing good, before the good enters the importing country'.[67] Therefore, the 'mode 5 services' actually are the services that are embedded in the goods (discussed above as the first scenario of digital products in this chapter). In the analysis by Antimiani and Cernat, the products analysed in the second scenario in this section are considered to be services.[68] Their analysis indicates that there is a paradox that 'mode 5 services' pay customs duties and are subject to a different set of trade rules compared to the same content which is traded in intangible carriers.

---

[64] China – Publications and Audiovisual Products AB Report, para 412.

[65] Willemyns (2019), p. 62.

[66] General Council, Work Programme on Electronic Commerce, WTO Doc. WT/L/274 (Sep. 30, 1998).

[67] Antimiani and Cernat (2018), p. 67.

[68] Antimiani and Cernat (2018), p. 80.

Essentially, the 'mode 5 service' proposal points out the exact classification difficulty rather than solving the problem.

After searching for possible solutions from the WTO case-law and academic writings, this chapter draws inspiration from RTAs for transferrable lessons for WTO negotiations. In the field of RTAs, there is a promising trend where some states are actively promoting digital trade rule negotiations. Substantial innovation has emerged in the rules relating to the free flow of information, digital trade facilitation, etc.[69] Nevertheless, with regard to the classification issue, little experience can be extracted from RTAs.

First, even in the RTAs which include advanced digital trade rules, there is a clear indication of avoidance in answering the classification question. For instance, the United States—Mexico—Canada Agreement defines a digital product as 'a computer program, text, video, image, sound recording, or other product that is digitally encoded, produced for commercial sale or distribution, and that can be transmitted electronically'.[70] It is vital to read the footnote following this definition provision. It states that 'this definition should not be understood to reflect a Party's view that digital products are a good or a service'.[71] The same provision and footnote are also included in Article 14.1 of the Comprehensive and Progressive Agreement for Trans-Pacific Partnership[72] and Article 3.1 of the Digital Economy Partnership Agreement between New Zealand, Chile, and Singapore.[73] Second, more and more RTAs adopt a negative list approach to subscribe to national treatment and market access obligations, which has few directly transferrable lessons for the WTO negotiation.[74] When adopting the negative list approach, states do not need to choose the service sectors for which they commit to liberalising. Instead, states typically use annexes to list their reservations. All sectors that are not listed in the annexes are by default liberalised. In the annexes, states usually list the reserved domestic legislations and the reserved sectors.[75] The classifications of the reserved sectors are usually based on the domestic service classification system of the parties to the RTAs, which are unharmonised and diverse.[76]

As explained above, classifying certain digital products as goods or services is a complex and difficult task. There is no straightforward or 'one size fits all' answer to

---

[69] Burri (2021), p. 99.

[70] Agreement between the United States of America, the United Mexican States, and Canada, art 19.1, Nov. 30, 2018, 107 Stat. 2116, [hereinafter USMCA].

[71] Art 19.1, USMCA.

[72] Comprehensive and Progressive Agreement for Trans-Pacific Partnership, Mar. 8, 2018, [hereinafter CPTPP].

[73] Digital Economy Partnership Agreement, Nov. 11, 2020, [hereinafter DEPA].

[74] See e.g., Gagné (2011), p. 1267.

[75] See, e.g., European Commission (2016), Services and investment in EU trade deals: Using "positive" and "negative" lists, http://ec.europa.eu/eurostat/documents/2995521/7142952/2.

[76] See, e.g., State Development and Reform Commission of PRC & Ministry of Commerce of PRC (2021), The Special Administrative Measures (Negative List) for Foreign Investment Access (2021 Edition).

this question. However, the 'cluster approach' might be an operational approach to advance the negotiation on this issue.[77] The 'cluster approach' was firstly proposed by the European Communities and Australia in 2000.[78] The 'cluster approach' itself is not a defined classification framework. It is a negotiation instrument, which can be used to negotiate the classification issue and the treatment of certain groups of related products, such as digital products.

The European Communities explained that 'a cluster was a group of sectors or sub-sectors which were related and for which negotiators would agree to seek a harmonized and coherent set of commitments'.[79] The European Communities envisaged two circumstances in which clusters might be needed.[80] The first circumstance was 'when economic activities were cutting across several sectors but were not covered anywhere'. The second circumstance was 'where a core sector was dependant on key inputs in other sectors or sub-sectors'.[81] The proposal was still a preparatory report, so there were concerns expressed by other Members that it was not clear whether the cluster was intended for classification purpose.[82]

I am of the view that the 'cluster approach' can be an operational method to drive the discussion on the classification issue. In the first place, it would be necessary to identify a cluster or multiple clusters of digital products, based on their technical and economic linkages. Next, it is vital to establish negotiating guidelines and procedures to ensure a structured classification negotiation. Four elements of the 'cluster approach' can support the feasibility of this approach for classifying digital products. First, the negotiation should be conducted on the basis of pre-decided clusters, which could include closely-related digital products. Under the umbrella of clusters, it might be more obvious that it is necessary to address the overlap and the inadequacy of the current classification for digital products. Second, the 'cluster approach' has already been discussed by WTO Members. Therefore, there is a substantial possibility that Members would be willing to engage in further discussion on refining this approach. Third, as has been stated by various Members in the communication, participation in the cluster negotiation shall be voluntary.[83] This is a demand

---

[77] Gao (2014), p. 350.

[78] Special Session of the Council for Trade in Services, Note by the Secretariat: Report of the Meeting Held on 26 May 2000, WTO Doc. S/CSS/M/3 (June 26, 2000), [hereinafter Report of the Meeting Held on 26 May 2000].

[79] Report of the Meeting Held on 26 May 2000, para 115.

[80] Report of the Meeting Held on 26 May 2000, para 115.

[81] Report of the Meeting Held on 26 May 2000, para 115.

[82] There are different positions regarding whether the cluster approach addresses the classification issue. See Report of the Meeting Held on 26 May 2000, para 116, India expressed the concern regarding the competent body for addressing the classification issue. See Report of the Meeting Held on 26 May 2000, para 117, Norway was of the view that classification is one of the elements of the cluster approach. See Report of the Meeting Held on 26 May 2000, para 114, Australia emphasised that classification issue shall not be confused with the negotiation proposal for cluster approach.

[83] See e.g., Report of the Meeting Held on 26 May 2000, paras 116, 122.

especially emphasised by developing countries.[84] Sufficient flexibility should be provided under the principle of progressive liberalisation. Fourth, the objective of adopting the 'cluster approach' for negotiating the classification issue is to supplement and clarify the current classification system. It does not aim to conduct an overhaul of the existing regime, which would reduce the political reluctance in the negotiation process.

In sum, this subsection discussed the first classification challenge brought by digital products under WTO law. The challenge is categorising certain digital products, such as video game software, as goods or services. The 'good or service' classification issue is an issue that has attracted increasing attention in recent years. Existing research on this issue can be broadly grouped into three different proposals. This section critically assessed each of these three proposals and conducted an analysis following a two-scenario structure. The first scenario analysed is when a digital service is embedded in a good. After a legal analysis of existing WTO dispute rulings, this chapter argues that the current GATT and GATS rules can apply to measures related to goods and services simultaneously and there is no need to break down the current GATT and GATS regimes. The second scenario is when a digital product is a good transformed into a 'service-like' intangible product. The analysis of the WTO case-law, existing research, and the developments of RTAs do not prove to be particularly helpful for addressing the challenge arising from the second scenario. I argue that the 'cluster approach' could be a feasible negotiation method to address the complex classification issue in groups.

2.2.2 Challenge 2: Digital Products in the Current Service Classification System

There is still a long way to go before finding a clear answer to challenge 1 analysed above. Without an answer to the 'good or service' classification issue, it is still common to adopt the old 'characteristic-based' approach and classify video game software as a service. The main argument in this section points out that even in cases where the video game software is treated as a service, it is still challenging to classify it into one specific service sector according to the GATS classification system (W/120). There is no plain answer to this question. Three possible categories for classifying video game software are discussed below.

Is It Possible to Classify Video Game Software as Computer and Related Services?

The short answer is no. According to the W/120, computer and related services include:

---

[84] Report of the Meeting Held on 26 May 2000, paras 116, 122, 127.

a. Consultancy services related to the installation of computer hardware (841)
b. Software implementation services (842)
c. Data processing services (843)
d. Data base services (844)
e. Other (845+849)[85]

After consulting the detailed description in the CPC Provisional, we find that software implementation services refer to the services 'involving *consultancy* services on development and implementation of software' according to the CPC Provisional. This is different from downloading video game software. It is also hard to conceive software as a data processing service. According to the CPC Provisional, data processing services include: (a) input preparation services; (b) data-processing and tabulation services; (c) time-sharing services; (d) other data processing services. The description from the CPC Provisional does not provide a clear meaning of data processing services. To assess whether downloading software is a type of data processing service, it is necessary to conduct an interpretative analysis under Articles 31 and 32 of the Vienna Convention on the Law of Treaties.[86] Firstly, the ordinary meaning of 'data processing' can be 'the collection and manipulation of items of data *to produce meaningful information*'.[87] However, the primary objective of downloading video game software is not to produce information. Instead, the primary objective of downloading video game software is storing the programming and for later execution. Besides, a background note prepared by the WTO Council for Trade in Services can be consulted as supplementary means of interpretation. This background note provides information on computer and related services for discussion.[88] In the section clarifying the 'definition of the sector', it is clearly provided that 'with respect to computer software, it would appear not to be covered in the existing classification scheme'.[89] This clarification seems to go beyond the scope of computer and related services and states that computer software (including computer video game software) is not covered by the GATS classification at all. In any case, it shows that it is not the purpose of the computer and related service sectors to cover the computer software.

[85] When discussing the classification system iin the W/120, the CPC numbers refer to the classification code of the CPC Provisional version.

[86] Vienna Convention on the Law of Treaties, Jan. 27, 1980, U.N.T.S. 1155 [hereinafter VCLT]. WTO case-law has confirmed that the only rules which may be applied to interpret the Service Schedules of Members are the general rules of treaty interpretation set out in the VCLT. See Appellate Body Report, European Communities - Customs Classification of Certain Computer Equipment, para 84, WTO Doc. WT/DS62/AB/R ; WT/DS67/AB/R; WT/DS68/AB/R (adopted June 5, 1998).

[87] French (1996), p. 2.

[88] Council for Trade in Services, Computer and Related Services, Background Note by the Secretariat, WTO Doc. S/C/W/45, (July 14, 1998).

[89] Council for Trade in Services, Computer and Related Services, Background Note by the Secretariat, WTO Doc. S/C/W/45, (July 14, 1998), para 9.

Is It Possible to Classify Video Game Software as Telecommunication Services?

Once again, the short answer is no. Telecommunication services can be divided into two sub-categories. The first sub-category is basic telecommunications, which involves the end-to-end transmission of customer and supplier information. In other words, basic telecommunications refer to the relay of voice or data from sender to receiver. The second sub-category is value-added services, which are telecommunications for which suppliers 'add value' to the customer's information by enhancing its form or content or by providing for its storage and retrieval.[90] According to the W/120, telecommunication services include:

a. Voice telephone services (7521)
b. Packet-switched data transmission services (7523)
c. Circuit-switched data transmissions services (7523)
d. Telex services (7523)
e. Telegraph services (7522)
f. Facsimile services (7521+7529)
g. Private leased circuit services (7522+7523)
h. Electronic mail (7523)
i. Voice mail (7523)
j. On-line information and data base retrieval (7523)
k. Electronic data interchange (EDI) (7523)
l. Enhanced/value-added facsimile services, incl. store and forward, store and retrieve (7523)
m. Code and protocol conversion (n.a.)
n. On-line information and/or data processing (incl. transaction processing) (843)
o. Other

At first glance, video game software does not neatly fit into any of these sub-sectors. Moreover, further interpretation of the telecommunication sector based on other supplementary material does not provide a promising result either. It is challenging to classify video game software under the telecommunication sector mainly because there is no mention of the content aspect in this service sector. The GATS Annex for Telecommunication defines 'telecommunication' as the transmission and reception of signals by any electronic means.[91] This indicates that in the context of the GATS, telecommunication services mean the services that transmit signals. There is no clear guidance about whether content and transmission of content shall be treated

[90] WTO | Services, Telecommunications - Coverage of basic telecommunications & value-added services, https://www.wto.org/english/tratop_e/serv_e/telecom_e/telecom_coverage_e.htm#value.

[91] WTO, WTO analytical index GATS – Annex on telecommunicaitons (jurisprudence) para 3 (a). https://www.wto.org/english/res_e/publications_e/ai17_e/ai17_e.htm.

separately. This question has been troubling the ongoing negotiations in the telecommunication sector because WTO Members hold opposite answers to this question.[92]

We can only observe that the GATS tends to carve the content element out of the coverage of the telecommunication sector. It is explicitly stated in the GATS Annex for Telecommunication that this Annex shall not apply to measures affecting the cable or broadcast distribution of radio or television programming.[93] There is no mention of any other online content. Therefore, I argue here that it would be improper to classify video game software into the telecommunication service sector since the essential function of video game software is the distribution of the game content and programming. This conclusion differs when it comes to online games, which will be discussed in the following section.

Is It Possible to Classify Video Game Software as Audiovisual Services?

Here, the answer is yes. According to the W/120, audiovisual services include:

a. Motion picture and video tape production and distribution services (9611)
b. Motion picture projection service (9612)
c. Radio and television services (9613)
d. Radio and television transmission services (7524)
e. Sound recording (n.a.)
f. Other

The first five sub-categories of audiovisual services cannot cover video game software because they all have explicitly targeted groups, including motion pictures, video tape, radio programmes, television programmes and sound recording. However, it is possible to classify video game software into the sub-category of 'other'. The reasoning is two-fold. Firstly, the content of the audiovisual services, video games and other audiovisual products all are cultural multimedia products. The core and defining element of video games and other audiovisual products is the cultural and creative content created by the designers, artists, programmers, etc. Secondly, from the perspective of the coverage of the audiovisual services in the W/120, video game software can fall within this sector because it is a distribution method of video games. As provided in the W/120, the audiovisual services sector covers the production and distribution services of audiovisual products. For different audiovisual products, different customised distribution methods are included. For instance,

[92] For a detailed analysis of Members' positions on the issue of treatment of content in the telecommunication service sector, see Wunsch-Vincent (2006a), p. 72.

[93] An audiovisual service background note prepared by the Council for Trade in Services secretariat also confirms that 'it has become accepted that commitments involving programming content are classified under audiovisual services, while those purely involving the transmission of information are classified under telecommunications'. See Council for Trade in Services, Audiovisual Services Background Note by the Secretariat, WTO Doc. S/C/W/40 (June15, 1998), para 5.

motion picture distribution includes theatre projection, television broadcasting, and sale or rental of video tape. This indicates that there is certain flexibility with regard to the distribution method of the audiovisual product. As for video games, nowadays, the primary distribution method is software.

Hence, I argue that it is possible to classify video game software under the 'other' sub-category based on the audiovisual content and the distribution function of video game software. Nevertheless, it is necessary to note that this is not an ideal classification as the 'other' sub-category is ambiguous. It is extremely scarce that WTO Members have liberalisation commitments in the 'audiovisual - other' sub-category.[94] Updating the GATS classification system to properly classify software services and content-related activities is needed.

2.3 Online Games

Online games refer to computer-based games played over the internet, including PC, console, and wireless games.[95] The reason to differentiate between online games and video game software is that they involve significantly different types of digital technology, which are usually classified as different service sectors. For online games, a connection to the internet is indispensable. Online games include standalone games which can be played by a small group of players and Massively Multiplayer Online Role Playing Games, with more than ten thousand players playing simultaneously and more than one million players registered.[96] The amount of data produced and processed in online games can be far more complex than by downloading video game software. Besides, online games and video game software correspond to different phases of accessing video games. Software downloading is the phase of storing video games on local devices. Online gaming is the phase of executing the downloaded software. Under the W/120, there is no such entry as 'online games'. This section explores the most appropriate service sector(s) to categorise online games.

First, is it possible to classify online games as computer and related services? The answer is yes. Given the interactive nature of online games, data input and data processing are critical to the operation of online games. Therefore, it is possible to classify online games under the data processing services sector (843). The CPC Provisional further divides the 843 sector into:

a. Input preparation services (8431)
b. Data-processing and tabulation services (8432)

---

[94] Only Central African Republic and United States of America have liberalisation commitments in the 'audiovisual - other' sub sector, see the I-TIP services WTO database, http://i-tip.wto.org/services/default.aspx.

[95] OECD (2005), p. 9.

[96] OECD (2005), p. 9.

c. Time-sharing services (8433)
d. Other data processing services (8439)

Online games could fall within the scope of 8431 and 8432 sectors.

Second, is it possible to classify online games as telecommunication services? The answer is yes. Firstly, in the W/120, telecommunication services also include data processing services (843). Therefore, because of this overlapping between computer-related services and telecommunication services, online games can also fall within the scope of telecommunication services. Secondly, the CPC Version 2.1 can provide some guidance in this regard, as it is the most likely classification system to be used for updating the W/120.[97] The CPC Version 2.1. classifies online games under the division of telecommunications, broadcasting, and information supply services (84). Though the CPC Version 2.1. categorises online games under the entry of online content (843), which does not appear in the W/120. Under such a circumstance, we might be able to classify online games under the W/120 entry 'enhanced/value-added facsimile services, incl. store and forward, store and retrieve'. It is worth noting that I argue that video game software should not be classified as telecommunication services in the previous analysis. The main reason is that telecommunication services as designed in the W/120 exclude the *distribution of radio or television programming*. We can understand that the distribution of audiovisual content (including video game software) is excluded from telecommunication services. However, as mentioned above, an online game is the execution or operation of the video game software, which is not excluded from the telecommunication sector in W/120. As a result, it is possible to classify online games as telecommunication services, falling within the scope of the online information and/or data processing services and enhanced/value-added facsimile services.

Third, is it possible to classify online games as audiovisual services? The answer is yes. To support this point, one can argue that playing video games online still involves the distribution of audiovisual programming. Because of the interactive nature of video games, the boundary between game delivery and game consumption is blurred. Following the same logic used for classifying video game software, online games might also fall within the scope of 'other' audiovisual services.

In sum, under the current GATS service classification system, it is possible to classify online games as computer and related services, telecommunication services, and audiovisual services. Clearly, such an overlapping system does not provide a precise and coherent framework for classifying services and bringing trade liberalisation negotiations forward.

---

[97] Wunsch-Vincent (2006a), p. 76.

3 Conclusion

As presented above, classifying digital cultural products under the current WTO framework is a highly complex task. Uncertainty and overlaps are inevitable, which calls for an update of the current classification system. With video games as a case study, this chapter explored the classification possibilities of three types of video games. For digitally ordered video games in tangible carriers, the classification is relatively easy. For video game software, the challenge of classification lies in two aspects. The first challenge is the difficulty of classifying digital products as goods or services. This chapter addresses this challenge by examining two scenarios. For digital services embedded in goods, this analysis proves that there is no need for reclassification, because the GATT and GATS can co-apply. For the digital products which are transformed from physical to non-physical, this analysis shows there is no immediate answer to whether these products are goods or services. This chapter suggests the adoption of a 'cluster approach' to advance the classification negotiation. The second challenge arises from the observation that it is difficult to change the 'good or service' dichotomy in the near future, and therefore, it is possible that products like software will be classified as services because they are intangible. The second challenge lies in the difficulty of classifying video game software into one proper service sector. For online games, the situation is that this service can be classified into multiple service sectors simultaneously under the current GATS classification system, which leads to an overlapping classification result.

My line of enquiry here further suggests that four factors may be warranted to update the GATS service classification system, especially for classifying digital video games. First, it is necessary to update the understanding regarding the difference between goods and services. Shall we consider video games as services once they break away from tangible carriers and are digitally encoded into intangible software? Second, if we consider many types of software as services, it will be necessary to clarify the service sector of software and to design a detailed classification system for it. Third, it is also necessary to specify the relationship between telecommunication services and audiovisual services in the digital age. Increasingly, audiovisual content (including video games) is fully functioning online and involves an enormous amount of data transmission, blurring the boundary between telecommunication services and audiovisual services. Fourth, it is necessary to adopt a more detailed classification list of audiovisual services. The current audiovisual sector might be underinclusive and overinclusive at the same time because of the limited specified entries and the inclusion of the 'other' entry.

Protection of cultural diversity consideration plays a vital role in current digital trade rule negotiations. It even can be said that some WTO Members' cultural exception strategy has a 'spillover' effect on the digital trade rule-making process. For instance, the EU does not undertake any liberalisation commitments in the audiovisual sector and insists that the audiovisual sector should remain outside of the scope of digital trade rules negotiations.[98] If the audiovisual sector is excluded from the negotiations, it would be challenging to proceed and classify digital audiovisual services. Some WTO Members could step beyond path dependence regarding the culture and trade issue, namely the path of insisting on a cultural exception in the whole audiovisual services sector. As Natens rightly argues, not all audiovisual services are necessarily covered by a cultural exception.[99] For instance, the video game industry is a relatively well balanced and international industry sector with less need for domestic cultural protection,[100] at least from the perspective of the EU.[101] The EU's whole-package cultural exception conception in the audiovisual service sector may have unwarranted political cost in the negotiations.[102] In the meantime, sufficient flexibility should be guaranteed for developing countries to adopt legitimate national cultural policies. More precisely, cluster negotiations should be conducted on a voluntary basis, to meet the cultural diversity protection needs of developing countries.

WTO Members might want to put more effort and commitment into updating a refined, detailed WTO classification system. A sufficiently detailed classification system can respond to WTO Members' cultural protection demands in a more targeted manner. The sectors which have less need for cultural protection will probably have a better chance of being identified and liberalised. Eventually, under an updated and detailed negotiation framework, hopefully, WTO Members can proceed with more trade liberalisation commitments without compromising their cultural diversity protection needs.

References

Antimiani A, Cernat L (2018) Liberalizing global trade in mode 5 services: how much is it worth? J World Trade 52(2):65–84

Brook O, O'Brien D, Taylor M (2020) Culture is bad for you: inequality in the cultural and creative industries. Manchester University Press, Manchester

Burri M (2021) Towards a new treaty on digital trade. J World Trade 55(1):77–100

Burri M, Weber RH (2012) Classification of services in the digital economy. Springer, Berlin

Burri-Nenova V (2008) Trade versus culture in the digital environment: an old conflict in need of a new definition. J Int Econ Law 12(1):17–62

[98] Joint Statement on Electronic Commerce - EU Proposal for WTO Disciplines and Commitments Relating to Electronic Commerce - Communication from the European Union, WTO Doc. INF/ECOM/22, (Apr. 26, 2019).

[99] Natens (2014), p. 373.

[100] It is usually the film industry and television industry that are calling for cultural policy measures' protection.

[101] In 2002 the United States represented 37%, Europe 36% and Japan 27% of their combined videogame markets. OECD (2005), p. 13.

[102] Natens (2014), p. 373.

Cernat L, Kutlina-Dimitrova Z (2014) Thinking in a box: a 'mode 5' approach to service trade. J World Trade 48(6):1109–1126
Chander A (2019) The internet of things: both goods and services. World Trade Rev 18(1):9–22
Farrokhnia F, Richards C (2016) E-commerce products under the World Trade Organization agreements: goods, services, both or neither? J World Trade 50(5):793–818
Fleuter S (2016) The role of digital products under the WTO: a new framework for GATT and GATS classification. J Int Law Chi 17(1):153–177
French C (1996) Data processing and information technology, 10th edn. Cengage Learning EMEA
Gagné G (2011) Free trade and cultural policies: evidence from three US agreements. J World Trade 45(6):1267–1284
Gagné G (2019) Trade and culture: the United States. Int J Cult Policy 25(5):615–628
Gao H (2014) Can WTO law keep up with the internet? In: Proceedings of the 14th ASIL annual meeting, American society of international law, vol 108. Cambridge University Press, New York, pp 350–352
Natens B (2014) Chronicle of a death foretold? The cultural exception for audio-visual services in EU trade negotiations. Leg Issues Econ Integr 41(4):367–388
Ochai O (2022) New opportunities and challenges for inclusive cultural and creative industries in the digital environment. In: Portolés JB (ed) Reshaping policies for creativity - addressing culture as a global public good. UNESCO, Paris, pp 91–116
OECD (2005) Online computer and video games, OECD Digital Economy Papers, No. 98. OECD Publishing, Paris, p 9. https://doi.org/10.1787/232164517856
Peng S (2020) A new trade regime for the servitization of manufacturing: rethinking the goods-services dichotomy. J World Trade 54(5):688–726
Sauvé P (2019) To fuse, not to fuse, or simply confuse? Assessing the case for normative convergence between goods and services trade law. J Int Econ Law 22(3):355–371
Steiner T (2009) Online games under WTO law: unresolved classification issues. NCCR TRADE Working Papers 17
Voon T (2007) A new approach to audiovisual products in the WTO: rebalancing GATT and GATS. UCLA Law Rev 14(1):1–32
Willemyns I (2019) GATS classification of digital services - does "the cloud" have a silver lining? J World Trade 53(1):59–82
Willemyns I (2021) Digital services in international trade law. Cambridge University Press, Cambridge
WTO (2018) World trade report 2018: the future of word trade: how digital technologies are transforming global commerce. Geneva, p 7
Wunsch-Vincent S (2006a) The WTO, the internet and trade in digital products: EC-US perspectives, 1st edn. Hart, Oxford
Wunsch-Vincent S (2006b) The internet, cross-border trade in services, and the GATS: lessons from US-Gambling. World Trade Rev 5(3):319–355
Zhang R (2015) Covered or not covered: that is the question - services classification and its implications for specific commitments under the GATS. World Trade Organisation Economics Research and Statistics Division Staff Working Paper ERSD-2015-11

Siqi Zhao is a PhD researcher at the Leuven Centre for Global Governance Studies and the Institute for International Law, KU Leuven, Belgium. Siqi's research addresses international trade law, international cultural law, and Chinese practices in global economic governance, with an emphasis on creative and cultural industries and digital trade.

E-commerce Provisions in Regional Trade Agreements and What They Mean for African MSMEs

Check for updates

Martin Luther Munu

Contents

Abstract The e-commerce negotiations at the World Trade Organization (WTO) are taking place at a time when other members have entered into Regional Trade Agreements (RTAs) with e-commerce chapters. By 19 July 2022, 193 RTAs covering e-commerce had been notified to the WTO. The most relevant RTAs with e-commerce chapters include the United-States-Mexico-Canada Agreement (USMCA), the Comprehensive and Progressive Agreement for Trans-Pacific Partnership Agreement (CPTPP), the Regional Comprehensive Economic Partnership

M. L. Munu (✉)
Maastricht University, Institute for Globalisation and International Regulation (IGIR), Faculty of Law, Maastricht, The Netherlands
e-mail: m.munu@maastrichtuniversity.nl

M. de Amstalden et al. (eds.), *International Economic Law*, Special Issue,
https://doi.org/10.1007/978-3-031-41996-6_7

(RCEP), and the European Union (EU)-United Kingdom (UK) Trade and Cooperation Agreement (TCA). This chapter identifies the main e-commerce-related provisions in the USMCA, EU-UK TCA, CPTPP, and RCEP, and discusses the spillover effects on African Micro, Small and Medium-sized Enterprises (MSMEs), particularly in Kenya, Rwanda, and Uganda. The chapter structures the analysis around the indirect implication of these rules on six parameters including facilitating imports and exports; addressing tariffs as a form of government revenue, attracting investment; preserving policy space for digital industrialization; providing for development assistance; and providing for different rights and obligations according to development levels. The RTAs are likely to play a significant role in setting standards for e-commerce rules both at the WTO and the AfCFTA level. The chapter concludes that if the RTAs shape e-commerce rules in their current form, it is likely to offer more opportunities for bigger players in the digital economy, especially from the US and China to continue with their dominance of global e-commerce. Moreover, MSMEs from African countries would struggle in building their competitiveness to take advantage of the opportunities brought by e-commerce.

Keywords E-commerce · Regional Trade Agreements · African MSMEs

1 Introduction

The e-commerce negotiations at the World Trade Organization (WTO) are taking place at a time when other members already have entered into Regional Trade Agreements (RTAs) covering e-commerce. As of 19 July 2022, there are 193 RTAs with e-commerce chapters.[1] The most relevant RTAs with e-commerce chapters include the United-States-Mexico-Canada Agreement (USMCA),[2] the Comprehensive and Progressive Agreement for Trans-Pacific Partnership Agreement (CPTPP),[3] and the Regional Comprehensive Economic Partnership (RCEP)[4] and the European Union (EU)-United Kingdom (UK) Trade and Cooperation Agreement (TCA).[5] The United States is the world's largest digital market,[6] while

[1]WTO, "Regional Trade Agreements Database", available at: http://rtais.wto.org/UI/PublicMaintainRTAHome.aspx.

[2]USMCA (2020): Agreement between the United States of America, the United Mexican States, and Canada, 1 July 2020 [hereinafter USMCA].

[3]CPTPP (2018) Comprehensive and Progressive Agreement for Trans-Pacific Partnership, 8 Mar 2018 [hereinafter CPTPP].

[4]RCEP (2020) Regional Comprehensive Economic Partnership Agreement, 15 Nov 2020 [hereinafter RCEP].

[5]TCA (2020) The EU–UK Trade and Cooperation Agreement, 30 Dec 2020 [hereinafter TCA].

[6]Leblond (2022) "USMCA Forward: Building a More Competitive, Inclusive, and Sustainable North American Economy – Digital", available at: https://www.brookings.edu/essay/usmca-forward-building-a-more-competitive-inclusive-and-sustainable-north-american-economy-digital/.

both CPTPP and RCEP Parties, combined are large economies,[7] with huge populations.[8] The UK and EU are big players in services trade and data flow, which is central to the digital economy. The regulatory agreements regarding the free flow of data and data protection between the EU and UK have a significant economic and social impact, affecting digital trade on a global scale, including in Africa, given that 11.5% of global cross-border data flows pass through the UK, of which 75% are with the EU.[9]

This chapter examines the e-commerce chapters of the four RTAs enumerated above with the aim of identifying the main provisions, and the spill-over effects of these RTAs on ongoing WTO e-commerce negotiations as well as on the African Continental Free Trade Area (AfCFTA) negotiations. Section 2 presents a brief typology of e-commerce regulation approaches shaping the RTAs, while Sect. 3 highlights an overview of USMCA, TPP, RCEP, and TCA. Section 4 analyses the spillover effects of e-commerce provisions in RTAs on African Micro, Small, and Medium-sized Enterprises (MSMEs), while Sect. 5 examines the effect of RTAs on e-commerce negotiations at the WTO and what they mean for African MSMEs. Section 6 provides a conclusion.

2 A Typology of e-Commerce Regulation Approaches Shaping the RTAs

There are different approaches to the regulation of the digital economy, which in effect shape the RTAs. Although different countries have their distinct approaches to e-commerce regulation, three approaches are dominant: the US approach, the Chinese approach, and the EU approach.[10] In as much as the various e-commerce regulation approaches are different, there are similarities which means they converge in certain areas that are crucial in formulating e-commerce rules in the RTAs.[11]

The highly liberal agenda for regulating the digital economy informs the US position in e-commerce negotiations, whereby they seek to sustain an open, interoperable, and dependable global network.[12] The US approach promotes cross-border transfer of information by placing a ban on measures requiring the localization of

[7] Government of Australia Department of Foreign Affairs and Trade, "CPTPP Text and Associated Documents," Australian Government Department of Foreign Affairs and Trade, available at: https://www.dfat.gov.au/trade/agreements/in-force/cptpp/official-documents.

[8] Government of Australia Department of Foreign Affairs and Trade, "Regional Comprehensive Economic Partnership," available at: https://www.dfat.gov.au/trade/agreements/in-force/rcep.

[9] Borchert and Morita-Jaeger (2021), Petropoulos (2020), pp. 8–9.

[10] Willemyns (2020), p. 227.

[11] Ibid., 222.

[12] Fefer (2020), p. 9.

cloud computing facilities.[13] Conversely, the Chinese approach to trade and internet policies embodies the increased role of the state in formulating digital industrial policy, restricting the free flow of information, and personal privacy while promoting the growth and development of domestic firms in the digital economy.[14] The EU's approach to internet regulation, including digital trade, is more regulated and prescriptive than the US approach although it is less state-controlled than China's approach.[15]

3 An Overview of USMCA, TPP, RCEP, and TCA

The USMCA is an agreement among three countries (United States, Mexico, and Canada) that came into force in 2020[16] and offers the strongest disciplines on digital trade of any international agreement.[17] The CPTPP incorporates the e-commerce provisions of the Trans-Pacific Partnership Agreement (TPP) covered under Chapter 14 of the agreement,[18] with parties to the agreement consisting of Australia, Brunei Darussalam, Canada, Chile, Japan, Malaysia, Mexico, Peru, New Zealand, Singapore, and Vietnam.[19] RCEP is an agreement among the Association of Southeast Asian Nations (ASEAN) members which include Brunei Darussalam, Cambodia, Indonesia, Laos, Malaysia, Myanmar, Philippines, Singapore, Thailand, and Vietnam, and ASEAN's free trade agreement partners which include Australia, China, India, Japan, New Zealand, and the Republic of Korea.[20] The TCA which came into force on 1 January 2021 resulted from negotiations between the EU and the UK following the withdrawal of the UK from the EU in January 2020.[21]

---

[13] Huang (2017), p. 328.

[14] Fefer (2020), p. 10.

[15] Fefer (2020), p. 12 and Article 44 of the Regulation (EU) 2016/679 of the European Parliament and of the Council of 27 April 2016 on the Protection of Natural Persons with Regard to the Processing of Personal Data and on the Free Movement of Such Data, and Repealing Directive 95/46/EC (General Data Protection Regulation), L 119/1 § (2016).

[16] Gantz (2018), p. 1.

[17] Wragg (2020).

[18] Chaurasia (2018), p. 25.

[19] Government of Australia Department of Foreign Affairs and Trade, "Comprehensive and Progressive Agreement for Trans-Pacific Partnership (CPTPP)," Australian Government Department of Foreign Affairs and Trade, available at: https://www.dfat.gov.au/trade/agreements/in-force/cptpp/comprehensive-and-progressive-agreement-for-trans-pacific-partnership.

[20] Ministry of Economy, Trade and Industry, "Regional Comprehensive Economic Partnership (RCEP) Signed," Japan Government, available at: https://www.meti.go.jp/english/press/2020/1115_001.html.

[21] Hallak (2022), p. 1.

3.1 Principle and Objectives

The principles of RTAs are related to promoting internet access as an instrument for facilitating e-commerce. Article 19.10 of USMCA tackles the principles of access and the use of the internet for digital trade. RCEP also covers internet access and use for e-commerce under Article 12.2 of the agreement. The USMCA and RCEP recognize the importance of consumers accessing and utilizing consumer-selected services and applications available on the internet, allowing parties to adopt or maintain measures such as comprehensive privacy, personal information, or personal data protection laws, sector-specific privacy laws, or laws that provide for the enforcement of voluntary privacy commitments by businesses.[22] The TTP covers the protection of personal information within the principles and guidelines of relevant international bodies.[23] The TCA takes the EU approach to e-commerce regulation by emphasizing the protection of personal data as stipulated under Paragraph 11 of the Preamble where each party is to respect the autonomy of the other to regulate the digital economy. The TCA recognizes the need of removing unjustifiable obstacles to data flows and facilitating trade using electronic means while maintaining the Parties' policies regarding the protection of personal data.[24]

3.2 Scope

The USMCA and TPP describe a digital product as a digitally encoded computer program, text, video, image, sound recording, or other digitally or electronically transmitted product, generated for commercial sale or distribution.[25] of the USMCA and TPP stipulate that the chapter on digital trade applies to a measure that affects trade by electronic means.[26] The TCA has a unique provision that identifies services that must be regarded as computer and related services to liberalize trade in services and investment, regardless of whether they are delivered via a network, including the internet.[27] The identified services include consulting, adaptation, strategy, computer programs, data processing, data storage, data hosting or database services, maintenance and repair services for office machinery and equipment, and training services for staff of clients, related to computer programs, computers, or computer systems.[28]

---

[22] Article 19.10 USMCA (2018); Article 12.2 RCEP (2020).

[23] Article 14.8 CPTPP, TPP § (2016), para. 2, available at: https://www.dfat.gov.au/trade/agreements/not-yet-in-force/tpp/Pages/tpp-text-and-associated-documents.

[24] "TCA," L 149/10 § (2021), para. 11.

[25] Article 19.1 USMCA; Article 14.1 CPTPP (2016).

[26] Article 19.2 USMCA, para. 2; Article 14.2. CPTPP (2018).

[27] Article 212 TCA, para. 1.

[28] Article 212 ibid.

3.3 Obligations

RTAs cover obligations to digitalize trade, obligations to increase trade in digital products, services, and information/data, and obligations to increase transparency and cooperation in the digital economy.

3.3.1 Digitalize Trade

RTAs have specific provisions covering electronic transactions. The RTAs observe that Parties shall maintain a legal framework for electronic transactions in a manner consistent with the principles of the 1996 United Nations Commission on International Trade Law (UNCITRAL) Model Law on Electronic Commerce.[29] In addition, Parties to USMCA and CPTPP shall endeavor to reduce the regulatory burden on electronic transactions.[30] RCEP and the TCA however, emphasize the right to regulate a wide range of public policies,[31] all four RTAs reflect the three approaches to e-commerce regulation which facilitate e-commerce as they provide for the digitalization of trade through the recognition of e-signatures.[32] These RTAs also seek to digitalize trade by facilitating paperless trading, a measure that covers the acceptance of electronic trade documents as a legal equivalent of paper versions.[33]

3.3.2 Increase Trade in Digital Products, Services, and Information/Data

These RTAs have provisions covering measures such as cross-border transfers of information, limiting data localization measures, promoting openness in terms of providing information to users or consumers, banning customs duty on electronic transmissions, and ensuring non-discrimination of digital products.[34] The provisions promote the cross-border transfer of information by electronic means by forbidding any restriction or prohibition on cross-border information transfer via electronic means, including personal information, provided the action is for the conduct of the business of a covered person.[35] However, a Party can still restrict or ban the cross-border flow of information if doing so is necessary to a legitimate public policy

[29] Article 19.5 USMCA; Article 14.5 CPTPP, 2018.

[30] Article 19.5 USMCA, para. 2; Article 14.5 CPTPP, 2018, para. 2.

[31] Article 12.10 RCEP, para. 2; Article 198 TCA.

[32] Article 19.6 USMCA; Article 14.6 CPTPP, 2016; Article 12.6 RCEP; Article 206 TCA.

[33] Article 19.9 USMCA; Article 14.9 CPTPP, 2016; Article 12.5 RCEP.

[34] Articles 19.3, 19.4, 19.11, 19.12. USMCA; Articles 14.3, 14.4, 14.11, 14.13. CPTPP, 2018; Articles 12.7, 12.11, 12.14, 12.15. RCEP; Articles 201.1, 203.2, TCA.

[35] Article 19.11 USMCA; Article 14.11 CPTPP, 2018; Article 12.15 RCEP; Article 201 TCA, para. 1.

objective, as long as the measure is not used in a way that amounts to arbitrary or unreasonable discrimination or a disguised trade restriction and does not place more limits on information transfers than are necessary to achieve the goal.[36]

These RTAs promote openness in terms of availing information to consumers. USMCA promotes openness in the provision of government data as per Article 19.18 of the agreement since public access to and use of government data promotes economic and social growth, as well as competitiveness, productivity, and innovation.[37] However, TTP and RCEP do not have specific provisions dealing with open government data.

In addition, RTAs ban the imposition of customs duties on electronic transmission, which increases trade in digital products -as seen in the USMCA.[38] The elimination of customs duties on electronically transmitted digital products also includes any other fees or charges related to imports or exports.[39] While the CPTTP and TCA have similar provisions to the USMCA regarding the elimination of customs duties on electronic transmission,[40] RCEP in line with the Chinese cautious approach to e-commerce regulation adopts a different approach, stipulating that each Party shall maintain the current practices of not imposing customs duties on electronic transmissions between the Parties.[41] Moreover, the RCEP leaves room for changes in customs duties by observing that each Party may alter its practice in light of any additional WTO decisions.[42]

The USMCA and the CPTPP stipulate that no Party shall treat a digital product created, produced, published, contracted for, commissioned, or first made available on commercial terms in another Party's territory, or a digital product whose author, performer, producer, developer, or owner is a person of another Party, any less favorably than it treats other similar digital products.[43] The RCEP does not have a hard non-discrimination obligation, instead taking quite a different approach to non-discrimination in terms of the treatment of digital products, taking the China approach to e-commerce regulation by placing it under areas for dialogue on e-commerce.[44]

Moreover, obligations to increase digital trade in RTAs consider the protection of consumers or users, address unsolicited commercial communications, and provide for cyber security measures.[45] All the RTAs provide for online consumer protection,

[36] Article 19.11 USMCA, para. 2; Article 14.11 CPTPP, 2016, para. 3; Article 12.15 RCEP, para. 3.

[37] Article 19.18 USMCA, para. 1; Article 210 TCA, para. 1.

[38] Article 19.3 USMCA, para. 1.

[39] Article 19.3 ibid., para. 2.

[40] Article 19.3 ibid., para. 1; Article 14.3 CPTPP, 2018, para. 1; Article 203 TCA, para. 2.

[41] Article 12.11 RCEP, para. 1.

[42] Article 12.11 ibid., 3.

[43] Article 19.4 USMCA, para. 1; Article 14.4 CPTPP, 2018, para. 1.

[44] Article 12.16 RCEP.

[45] Articles 19.7.1, 19.8, 14.13 USMCA; Articles 14.7, 14.8, 14.14 CPTPP, 2016; Articles 12.7.2, 12.8, 12.9, 12.13 RCEP; Articles 208.1(a), 209, 703 TCA.

which is in recognition of the need to protect digital economy consumers from fraudulent or deceptive commercial activities that cause or potentially cause harm to consumers.[46]

The RTAs also cover measures to address unsolicited commercial communications, which obligates each Party to adopt or maintain measures providing for the limitation of unsolicited commercial electronic communications.[47] With similar language, the provisions under various Articles mentioned above state that Parties shall endeavor to adopt or maintain systems that allow customers to decrease or eliminate unwanted commercial electronic communications addressed to addresses other than their email addresses.[48]

All four RTAs provide for the protection of personal information or data. While USMCA and CPTTP start by acknowledging the economic and social benefits of protecting users' personal information in digital trade, as well as the role that this plays in boosting consumer trust in e-commerce, RCEP does not and instead focuses on the protection of personal information by adopting a common language with USMA and CPTTP.[49] The TCA, in line with the EU approach, acknowledges that people have a right to the protection of their personal information and privacy and that high standards in this area help build public confidence in the digital economy.[50]

The RTAs also have provisions related to cybersecurity, particularly the USMCA, CPTPP, and RCEP. Under the three RTAs, Parties shall endeavor to enhance the cybersecurity incident response capabilities of their respective national institutions.[51] In terms of disclosure of source codes, the USMCA CPTPP and TCA stipulate that as a condition for the import, distribution, sale, or use of such software, or of products including that software, no Party shall require the transfer of, or access to, a source code of software owned by a person of another Party, or to an algorithm expressed in that source code.[52]

While CPTTP, RCEP, and TCA do not have specific provisions related to interactive computer services, USMCA, in line with the US approach to e-commerce rules through disciplines that seek to constrain governments' regulatory powers has obligations covering interactive computer services.[53] Under USMCA's obligations on interactive computer services, the Parties agree that promoting interactive computer services, including for small and medium-sized businesses, is critical for the growth of digital trade.[54]

---

[46] Article 19.7 USMCA, para. 1; Article 14.7 CPTPP, 2016, para. 1; Article 12.7 RCEP, para. 2; Article 208 TCA, para. 1 (a).

[47] Article 19.13 USMCA; Article 14.14 CPTPP, 2018; Article 12.9 RCEP; Article 209 TCA.

[48] Article 19.13 USMCA; Article 14.14 CPTPP, 2018; Article 12.9 RCEP; Article 209 TCA.

[49] Article 19.8 USMCA, para. 1; Article 14.8 CPTPP, 2018, para. 1; Article 12.8 RCEP, para. 1.

[50] Article 203 TCA, para. 1.

[51] Article 19.15 USMCA, para. 1; Article 14.16 CPTPP, 2016; Article 12.13 RCEP.

[52] Article 19.16 USMCA, para. 1; Article 14.17 CPTPP, 2016, para. 1; Article TCA, para. 1.

[53] Article 19.17 USMCA.

[54] Article 19.17 ibid., para. 1.

3.3.3 Increased Transparency and Cooperation

All four RTAs have provisions related to the promotion of transparency and cooperation among Parties, which demonstrate the US, EU, and Chinese approaches to seeking cooperation to govern the digital economy. Of these RTAs, the USMCA, CPTPP, and RCEP promote cooperation for enhancing digital trade.[55] In promoting cooperation, Parties agree to share knowledge and experiences on digital commerce regulations, policy, enforcement, and compliance, including personal data protection, notably to bolster current international mechanisms for cooperating in the enforcement of privacy legislation, electronic communication security, authentication, and the use of digital tools and technologies by the government to improve government performance.[56] Conversely, the TCA binds the Parties to cooperate on regulatory matters of e-commerce, including the recognition and facilitation of interoperable electronic authentication and electronic trust services, the handling of direct marketing communications, consumer protection, and any other matter pertinent to the growth of electronic commerce, including emerging technologies.[57] However, other than other RTAs, provisions for cooperation in the TCA do not apply to a Party's privacy and data protection policies, particularly those governing cross-border transfers of personal data.[58]

3.4 Exceptions

These RTAs provide exceptions that reflect the level of negotiations and the different interests of the Parties to the agreement. The exceptions are meant to allow Parties to deviate from the obligations of the agreements due to general reasons, known as general exceptions, security reasons, known as security exceptions, and prudential reasons.[59] One of the main exceptions is the cross-border transfer of information

[55] Article 19.4 ibid.; Article 4.15 CPTPP, 2016; Article 12.4 RCEP, para. 1.

[56] Article 19.4 USMCA, para. 1; Article 4.15 CPTPP, 2016; Article 12.4 RCEP, para. 1.

[57] Article 211 TCA, para. 1.

[58] Article 211 ibid., para. 2.

[59] Article 19.17 USMCA: this is covered under Article 32.1 which deals with General Exceptions. CPTPP (2018): the exception incorporates those covered under Chapter 9 (Investment), Chapter 10 (Cross-Border Trade in Services) and Chapter 11 (Financial Services). RCEP: the exceptions are applicable to the obligations in chapter 8, covering trade in services or chapter 10, covering investment. Article 199 TCA: the exceptions apply to three areas, namely (1) measures for prudential reasons (Article 184] such as for the protection of investors, depositors, policy-holders, or persons to whom a fiduciary duty is owed by a financial service supplier; or ensuring the integrity and stability of a Party's financial system; (2) measures compatible with Article XX of GATT 1994, which are related to those necessary to protect human life or health (covered under Article 412); and (3) measures necessary for security reasons covered under Article 415.

obligations.[60] Through the exceptions, all Parties to the RTAs have the right to restrict cross-border transfer of data if such restrictions are necessary to achieve a legitimate public policy objective, and as long as such measures are not applied discriminately or impose restrictions beyond the levels necessary for achieving such legitimate policy objectives.[61]

3.5 *Special and Differential Treatment*

Provisions related to special and differential treatment in the RTAs cover different areas including interactive computer services, dispute resolution, and other obligations on paperless trading, and electronic transactions.[62] While all the other RTAs have elements of SDT, the TCA does not offer any SDT provisions. In the USMCA, provisions related to interactive computer services were not to immediately apply to Mexico but rather three years upon entry into force of the agreement.[63] Moreover, as a less developed country member with an ambition to build its digital economy, Mexico's compliance with the provisions under interactive computer services will be in line with the country's constitutional provisions, which guarantee free access to plural and timely information, access to information and communication technology, access to the services of a radio broadcast, telecommunications, and broadband internet,[64] as well as and protects freedoms of speech, opinion, ideas, and information.[65] In the CPTPP, Brunei Darussalam and Vietnam, two of the less developed Parties in this RTA, are not under obligation to apply provisions related to personal data protection before the date on which they implement their legal frameworks that protect personal data for e-commerce.[66] CPTPP also exempts Brunei Darussalam from implementation measures regarding unsolicited commercial electronic messages before implementing its laws regarding the same.[67]

The CPTPP covers SDT measures in the dispute resolution mechanism of the agreement.[68] The CPTPP SDT dispute settlement measure specifically stipulates that Malaysia and Vietnam shall not be subjected to dispute settlement under chapter

---

[60] Article 19.11 USMCA, para. 2; Article 14.11 CPTPP, 2016, para. 3; Article 12.15 RCEP, para. 3; Article 199 TCA.

[61] Article 19.11 USMCA, para. 2; Article 14.11 CPTPP, 2016, para. 3; RCEP, para. 3; Article 199 TCA.

[62] Articles 19.17, 19.9, 19.5 Annex 19-A.2. USMCA; Articles 14.5, 14.11 CPTPP, 2016; Articles 12.5, 12.6,12.15, 12.17 RCEP, para. 3.

[63] Annex 19-A USMCA, para. 1.

[64] Article 6, Mexico's Constitution of 1917 with Amendments through 2015 (1917), available at: https://www.constituteproject.org/constitution/Mexico_2015.pdf?lang=en.

[65] Article 7 ibid.

[66] Article 14.8 CPTPP, 2018.

[67] Article 14.14 ibid.

[68] Article 14.18 ibid.

28 of the agreement concerning their obligations related to the non-discriminatory treatment of digital products, and cross-border transfer of information by electronic means for a period of two years after the date of the agreement's entry into force.[69] Vietnam is further exempted from dispute settlement under obligations related to the location of computing facilities, for an additional two years after the date of entry into force.[70] For the RCEP, although the agreement provides for dispute resolution, there are no specific SDT provisions.[71]

The most extensive SDT in the RTAs is in the RCEP. For instance, obligations on paperless trading,[72] electronic authentication, and electronic signature[73] exempt poorer countries namely Cambodia, Lao PDR, and Myanmar for a period of five years upon the agreement entering into force. In addition, the agreement exempts the three countries from the obligation to implement provisions related to the protection of consumer fraud,[74] protection of personal information,[75] or recourse against suppliers of unsolicited commercial electronic messages[76] until five years after the agreement enters into force. Regarding recourse for unsolicited commercial electronic messages, RCEP exempts Brunei Darussalam from implementing any measure for a period of three years from the date of entry into effect of the Agreement.[77] Regarding the domestic regulatory framework, the RCEP exempts Cambodia from maintaining or adopting electronic transactions for a period of five years upon the agreement entering into force.[78] Even greater flexibility is provided for obligations related to the location of computing facilities and cross-border transfer of information where Cambodia, Lao PDR, Myanmar, and Vietnam maintain the right to require the location of computing facilities within their respective jurisdictions for a period of five years upon entry into force of the agreement.[79] Moreover, Cambodia, Lao PDR, and Myanmar are provided with an additional three years to require the domestic location of cloud computing facilities as a condition for companies conducting businesses within their territories if necessary.[80]

In terms of data localization and data privacy, the CPTPP's approach is more liberal than the RCEP's, but not as much as the USMCA's. The RCEP's approach acknowledges the Parties' freedom to implement restrictive measures when they

[69] Article 14.18 CPTPP, 2016, paras. 1 and 2.

[70] Article 14.18 ibid., para. 2.

[71] Article 12.17 RCEP.

[72] Article 12.5 ibid.

[73] Article 12.6 ibid.

[74] Article 12.7 ibid., para. 6.

[75] Article 12.8 ibid., para. 1.

[76] Article 12.9 ibid., para. 2.

[77] Article 12.9 ibid.

[78] Article 12.10 RCEP.

[79] Article 12.14 ibid., para. 2; Article 12.15 ibid.

[80] Article 12.14 RCEP, para. 2.

consider their essential security interests.[81] These obligations also have exceptions and important special and differential treatment obligations, especially for RCEP.[82] Other critical issues in the RTAs, particularly the USMCA, cover regulation for SMEs, state-owned enterprises, and data localization, which could set a precedence for future digital trade agreements.[83]

4 Spillover Effects of e-Commerce Provisions in RTAs on African MSMEs

This section examines the spillover effects of e-commerce provisions in USMC, TPP, and RCEP on MSMEs in African countries using six factors as normative criteria. These include (1) facilitating imports and exports,[84] (2) addressing tariffs as a form of government revenue,[85] (3) attracting investment,[86] (4) preserving policy space for digital industrialization,[87] (5) providing for development assistance,[88] and (6) providing for different rights and obligations according to development levels.[89] The six factors have been chosen for analysis because they incorporate sustainable development issues in addressing e-commerce,[90] Moreover, several international policy processes focus on the impact of digitalization on industrial activities, foreign direct investment, trade, and sustainable development.[91] I elaborate below.

4.1 Facilitating Imports and Exports

The RTAs provide opportunities for increased imports and exports among the Parties. Despite not using the term non-discrimination, the regulations on

[81] Article 12.15 ibid., 3 (b).

[82] Articles 12.15.2, 12.15.3 (b), 12.14 (2-3). RCEP.

[83] Gantz (2018), p. 1.

[84] Terzi (2011), p. 747.

[85] Darsinouei and Kaukab (2017), p. 21.

[86] Foster and Azmeh (2019), p. 4.

[87] Mayer (2009), p. 337; Chang (2006), p. 630.

[88] Development assistance in this case means building and strengthening provisions in an agreement to better achieve the objectives of the Aid for Trade initiative, which was launched at the Hong Kong Ministerial Conference in December 2005. See: WT/MIN(15)/DEC.

[89] This borrows the approach from the Trade Facilitation agreement, WT/L/940.

[90] Leal-Arcas et al. (2015), p. 99.

[91] UN, "Maximizing the Development Gains from E-Commerce and the Digital Economy," Note by the Secretariat, TD/B/EDE/1/2 (Geneva: United Nations Conference on Trade and Development, July 26, 2017), 9, available at: https://unctad.org/meetings/en/SessionalDocuments/tdb_ede1d2_en.pdf.

cross-border data flow in the chapters on digital trade arguably have the same effect.[92] RTAs increase import and export through trade creation since they generate opportunities for distance teaching and education for instructors, remote employment for office workers, online shopping without leaving home, and delivery of cashless takeaways, especially during the COVID-19 pandemic -all of which demonstrate the enormous potential of cross-border e-commerce and the digital economy among Parties.[93] However, this increased trade may lead to trade diversion as previous would-be markets for African MSMEs have less trade restrictive and e-commerce facilitative frameworks than other Parties to the RTAs. Therefore, for African countries, increased imports and exports for both goods and services resulting from the RTAs reduce their potential markets for trade in both goods and services. The reduced potential markets result from the fact that more market opportunities are created by the RTAs through reduced digital trade barriers while such barriers remain for Third Parties.

4.2 *Addressing Tariffs as a form of Government Revenue*

The RTA provisions on tariffs are likely to inform the position of Parties to the agreements in the WTO e-commerce negotiations, particularly the 1998 Work Programme that has since been extending the moratorium on customs duties on electronic transmissions.[94] Parties to the RTAs, being influential WTO, Members are likely to use their RTA rulebook as motivation for making the WTO moratorium on customs duties on electronic transmission permanent. If the moratorium is made permanent, African countries, which rely on customs duties for revenue generation, may continue to lose revenues, denying them opportunities to generate revenue for building capabilities in the digital economy for the benefit of MSMEs.[95] Moreover, the loss of customs revenue to Sub-Saharan nations has increased over time, doubling the potential loss of tariff revenue to WTO developed-country Members,[96] potentially denying them opportunities to generate revenue for building capabilities in the digital economy for the benefit of MSMEs.[97]

[92]Lester (2022), "Non-Discriminatory Treatment of Digital Trade Products in the EU-NZ FTA", available at: https://ielp.worldtradelaw.net/2022/07/non-discrimination-on-digital-trade-in-the-eu-nz-fta.html.

[93]Liu et al. (2022), p. 3.

[94]WTO, "Work Programme on Electronic Commerce: General Council Decision Adopted on 10 December 2019," December 11, 2019b, available at: https://docs.wto.org/dol2fe/Pages/SS/directdoc.aspx?filename=q:/WT/L/1079.pdf&Open=True.

[95]Banga (2019), p. 23.

[96]Abendin and Duan (2021), p. 716.

[97]Banga (2019), p. 23.

4.3 Attracting Investment

RTA e-commerce chapters have no specific provisions for attracting investment. However, the agreements play a significant role in attracting investment in the digital economy of Parties, since they cover key obligations on digitalizing trade and promoting trade in digital products. This is also evidenced by increased interest from large investment banks and sovereign investors in the digital economy.[98] RTAs can enable Parties to attract investment in their services sector such as telecommunications and logistics, as well as professional, financial, and computer-related services which are all crucial for building capabilities in the digital economy.[99] The RTAs would be expected to increase trade opportunities, incentivizing investments in the digital economy since, arguably, the future of trade and investment decisions lie in digital trade, which can use blockchain technology, artificial intelligence, and the Internet of Things to steer the spread of e-commerce and cross-border payments.[100]

The RTAs build a global network of digital trade rules that reinforce the dominant position of big technology firms such as those from the US and China, hindering the emergence of smaller companies such as MSMEs from African countries.[101] As a result, RTAs will build even more capacities for digital economy big players to enable them to widen their dominance in the respective regions, and possibly expand this dominance to African countries through investment.[102]

4.4 Preserving Policy Space for Digital Industrialization

RTA e-commerce rules appear to have been carefully crafted to limit the government's ability to regulate various issues in the digital economy.[103] These issues, under regulation in the digital economy as per RTAs, have potential spillover effects on the policy space of African countries. While Parties to the RTAs enforce these rules, they are likely to determine global standards and practices, since they encourage countries to provide e-commerce businesses with specific technical controls and standards to implement.[104]

RTA e-commerce provisions promote market access opportunities for big players in the digital economy with less attention to smaller players from developing

[98] Peters (2022) p. 1.

[99] Tham (2022) "Harnessing RCEP to Harvest ASEAN's Unicorns", available at: https://fulcrum.sg/harnessing-rcep-to-harvest-aseans-unicorns/.

[100] Peters (2022), p. 7.

[101] Alamilla and Cabañas (2022); Liu et al. (2022), p. 1.

[102] James (2020), p. 35.

[103] Monteiro and Teh (2017), p. 4.

[104] Bieron and Ahmed (2012), p. 568.

countries, Africa inclusive. For instance, it has been argued that implementing a strong TPP and developing other high-standard agreements will help ensure that US businesses, many of which pioneered the Internet and other digital technologies, have more open access to their partners' markets and can transfer data across international borders more seamlessly.[105] Such an argument carries much significance considering that RTAs are dominated by big players such as the US and China, meaning that by design, they do not focus on the offensive trade interests of MSMEs from African countries. Despite not focusing on their interests, MSMEs from African countries would be expected to abide by standards set by the RTAs if they are to trade with Parties to such agreements.

4.5 *Provide for Development Assistance*

The RTAs do not provide for development assistance but rather cooperation and capacity building, ranging from obligations such as market access and regulatory issues to overcoming obstacles faced by MSMEs' participation in e-commerce.[106] Cooperation allows parties to the agreements to share information, coordinate both domestic and international policy measures, and negotiate the removal of e-commerce barriers.[107] The RTAs provide an avenue for Parties to cooperate and build digital capabilities at the respective national levels, which in turn increases the competitiveness of companies from these countries. Such cooperation measures would widen the digital divide since African countries, in addition to not being Parties to the RTAs, have low levels of digitalization and would see their MSMEs having to compete with counterparts from countries benefiting from cooperation with other established players in the digital economy.

4.6 *Providing for Different Rights and Obligations According to Development Levels*

The spill-over effects of RTAs regarding the provision for different rights and obligations according to development levels are two-fold. On one hand, the approach which ignores SDT, taken by USMCA and TPP, if it is to shape the global standards for e-commerce agreements, would mean that such agreements would be

[105] Buxbaum (2016), "TPP Critical for Ensuring Digital Trade", available at: https://www.globaltrademag.com/tpp-critical-for-ensuring-digital-trade/.

[106] Herman (2010), p. 15.

[107] Leblond (2022), "USMCA Forward: Building a More Competitive, Inclusive, and Sustainable North American Economy – Digital", available at: https://www.brookings.edu/essay/usmca-forward-building-a-more-competitive-inclusive-and-sustainable-north-american-economy-digital/.

designed in such a way that African countries would lack flexibility periods to build their domestic capacity for MSME growth and competitiveness for a longer transition. On the other hand, however, if the RCEP approach is to inform global standards for e-commerce agreements,[108] it implies that African countries have a leeway to demand longer transition periods similar to the provisions under Article 66.1 of the Trade-Related Aspects of Intellectual Property Rights (TRIPS) agreement.[109]

5 The Effect of RTAs on e-Commerce Negotiations at the WTO and What They Mean for African MSMEs

Adopting the RTA e-commerce would be a big step forward for trade governance, especially given the fact that CPTPP and the USMCA both contain comprehensive and binding next-generation standards for e-commerce.[110] The USMCA is aimed at promoting and facilitating the development of digital trade and the US is working on establishing rules and dialogues governing digital trade with its partners.[111] Other big players in the digital economy, for instance, China and India joining hands in RCEP, also indicate that the ASEAN region is stepping up into a leadership role in global trade negotiations.[112] As a result, RTAs shape the WTO e-commerce negotiations as per the e-commerce negotiations consolidated negotiating text that was released by WTO Members under the Joint Statements Initiative (JSI) on e-commerce.[113] The RTAs are also likely to shape e-commerce negotiations under the AfCFTA.[114]

5.1 *The Effect of RTAs in Shaping the WTO e-Commerce Agreement*

The RTAs members, except Cambodia and Viet Nam, are active members of the WTO JSI on e-commerce negotiations, which increases the likelihood of shaping a

[108]Umezaki (2022).

[109]TRIPS: Agreement on Trade-Related Aspects of Intellectual Property Rights, Apr. 15, 1994, Marrakesh Agreement Establishing the World Trade Organization, Annex 1C, 1869 U.N.T.S. 299, 33 I.L.M. 1197 (1994).

[110]Froese (2019), p. 789.

[111]Nesamani (2021), "Talking Trade with Ambassador Tai", available at: https://nwasianweekly.com/2021/08/talking-trade-with-ambassador-tai/.

[112]Tobin (2019), "Explained: The Difference between the RCEP and the CPTPP", available at: https://www.scmp.com/week-asia/geopolitics/article/3017487/explained-difference-between-rcep-and-cptpp.

[113]WTO, WTO Electronic Commerce Negotiations Consolidated Negotiating Text -December 2020, INF/ECOM/62 (World Trade Organization, December 7, 2020b).

[114]Banga et al. (2021), p. 15.

future WTO e-commerce agreement.[115] Moreover, the three coordinators for the JSI on e-commerce Japan, Australia, and Singapore, are all members of the RCEP.[116]

The e-commerce chapters in RTAs play a dual role in the landscape of trade rules in the digital era. On the one hand, they represent an attempt to compensate for the lack of progress in the WTO and remedy the ensuing uncertainties while on the other hand, they also set the standards for WTO e-commerce rules.[117]

RTA provisions included in the e-commerce negotiations consolidated negotiating text include provisions on paperless trading, electronic authentication and electronic signatures, customs duties, cross-border data flows, location of computing facilities, consumer protection, personal information protection, transparency, cybersecurity, and dispute settlement, all of which are similar or identical to the RTAs. Due to the similar nature of RTA e-commerce provisions to the JSI consolidated negotiating text, the JSI proposals do not explicitly cover the most critical issue for bridging the digital divide capacity building. Instead, the JSI takes the best endeavor language for cooperation and capacity building that appears not to offer meaningful outcomes for the growth and development of MSMEs from African countries.[118]

5.2 The Effect of RTAs in Shaping the AfCFTA e-Commerce Protocol

Under Phase III of the AfCFTA negotiation, an e-commerce protocol is to be included.[119] RTAs shape e-commerce issues related to definitions, application of WTO rules, non-discrimination, transparency, and a moratorium on customs duties on e-commerce transactions.[120] It also deals with domestic regulation issues such as regulatory barriers, electronic authentication, and consumer protection.[121] Consequently, market access, rules and regulations, and facilitation are the main issues identified as forming the core structure of a future AfCFTA e-commerce protocol.[122] What is, however, unclear at present is how African countries can balance their

---

[115] WTO, "Joint Statement on Electronic Commerce," WT/L/1056 (World Trade Organization, January 25, 2019a), available at: https://docs.wto.org/dol2fe/Pages/SS/directdoc.aspx?filename=q:/WT/L/1056.pdf&Open=True.

[116] Oh (2021), pp. 417–18.

[117] Burri (2021), p. 82.

[118] Ismail (2020), p. 21.

[119] Banga et al. (2021), p. 10.

[120] Ibid., 15.

[121] Herman (2010), p. 4.

[122] Sasi (2022), "AfCFTA Protocol on Digital Trade: Core Provisions That Drafters Should Address - Fie-Consult", available at: https://fieconsult.com/afcfta-protocol-on-digital-trade-core-provisions-that-drafters-should-address/.

digital development ambition to bridge the digital divide, build domestic MSME competitiveness on one side, and the non-discrimination principles as well as the other obligations in the RTAs that constrain the policy space for digital industrialization on the other side.[123]

Since African countries are at relatively similar levels of development, it may appear that the AfCFTA e-commerce protocol application of non-discrimination principles is not a complex issue. However, tackling non-discrimination in the e-commerce agreement is important because the world's largest digital platforms, which are primarily established in the US and China, display monopolistic trends and growing market dominance due to network effects, data access, and economies of scale and scope.[124] This means that if the AfCFTA e-commerce protocol adopts the RTA approach, it would lock in the dominance of external big players in Africa's e-commerce agenda while making it harder for African MSMEs to build a competitive edge in the domestic markets before taking advantage of international markets.

The Africa Group[125] has always emphasized that e-commerce and digital trade must be developed in an inclusive way to avoid exacerbating the current global trade imbalances.[126] The Africa Group's position at the WTO implies that the AfCFTA e-commerce protocol is likely to adopt the SDT approach taken by RCEP since countries such as Kenya are more developed and attract more investment in the digital economy than others such as Uganda.[127] Moreover, RCEP recognizes that its members' readiness for quick adoption of e-commerce obligations varies, hence it provides flexibility.[128] Therefore, future free trade agreements such as the AfCFTA e-commerce protocol would be expected to adopt the RCEP approach and include robust exceptions for less developed county members inclusive of their MSMEs from complying with certain provisions of the agreement.[129]

The RTAs also have the potential to shape the AfCFTA e-commerce protocol, not only by what they cover but by what they do not cover, especially on the issue of cooperation and capacity building. The RTA approach for cooperation is more oriented toward dialogue and collaboration but the AfCFTA e-commerce protocol,

[123]The e-commerce agreement issues constraining policy space include the provisions to digitalise trade, increase trade in digital products and the obligations therein, as per the JSI on e-commerce consolidated negotiating text and the e-commerce chapters in the various RTAs.

[124]UNCTAD, Digital Economy Report 2021: Cross-Border Data Flows and Development: For Whom the Data Flow, UNCTAD/DER/2021 (New York: United Nations Conference on Trade and Development), 22, available at: https://unctad.org/system/files/official-document/der2021_en.pdf.

[125]This is a group of WTO Members and Observers from Africa. More information is available at: https://www.wto.org/english/tratop_e/dda_e/negotiating_groups_e.htm.

[126]WTO, Strengthening the WTO to Promote Development and Inclusivity: Communication from the African Group, Cuba and India, WT/GC/W/778/Rev.3 (World Trade Organization, December 4, 2020a), para. 4.3.

[127]Collins (2022), "Can Uganda's Tech Scene Compete with Kenya?", available at: https://african.business/2022/04/technology-information/ugandas-tech-scene-slowly-matures/.

[128]Oh (2021), p. 423.

[129]Bieron and Ahmed (2012), p. 566.

considering the low levels of digital capabilities in the continent compared to other continents needs more capacity building.[130] Moreover, since many small developing countries need support to reach the necessary scale and critical mass for digitalization, capacity-building efforts may be better addressed through a regional approach.[131]

Globally, different countries are at various stages of readiness to participate in and profit from the e-commerce and data-driven digital economy.[132] Most of the developing and least developed countries, especially in Africa must improve their ability to digitalize and process data into digital intelligence to support their MSMEs which emphasizes the importance of capacity building to bridge the digital and data barriers.[133]

6 Conclusion

There are 193 RTAs with explicit e-commerce provisions, with the USMCA, CPTPP, RCEP, and TCA being the most significant to African countries. This chapter examined the e-commerce chapters of the RTAs with the aim of identifying the main provisions and the potential effects of these RTAs on the WTO e-commerce negotiations as well as the AfCFTA e-commerce protocol. The RTAs do not cover SDTs, a critical issue for African countries, except for the RCEP. They instead focus on cooperation among the parties to address barriers to SME participation in e-commerce. The RTAs are likely to play a significant role in setting standards for e-commerce rules both at the WTO and the AfCFTA level. These standards converge in areas where the Parties agree on liberalization to facilitate digital trade but also differ in areas where the Parties take more protectionist and cautious measures to e-commerce regulation. At the WTO, the JSI on e-commerce consolidated negotiating text has similar provisions to the RTAs, with the three coordinators-Australia, Japan, and Singapore all Parties to the RTAs. If the RTAs shape e-commerce rules in their current form, it is likely to offer more opportunities for bigger players in the digital economy, especially from the US and China to lock in their dominance of global e-commerce while making it harder for African countries to build the competitiveness of the MSMEs to take advantage of the opportunities brought by e-commerce.

[130]UNCTAD, Digital Economy Report 2021: Cross-Border Data Flows and Development: For Whom the Data Flow, UNCTAD/DER/2021, p. 190, available at: https://unctad.org/system/files/official-document/der2021_en.pdf.

[131]Ibid.

[132]Ibid., 189.

[133]Ibid.

References

Abendin S, Duan P (2021) Global E-commerce talks at the WTO: positions on selected issues of the United States, European Union, China, and Japan. World Trade Rev 20(5):707–724. https://doi.org/10.1017/S1474745621000094

Alamilla M, Cabaña G (2022) Digital Trade under the USMCA: A Modern Opportunity for North American Economic Growth. Wilson Center, March 21, 2022. Available at: https://www.wilsoncenter.org/article/digital-trade-under-usmca-modern-opportunity-north-american-economic-growth

Banga K et al (2021) E-Commerce in Preferential Trade Agreements: Implications for African Firms and the AfCFTA. Research Report. ODI Report, 2021. Available at: https://www.econstor.eu/handle/10419/251135

Banga R (2019) Growing Trade in Electronic Transmissions: Implications for the South. UNCTAD/SER.RP/2019/1/Rev.1. Geneva: United Nations Conference for Trade and Development

Bieron B, Ahmed U (2012) Regulating E-commerce through international policy: understanding the international trade law issues of E-Commerce. J World Trade 46(3):545–570

Borchert I, Morita-Jaeger M (2021) Taking Stock of the UK-EU Trade and Cooperation Agreement: Trade in Services and Digital Trade. Briefing Paper. Available at: https://blogs.sussex.ac.uk/uktpo/files/2021/01/BP53.pdf

Burri M (2021) Towards a new treaty on digital trade. J World Trade 1(55):77–100

Buxbaum P (2016) TPP Critical for Ensuring Digital Trade. Global Trade Magazine, July 20, 2016. Available at: https://www.globaltrademag.com/tpp-critical-for-ensuring-digital-trade/

Chang HJ (2006) Policy space in historical perspective with special reference to trade and industrial policies. Econ Polit Weekly 41(7):627–633

Chaurasia S (2018) Impact of TPP's E-Commerce Chapter on APEC's E-Commerce. Asia-Pacific Economic Cooperation Secretariat, Singapore. Available at: https://www.academia.edu/38115684/Impact_of_TPPs_E_commerce_Chapter_on_APECs_E_commerce_APEC_Electronic_Commerce_Steering_Group

Collins T (2022) Can Uganda's Tech Scene Compete with Kenya? African Business, April 8, 2022. https://african.business/2022/04/technology-information/ugandas-tech-scene-slowly-matures/

Darsinouei AE, Kaukab R (2017) Understanding E-Commerce Issues in Trade Agreements: A Development Perspective Towards MC11 and Beyond. Research Study. CUTS International, Geneva, 2017. Available at: http://www.cuts-geneva.org/pdf/STUDY%20-%20E-Commerce%20Towards%20MC11.pdf

E-Commerce Law of the People's Republic of China (Adopted at the Fifth Session of the Standing Committee of the 13th National People's Congress on August 31, 2018). Available at: https://ipkey.eu/sites/default/files/documents/resources/PRC_E-Commerce_Law.pdf

Fefer R (2020) Internet Regimes and WTO E-Commerce Negotiations. Congressional Research Service, Washington DC

Foster C, Azmeh S (2019) E-Commerce and the African Continental Free Trade Agreement (AfCFTA). Discussion Paper. Pretoria, South Africa: GEG Africa. Available at: https://infomediation.net/wp-content/uploads/2020/10/Geg_final.pdf

Froese MD (2019) Digital trade and dispute settlement in RTAs: an evolving standard? J World Trade 53(5):783–810

Gantz, D.A. (2018) The United States-Mexico-Canada Agreement: overview and analysis. Baker Institute. Report no.12.11.18. Rice University's Baker Institute for Public Policy, Houston, Texas

Government of Australia Department of Foreign Affairs and Trade. Comprehensive and Progressive Agreement for Trans-Pacific Partnership (CPTPP). Australian Government Department of Foreign Affairs and Trade. Available at: https://www.dfat.gov.au/trade/agreements/in-force/cptpp/comprehensive-and-progressive-agreement-for-trans-pacific-partnership

Government of Australia Department of Foreign Affairs and Trade. CPTPP Text and Associated Documents. Australian Government Department of Foreign Affairs and Trade. Available at: https://www.dfat.gov.au/trade/agreements/in-force/cptpp/official-documents

Government of Australia Department of Foreign Affairs and Trade. Regional Comprehensive Economic Partnership. Available at: https://www.dfat.gov.au/trade/agreements/in-force/rcep

Hallak I (2022) EU-UK Trade and Cooperation Agreement. Legislative Train. European Parliament, June 23, 2022. Available at: https://www.europarl.europa.eu/legislative-train/carriage/eu-uk-trade-and-cooperation-agreement/report?sid=6001

Herman L (2010) Multilateralising regionalism: the case of E-commerce. OECD Trade Policy Papers. OECD, Paris

[Japan] Ministry of Economy, Trade and Industry. Regional Comprehensive Economic Partnership (RCEP) Signed. Available at: https://www.meti.go.jp/english/press/2020/1115_001.html

Huang J (2017) Comparison of E-Commerce regulations in Chinese and American FTAs: converging approaches, diverging contents, and polycentric directions? Neth Int Law Rev 64(2): 309–337

Ismail Y (2020) E-Commerce in the World Trade Organization: history and latest developments in the negotiations under the joint statement. International Institute for Sustainable Development and CUTS International, Geneva

James D (2020) Digital trade rules; a disastrous new constitution for the global economy written by and for Big Tech. Rosa-Luxemburg-Stiftung, Brussels. Available at: https://www.rosalux.eu/en/article/1742.digital-trade-rules.html

Leal-Arcas R et al (2015) Strengthening sustainable development through regional trade agreements. In: Marx A (ed) Wouters, J. Edward Elgar Publishing, Global governance through trade, pp 92–123

Leblond P (2022) USMCA Forward: Building a More Competitive, Inclusive, and Sustainable North American Economy – Digital. Brookings (blog), February 28, 2022. Available at: https://www.brookings.edu/essay/usmca-forward-building-a-more-competitive-inclusive-and-sustainable-north-american-economy-digital/

Lester S (2022) Non-Discriminatory Treatment of Digital Trade Products in the EU-NZ FTA. International Economic Law and Policy Blog (blog). Available at: https://ielp.worldtradelaw.net/2022/07/non-discrimination-on-digital-trade-in-the-eu-nz-fta.html

Liu Y et al (2022) Modelling the impact of RCEP agreement on the economic and trade environment of Beijing. Disc Dyn Nat and Soc 2022:1–7. https://doi.org/10.1155/2022/9237940

Mayer J (2009) Policy space: what, for what, and where? Dev Policy Rev 27(4):373–395. https://doi.org/10.1111/j.1467-7679.2009.00452.x

Monteiro J, Teh R (2017) Provisions on Electronic Commerce in Regional Trade Agreements. WTO Working Paper ERSD-2017-11. World Trade Organization

Nesamani J (2021) Talking Trade with Ambassador Tai. Northwest Asian Weekly, August 19, 2021. Available at: https://nwasianweekly.com/2021/08/talking-trade-with-ambassador-tai/

Oh E (2021) Digital Trade Regulation in the Asia-Pacific: where does it stand? Comparing the RCEP E-Commerce Chapter with the CPTPP and the JSI. Legal Issues Econ Integr 48(4): 403–430

Peters MA (2022) Digital trade, digital economy and the digital economy partnership agreement (DEPA). Educ Philos Theory 1–9. https://doi.org/10.1080/00131857.2022.2041413

Petropoulos G (2020) Socio-economic effects of digital trade and artificial intelligence on EU industries including their value chains and EU imports and exports with major trade partners. In: Reiss B (ed) Two briefings and an in-depth analysis on data flows, artificial intelligence and international trade: impacts and prospects for the value chains of the future. Policy Department for External Relations, Directorate General for External Policies of the Union, Belgium, pp 7–11. https://doi.org/10.2861/23699

Regulation (EU) 2016/679 of the European Parliament and of the Council of 27 April 2016 on the protection of natural persons with regard to the processing of personal data and on the free

movement of such data, and repealing Directive 95/46/EC (General Data Protection Regulation), L 119/1 § (2016)
Sasi I (2022) AfCFTA Protocol on Digital Trade: Core Provisions That Drafters Should Address - Fie-Consult" May 10, 2022. Available at: https://fieconsult.com/afcfta-protocol-on-digital-trade-core-provisions-that-drafters-should-address/ (last accessed: 21 May 2022)
Terzi N (2011) The impact of E-commerce on international trade and employment. Procedia-Soc Behav Sci 24:745–753
Tham Y (2022) Harnessing RCEP to Harvest ASEAN's Unicorns. FULCRUM, February 15, 2022. Available at: https://fulcrum.sg/harnessing-rcep-to-harvest-aseans-unicorns/
Tobin M (2019) Explained: The Difference between the RCEP and the CPTPP. South China Morning Post, July 6, 2019. Available at: https://www.scmp.com/week-asia/geopolitics/article/3017487/explained-difference-between-rcep-and-cptpp
Umezaki S (2022) E-Commerce Provisions in the Regional Comprehensive Economic Partnership: A Milestone for a Global Rule?" Institute of Developing Economies, August 2022. Available at: https://www.ide.go.jp/English/ResearchColumns/Columns/2022/so_umezaki.html
UNCTAD (2021) Digital Economy Report 2021: Cross-Border Data Flows and Development: For Whom the Data Flow. UNCTAD/DER/2021. New York: United Nations Conference on Trade and Development. Available at: https://unctad.org/system/files/official-document/der2021_en.pdf
United Nations (2017) Maximizing the Development Gains from E-Commerce and the Digital Economy. Note by the Secretariat. TD/B/EDE/1/2. Geneva: United Nations Conference on Trade and Development, July 26, 2017. Available at: https://unctad.org/meetings/en/SessionalDocuments/tdb_ede1d2_en.pdf
Willemyns I (2020) Agreement forthcoming? A comparison of EU, US, and Chinese RTAs in Times of Plurilateral E-Commerce negotiations. J Int Econ Law 23(1):221–244
Wragg E (2020) USMCA: A High-Water Mark for Digital Trade? Global Trade Review (GTR). available at: https://www.gtreview.com/magazine/volume-18-issue-3/usmca-high-water-mark-digital-trade/
WTO (2019a) Joint Statement on Electronic Commerce. WT/L/1056. World Trade Organization, January 25, 2019. Available at: https://docs.wto.org/dol2fe/Pages/SS/directdoc.aspx?filename=q:/WT/L/1056.pdf&Open=True
WTO (2019b) Work Programme on Electronic Commerce: General Council Decision Adopted on 10 December 2019, December 11, 2019. Available at: https://docs.wto.org/dol2fe/Pages/SS/directdoc.aspx?filename=q:/WT/L/1079.pdf&Open=True
WTO (2020a) Strengthening the WTO to Promote Development and Inclusivity: Communication from the African Group, Cuba and India. WT/GC/W/778/Rev.3. World Trade Organization, December 4, 2020. Available at: https://web.wtocenter.org.tw/DownFile.aspx?pid=348799&fileNo=0
WTO (2020b) WTO Electronic Commerce Negotiations Consolidated Negotiating Text -December 2020. INF/ECOM/62. World Trade Organization, December 7, 2020. Available at: https://www.bilaterals.org/IMG/pdf/wto_plurilateral_ecommerce_draft_consolidated_text.pdf
WTO (2022) Regional Trade Agreements Database. World Trade Organization. Available at: http://rtais.wto.org/UI/PublicMaintainRTAHome.aspx

Martin Luther Munu is a PhD Candidate at the Institute for Globalisation and International Regulation (IGIR), Faculty of Law, Maastricht University. His research focuses on e-commerce negotiations at the WTO and their potential impact on micro, small and medium-sized enterprises growth in African countries. At Maastricht University, he taught and supervised students in various courses namely: International Relations: Themes and Theories; Skills: Legal Research and Reasoning; and International Trade Law: Globalisation Trade and Development. Previously, he worked with the Economic Policy Research Centre (EPRC) in Uganda researching on trade and regional integration issues and the Southern and Eastern African Trade, Information and Negotiations Institute (SEATINI) on bilateral and multilateral trade negotiations. Martin has attended and made several presentations during stakeholder initiatives seeking to promote development outcomes in the multilateral trading system. He also worked with Consumer Unity & Trust Society (CUTS) International, Nairobi on trade and development issues.

Part III
Public Policy and International Economic Law

Pursuing Geo-political Interests Through Investment Policies: Undesirable and (Un)feasible

Najibullah Zamani

Contents

Abstract The post-Cold War era saw the foundations being laid for a new global order in which the realms of politics and security on the one hand and the economic domain on the other, were relatively well-defined and distinct from one another. Security issues no longer dictated international relations and trade and investment decisions were mainly taken on the basis of economic considerations. However, recent developments suggest a significant shift with the emergence of geo-economics. In the contemporary environment, states increasingly pursue geo-political and security interests through trade and investment policies, thereby diverging from traditional reliance on political and military policies. Consequently, geopolitical power is increasingly derived from and dependent on economic power.

While employing trade and investment policies to address geopolitical and security matters presents an appealing and potentially effective alternative to direct military confrontation, this approach simultaneously poses challenges and partially undermines the established liberal international economic order and its associated institutions and norms developed in the post-Cold War era. Moreover, despite the significant influence of geopolitical and strategic motives in state decisions to enter into preferential trade agreements, international economic law offers limited leeway

N. Zamani (✉)
Radboud University, Nijmegen, The Netherlands
e-mail: najib.zamani@ru.nl

M. de Amstalden et al. (eds.), *International Economic Law*, Special Issue,
https://doi.org/10.1007/978-3-031-41996-6_8

for states to employ trade and investment mechanisms in pursuit of geopolitical and security objectives once such agreements have been concluded.

Keywords International economic law · Liberal international economic order · Geo-economics · Geopolitics · Politicization · Securitization

1 Introduction

With the collapse of the Soviet-Union, the end of the Cold war, the adoption of the General Agreement on Trade in Services (GATS) and the creation of the World Trade Organization (WTO), the world entered in the 1990s a new era of 'true economic liberalism' and (hyper) economic globalization. The term economic liberalism is frequently employed to make a reference to the classical school of economic thought, which began in 1776 when Adam Smith published *the Wealth of Nations*.[1] One of the main tenets of economic liberalism is a strong support for a market economy which should be based on a free, competitive market without protectionism and the law of comparative advantage.[2] While Adam Smith was the first to propose free foreign trade without impediments, David Ricardo offered the underlying economic arguments for it with his law of comparative advantage.[3] According to this economic law, free trade between states is mutually beneficial even if one of the states can produce all goods more efficiently than the other states.[4] The law of comparative advantage thus formed the basic rationale for trade liberalization. Accordingly, a liberal international economic order was established that was rules-based and "enshrined in institutions such as the United Nations and norms such as multilateralism".[5] In this liberal international economic order, the realms of geopolitics and economics were relatively well separated and trade and investment decisions were mainly taken on economic grounds.

In recent years however, there has been a visible tendency wherein states through trade and investment policies pursue geopolitical interests that were formerly pursued through military or political policies. Trade and investment policies have thus taken on the characteristics of tools rather than being mere objectives. A prime example of this tendency has been the trade restrictions put in place by China vis-à-vis Lithuania. According to China, these trade restrictions are justified because Lithuania has violated the one-China principle.

In the present chapter, it will be argued that this process of geo-politicization is undermining international economic law and that states currently have, little to no

---

[1]Smith (1776).

[2]Bruce and Grant (2013), p. 53.

[3]Ricardo (1817).

[4]It is outside the scope of the present chapter to discuss (in depth) the law of comparative advantage. See, for such a discussion Bruce and Grant (2013), *supra* note 2, pp. 123–126.

[5]Ikenberry (2011), p. 56; Ikenberry (2018), p. 12.

room to pursue geopolitical interests through trade and investment policies. In order to build this argument, it is first of all necessary to make some preliminary observations and provide some definitions (Sect. 2). Then in Sect. 3, the concept of geo-economics, which refers to the geo-politicization of trade and investment policies, will be discussed. Section 4 will discuss the possibilities for states to pursue geopolitical interests under international economic law. A distinction will be made in this regard between the pre- and post-conclusion phases of Preferential Trade Agreements (PTAs). Section 5 will explain why geo-economics is undermining international economic law and finally, Sect. 6 will conclude.[6]

2 Preliminary Observations

In order to define and demark the scope of the present article, it is necessary to make some preliminary observations. As stated earlier, geo-economics is the use of trade and investment policies to pursue geo-political interests. The focus of the present chapter is solely on investment policies and more specifically on commercial presence. Commercial presence is one of the four modes through which services are supplied. Pursuant to Article I(2)(c) of the GATS, Mode 3 is concerned with the supply of a service *by a service supplier of one Member, through commercial presence in the territory of any other Member*. Mode 3 thus entails the commercial presence of a company from one Member on the territory of another Member. Commercial presence means thus that a service supplier of one Member (Member A) provides services through a professional establishment (i.e. commercial presence) on the territory of another Member (Member B). The fact that services are provided through a fixed establishment, implies that the commercial presence (i.e. professional establishment) on the territory of Member B, must be owned or controlled by a natural or juridical person from Member A (i.e. the service supplier).[7] A necessary precondition for commercial presence is the existence of Foreign Direct Investments (FDI),[8] which are investments made by an individual or a firm in one country into an undertaking in another country with the intention to establish lasting and direct economic links between the investor and the undertaking to whom the capital is provided. If for instance a service supplier from Member A wants establishes a commercial presence in Member B through acquisition, then this transaction

[6] See, with regard to the one-China policy, *inter alia:* Statement of the Ministry of Foreign Affairs of the People's Republic of China, 2 August 2022. Accessible via: https://www.fmprc.gov.cn/eng/zxxx_662805/202208/t20220802_10732293.html. See, for a short historical overview, *inter alia*: Green, 'What is the U.S. "One China" policy, and why does it matter?', CSIS (2017). Retrieved from: https://www.csis.org/analysis/what-us-one-china-policy-and-why-does-it-matter; BBC, 'What is the "One China" policy?', 6 October 2021. Retrieved from: https://www.bbc.com/news/world-asia-china-38285354.

[7] See Article XXVIII(m)(ii) GATS.

[8] Zacharias (2008), pp. 51–52.

entails FDI. The service supplier has to pay a certain amount of capital in order to acquire the juridical person in Member B. Due to this, it is assumed that commercial presence and FDI concern the same concept.[9] From an EU law perspective, the European Commission (Commission) considers commercial presence as the equivalent of FDI.[10] Accordingly, any commitment regarding commercial presence can generally be considered to be a commitment regarding FDI.[11]

Secondly and following on from the above, the present chapter takes the GATS as its starting point since it is the model agreement in international trade law when dealing with commercial presence. Many PTAs either resemble or incorporate by reference[12] GATS provisions.[13] Accordingly, the case law and literature developed under the GATS is often directly relevant for the interpretation of provisions of PTAs.[14] It is important to bear in mind though that the approaches of the GATS and some PTAs toward the liberalization of investments differ significantly from each other, despite the fact that they contain both similar, and in some cases even identical provisions. Three approaches can be distinguished in this regard.[15] The first one is the positive list approach, whereby parties explicitly list the (sub) sectors in which they undertake specific commitments. The GATS features this approach. The second one is the negative list approach, whereby parties list reservations, often called nonconforming measures, to the core obligations in an agreement. Accordingly, parties are not required to list the (sub) sectors wherein they take commitments. All (sub) sectors are by default liberalized unless they are listed in the Annexes. The North American Free Trade Agreement (NAFTA) is a prime example of this approach. Finally, the last approach concerns a hybrid one, which is a combination of the previous two approaches. In the Trade in Services Agreement (TiSA) the hybrid approach was adopted. The EU has used both the positive (in for instance the EU-Singapore Free Trade Agreement) and negative list (in for instance the EU-Japan Economic Partnership Agreement) approaches.

Finally, the present chapter deals with the geo-politicization rather than the politicization of international economic law. The question is obviously what geo-politicization, and more generally geopolitical or geopolitics mean. In this regard, it is helpful to first pay attention to the word 'political', that is derived

---

[9]See *inter alia*: Chaisse (2015) and Pasini (2012).

[10]European Commission, *Towards a comprehensive European international investment policy*, COM(2010)343 final, footnote 16 (7 July 2010).

[11]Zacharias (2008), *supra* note 8, p. 52.

[12]See, for instance, Articles 1.5 and 8.3 of the EU – Japan agreement, Articles 1 and 4 of Part 2, Articles 412 and 415 of the EU – UK agreement and Articles 224 and 225 of the EU – CARIFORUM agreement with regard to the exception grounds.

[13]Allee et al. (2017), provide empirical evidence that nearly all PTAs either copy-and-paste relevant provisions from the WTO agreements or employ similar language as the WTO provisions.

[14]See, for an extensive analysis of this proposition: e.g. Hsu (2006), p. 526; Lanyi and Steinbach (2017), p. 80.

[15]See, for instance, Zhang et al. (2022).

from the Greek word *politikos*, which can be translated as "of, or pertaining to, the *polis*", whereby *polis* means a city-state.[16] Hence, political means of, or pertaining to the city-state. In common parlance, the words politics and political refer to how a state is governed. For the purpose of the present chapter, politics, political and politicization are terms that refer to the internal process within a state with regard to international economic law. So it concerns for instance questions such as which political parties on the domestic level are or are not in favor of concluding trade agreements. The politicization of international economic law is in this regard nothing new and is a process that has been ongoing for decades. Geopolitics refers according to the Oxford English Dictionary, to the political relations between states as influenced by geographical factors, whereby geographical factors means the physical features of states, such as the climate and natural resources.[17] While this definition of geopolitics is solely focused on the geographical factors of states, the Britannica is a bit elaborative and includes also the economic factors of states. Accordingly, geopolitics is defined as "the study of how geography and economics have an influence on politics and on the relations between nations".[18] Hence, geo-politicization is, as it will become clear from the next section, an external process and refers to the use of economic policies for geopolitical purposes.[19]

3 Geo-economics: The Geo-politicization of Investment Policies

As stated above, in the late 1980s and especially the early 1990s, world politics fundamentally changed due to the collapse of the Soviet-Union and the subsequent end of the Cold War. Accordingly, security issues no longer dictated international relations.[20] It was in this period that Edward Luttwak argued that geopolitical and security issues were still salient; the only thing that had changed were the means through which states would pursue geopolitical and security objectives. According to him "the methods of commerce are displacing military methods- with disposable capital in lieu of firepower, civilian innovation in lieu of military-technical advancement, and market penetration in lieu of garrisons and bases [. . .] [which has led to] the emergence of geo-economics [. . .] the best term I can think of to describe the admixture of the logic of conflict with the methods of commerce".[21] Geo-economics entailed in the view of Luttwak thus "the admixture of the logic of conflict with the

[16] Aristotle's political theory: https://plato.stanford.edu/entries/aristotle-politics/.

[17] Oxford English Dictionary: geopolitics (oed.com).

[18] Britannica Dictionary: Geopolitics Definition & Meaning | Britannica Dictionary.

[19] Meunier and Nicolaidis (2019), pp. 102–113.

[20] Cai (2010), pp. 57–58.

[21] Luttwak (1990), pp. 17–19.

methods of commerce".[22] Blackwill and Harris have provided an even more precise definition of geo-economics which fits current trends quite well. According to them, geoeconomics means "the use of economic instruments to promote and defend national interests, and to produce beneficial (geo)political results; and the effects of other nations' economic actions on a country's (geo)political goals". Geo-economics refers to the politization of economic policy whereby "fewer and fewer cross-border trade and investment decisions are taken on solely economic grounds [i.e. what is economically most beneficial] [...] [but rather are taken] with an eye to what strategic advantages they will bring".[23] Economic policy is thus becoming merely a tool rather than an objective: through economic policies, states pursue geopolitical interests.

Considering the recent developments in the field of international and European economic law, there is indeed a tendency visible wherein economic policies are used to pursue geopolitical and security interests. China is using trade and investment policies to (inter alia) enforce adherence to the one-China principle. The recent trade restrictions vis-à-vis Lithuania form a clear example.[24] The spokesman of the Chinese Foreign Ministry explicitly stated that the conflict between China and Lithuania is not of an economic but rather of a political nature and the responsibility should be borne entirely by Lithuania since the "Lithuanian government blatantly violated the one-China principle".[25] In Africa, the one-China principle is pursued by the Chinese government through investments.[26] In the same vein, China and its state-backed companies have in recent years made geo-economically motivated investments in the EU, in order to reduce its technology gap with the developed world by acquiring *inter alia* EU companies with key technologies.[27] In 2016 for instance the Chinese Midea Group Co. Ltd. acquired Kuka, a leading German robotics maker.[28] The acquiring investors are in most cases state-owned or backed

---

[22] Ibid.

[23] Wesley (2016), p. 4.

[24] European Commission, press release: 'EU refers China to the WTO following its trade restrictions on Lithuania' (27 January 2022). Retrieved from: EU refers China to WTO following its trade restrictions (europa.eu).

[25] Foreign Ministry spokesperson Zhao Lijian at a press conference on 31 December 2021. Retrieved from: Foreign Ministry Spokesperson Zhao Lijian's Regular Press Conference on December 31, 2021 (china-embassy.gov.cn).

[26] Blackwill and Harris (2016), p. 56.

[27] See, for an overview of China's geo-economically motivated FDI in the EU: Zeneli, 'Mapping China's Investments in Europe', *The Diplomat,* 14 March 2019. Accessible via: <https://thediplomat.com/2019/03/mapping-chinas-investments-in-europe/>.

[28] P. Basu, 'Midea completes acquisition of German robot maker Kuka', 8 January 2017. Retrieved from: <https://www.spglobal.com/marketintelligence/en/news-insights/trending/gjozjwvrkhepx0jql2sshw2>. See, for an overview of (mainly) German companies acquired by Chinese investors: Wübbeke et al. (2016), p. 52.

by the Chinese government. Accordingly, the Chinese government has access to these key technologies and can use them for geopolitical purposes.[29]

Russia is using the dependency of (mainly) Western countries on Russian oil and gas as leverage to soften the sanctions imposed on it for its invasion in Ukraine. Economic sanctions are imposed by the West on Russia because of the invasion of Ukraine and on Iran and North Korea for their nuclear capabilities. The trade wars[30] of former president Trump, with his America First policies, were also geo-economically motivated. From an economic perspective, the trade wars did not make any sense. Indeed, it is even suggested that the trade wars were economic failures and adversely affected the economy and consumers of the United States.[31] Launching trade wars despite the lack of economic benefits, can however (partially) be explained from a political economy perspective according to which tariffs are imposed for electoral gains.[32] Under the Biden administration, there is this phenomenon called friend or ally-shoring, which means that the United States is leaning into economic relations with states with whom it shares common values and strategic interests.[33] Finally, the EU is also not without sin. It is argued that the conditionality of trade aid (GPS+) to third countries can be considered as a form of economic coercion. The receiving countries have to adopt certain policies regarding issues such as the environment, labour and/or human rights, in order to receive the aid.[34] Hence, trade aid is used by the EU to pursue geopolitical interests, although one can argue to what extent environmental, labour and human rights norms can be considered to fall under the scope of geopolitics.

Overall, states are increasingly employing trade and investment policies to pursue geopolitical and security interests. It is important to note however that geo-economics as a statecraft, with trade and investment policies as instruments to achieve geopolitical and security ends, is in itself nothing new. Throughout history, trade and investment policies were often used by states to pursue geopolitical and security interests. The British Empire and the Kingdom of the Netherlands have for instance used the East Indian Companies to acquire geopolitical power. The United

[29] See, for instance: Gagnon, 'Are European academics helping China's military?' Accessible via: https://www.dw.com/en/are-european-academics-helping-chinas-military/a-61834716.

[30] See, for an overview of the trade wars of Trump: Bown and Kolb, 'Trump's trade war timeline: An up-to-date guide', *Peterson Institute for International Economics* (Updated 10th of May 2022). Retrieved from: Trump's Trade War Timeline: An Up-to-Date Guide (piie.com).

[31] See inter alia: Amiti et al. (2020); Fajgelbaum et al. (2019); Milberg (2020) and Zandi et al., 'Trade war chicken: The tariffs and the damage done', September 2019.

[32] Fetzer and Schwarz (2021), Kim and Margalit (2021) and Di et al. (2019).

[33] Dezenski and Austin, 'Re-forge strategic alliances and check China abroad, rebuild economy at home', 13 July 2020. Retrieved from https://www.fdd.org/analysis/2020/07/13/check-china-abroad-rebuild-economy-at-home/; Dezenski and Austin, 'Rebuilding America's economy and foreign policy with ally-shoring', 8 June 2021. Retrieved from https://www.brookings.edu/blog/the-avenue/2021/06/08/rebuilding-americas-economy-and-foreign-policy-with-ally-shoring/.

[34] F. Baetens and M. Bronckers, 'The EU's Anti-Coercion Instrument: A big stick for big targets', 19 Jan 2022, EJIL!Talk, Blog of European Journal of International Law.

States pursued geopolitical and security interests via the Marshall Plan, which helped to rebuild the Western European economies and by doing so protected them from the influence of communism. Moreover, the United States has used and continues to use international institutions to pursue its own national interests.[35] While every state does so to a certain extent, it becomes problematic when the international economic legal order is undermined as evidences by inter alia the paralyzed Appellate Body (AB) of the WTO because the United States blocks the appointment of new judges.[36] The current rise of geo-economics is unique in that it represents a break with the post-Cold War liberal international economic order.

4 Pursuing Geopolitical Interests Under International Economic Law

In order to analyse the main question of the present chapter, it is helpful to make a distinction between the pre-conclusion and the post-conclusion phases of PTAs and other multilateral trade and investment agreements.

4.1 Pre-conclusion Phase: Geopolitical Motivations for Entering into PTAs

The pre-conclusion phase is the phase wherein a PTA has not yet been concluded. States generally conclude PTAs for economic reasons, although other considerations may also be in play. As stated previously, the law of comparative advantage provides the underlaying rationale for free trade and specialization among states.[37] Through PTAs, tariffs are reduced or eliminated. Companies can access new markets, consumers can access new products and this leads to economic growth, employment and the efficient allocation of capital and other resources. Based on this line of argumentation, i.e. PTAs are concluded for (purely) economic reasons, a state chooses its trading partners on the basis of economic benefits. The economic literature however provides evidence that geopolitical considerations play a significant role in the choice of trading partners. Indeed, for some states geopolitical considerations

---

[35] M. Beeson, 'Geoeconomics isn't back - it never went away', 22 Aug 2018. Accessible via: https://www.lowyinstitute.org/the-interpreter/geoeconomics-isnt-back-never-went-away.

[36] Center for Strategic & International Studies, 'The World Trade Organization: The Appellate Body crisis'. Retrieved from https://www.csis.org/programs/scholl-chair-international-business/world-trade-organization-appellate-body-crisis#:~:text=For%20roughly%20two%20years%2C%20the,and%20concerns%20over%20U.S.%20sovereignty.

[37] Ricardo (1817), *supra* note 3.

might even form the dominant motivation.[38] Hillary Clinton summarized this in 2012 perfectly by stating that "[the] connection between economic power and global influence explains why the United States is placing economics at the heart of our foreign policy".[39] This explains why the United States has more agreements with countries in the Middle East, which are of great geopolitical and strategic importance, than with East Asian countries.[40] Furthermore, the agreements it has in in place tend to be deeper with its partners in the Middle East.

In the pre-conclusion phase, states can pursue geopolitical interests by choosing the contracting parties. The pre-conclusion phase is thus quite important since the choice of the contracting parties is mainly influenced by geopolitical considerations. Once a state has chosen its contracting parties, discussions start wherein the parties explore areas of mutual interest for inclusion in the agreement. The exploratory discussions, and the subsequent negotiations, form yet another opportunity for states to pursue geopolitical interests. The Transatlantic Trade and Investment Partnership (TTIP) is illustrative for the geopolitical considerations in choosing contracting parties for PTAs. This US-EU agreement is perceived to be, at least partially, geopolitically motivated. First of all, the choice of the contracting parties was, besides economically also geopolitically motivated. Through TTIP the US and the EU wanted to reinvigorate the transatlantic alliance that emerged after World War II in the form of the NATO.[41] Hence, TTIP was meant to build on the previous relations (in the context of inter alia the NATO) that were faltering. This was particularly important since the support for the transatlantic partnership was eroding after the end of the Cold War.[42] Moreover, with the TTIP the US and the EU aimed for setting common rules, regulations and standards which would set a precedent for future negotiations. The rationale was thus that if the US and the EU did not "write the rules today, China will write them tomorrow".[43] Finally, TTIP was meant to reinforce and promote the "core values of the Western liberal economic and political order such as the rule of law, human rights and democratic governance".[44] These geopolitical objectives of TTIP were expressed clearly by Eizenstat, former US Deputy Secretary of the Treasury and ambassador to the EU. According to him, "[t]here are essentially two competing models of governance in the post-Communist world. One is the transatlantic model shared by many other countries, based upon democratic governance, with free peoples, free markets, and free trade; the other is autocratic governance, state-controlled or dominated economies, and managed trade. The TTIP is an opportunity to show the world that our model of governance can

[38] Hinz (2023) and Eichengreen et al. (2019).

[39] Clinton, 'Delivering on the promise of economic statecraft', 17 Nov 2012. Retrieved from: https://2009-2017.state.gov/secretary/20092013clinton/rm/2012/11/200664.htm.

[40] Hinz (2023), *supra* note 38.

[41] Kirisci (2014), p. 76.

[42] Hormats (2014), p. 15.

[43] Dieter (2014).

[44] Kirisci (2014), supra note 41, p. 77.

produce tangible gains for our people on both sides of the Atlantic and more broadly are the best model to meet the challenges of the 21st century".[45]

A more recent example concerns the EU-New Zealand Trade Agreement that was concluded on 30 June 2022. While the agreement itself is of an economic nature and is expected to increase the trade between the EU and New Zealand by 30%,[46] it has also clear geopolitical components. According to the Commission, the agreement will, besides creating economic opportunities, "cement EU ties with a like-minded ally".[47] It is quite obvious that the like-mindedness refers to common geopolitical interests. In his speech, Executive Vice-President Dombrovskis stated explicitly that "the deal sends a strong geopolitical signal".[48] In conclusion, geopolitical considerations seems to become the dominant motivation behind the conclusion of PTAs and the choice of trading partners.

4.2 Post-conclusion Phase: Invoking the Public Morals, Public Order and Security Exceptions

With the conclusion of a PTA, states commit themselves to open their domestic markets for foreign service suppliers. Market access and national treatment provisions play in this regard an important role. Market access provisions ensure that service suppliers of one party to an agreement have access to the domestic market of the other parties to the agreement. Moreover, market access provisions prohibit states from taking certain measures that are considered to restrict access to the market. Article XVI(2)(f) GATS for instance prohibits states from putting in place measures that limit the participation of foreign capital in terms of maximum percentages of shareholdings. States are thus not allowed to take measures limiting the shareholdings of foreign service suppliers in domestic companies to a certain maximum percentage. Once foreign service providers have access to the domestic market, national treatment provisions (such as Article XVII GATS), which are almost universal in the services chapters of PTAs, ensure that there is equal treatment between them and 'like' domestic service suppliers.[49] If states were to deviate from these obligations by adopting investment restrictive measures, they would be in

---

[45] The quote is taken from Kirisci (2014), *supra* note 41, footnote 2.

[46] European Commission, Factsheet EU-NZ trade agreement: https://ec.europa.eu/commission/presscorner/detail/en/ip_22_4158.

[47] European Commission, EU-New Zealand Agreement: https://policy.trade.ec.europa.eu/eu-trade-relationships-country-and-region/countries-and-regions/new-zealand/eu-new-zealand-agreement_en.

[48] Speech by Executive Vice-President Dombrovskis following the conclusion of EU-New Zealand Trade Agreement: https://ec.europa.eu/commission/commissioners/2019-2024/dombrovskis/announcements/speech-executive-vice-president-dombrovskis-following-conclusion-eu-new-zealand-trade-agreement_en.

[49] See *inter alia* Bjorklund and Vanhonnaeker (2019).

violation of (inter alia) the market access and national treatment provisions of the agreement. If for instance China blocks FDI from Taiwan or the US from China and Russia because of (obvious) geopolitical reasons, then that in principle violates the market access provision if specific commitments are made and no reservations are applicable. The participation of foreign capital is namely set at zero (Article XVI(2)(f) GATS).

A prima facie violation of one of these provisions may however be justified under a treaty exception. The GATS contains a couple of justification grounds in Articles XIV and XIVbis. For the purpose of the present chapter, the public morals, public order and security exceptions are the most relevant due to their vague and open nature. Accordingly, it is, at least in theory, possible that these exceptions cover geopolitical interests. This cannot be said about for instance the animal or plant life and health ex Article XIV(b) GATS since it is obvious that it does not cover geopolitical interests. Public morals, public order and security are general exceptions that are meant to protect the legitimate interests of states. Hence, the question becomes whether the public morals, public order and security exceptions of the GATS cover geopolitical interests. It is thus necessary to consider the scope of these exceptions and the conditions under which they can be invoked.

In order to invoke public morals, public order or security, it is first of all necessary that a certain interest falls within the scope of these exception grounds. If that is the case, then it should be assessed whether the conditions are satisfied since these exceptions do not provide a *carte blanche* to states. Rather, certain conditions, such as the proportionality requirement, should be met before a state can invoke them successfully. For the purpose of the present chapter, the scope of the public morals, public order and security exceptions to the GATS is important as the research question concerns whether geopolitical interests fall within the scope of these exceptions. Whether for in stance the proportionality requirement is met, must be assessed on a case by case basis. Therefore, the focus in the subsequent sections will be on the scope of the public morals, public order and security exceptions. By discussing the scope, it can be assessed to what extent geopolitical interests can be covered by these exception grounds.

4.2.1 Public Morals and Public Order

Article XIV(a) GATS contains the public morals and public order exceptions. In *US – Gambling*[50] the Appellate Body (AB) ruled that the term public morals refer to principles of right and wrong in a society which "can vary in time and space, depending upon a range of factors including prevailing social, cultural, ethical and

[50] Appellate Body Report WT/DS285/AB/R *United States – Measures affecting the cross-border supply of gambling and betting services* [7 April 2005], para. 296.

religious values".[51] Due to this, the AB in *EC – Seal products*[52] did not sanction (and thus implicitly approved) the ruling of the Panel that "the Members [i.e. countries] should be given some scope to define and apply for themselves the concept of public morals according to their own systems and scales of values". Furthermore, countries were supposed to have the right to determine the level of protection of public morals that they considered necessary.[53] Due to the fact that public morals vary over time and geographically, no exact definition or universal examples can be provided. In Islamic countries for instance, a ban on drinking alcohol, charging interest or eating pork can be considered as public morals while issues related to transgenderism for instance are typically morals of the west.[54]

Public order is closely related to public morals. Indeed, there is a certain overlap between these two concepts since both intend to protect similar values.[55] The Panel in *US – Gambling* held that "public order refers to the preservation of the fundamental interests of a society, as reflected in public policy and law, [...] [whereby] these fundamental interests can relate, inter alia, to standards of law, security and morality".[56] Considering the formulation of the Panel in *US – Gambling case*, Cottier and others conclude that public morals and public order are not fundamentally different concepts; rather public order is the overarching concept which also encompasses public morals. Hence, public order is broader than public morals and can thus be considered as a catch-all term.[57] In this regard, any interests (such as the protection of underage gamblers) that falls under public morals falls also under public order. However, interests that are protected by public order do not need necessarily to be encompassed by public morals. For instance, access to essential facilities and the fight against organized crime are only related to public order but not to public morals.[58]

Given the fact that public order can be considered as a catch-all term, the question arises with respect to the *raison d'être* of public morals as an exception ground on itself. In other words: what is the added value of public morals, given the fact that all interests that are encompassed by public morals are also protected by public order? The answer to this question is related to the conditions under which public order and

---

[51] See also: Appellate Body Report WT/DS363/AB/R *China – Measures affecting trading rights and distribution services for certain publications and audiovisual entertainment products* [21 December 2009].

[52] Appellate Body Report WT/DS400/AB/R *European Communities – Measures prohibiting the importation and marketing of seal products* [22 May 2014], para. 5.199.

[53] Appellate Body Report WT/DS400/AB/R *European Communities – Measures prohibiting the importation and marketing of seal products* [22 May 2014], para. 5.200.

[54] Yeasmeen (2015), p. 43.

[55] Cottier et al. (2008), p. 295 where a reference is made to Panel Report WT/DS285/R *US – Gambling*, para. 6.468.

[56] Cottier et al. (2008), *supra* note 55, p. 295 where is referred to Panel Report WT/DS285/R *US – Gambling*, para. 6.467.

[57] Cottier et al. (2008), *supra* note 55, p. 296.

[58] Cottier et al. (2008), *supra* note 55, p. 297.

public morals can be invoked as exception grounds. To invoke public morals as an exception, the necessity test must be met. However, to invoke public order as an exception ground, an additional test must be met besides the necessity test. Pursuant to footnote 5 to Article XIV(a) GATS, states may rely only on public order if there is a genuine and sufficiently serious threat to one of the fundamental interests of the society. Accordingly, this is a higher threshold than the necessity test. Hence, the existence of public morals is meant to provide parties more room and flexibility.[59]

In the case law, the Panel and the AB have further clarified the concepts of public morals and public order and their interrelationship. In the *US – Gambling* case, the United States argued there that the measures it had taken, were related to (1) organized crime, (2) money laundering, (3) fraud and other criminal activities, (4) risks to children given the availability of remotely supplied gambling and betting services to children and (5) particular health risks.[60] According to the Panel, preventing underage persons and pathological gamblers from gambling can be considered as an interest covered by public morals. The fight against organized crime on the other hand, is a matter of public order while the fight against money laundering and fraud schemes may relate to both public morals and public order.[61] On appeal, the AB left the findings of the Panel untouched.[62] Moreover, from the *EC – Seal Products,*[63] *Columbia – Textiles*[64] and *Brazil – Taxation and Charges*[65] cases, it can inferred that animal welfare, bridging the digital divide in a society, the promotion of social inclusion and the security of energy supply within the scope of public order. Finally, it is argued in the literature that measures related to alcohol, sex, drugs and slavery are also covered by the scope of the public order exception.[66]

The *EC – Energy Package*[67] case is a rare example wherein only the public order exception ex Article XIV(a) GATS is invoked. At issue was EU legislation regulating the natural gas sector within the EU. The EU invoked the public order exception in order to justify the restrictive measures. It argued that "security of energy supply is

[59] Cottier et al. (2008), *supra* note 55, p. 298.

[60] Panel Report WT/DS285/R *US – Gambling*, para. 6.479.

[61] Panel Report WT/DS285/R *US – Gambling*, para. 6.469.

[62] Appellate Body Report, WT/DS285/AB/R, *United States – Measures affecting the cross-border supply of gambling and betting services* [7 April 2005], para. 296.

[63] Panel Report, WT/DS400/R, *European Communities – Measures prohibiting the importation and marketing of seal products* [25 November 2013], para. 5.199.

[64] Panel Report, WT/DS461/R, *Columbia – Measures relating to the importation of textiles, apparel and footwear* [27 November 2015], paras. 7.338–7.339.

[65] Panel Report, WT/DS492/R, *Brazil – Certain measures concerning taxation and charges* [30 August 2017], paras. 7.568.

[66] Charnovitz (1998).

[67] Panel Report, WT/DS476/R, *European Union and its Member States – Certain measures relating to the energy sector* [10 August 2018].

a fundamental interest of society [...] [whereby] disruptions in supply potentially having severe social, economic and, ultimately, political consequences".[68] The Panel agreed with the EU and concluded that the security of energy supply can indeed be covered by the public order exception ex Article XIV(a) GATS.[69]

4.2.2 Essential Security

The security exception is one of the oldest defences and present in almost all trade and investment agreements.[70] Even Adam Smith, one of the most prominent proponents of free trade, argued that the Navigation Act, which restricted colonial trade to England, was "[a]s defence [...] of much more importance than opulence [and] perhaps the wisest of all commercial regulations of England".[71] The purpose of the security exception is thus to provide room for states to protect their vital interests related to the core of their sovereignty.[72] The security exception of the GATS is contained in Article XIVbis and reads as follows:

1. Nothing in this Agreement shall be construed:
    a. To require any Member to furnish any information, the disclosure of which it considers contrary to its essential security interests; or
    b. To prevent any Member from taking any action which it considers necessary for the protection of its essential security interests:
        i. Relating to the supply of services as carried out directly or indirectly for the purpose of provisioning a military establishment
        ii. Relating to fissionable and fusionable materials or the materials from which they are derived;
        iii. Taken in time of war or other emergency in international relations; or
    c. To prevent any Member from taking any action in pursuance of its obligations under the United Nations Charter for the maintenance of international peace and security.

As is clear from the above, Article XIVbis(1) GATS contains in essence three separate security exceptions. According to Article XIVbis(1)(a) GATS, states are not obliged to *furnish any information, the disclosure of which it considers contrary*

[68] Panel Report, WT/DS476/R, *European Union and its Member States – Certain measures relating to the energy sector* [10 August 2018], para. 7.1145.

[69] Panel Report, WT/DS476/R, *European Union and its Member States – Certain measures relating to the energy sector* [10 August 2018], para. 7.1156. See for an extensive discussion of the case and background information with regard to energy security: Marhold (2021).

[70] This section is loosely based on Zamani (2022).

[71] Smith (1776), p. 356. The book of Adam Smith can be consulted online via: https://www.ibiblio.org/ml/libri/s/SmithA_WealthNations_p.pdf.

[72] Delimatsis and Hrynkiv (2020), para. 1.

to its essential security interests. Pursuant to Article XIVbis(1)(c) GATS, states can take *any action in pursuance of its obligations under the United Nations Charter for the maintenance of international peace and security*. Finally, Article XIVbis (b) GATS allows states to take any action that they consider necessary for the protection of its essential security interests as long as these interests are related to the provisioning of military establishments, nuclear fission or fusion or are taken in time of war or other emergency in international relations.

The first and third paragraph of Article XIVbis(1) GATS deal with very specific situations. Pursuant to paragraph (a), states are not obliged to provide sensitive information if the disclosure of it may jeopardize its essential security interests. According to paragraph (c), states can take *any* action that is necessary to pursue their obligations under Chapter VII and/or VIII of the Charter of the United Nations. Sub (c) thus articulates Article 103 of the Charter of the United Nations, according to which *in the event of a conflict between the obligations of the Members of the United Nations under the present Charter and their obligations under any other international agreement, their obligations under the present Charter shall prevail*. Pursuant to Article 41 of the Charter of the United Nations, the Security Council can inter alia decide that economic relations are completely or partially interrupted to give effect to its decisions. Hence, measures, even though incompatible with the GATS and other PTAs, ordered by the Security Council can be justified by Article XIVbis(1)(c) GATS.

Article XIVbis(1)(b) GATS, in contrast to the first and third paragraph, appears to be construed more broadly since it is not dealing with very specific and well demarked situations. The scope of paragraph (b) is however limited in another way. Like paragraph (a), Article XIVbis(1)(b) GATS is concerned with *essential security interests*. In order to rely on Article XIVbis(1)(a) and (b) GATS, states have to prove that essential security interests are at stake. The security interests must thus not be ordinary, but essential.[73] In the *Russia – Traffic in Transit* case, the Panel argued that "essential security interests, which is evidently a narrower concept than security interests, may generally be understood to refer to those interests relating to the quintessential functions of the state, namely, the protection of its territory and its population from external threats, and the maintenance of law and public order internally".[74] Essential security interests concern thus military interests, such as the fight against terrorism,[75] and the maintenance of law and order (internal security).[76] The exact definition of the essential security interests in specific cases, is left

[73]Delimatsis and Hrynkiv (2020), para. 1.

[74]Panel Report, WT/DS512/R, *Russia – Measures concerning traffic in transit* [5 April 2019], para. 7.130.

[75]Panel in Panel Report, WT/DS567/R, *Saudi Arabia – Measures concerning the protection of intellectual property rights* [16 June 2020], para. 7.280–7.282.

[76]Delimatsis and Hrynkiv (2020), *supra* note 72, para. 28.

to the states as they have a certain margin of discretion to define for themselves what they consider to be essential security interests.[77] The margin of discretion does not provide however a *carte* blanche since the discretion provided is limited by the principle of good faith[78] whereby the WTO judiciary is also competent to review the decisions taken by states.[79] Moreover, economic interests can never be qualified as essential security interests and states are not allowed to rephrase commercial interests as essential security interests.[80] Accordingly, the scope of Article XIVbis(1)(b) GATS is limited to military affairs and defence and the maintenance of law and order.[81]

The fact that the scope of Article XIVbis(1)(b) GATS is limited to military affairs and defence and the maintenance of law and order, is also exemplified by the three subs under paragraph b which are all dealing with military and defence related matters. Under sub (i), states can take any measures that they consider necessary in order to protect their essential security interests that are related to the supply of services which directly or indirectly provision a military establishment. One can think of the procurement of military materials such as weaponry. Sub (ii) is concerned with nuclear materials while sub (iii) entails a broad carve out which justifies any measures that is necessary to protect essential security interests and is taken in time of war or other emergency in international relations. In *Russia – Traffic in Transit,*[82] the Panel took as starting point the notion that "'emergencies in international relations' is the broader category, which include inter alia war, whereby war entails an armed conflict".[83] It then held that "an emergency in international relations would, therefore, appear to refer generally to a situation of armed conflict, or of latent armed conflict, or of heightened tension or crises, or of general instability engulfing or surrounding a state".[84] According to the Panel, political or economic differences between states do not constitute in this regard 'other emergencies in international relations', even though they might entail serious political disagreements.[85] However "one Member's severance of all diplomatic and economic ties

[77] Panel Report, WT/DS512/R, *Russia – Measures concerning traffic in transit* [5 April 2019], para. 7.131.

[78] Panel Report, WT/DS512/R, *Russia – Measures concerning traffic in transit* [5 April 2019], para. 7.132–7.133.

[79] Panel Report, WT/DS512/R, *Russia – Measures concerning traffic in transit* [5 April 2019], para. 7.102.

[80] Panel Report, WT/DS512/R, *Russia – Measures concerning traffic in transit* [5 April 2019], para. 7.132–7.133.

[81] Prazeres (2020), p. 143.

[82] Panel Report, WT/DS512/R, *Russia – Measures concerning traffic in transit* [5 April 2019].

[83] Panel Report, WT/DS512/R, *Russia – Measures concerning traffic in transit* [5 April 2019], paras. 7.71–7.72.

[84] Panel Report, WT/DS512/R, *Russia – Measures concerning traffic in transit* [5 April 2019], para. 7.76.

[85] Panel Report, WT/DS512/R, *Russia – Measures concerning traffic in transit* [5 April 2019], para. 7.75.

with another Member could be regarded as the ultimate state expression of the evidence of an emergency in international relations".[86] Overall, the interpretation of the Panel of 'other emergencies in international relations' is quite strict and does not cover political or economic disagreement.

5 Geo-economics and International Economic Law: An Unhappy Marriage

Due to the rise of geo-economics, states increasingly use trade and investments policies to pursue geopolitical interests. The reason for this is quite straightforward: trade and investment policies are an effective alternative for a direct military conflict.[87] Accordingly, the geopolitical power of states is increasingly dependent on and derived from economic power rather than military power.[88] While trade and investment policies might be a desirable and effective alternative for a direct military conflict, geo-economic practices challenge, and to in certain circumstances undermine, international economic law.

First of all, geo-economics contributes to the already existing threats that are faced by multilateralism and multilateral institutions.[89] Given the fact that in the geo-economic doctrine geopolitical power is derived from economic power, multilateralism and multilateral institutions are perceived by states to be instruments. Accordingly, it becomes harder to reach multilateral agreements. Instead bilateral or regional agreements have become more common. In this sense, geo-economics contributes to the already ongoing process of fragmentation of international economic law. Moreover, multilateral institutions, such as the WTO, are perceived by states to be instruments to further the pursuit of their own geopolitical interests rather than as institutions that safeguard the liberalization and promotion of free trade and investments.[90] Due to this, the credibility and importance of these institutions is questioned and their functioning may become paralyzed. The refusal of the United States to allow the appointment of new adjudicators to the Appellate Body of the WTO, which is (at least partially) geo-economically motivated, is telling in this regard and "has pushed the WTO into an existential crisis".[91]

---

[86]Panel Report, WT/DS512/R, *Russia – Measures concerning traffic in transit* [5 April 2019], para. 7.259.

[87]Peksen (2019), pp. 635–647.

[88]Cai (2010), *supra* note 20, pp. 57–58.

[89]See in this regard *inter alia*: Roberts et al. (2019), p. 16.

[90]Leonard, 'Geopolitics vs globalization: How companies and states can become winners in the age of geo-economics' (2015) World Economic Forum, p. 12.

[91]See for instance: Schott and Jung, 'The WTO's existential crisis: How to salvage its ability to settle trade disputes?' (2019) Peterson Institute for International Economics, Policy Brief 19-19. Retrieved from: https://www.piie.com/sites/default/files/documents/pb19-19.pdf.

Secondly, geo-economically motivated FDI has led to the adoption of investment restrictive legislation. In 2020, the OECD noticed in a research note that more and more countries were adjusting existing mechanisms and adopting new policies in order to safeguard their national security interests.[92] A review of the policies of 62 economies by the OECD revealed that security risks associated with mergers and acquisitions were increasingly managed through the introduction of concepts such as essential or national security, national interests or public order.[93] By adopting Regulation 2019/452,[94] the EU and its Members States have joined the ranks of these countries. The series of takeovers of EU companies with key technologies by Chinese investors, as mentioned above, seems to be the trigger event for the adoption of Regulation 2019/452.[95] This Regulation provides the means to Member States to screen, and eventually prohibit or even unwind inward FDI that adversely affects security and public order.[96] Also, the competencies of the Committee on Foreign Investment in the United States (CIFUS) are significantly expanded.[97] Moreover, the United States is preparing legislation to screen outward FDI as well as inward FDI.[98]

Finally, geo-economics has led to an increased invocation of the exceptions as laid down in the various agreements. Until recently the security exception was invoked only marginally. States were aware that excessive reliance on the security exception would set a precedent and pave the way for others to abuse the exception.[99] Hence, the realms of geopolitics and security on the one hand and economics on the other were relatively well separated from each other.[100] However, since 2016 states are increasingly relaying on the security exception and trying to expand the scope of it.[101] In 2016 requested Ukraine consultations with the Russian Federation with regard to the restrictions on traffic in transit put in place by Russia. Ukraine claimed that these restrictions were inconsistent with the obligations of Russia under

[92]Organization for Economic Cooperation and Development research note on current and emerging trends, 'Acquisition- and ownership- related policies to safeguard essential security interests' (May 2020), p. 14.

[93]Organization for Economic Cooperation and Development research note on current and emerging trends, 'Acquisition- and ownership- related policies to safeguard essential security interests' (May 2020), p. 65.

[94]Regulation 2019/452 of the European Parliament and of the Council establishing a framework for screening of foreign direct investments into the European Union [2019] OJ L791/1.

[95]European Commission, Explanatory Memorandum to Regulation 2019/452, p. 10.

[96]See Article 1(1) Regulation 2019/452.

[97]See for instance Sprich, 'Tightening the net: Investment screening in the United States'. Accessible via: https://english.bdi.eu/article/news/tightening-the-net-investment-screening-in-the-united-states/.

[98]Bauerle-Danzman, 'Is the US going to screen outband investment?'. Accessible via: https://www.atlanticcouncil.org/blogs/econographics/is-the-us-going-to-screen-outbound-investment/.

[99]Delimatsis and Hrynkiv (2020), *supra* note 72, para. 3.

[100]Roberts et al., 'Geo-economics: The variable relationship between economics and security' (2018). Accessible via: https://www.lawfareblog.com/geoeconomics-variable-relationship-between-economics-and-security.

[101]Delimatsis and Hrynkiv (2020), *supra* note 72, para. 4.

WTO law. Russia invoked the security exception to justify the restrictions.[102] In 2017, the United Arab Emirates (UAE), Bahrain and Saudi Arabia relied on the security exception to justify measures that were meant to economically isolate Qatar.[103] In 2018, the United States under the Trump administration imposed tariffs on steel and aluminium and argued that these tariffs could be justified by the security exception.[104] Finally, in 2019 Japan took trade restrictions vis-à-vis South Korea. It delisted South Korea as a favoured destination for the export of materials used in the production of inter alia smartphones and computer chips.[105] It is argued that Japan arguably has imposed these restrictions because of security concerns.[106]

6 Conclusion

As evidenced by recent trends, geo-economics is on the rise. Due to the fundamental changes in post-Cold War international politics, geopolitical power is more and more dependent on and derived from economic power. Accordingly, states are increasingly eager to pursue geopolitical and security interests through trade and investment policies. The question thus arises what the effects are of this geo-politicization of trade and investment policies on international economic law and whether states can pursue geopolitical interests under international economic law.

With regard to the first part of the question, it can be concluded that pursuing geopolitical and security interests through trade and investment policies may well be a desirable and an effective alternative to direct military confrontations. Nevertheless this pursuit challenges the liberal international economic order, its institutions and undermines, to a certain degree, the trade rules aimed at liberalizing investments in at least three ways. First of all, multilateralism is replaced by bilateralism and regionalism and the credibility, importance and functioning of multilateral institutions is eroded. Secondly, where states adopt FDI restrictive legislation, this hampers investment liberalization. Finally, where states invoke the exceptions laid down in various

102 Panel Report, WT/DS512/R, *Russia – Measures concerning traffic in transit* [5 April 2019].

103 Panel Report, WT/DS567/R, *Saudi Arabia – Measures concerning the protection of intellectual property rights* [16 June 2020].

104 See inter alia Globerman, 'Trump administration summons national security to justify tariffs' (18 July 2018). See also: A. Buser, 'Justiciability of security exception in the US Steel (and other) disputes: Some middle ground options and the requirements of Article XXI lit. b (i)-(iii)', accessible via https://www.ejiltalk.org/justiciability-of-security-exceptions-in-the-us-steel-and-other-disputes-some-middle-ground-options-and-the-requirements-of-article-xxi-lit-b-i-iii/, where references ae made to additional literature.

105 Request for consultations by the Republic of Korea, WT/DS590/1, *Japan – Measures related to the exportation of products and technology to Korea* [16 September 2019].

106 Delimatsis and Hrynkiv (2020), *supra* note 72, para. 14.

agreements more often and where they seek to broaden the scope of these exceptions, this puts a strain on the operation of these international agreements.

Regarding the second part of the question, i.e. whether and if so to what extent states can pursue geopolitical interests under international economic law, it is important to make a distinction between two situations. In the pre-conclusion phase, i.e. when a PTA has not yet been concluded, states have considerable room to take into account geopolitical considerations. The choice of the contracting parties seems to be in this regard mainly geopolitically motivated. States tend to conclude PTAs with 'like-minded allies' and strategic partners, even though the economic rationale may often be lacking. Once a PTA is concluded (the post-conclusion phase), states have significantly less room to pursue geopolitical interests. Pursuing geopolitical interests, through for instance screening and eventually blocking FDI from certain countries, often entails a violation of the provisions (such as market access and National Treatment) of the concluded PTA.

Consider the following example. The United States has a longstanding one-China policy, meaning that the government of the Peoples Republic of China (PRC) is the sole government of China. Accordingly, it has recognized China and de-recognized Taiwan in 1979 and it considers since then Taiwan as part of China.[107] At the same time however, the United States considers Taiwan "[a]s a leading democracy and technological powerhouse [...] [and a] key U.S. partner in the Indo-Pacific, [...] [with whom it shares] similar values, deep commercial and economic links, and strong people-to-people ties".[108] Despite the lack of diplomatic relations, the United States has a robust unofficial relationship with Taiwan.[109] Suppose that the United States would decide to block investments in domestic companies by Chinese investors, in order to ensure the territorial integrity of Taiwan given the current tensions between China and Taiwan.[110]

This is a classic example of a geopolitical interest and illustrates well the concept of geo-economics: ensuring the territorial integrity of an (unofficial) ally is geopolitical interest that is pursued through investment policy rather than political or military policy. However, preventing Chinese investors from investing in U.-S. companies might violate the market access obligation of the United States under inter alia Article XIV(2)(f) GATS on the basis of which it is prohibited to

[107] See with regard to the United States position with respect to issue inter alia Green, 'What is the U.S. "One China" policy, and why does it matter?', CSIS (2017), retrieved from: https://www.csis.org/analysis/what-us-one-china-policy-and-why-does-it-matter and the communication of the United States Department of State, 'U.S. relations with Taiwan' (28 May 2022), retrieved from: https://www.state.gov/u-s-relations-with-taiwan/.

[108] Communication of the United States Department of State, 'U.S. relations with Taiwan' (28 May 2022), retrieved from: https://www.state.gov/u-s-relations-with-taiwan/.

[109] Communication of the United States Department of State, 'U.S. relations with Taiwan' (28 May 2022), retrieved from: https://www.state.gov/u-s-relations-with-taiwan/.

[110] Blanchard, 'China-Taiwan: why tensions are rising and what could happen in 2023' (6 December 2022), retrieved from: https://www.reuters.com/world/asia-pacific/yearender-eye-storm-taiwan-centre-sino-us-tensions-2022-12-06/.

limit the participation of foreign capital.[111] Such a violation needs to be justified and the GATS contains, as almost all PTAs, the public morals, public order and security exceptions. States can invoke these exceptions to justify the violation of provisions in order to pursue legitimate interests. The common thread in the case law is however that geopolitical interests cannot be accommodated in the public morals, public order or security exception.

References

Allee T et al (2017) The ties between the World Trade Organization and preferential trade agreements: a textual analysis. J Int Econ Law 20:333–363

Amiti M et al (2020) Who's paying for the US tariffs? A longer term perspective. AEA Papers Proc 110:541–546

Bjorklund A, Vanhonnaeker L (2019) National treatment. In: Mbengue M-M, Schacherer S (eds) Foreign investment under the Comprehensive Economic and Trade Agreement (CETA). Springer, Cham, pp 45–71

Blackwill R-D, Harris J-M (2016) War by other means: geoeconomics and statecraft. Harvard University Press, Cambridge

Bruce S-L, Grant R-R (2013) The evolution of economic thought, 8th edn. South-Western Cengage Learning

Cai K-C (2010) The politics of economic regionalism: explaining regional economic integration in East Asia. Palgrave Macmillan, London

Chaisse J (2015) Assessing the relevance of multilateral trade law to sovereign investments: sovereign wealth funds as "investors" under the general agreement on trade in services. Int Rev Law 2:9–27

Charnovitz S (1998) The moral exception in trade policy. Virginia J Int Law 38:689–746

Cottier T et al (2008) Article XIV GATS: general exceptions. In: Wolfrum R et al (eds) WTO-trade in services. Brill, Leiden, pp 287–329

Delimatsis P, Hrynkiv O (2020) Security exceptions under the GATS - a legal commentary on Article XIVbis GATS. TILEC discussion paper no. 2020-026

Di D et al (2019) Why did Trump launch a trade war? A (geo)political economy explanation from the perspective of financial constraint. Econ Polit Stud 7:203–216

Dieter H (2014) The return of geopolitics: trade policy in the era of TTIP and TPP. International Policy Analysis. https://library.fes.de/pdf-files/iez/global/11114.pdf

Eichengreen B et al (2019) Mars of Mercury redux: the geopolitics of bilateral trade agreements. World Econ 44:21–44

Fajgelbaum P-D et al (2019) The return to protectionism. Q J Econ 135:1–55

Fetzer T, Schwarz C (2021) Tariffs and politics: evidence from Trump's trade wars. Econ J 131: 1717–1741

Hinz J (2023) The ties that bind: geopolitical motivations for economic integration. Rev World Econ 159:51–100

Hormats R-D (2014) The geopolitical implications of TTIP. In: Hamilton D-S (ed) The geopolitics of TTIP: repositioning the transatlantic relationship for a changing world. Centre for Transatlantic Relations SAIS, Washington, pp 13–21

[111] It is important to note however, that first it should be assessed whether the United States has made commitments with regard to Mode 3. Such commitments can be found in the schedule of commitments.

Hsu L (2006) Applicability of WTO law in regional trade agreements: identifying the links. In: Bartel L, Ortino F (eds) Regional trade agreements and the WTO legal system. Oxford University Press, Oxford, pp 525–552
Ikenberry G-J (2011) The future of the liberal world order. Foreign Aff 90:56–68
Ikenberry G-J (2018) The end of liberal international order? Int Aff 94:7–23
Kim S-E, Margalit Y (2021) Tariffs as electoral weapons: the (geo)political geography of the US-China trade war. Int Organ 75:1–38
Kirisci K (2014) TTIP and Turkey: the geopolitical dimension. In: Hamilton D-S (ed) The geopolitics of TTIP: repositioning the transatlantic relationship for a changing world. Centre for Transatlantic Relations SAIS, Washington, pp 71–97
Lanyi P-A, Steinbach A (2017) Promoting coherence between PTAs and WTO through systemic integration. J Int Econ Law 61(20):61–85
Luttwak E-N (1990) From geopolitics to geo-economics: logic of conflict, grammar of commerce. Natl Interest 20:17–23
Marhold A-A (2021) Unpacking the concept of 'energy security': lessons from recent WTO case law. Leg Issues Econ Integr 48:147–170
Meunier S, Nicolaidis K (2019) The geopoliticization of European Trade and Investment Policy. J Common Mark Stud 57:103–113
Milberg W (2020) Trump's tariffs and U.S. workers. New Labor Forum 29:28–37
Pasini F-L (2012) Movement of capital and trade in services: distinguishing myth from reality regarding the GATS and the liberalization of the capital account. J Int Econ Law 15:581–619
Peksen D (2019) When do imposed economic sanctions work? A critical review of the sanctions effectiveness literature. Defense Peace Econ 30:635–647
Prazeres T-L (2020) Trade and national security: rising risks for the WTO. World Trade Rev 19: 137–148
Ricardo D (1817) On the principles of political economy and taxation. John Murray, London
Roberts A et al (2019) Toward a geo-economic order in international trade and investment law. J Int Econ Law 22:655–676
Smith A (1776) An inquiry into the nature and causes of the wealth of nationals
Wesley M (2016) Australia and the rise of geoeconomics. Centre Gravity 29:1–21
Wübbeke J et al (2016) Made in China 2025: the making of a high tech superpower and consequences for industrial countries. MERICS papers on China 2, pp 6–72
Yeasmeen N (2015) Interpretation of public morals under article XX of the GATT. IOSR J Humanit Soc Sci 20:33–43
Zacharias D (2008) Article I GATS. In: Wolfrum R et al (eds) WTO-trade in services. Brill, Leiden, pp 31–71
Zamani N (2022) The economization and politization of international economic law: toward a geo-economic world order? In: De Jong B-J et al (eds) The rise of public security interests in corporate mergers and acquisitions. Wolf Legal Publishers, Nijmegen, pp 63–85
Zhang R et al (2022) Means of liberalization and beyond: understanding scheduling approaches in services trade agreements. WTO Staff working paper no. ERSD-2022-13, pp 1–38

Najibullah Zamani is a Lecturer and PhD Candidate European and International Economic Law. N. Zamani holds a LLM degree in Corporate Law and a MSc degree in Corporate Finance and Control from Radboud University, Nijmegen.

The Anti-coercion Instrument: Is the EU Renouncing Its 'Multilateralist' DNA?

Cornelia Furculita

Contents

Abstract In the context of increased geopolitical tensions and the so-called 'weaponization' of international trade, the EU Commission tabled a proposal for an Anti-Coercion Instrument (ACI) to tackle instances of alleged economic coercion. Considering the tensions that it might come into with multilateral trade rules, this chapter analyses whether the ACI, as proposed by the Commission, is consistent with WTO procedural and substantive norms and whether it could be indeed justified under general customary international law on countermeasures. As the ACI would have consequences beyond legal ones, it will look into its potential broader implications of the instrument for the multilateral trading system and EU's self-declared multilateralist 'DNA'.

Keywords Anti-Coercion Instrument · EU and International Trade Law · WTO Dispute Settlement · Geopolitical European Union · Economic Coercion

---

C. Furculita (✉)
Speyer, Germany
e-mail: furculita@uni-speyer.de

M. de Amstalden et al. (eds.), *International Economic Law*, Special Issue,
https://doi.org/10.1007/978-3-031-41996-6_9

1 Introduction

Under its Trade Policy Review of 2021, the EU engaged to further strengthen its toolbox to protect itself from unfair trading practices, including through the preparation of an Anti-Coercion Instrument ('ACI'). Thereupon, in December 2021, the EU Commission proposed a new tool to oppose economic coercion exercised by third countries.[1] In April 2022, the EP's Committee on International Trade (INTA) endorsed the proposal by adopting a draft report suggesting multiple amendments,[2] which served as a negotiating mandate with the Council. Subsequently, in November 2022, the Council adopted its own negotiating position, which most notably enhances its involvement in the decision-making process.[3] In March 2023 the Council and the European Parliament reached a provisional political agreement on the ACI, seemingly agreeing to strengthen the involvement of the Council in the decision-making process.[4] The present chapter is, nevertheless, based on the Commission's initial proposal, the final agreed text pending publication at the moment of writing.

The need for an ACI emerged in the context of rising geopolitical tensions and international trade being increasingly 'weaponised'.[5] In 2021, China imposed blocks on Lithuanian exports and pressured companies in third countries to stopping doing business with the latter, after the Baltic state announced the opening of mutual diplomatic offices with Taiwan. This case is said to confirm the need for an ACI. As stated in President's von der Leyen's Political Guidelines to the Commission:

---

[1] Proposal for a Regulation of the European Parliament and of the Council on the protection of the Union and its Member States from economic coercion by third countries (ACI Proposal), COM (2021) 775 final, 8 December 2021.

[2] The most notable suggested amendments extend the scope of the proposal to also address situations when third countries fail to take measures affecting trade or investment, and to include measures to repair the injury caused by the coercion. In this respect, see European Parliament, Committee on International Trade, Draft Report on the Proposal for a Regulation of the European Parliament and of the Council on the Protection of the Union and its Member States from Economic Coercion by Third Countries (INTA Draft Report), 19 April 2022, 2021/0406(COD).

[3] Council of the European Union, Mandate for Negotiations with the European Parliament (Council Mandate for Negotiations), Proposal for a Regulation of the European Parliament and of the Council on the protection of the Union and its Member States from economic coercion by third countries, 16 November 2022, 2021/0406 (COD).

[4] Council of the EU, 'Trade: political agreement on the anti-coercion instrument', available at: https://www.consilium.europa.eu/en/press/press-releases/2023/03/28/trade-political-agreement-on-the-anti-coercion-instrument/.

[5] As stated by the Executive Vice-President and Commissioner for Trade, Valdis Dombrovskis, 'EU strengthens protection against economic coercion', available at: https://ec.europa.eu/commission/presscorner/detail/en/ip_21_6642.

'Multilateralism is in Europe's DNA'.[6] Nevertheless, the ACI may call into question EU's commitment to the WTO rules.

In what follows, this chapter will briefly introduce the proposal (Sect. 2), then it will analyse its conformity with WTO rules (Sect. 3). While the Commission justifies its instrument and potential anti-coercion measures under general customary rules of international law on countermeasures, those rules might be displaced by the more specific WTO rules. Furthermore, as it will be argued, even though they would not be displaced, specialised regimes such as the WTO may not give heed to the justification provided by the customary law within dispute settlement proceedings. Therefore, this chapter will analyse whether Article 23 of the WTO's DSU would be applicable to the instrument, and if so, whether it would be complied with. The ACI proposal and measures taken under it may also raise questions with respect to their legality under substantive WTO rules. Accordingly, this chapter will specifically analyse the conformity of the ACI proposal under WTO substantive rules and whether potential violations could be justified. It will also consider other consequences that the instrument could have and that might call into question EU's professed support for the multilateral trade rules (Sect. 4). Finally, this chapter will conclude by briefly summarizing the findings of the chapter and pondering how the instrument can be squared with EU's multilateralist DNA (Sect. 5).

2 Presenting the ACI

The ACI proposal is set to deal with measures of economic coercion, namely measures that comply with two conditions: (1) a third country applies or threatens to apply measures affecting trade or investment; and (2) it does so with the aim 'to prevent or obtain the cessation, modification or adoption of a particular act by the Union or a Member State', thereby interfering in the sovereign choices of the Union or a Member State (Article 2 (1)).[7] Additionally, the proposal provides in Article 2 (2) several elements that should be taken into consideration when determining whether the conditions for economic coercion are met, such as its intensity, severity, frequency, duration, breadth, the magnitude of the measure, the presence of a pattern of interference, and whether the third country tried to settle the matter through coordination or adjudication. According to the proposed ACI, in case the presence

[6] Ursula von der Leyen, 'A Union that Strives for More. My Agenda for Europe', Political Guidelines for the Next European Commission 2019–2024, p. 17, available at: https://ec.europa.eu/info/sites/default/files/political-guidelines-next-commission_en.pdf.

[7] While the INTA Draft Report suggests to define 'coercion' and 'third country action or measures' as separate elements of 'economic coercion', the essence of the conditions does not change, adding only the that such a measure could also be found in case of 'failure to act'.

of a measure of economic coercion is determined to have occurred,[8] the third country should be notified, a requested should be made to cease the coercive activity, and where appropriate, a request should be made to repair the injury caused (Article 4, para. 3). The Commission should then engage with the third country with the aim of bringing the coercive activity to an end via means such as negotiations, mediation, conciliation, good offices, or international adjudication (Article 5, para. 1). When these actions have not ceased within a reasonable period of time, countermeasures may be adopted (Article 7 (1) (a)). While, the ACI clearly favours encouraging the cessation of the coercion through other means, as a last resort under it, the Commission may impose countermeasures, seemingly even before the conclusion of international adjudication procedures. Annex I to the proposal contains a list of potential countermeasures, among them being the 'suspension of tariff concessions [...] and the imposition of new or increased customs duties, including [...] beyond the most-favoured-nation level', the 'introduction or increase of restrictions on the importation or exportation of goods', and most notably 'the suspension of applicable international obligations'. Accordingly, Annex I lists countermeasures that on their face seem to violate substantive WTO rules, such as Articles I, XI, and XIII of the GATT. Although Article 1 (2) of the ACI proposal requires that actions taken under it be consistent with international obligations, the Commission considers them justified under customary rules on countermeasures. From the proposal it is clear that the Commission would justify its actions as countermeasures taken against coercive economic measures, which presumably violate the international principle of non-intervention.[9] Indeed, under Article 49 of the ILC Draft Articles on State Responsibility '[a]n injured State may only take countermeasures against a State which is responsible for an internationally wrongful act'. Since WTO DSU rules are *lex specialis vis-à-vis* general rules on countermeasures under Article 55 of the ILC Draft Articles, it is necessary to see, however, whether the first are applicable to the case at hand. Were the WTO rules on countermeasures to be the applicable norms, the general customary rules on countermeasures contained in the ILC Draft Articles would be displaced. The Commission, however, fails to clarify in its proposal the relationship between WTO and general customary rules on countermeasures.

[8] The Council's negotiating mandate, which seems to have found its way in the agreed version of the instrument, confers the power to adopt an implementing act determining the existence of such measures to itself (Council Mandate for Negotiations modifying Art. 4 (1) of the ACI Proposal).

[9] Article 2 (1) read in conjunction with the Preamble, recital (11) of the ACI Proposal. The Council Mandate for Negotiations explicitly adds Recital 10bis to the proposal in which it states that '[c] ustomary international law, as reflected in Articles 22 and 49 to 53 of the Articles on Responsibility of States for Internationally Wrongful Acts [...] allows, under certain conditions [...] the imposition of countermeasures. Accordingly, Union response measures could consist [...] in the non-performance of international obligations towards the third country concerned insofar as the measures of economic coercion of the third country constitute an internationally wrongful act'.

3 Legality Under WTO Rules

3.1 Applicable Law and Article 23 of the DSU

Article 23.1 of the DSU generally mandates the use of WTO dispute settlement to the exclusion of the customary rules on countermeasures codified in the ILC Draft Articles. Nevertheless, it does so only when WTO Members 'seek the redress of a violation [. . .] under the covered agreements'. Similarly, Article 23.2 (a) of the DSU contains the more specific prohibition on unilateral determinations of *inconsistency with WTO rules* prior to exhaustion of DSU proceedings,[10] while Article 23.2 (c) 'prohibits any suspensions of concessions or other obligations (taken as measures seeking to redress a *WTO violation*), prior to a relevant DSB authorization' (emphasis added).[11] The panel in *US – Certain EC Products* expressly stated that 'the criterion for determining whether Article 23 is applicable is whether the Member that imposed the measure was "seeking the redress of" a WTO violation'.[12] This approach was also confirmed in the *EC – Commercial Vessels* case where the panel said that 'the phrase "seek the redress of a violation . . ." covers any act of a Member *in response to what it considers to be a violation of a WTO obligation* by another Member' (emphasis added).[13] The ACI proposal however, does not necessarily deal with cases related to alleged WTO illegalities.[14] In fact the proposal's purpose is to deal with measures of economic coercion, which presumably violate the customary principle of non-intervention, regardless of whether these measures simultaneously violate WTO rules. Accordingly, in case of countermeasures imposed under the ACI, the EU's legal claim would not be based on WTO rules. Hence, the *lex specialis* in the form of Article 23 of the DSU, requiring the use of the WTO dispute settlement for disputes on WTO law, might not be considered applicable 'as such' to the ACI, which deals with other breaches of international law. Similarly, outside the ACI context, there seems to be an agreement that when RTAs contain their own dispute settlement rules, Article 23.1 of the DSU is not deemed to have been violated even when the legal basis for the dispute at issue is an RTA norm replicating a WTO norm, due to the fact that the legal basis is still different.[15] Thus, Article 23 of the DSU does not seem applicable to the ACI 'as such' and the customary rules on countermeasures would not be displaced. The question of whether the conditions for imposing unilateral countermeasures under customary

---

[10] Panel Report, *US – Section 301*, WT/DS152/R, 22 December 1999, para. 7.59.

[11] Panel Report, *US – Certain EC Products*, WT/DS165/R, 17 July 2000, para. 6.37.

[12] Panel Report, *US – Certain EC Products*, para. 6.21.

[13] Panel Report, *EC – Commercial Vessels*, WT/DS301/R, 22 April 2005, para. 7.196.

[14] Impact Assessment Report Accompanying the Document Proposal for a Regulation of the European Parliament and of the Council on the protection of the Union and its Member States from Economic Coercion by Third Countries (Impact Assessment Report), 8.12.2021, SWD(2021) 371 final, fn. 18, p. 23.

[15] Apaza Lanyi and Steinbach (2014), p. 397; Flett (2015), pp. 557–558.

rules are met, such as whether the principle of non-interference is breached in case of economic coercion, lies outside the scope of this chapter.

Nevertheless, besides the statutory language of the measure, the panel could also take into consideration other internal elements legally relevant for the construction of legislation as it did in *US – Section 301* case, namely an administrative act accompanying the legislation, US statements before the panel, and US practice.[16] While currently there is little evidence to reverse the conclusion that Article 23 of the DSU is not 'as such' applicable to the ACI, in time if, for example, there is extensive practice showing that the EU is regularly using the instrument to adopt countermeasures before it challenges the same measures at the WTO or before exhausting the DSU proceedings and without obtaining the DSB's authorization, an 'as such' violation could be found.

Even if the ACI proposal is found to be 'as such' in conformity with Article 23 of the DSU, the assessment could be different when considering its application in individual instances. Thus, if a WTO panel determines that the evidence shows that EU's response measures under the ACI actually seek the redress of a WTO violation, Article 23 of the DSU could be applicable to the measures at issue. For example, in *US – Certain EC Products*, the panel established that there was 'ample evidence', consisting of the USTR Press Release announcing the measure, the request from USTR to the US Customs Service, memoranda of US Customs Service officials, and a press conference by the Deputy USTR, demonstrating that the measure at issue was seeking redress for a perceived WTO violation within the meaning of Article 23.1 of the DSU.[17] Hence, although under the ACI, the imposed unilateral measures theoretically should address violations of customary law, the WTO panel could analyse whether they are in fact seeking the redress of a WTO violation. In case a coercive measure is simultaneously challenged by the EU within WTO proceedings, as recently happened in the EU's conflict with China in relation to restrictions taken against Lithuania,[18] it might be more difficult for the EU to argue that its countermeasures are not taken against a WTO violation. In case there will be sufficient evidence, the panel could conclude that EU's measure seeks redress against a breach of the WTO agreements, rendering applicable the more special WTO rules, which constitute *lex specialis*. Hence, the conformity of a countermeasure adopted under the ACI with Article 23 of the DSU will depend on the specific facts of the case, in particular the available evidence, such as the text of the measure or official statements. If Article 23 of the DSU is applicable to a specific anti-coercion measure taken before obtaining the authorisation of the Dispute Settlement Body (DSB) in accordance with Article 22 procedures, Article 23 would be clearly violated. Therefore, specific unilateral response measures taken under the ACI, might be found to be incompatible with Article 23 of the DSU. Although,

[16] Panel Report, *US – Section 301*, paras. 7.110–7.130.

[17] Panel Report, *US – Certain EC Products*, paras. 6.25–6.34.

[18] Request for the establishment of a panel by the European Union, *China – Measures Concerning Trade in Goods and Services*, WT/DS610/8, 9 December 2022.

Article 1 (2) of the ACI proposal requires that actions taken under it be consistent with international obligations, in the Impact Assessment Report, the Commission itself stated that there can be cases in which the coercive measures are simultaneously in breach of WTO obligations,[19] and affirmed that in these cases 'the EU would continue to take to the WTO any grievances [. . .] if the EU considers those to be at odds with WTO disciplines'.[20] Therefore, the EU intends to make use of countermeasures under the ACI even in instances where the situations that the measures address amount to breaches of WTO law.

To conclude, while the ACI proposal 'as such' could currently pass the legality test under Article 23 of the DSU, specific measures in the form of suspension of WTO concessions or obligations could violate Article 23 of the DSU, provided that there will be sufficient evidence to support this conclusion.

3.2 *Legality Under WTO Substantive Rules*

The ACI proposal and measures taken under it may not only raise questions with respect to their legality under Article 23 of the DSU, but also under substantive WTO rules.

The first question is whether the ACI Proposal could be considered violating 'as such' substantive WTO norms. In order to answer this question, the mandatory/discretionary distinction often applicable in the analysis of 'as such' claims will be used. The value of this distinction, however, is not entirely clear.[21] According to the more traditional view originating under the GATT, only mandatory legislation can violate WTO law 'as such'. However, according to a more recent view, largely put forth in *US – Section 301*, discretion in legislation would not preclude the finding of an 'as such' violation.[22] Under this more recent view, the importance of the mandatory/discretionary distinction may vary from case to case and cannot be applied in an automatic manner.[23] Therefore, how the distinction is applied will also depend on the specific claims and context at issue. Nevertheless, the conclusion that the more discretion contained in legislation, the lower the likelihood that it will be found 'as such' inconsistent with the WTO rules seems valid, and this approach is supported in academic writings.[24] More recent WTO cases also seem to confirm that

[19] Impact Assessment Report, 8.12.2021, SWD(2021) 371 final, p. 23.

[20] ibid, p. 43.

[21] See generally Lockhart and Sheargold (2010), pp. 378–421; Lester (2011), pp. 369–402; Kang (2012), pp. 879–912.

[22] Lester (2011), p. 370.

[23] Panel Report, *US – Section 301*, para. 7.53; Panel Report, *Brazil – Aircraft (Article 21.5 – Canada II)*, T/DS46/RW2, 26 July 2001, paras. 5.9, 5.12; Appellate Body Report, *US – Corrosion-Resistant Steel Sunset Review*, T/DS244/AB/R, 15 December 2003, para. 93; Appellate Body Report, *EU – Biodiesel*, WT/DS473/AB/R, 6 October 2016, para. 6.227.

[24] Lockhart and Sheargold (2010), pp. 410 et seq.; Lester (2011), p. 399.

the degree of discretion matters, although the mere discretionary nature of legislation is no impediment for a finding of violation and each case should be considered separately. Most recently, the Appellate Body (AB) in *EU – Biodiesel*, as well as the panel in *US – Olives* stated that for an 'as such' violation, the legislation in question should *require* a breach of the WTO agreements or otherwise *restrict in a material way* the Member's discretion to act in a manner that is consistent with the agreements.[25] Still, it has also been argued in academic writings that when a WTO-inconsistent action is *expressly* mentioned in the legislation as the only possible action or one of the possible actions, it is more likely that it will be found in violation of a WTO substantive rule.[26]

Although the ACI Proposal establishes when economic coercion is found, the first step should be engagement with the state concerned. Where engagement is unsuccessful, and when it is necessary to protect Union's and its Member States' interests and rights; and action is in the Union's interest, the Commission '*shall* adopt an implementing act determining that it *shall* take a Union response measure' (Article 7 (1), first paragraph, emphasis added).[27] Accordingly, there is no discretion whether or not to act if certain conditions are fulfilled. Still, the Commission enjoys discretion in determining whether the relevant conditions have been met, e.g. whether the action is in the interest of the Union. Under the agreed final text, the Commission also has the discretion whether to submit a proposal to the Council to adopt an implementing act determining that a measure meets the conditions for economic coercion. Furthermore, the Council also seems to enjoy a high degree of discretion, being able to establish by qualified majority voting whether there are 'measures of economic coercion'.[28] Consequently, the proposal leaves the EU with discretion as to whether it shall take any action at all in a particular case. If the first-tier diplomatic efforts are unsuccessful, the ACI entails a high degree of discretion with respect to which countermeasures to apply from the list contained in Annex I. According to the ACI Proposal, the Commission may take measures pursuant to other legal instruments, and is even empowered in certain circumstances to amend the list from Annex I to provide additional types of measures via delegated acts (Article 7 (1) second paragraph, (7)—provision that might not be present in the final text of the Regulation, as the Council sought to delete it).[29] Hence, the Commission enjoys a high degree of discretion, especially with respect to choosing the response measures when non-interventionist measures are not successful. It can choose and

---

[25] Appellate Body Report, *EU – Biodiesel*, paras. 6.229, 6.281; Panel Report, *US – Olives*, WT/DS577/R, 19 November 2021, para. 7.146. Referring to older Appellate Body Reports from *US – Corrosion-Resistant Steel Sunset Review*, para. 100 and *US – Carbon Steel*, WT/DS/213/AB/R, 28 November 2002, para. 162.

[26] Lockhart and Sheargold (2010), pp. 415–418; Lester (2011), p. 399.

[27] The INTA Draft Report, 19 April 2022, 2021/0406(COD), suggests changing the text as following: '[t]he Commission *shall* adopt an implementing act taking a Union response measure on the following conditions' (emphasis added). Still, the mandatory language remains intact.

[28] Dreyer (2023).

[29] The Council Mandate for Negotiations deleting Art. 7 (7) of the ACI Proposal.

design measures that are consistent with WTO rules, especially considering that when selecting and designing measures it shall *inter alia* take into account 'any other relevant criteria established in international law' (Article 9 (2) (g)), including those from the WTO agreements. Therefore, the Commission is not *required* to act in violation of WTO norms; in fact Article 1 (2) of the proposal requires the Commission to act according to its international commitments. Thus, the Commission's discretion is not *restricted in a material way* to acting consistently with its WTO obligations. Still, Annex I expressly mentions 'the suspension of applicable international obligations' and contains explicit potential future measures that on their face are WTO-inconsistent,[30] which, unless justified, could lead to a finding of an 'as such' violation according to some cited academic writings.[31]

Therefore, considering the increased ambiguity around how 'as such' claims are evaluated, it is not entirely clear whether the ACI proposal would be found 'as such' consistent under WTO law. Nevertheless, its high degree of discretion considerably increases the proposal's likelihood of passing the 'as such' legality test under substantive WTO norms. The EU could also face 'as applied' claims of substantive violations, resulting from the specific application of the ACI, namely if the EU were to impose WTO-inconsistent countermeasures where first-tier efforts have failed. However, the assessment of such measures would have to be done in the context of the relevant dispute, with reference to how the measure in question has been applied—and this is outside the scope of this chapter.

3.3 *Justifications for Potential WTO Violations*

In case a violation of WTO rules is found, the EU would most likely try to justify it by invoking non-WTO or/and WTO law. It seems that the EU intends to justify its potential WTO-breaching measures under international customary rules on countermeasure. However, justifications based on non-WTO law, i.e. customary rules of international law, might not be recognized within WTO proceedings. WTO panels and the AB are known for their reticence in applying non-WTO law within WTO proceedings.[32] Thus, even though ILC Draft Articles on State Responsibility have been used for interpretative purposes, they have never been used by a panel or the AB as applicable law within WTO proceedings.[33] Accordingly, unilateral countermeasures in violation of substantive WTO obligations, are less likely to be justified by international customary norms.

---

[30] See Sect. 2.

[31] Lockhart and Sheargold (2010), pp. 415–418; Lester (2011), p. 399.

[32] Weiß and Furculita (2020), p. 875; Pauwelyn (2003), pp. 997–1030; Bartels (2016), pp. 1–21; Weiß (2020), pp. 412–419. For arguments in favour of considering countermeasures against non-WTO law violations as justifications for WTO law breaches, see Azaria (2022), pp. 389–423.

[33] Sánchez (2012), p. 292.

WTO justifications have not been given consideration in official ACI-related documents that have been made public by the EU to date. Still, the EU could also try to invoke WTO justifications, such as those contained in Article XX (a) of the GATT permitting measures that are 'necessary to protect public morals'. According to the WTO jurisprudence the term 'public morals' refers to standards of 'right and wrong conduct' belonging to a community or nation.[34] WTO Members enjoy wide discretion in defining their own public morals, as they are influenced by each Member's prevailing values.[35] Accordingly, while WTO agreements 'do not tackle the question of coercion',[36] they offer leeway to justify measures taken against them. When determining a measure's objective and establishing that it falls under the concept of 'public morals', a Member can invoke the relevant domestic regulations and legislative history.[37] Considering that the ACI is set to deal with measures that interfere with the EU's or its Member States' sovereign choices, the EU could argue that anti-coercion measures were taken to protect such values as the sovereign equality of states, mutual respect among peoples, and observance of international law, along with economic values.[38] These values are widely recognized as principles of international law being explicitly mentioned in Articles 1 (2) and 2 of the UN Charter[39] and in the Helsinki Final Act.[40] These values and principles are also enshrined in Articles 3(5), 21(1) and (2) of the TEU. The ACI proposal, pursuant to Articles 3 (5) and 21 (1) and (2) of the TEU, also specifically refers to the principles of equality, mutual respect among peoples, and strict observance of international law.[41] Since these values are consecrated in EU Constitutional treaties and in the ACI's preamble, and are recognized principles of international law, the claim that they represent 'public morals' is likely to be accepted without much debate, especially considering the leeway the concept allows. Even if the specific

---

[34] Panel Report, *China – Publications and Audiovisual Products*, WT/DS363/R, 12 August 2009, para. 7.759; Appellate Body Reports, *EC – Seal Products*, WT/DS400/AB/R, WT/DS401/AB/R, 22 May 2014, para. 5.199; Panel Report, *US – Tariff Measures*, WT/DS543/R, 15 September 2020, para. 7.140.

[35] Panel Report, *China – Publications and Audiovisual Products*, para. 7.763; Appellate Body Reports, *EC – Seal Products*, para. 5.199; Panel Report, *US – Tariff Measures*, para 7.116.

[36] Impact Assessment Report, 8.12.2021, SWD(2021) 371 final, p. 23.

[37] Conconi and Voon (2015), pp. 16–17; Panel Report, *EC – Seal Products*, WT/DS400/R, WT/DS401/R, 25 November 2013, para. 7.398.

[38] After *EC – Seals*, it is clear that the defendant does not have to establish that the measure was solely motivated by public morals; see Conconi and Voon (2015), p. 7.

[39] Article 1 (2) of the UN Charter mentions 'friendly relations among nations based on respect for the principle of equal rights and self-determination of peoples', while Article 2 of the UN Charter provides that '[t]he Organization is based on the principle of the sovereign equality of all its Members'.

[40] Conference on Security and Co-Operation in Europe Final Act, Helsinki, 1 August 1975. The first principle that it enshrines is the 'sovereign equality, respect for the rights inherent in sovereignty', while the tenth is 'fulfilment in good faith of obligations under international law'.

[41] ACI Proposal, Preamble, recitals (1), (2), (4).

instrument implementing the measure does not explicitly reference public morals, this should not be determinative for the justification.[42]

Although the values at stake would constitute public morals, other conditions established in subparagraph (a) and the chapeau of Article XX might be more difficult to meet.[43] According to subparagraph (a), the measures at issue should be 'designed', i.e. not incapable of, and 'necessary' to protect public morals.[44] While the threshold set for proving that a measure was 'designed' to protect public morals is lower and might not even be a helpful step for the analysis,[45] evaluating whether a measure is 'necessary' represents a 'holistic approach', involving the 'weighing and balancing' of a series of factors: the relative importance of the pursued objective, the restrictiveness of the measure, and the degree of contribution to the objective, followed by an assessment of whether there were potential WTO-consistent or less restrictive alternatives.[46] In view of the inclusion of the interests and values at issue in UN Charter and Helsinki Final Act, as well as EU's constitutional treaties, it is reasonable to expect that the pursued objectives will be qualified as vital and highly important. The assessment of other factors, however, can be performed only when specific measures will be known. However, for a justification to be accepted, the measures chosen should be connected to the objective pursued and actually contribute to it, including through the products covered by the measures to be justified.[47] Thus, the specified products covered by the measures should be connected to the morally wrong conduct or otherwise contribute to the invoked objectives.[48] Furthermore, the EU would have to demonstrate that a proposed less restrictive measure was not reasonably available to it.[49] Finally, if the measure is considered provisionally justified under one of the paragraphs of Article XX of the GATT, the measure still should not be '*applied* in a manner which would constitute a means of arbitrary or unjustifiable discrimination between countries where the same conditions prevail, or a disguised restriction on international trade' (emphasis added). Accordingly, a

[42] Panel Report, *US – Tariff Measures*, para. 7.125.

[43] Article XX GATT involves a two-tier test; the measure at issue must not only fall under a particular exception contained in the paragraphs (a)–(j), but also should satisfy the chapeau; see: Appellate Body Report, *US – Gasoline*, WT/DS2/AB/R, 29 April 1996, p. 22.

[44] Appellate Body Report, *Colombia – Textiles*, WT/DS461/AB/R, 7 June 2016, para. 5.68; Panel Report, *US – Tariff Measures*, paras. 7.145–7.153.

[45] Panel Report, *US – Tariff Measures*, para. 7.151. If this initial threshold is not met, further examination would not be required; see: Appellate Body Report, *Colombia – Textiles*, para. 5.68.

[46] Appellate Body Report, *Colombia – Textiles*, para. 5.77; Appellate Body Report, *China – Publications and Audiovisual Products*, para. 244; Panel Report, *US – Tariff Measures*, para. 7.159.

[47] Panel Report, *US – Tariff Measures*, para. 7.178.

[48] The panel in *US – Tariff Measures* has not resolved the issue whether a measure would have to apply only to products that embody the morally offensive conduct to benefit from justification (para. 7.179).

[49] Appellate Body Report, *Korea – Measures Affecting Imports of Fresh, Chilled and Frozen Beef*, WT/DS161/AB/R, WT/DS169/AB/R, 11 December 2000, paras. 165–166; Appellate Body Report, *China – Publications and Audiovisual Products*, para. 246.

measure's conformity with the chapeau will depend on how it will be applied in practice. The cause and rationale behind the discrimination would have to bear a rational connection to the objective.[50] For example, if a measure were imposed on the products of a particular state and not those of others,[51] because of its potential to provide relief to EU economic operators (a criterion to be taken into account when selecting and designing a measure under the ACI proposal),[52] without a rational connection to the EU's alleged objective, it would not pass the chapeau test.

GATS violations could similarly be justified under Article XIV of the GATS, which contains an exception for measures 'necessary to protect public morals *or* to maintain public order' (emphasis added) and providing a chapeau with a similar language to that of Article XX of the GATT. Thus, the analysis under Article XIV of the GATS would be similar to that under Article XX of the GATT, except that it additionally covers measures necessary 'to maintain public order'.[53] Nevertheless, the conclusion reached under Article XX GATT (a) of the GATT that measures are necessary to protect public morals would be sufficient considering the use of the conjunction 'or' suggesting their alternative character.[54] Therefore, the difference in wording should not generally affect the analysis described above.

4 The EU's Multilateralist DNA Called into Question

Questions as to the credibility of the EU's multilateralist stance will arise not only in relation to the legality of the ACI under procedural and substantive WTO rules. The adoption of such a unilateral instrument, even if legal, could endanger the multilateral trading system.

The ACI confers credibility on the EU that it will act in the face of coercion and the Commission hopes that the instrument's deterrent effect will be successful enough to avoid the actual imposition of countermeasures in most cases.[55] However, allowing unilateral action without resorting to WTO proceedings or waiting for a

[50] Appellate Body Report, *Brazil – Retreated Tyres*, WT/DS332/AB/R, 3 December 2007, para. 227; Appellate Body Report, *US – Tuna II (Mexico) (Article. 21.5 – Mexico)*, WT/DS381/AB/RW, 20 November 2015, para. 7.316.

[51] Since the chapeau refers to the discrimination between countries with the same conditions that are relevant in light of the particular policy objective (Appellate Body Reports, *EC – Seal Products*, paras. 5.299–5.300), there will be discrimination if countries that engage in economic coercive measures, as defined by the ACI, are treated differently.

[52] ACI Proposal, Art. 9 (2) (b).

[53] Appellate Body Report, *US – Gambling*, WT/DS285/AB/R, 20 August 2005, para. 296.

[54] As sovereign equality and mutual respect among peoples are reflected in EU's law and will likely be recognized as fundamental interests of the society, measures under the ACI proposal could be considered besides 'necessary to protect public morals' also 'necessary to maintain public order', which would still keep the rest of the analysis intact.

[55] Impact Assessment Report, 8.12.2021, SWD(2021) 371 final, p. 21.

final WTO report would clearly undermine the WTO dispute settlement rules. Although the EU alleges that the ACI is designed to address economic coercion that it is not tackled by WTO law, the legislative history might indicate that the EU is in fact trying to circumvent multilateral trading rules. The INTA's proposal for additional amendments to Regulation 654/2014 on the trade enforcement regulation, the trigger behind the Commission's promise to introduce an anti-coercion tool, sought to address 'a clear breach of obligations of trade agreements', since '[d]ispute settlement provisions, including in regional or bilateral trade agreements, might not be sufficiently specific or explicit enough'.[56] The amendment on immediate action in the event of a unilateral measure imposed by a third country which represents a clear breach of international law was introduced by INTA 'against the background of the ongoing tension in international trade and the crisis in the WTO'.[57] Accordingly, the Committee seemed particularly concerned about the availability of a tool that would allow the EU to act swiftly as the WTO Appellate Body crisis continues and asked the Commission to table an anti-coercion proposal. Even if, unlike the INTA's initial proposal, which was clearly in violation of Article 23 of the DSU,[58] the ACI proposal has a better chance of withstanding the test of legality under WTO rules, it still shows the EU's turn towards unilateralism.

Additionally, there is an increased risk that by imposing countermeasures the dispute will escalate into a 'trade war' through retaliation against the EU. Since the ACI would contribute to the weaponization of international trade law, the exact phenomenon that it seeks to counter, the EU could be accused of hypocrisy. The instrument could also invite others to adopt similar unilateral legislation, further eroding the force of multilateral rules. Although the EU could act cautiously, others could often and recklessly adopt countermeasures against alleged economic coercion in a bid to escape accusations of WTO violations. Furthermore, powerful actors like the EU might similarly rely on their economic strength to pressure other countries into stopping economic coercion, but smaller countries cannot adopt similar legislation with a similar effect. Hence, there is a risk that international trade law will be ruled by the law of might,[59] with the EU contributing to this.

Thus, the ACI challenges the credibility of the EU's multilateralist DNA not only because of the question of its (i)legality under WTO rules, but also because of other consequences that would weaken the multilateral trading system.

[56] Report on the Proposal for a Regulation of the European Parliament and of the Council amending Regulation (EU) No. 654/2014 of the European Parliament and of the Council concerning the Exercise of the Union's Rights for the Application and Enforcement of International Trade Rules (INTA Report), COM(2019)0623, 6 July 2020, Amendments 3, 8, and 14.

[57] INTA Report, COM(2019)0623, 6 July 2020, Explanatory Statement, p. 19.

[58] For further detail, see Weiß and Furculita (2020), pp. 879–881.

[59] Brewster (2019), p. 65; Weiß and Furculita (2020), p. 880.

5 Conclusion

In light of the increasing tensions and rising unilateralism in the international trade arena, the EU is seeking to strengthen its toolbox by creating the ACI that would allow it to impose immediate countermeasures, without waiting for WTO procedures to unfold and the DSB's authorization for retaliation, which is necessary under WTO rules. The EU justifies its actions based on customary international law, arguing that these countermeasures are legal because they are taken against coercive economic measures presumably violating the international principle of non-intervention. However, the question arises whether EU's reasoning can be squared with WTO rules. The EU is a declared staunch multilateralist, however this new instrument allowing it to take unilateral countermeasures challenges this position.

As argued, Article 23 of the DSU does not seem to be currently applicable to the ACI proposal 'as such', since the Regulation is set to deal with violations of the customary principle of non-intervention, and not WTO violations. Its application in specific instances, however, might be considered as seeking redress for a WTO-violation, making Article 23 of the DSU the applicable law as *lex specialis*, to the detriment of general public international law. In such a case, countermeasures taken without following the relevant WTO procedures would clearly violate Article 23 of the DSU. In terms of substantive conformity, considering the high degree of discretion that it entails, the ACI could be found 'as such' consistent with the WTO rules, leaving the question of WTO conformity of potential future specific measures unanswered. Accordingly, it seems that despite the 'unilateral' character of the new instrument, the Commission put considerable effort into not making the ACI a blatant 'as such' violation of the WTO rules. Still, ACI's fate in terms of its WTO legality very much depends on how it will actually be used. Furthermore, even if the instrument would not overtly 'as such' breach WTO rules, the EU could be accused of hypocrisy, circumvention of these rules, and betrayal of its multilateralist DNA, since the ACI only contributes to the increased weaponization of international trade. Resort to unilateral trade measures to deal with economic coercion could make the EU less interested in reforming the WTO to address such issues, leading to the risk of further WTO redundancy. Furthermore, the ACI might provide incentives for others to follow suit, posing the risk that international trade law will be ruled by the law of might. Thus, it is hoped that the ACI has the desired deterrent effect on states that would otherwise seek to exert economic pressure on the EU and that this does not cause more damage to the WTO.

References

Apaza Lanyi P, Steinbach A (2014) Limiting jurisdictional fragmentation in international trade disputes. J Int Disput Settl 5:372–405

Azaria D (2022) Trade countermeasures for breaches of international law outside the WTO. ICLQ 71:389–423

Bartels L (2016) Jurisdiction and applicable law in the WTO. SIEL working paper no. 2016/18, pp 1–21

Brewster R (2019) Can international trade law recover? WTO dispute settlement: can we go back again? AJIL Unbound 113:61–66

Conconi P, Voon T (2015) EC – Seal Products: the tension between public morals and international trade agreements. EUI working paper RSCAS 2015/70, pp 1–20

Dreyer I (2023) EU capitals to decide on coercion in inter-institutional deal over new retaliatory instrument. https://borderlex.net/2023/03/28/eu-capitals-to-decide-on-coercion-in-inter-institutional-deal-over-new-retaliatory-instrument/

Flett J (2015) Referring PTA disputes to the WTO dispute settlement system. In: Dür A, Elsig M (eds) Trade cooperation: the purpose, design and effects of preferential trade agreements. World Trade Forum, Cambridge University Press, New York, pp 555–579

Kang J (2012) The presumption of good faith in the WTO 'as such' cases: a reformulation of the mandatory/discretionary distinction as an analytical tool. J World Trade 46(4):879–912

Lester S (2011) A framework for thinking about the 'discretion' in the mandatory/discretionary distinction. JIEL 14(2):369–402

Lockhart N, Sheargold E (2010) In search of relevant discretion: the role of the mandatory/ discretionary distinction in WTO law. JIEL 13(2):379–421

Pauwelyn J (2003) How to win a World Trade Organization dispute based on non-World Trade Organization law? Questions of jurisdiction and merits. J World Trade 37(6):997–1030

Sánchez A (2012) What trade lawyers should know about the ILC articles on state responsibility. GTCJ 7(6):292–299

Weiß W (2020) WTO law and domestic regulation. C.H. Beck, München

Weiß W, Furculita C (2020) The EU in search for stronger enforcement rules. Assessing the proposed amendments to Trade Enforcement Regulation 654/2014. JIEL 23(4):865–884

Cornelia Furculita, Dr. iur., is a postdoctoral researcher at the German University of Administrative Sciences Speyer. Her research interests lie in international trade law, international dispute settlement, and EU trade policy. Cornelia has successfully defended her PhD thesis (summa cum laude) in 2021. From September 2017 until August 2020, she was a Marie Curie Early Stage Researcher at the University of Speyer, funded by the EU Horizon Project EUTIP. During her PhD studies, she was a visiting researcher at the University of Passau (Germany), T.M.C. Asser Instituut (the Netherlands), NautaDutilh (the Netherlands), and BusinessEurope (Belgium). Cornelia is the author of 'The WTO and the New Generation EU FTA Dispute Settlement Mechanisms: Interacting in a Fragmented and Changing International Trade Law Regime' (Springer, 2021). She has also co-edited the book 'Global Politics and EU Trade Policy: Facing the Challenges to a Multilateral Approach' (Springer, 2020), and published several book chapters and articles in top international trade journals. She has also presented her research at numerous conferences, such as the World Trade Forum (2019), PEPA/SIEL (2019 and 2022), ESIL Workshops of the International Economic Law Interest Group (2019 and 2020), Jean Monnet Doctoral Workshops (2019), The EU in International Affairs VI (2018), and Transatlantic Perspectives: The Future of European Law and Policy VI (2018).

The Principle of Autonomy of EU Law in the Context of Investor-State Dispute Settlement: A Public Policy Norm?

Trajan Shipley

Contents

Abstract The principle of autonomy of EU law sits at the core of the current clash between EU law and ISDS. Considering the widespread rejection by investment arbitration tribunals of the Court of Justice's *Achmea* case law, this chapter examines the nature, scope and content of the principle of autonomy of EU law in the context of ISDS. It considers relevant case law of both the Court of Justice and arbitral tribunals together with literature on the nature of the EU legal order from an international law perspective and on the principle of autonomy. It also examines the possibility to claim the autonomy of EU law as a norm of public policy and the relevance of pursuing such an approach.

This chapter is written on the basis of my master's thesis, which was defended in June 2022. I would like to thank Prof. Isabelle van Damme and Michael De Boeck for their insightful comments and guidance during the drafting, as well as the editors of this volume for reviewing earlier versions of the chapter.

T. Shipley (✉)
Brussels, Belgium
e-mail: trajan.shipley@coleurope.eu

M. de Amstalden et al. (eds.), *International Economic Law*, Special Issue,
https://doi.org/10.1007/978-3-031-41996-6_10

Keywords EU law · Investment arbitration · Achmea · Public policy · Energy charter treaty

1 Introduction

EU law and international arbitration law have long been described as two bodies of law failing to intersect.[1] This is even more pronounced when it comes to investment arbitration law, particularly regarding 'intra-EU disputes', which occur between EU investors and EU Member States under bilateral investment treaties ('BITs') entered into by Member States. The reasons for this rocky relationship relate to the difficulties arising from the simultaneous coexistence of investment protection requirements under international law with substantive provisions of EU law. In its landmark *Achmea* judgment,[2] the Court of Justice of the EU ('CJEU') declared investor-state dispute settlement ('ISDS') provisions in intra-EU BITs incompatible with the autonomy of EU law, further widening the gap between the two legal regimes. Despite initial calls to read *Achmea* narrowly, the CJEU has recently confirmed that it also encompasses intra-EU disputes pursuant to the Energy Charter Treaty ('ECT') or individual arbitration agreements.[3]

Often raised as a so-called 'intra-EU objection' in ISDS proceedings, the *Achmea* case law has been systematically rejected by arbitral tribunals and foreign courts throughout the world,[4] with the only exception being the recent award in *Green Power v Spain*.[5] Many of these disputes are under the ECT, the largest multilateral agreement in the field of energy to which the EU is itself a party. The fate of the ECT, currently under a modernization process, is far from certain given the fact that several Member States have announced their withdrawal.[6] However, numerous

[1] Bermann (2011), p. 1193; Broberg and Fenger (2022), p. 87.

[2] CJEU Case C-284/16 *Slowakische Republik v Achmea BV* EU:C:2018:158.

[3] CJEU Case C-109/20 *Poland v PL Holdings Sàrl* EU:C:2021:875; CJEU Case C-741/19 *République de Moldavie v Komstroy LLC* EU:C:2021:655; CJEU Case C-638/19 P *Commission v European Food SA and Others* EU:C:2022:50.

[4] See, for instance *Infracapital v Kingdom of Spain*, ICSID Case No. ARB/16/18, Decision on Respondent's Request for Reconsideration Regarding the Intra-EU Objection and the Merits, 1 February 2022, paras. 108 and 113; Opinion & Order of the United States District Court of the Southern District of New York, 15 August 2015, *Micula v. Government of Romania*, 2015 WL 4643180 (S.D.N.Y. Aug. 5, 2015), para. 12.

[5] Green Power Partners K/S & SCE Solar Don Benito APS v Kingdom of Spain, SCC Case No. 2016/135, Award, 16 June 2022.

[6] At the time of the last review of this chapter, Poland, Spain, the Netherlands, France, Slovenia and Germany had publicly confirmed their intention to withdraw from the ECT, while the European Parliament had called for a coordinated EU withdrawal.

intra-EU arbitral proceedings continue their course, and a 20-year sunset clause applies even in the case of withdrawal.[7]

This leaves two vast bodies of case law, namely of arbitral tribunals and of the CJEU, that are plainly and mutually incompatible. On the one hand, the CJEU has resorted to the autonomy of the EU legal order to deny the compatibility with EU law of intra-EU arbitration clauses in a way that raises doubts on their compatibility with Articles 26 and 27 of the Vienna Convention on the Law of Treaties ('VCLT'). On the other, arbitral tribunals have used methods of interpretation under public international law that fail to grasp the EU legal order's *sui generis* nature as a legal order of both national and international law. At the heart of that cleavage sits the principle of autonomy of EU law, a unique and uncertain principle of jurisprudential creation that allows the EU legal order to distinguish itself from both national and international law by reference to the essential characteristics of the EU and its law.[8] It is the nature, scope and limits of this principle what this chapter seeks to address.

This chapter thus examines in a pluralistic way how the CJEU has defined the principle of autonomy of EU law and applied it to the context of international dispute resolution, and how arbitral tribunals have reacted to it. It also explores whether it is possible to consider the principle of autonomy as a norm of public policy deriving from the EU legal order for the purposes of establishing a framework to address the compatibility of EU and international investment law.

2 Grasping the Meaning of the Autonomy of EU Law

In a legal context, the notion of 'autonomy' is generally understood as the ability to abide by self-imposed norms shielded off from external influences. When referring to a given legal order, autonomy relates to its ability to limit the influences of other established legal orders with which it interacts or from which it is derived.[9] In EU law, the principle of autonomy is of jurisprudential creation and refers to a qualitative characteristic of the EU legal order, enabling it to claim its *sui generis* nature in respect of both national and international law. From an international law dimension, EU law is often considered a 'subsystem' of public international law,[10] and arbitral tribunals sometimes struggle to determine the nature of secondary EU law provisions.[11] As stressed by Advocate General Maduro, EU law is 'a municipal order of

---

[7] See Article 47(3) ECT.

[8] CJEU Opinion 1/17 (*CETA*) EU:C:2019:341, para. 109.

[9] See the concept of 'derivative autonomy' in Schilling (1996), p. 390.

[10] Binder and Hofbauer (2017), p. 140.

[11] *Vattenfall AB and Others v Germany*, ICSID Case No. ARB/12/12, Decision on the Achmea Issue, 31 August 2018, para. 149.

transnational dimensions',[12] and because of this it must be regarded in its dual dimension of forming part of both the national law in force in every Member State and as deriving from an international agreement between the Member States.[13] It is precisely through the principle of autonomy that the EU legal order claims its special nature and characteristics without being held hostage to the dichotomy of national versus international law.

The autonomy of EU law, which was only recently recognized as a principle in Opinion 1/20,[14] can be traced back to the CJEU's seminal judgments in *Van Gend en Loos* and *Costa v ENEL*,[15] where it stressed that the law stemming from the Treaty was 'a new legal order of international law', created from 'an independent source'. According to the CJEU, EU law is vested with special characteristics, including the fact that its subjects are not just Member States but also their citizens, and that through it Member States have in effect limited their sovereign rights.[16] As noted by Pescatore, it is the realization of the concept of solidarity between Member States and the creation of a specific set of internal structures, including the CJEU's compulsory jurisdiction, what truly distinguishes EU law from international law.[17]

The autonomy of EU law was initially claimed in respect of the national law of the Member States. However, with a series of decisions starting with Opinion 1/76[18] and all the way until *Kadi*[19] and *Achmea*,[20] the CJEU has asserted the autonomy of EU law *vis-à-vis* international law on key aspects of the EU legal order such as its exclusive jurisdiction pursuant to Article 344 TFEU, the preliminary reference procedure under Article 267 TFEU, or the system of protection of fundamental rights under EU law. In this 'external' dimension, the autonomy of the EU legal order purports to shield the essential characteristics of EU law from conflicting obligations under international law which may otherwise be opposed to them. As the CJEU first held in Opinion 2/13, the autonomy of EU law is violated when the essential characteristics of the EU legal order are adversely affected.[21] The content principle of autonomy of EU law is thus *prima facie* determined by the essential characteristics of EU law.

[12] Opinion of AG Poiares Maduro in Case C-402/05 P *Kadi* EU:C:2008:11, para. 21. See also the German Constitutional Court Case 1 BvR 248/63 and 216/67 §2(3)(c).

[13] *Achmea*, *supra* note 2, para. 41.

[14] Opinion 1/20 (*Draft Modernised ECT*) EU:C:2022:485, para. 47.

[15] CJEU Case C-26/62 *Van Gend en Loos* EU:C:1963:1; CJEU Case C-6/64 *Costa v ENEL* EU: C:1964:66.

[16] Ibid.

[17] Pescatore (1970), p. 167. For instance, compliance with the principle of energy solidarity is a condition of the legality of EU policies in the field of energy which can be subject to judicial review, see CJEU Case C-848/19 P *Germany v Poland* EU:C:2021:598, para. 44.

[18] CJEU Opinion 1/76 (*Inland Waterway Vessels*) EU:C:1977:63.

[19] CJEU Cases C-402/05 P and C-415/05 P Kadi and Al Barakaat International Foundation v Council and Commission EU:C:2008:461.

[20] *Achmea*, *supra* note 2.

[21] CJEU Opinion 2/13 EU:C:2014:2454, para. 200; Contartese (2017), p. 1670.

The CJEU has however not exhaustively defined what are exactly these essential characteristics of EU law.[22] In Opinion 1/17, it stressed that the autonomy of EU law resides in the fact that the EU has a unique constitutional framework that encompasses the founding values under Article 2 TEU, the general principles of EU law, the provisions of the Charter of Fundamental Rights, and the provisions of the EU Treaties.[23] It also noted that in order to preserve this autonomy, the EU Treaties provide for a judicial system comprising both national and EU courts with the preliminary ruling mechanism under Article 267 TFEU acting as its cornerstone.[24] The system is completed by the standstill obligation under Article 344 TFEU which prevents Member States from submitting disputes concerning the interpretation and application of the EU Treaties to external methods of dispute settlement, thus ensuring the exclusive jurisdiction of the CJEU in this regard.[25] However, the CJEU has also stressed that the autonomy of the EU would be undermined if the EU institutions were precluded by an international tribunal from establishing a level of protection of a public interest in accordance with its constitutional framework,[26] or if the interpretation of fundamental rights under the framework of the EU were impaired by obligations under international agreements.[27] As a result, the CJEU seemingly applies the principle of autonomy in a relational way, taking into account the nature of the envisaged relationship between the CJEU and other dispute settlement bodies which may be called to interpret or apply EU law.[28]

Given the lack of preciseness as to what are the essential characteristics of EU law in relation to its autonomy, there are two differing views in the academic literature that try to illustrate this point. Both of them share the fact that the autonomy of EU law operates, in essence, as a functional principle,[29] allowing the EU legal order to simultaneously shield itself from external interference and protect some of its key features. In this sense, some authors understand autonomy also as a 'structural' principle in that it protects the essential elements of the EU legal order's structure without defining its normative content. This allows the EU legal order to preserve its way of functioning and to establish itself as an international actor. In other words, the principle of autonomy protects the overall structure of the EU legal order from pressures coming from national and international law but does not define the content of that legal system.[30] Another line of scholarship sees autonomy as an 'existential' principle, linking autonomy to the EU's constitutional character. Here autonomy is seen as a premise upon which the existence and the qualitative nature of the EU legal

---

[22] See De Boeck (2022), pp. 275–306. Klabbers and Koutrakos (2019), p. 8.

[23] Opinion 1/17, *supra* note 8, para. 110.

[24] Ibid., para. 111.

[25] CJEU Case C-459/03 *Commission v Ireland* ECLI:EU:2006:345, paras. 123 and 124.

[26] Opinion 1/17, *supra* note 8, paras. 147–150.

[27] Opinion 2/13, *supra* note 21, para. 170; *Kadi*, *supra* note 19, paras. 281–285.

[28] Odermatt (2023), pp. 17–18.

[29] Lenaerts et al. (2021), p. 49; De Boeck (2022), p. 294.

[30] See Cremona (2018), p. 15; Odermatt (2016), p. 5; Shuibhne (2019), pp. 20–22.

order is founded. In other words, because EU law has special characteristics of a constitutional nature, it is autonomous. If it were not for the principle of autonomy, the EU legal order's qualitative components would be imperiled by national and international law.[31]

The choice between a 'structural' or an 'existential' view of the autonomy of EU law ultimately has important implications from the perspective of international law. A structural view that links autonomy to the essential characteristics of the architecture of the EU legal order as defined in the EU Treaties, could avoid being categorized as a constitutional exception at odds with Article 27 VCLT. On the contrary, an existential view of the autonomy of EU law may be presented as having an unlimited scope, as anything that operates in accordance with the EU Treaties could potentially be linked to the essential characteristics of EU law. It is here submitted that under the principle of autonomy, there are limits as to what the autonomous EU legal order can do without entering into potential breaches of international obligations by the EU itself as a subject of international law and/or by its Member States. This premise is not incompatible with accepting that the EU legal order, even if considered a subsystem of international law, has a constitutional dimension. Indeed, the CJEU has claimed that the Treaties are the 'basic constitutional charter' of the EU and that the measures adopted by its institutions and Member States must be in conformity with them and subject to judicial review.[32] Eckes argues that the CJEU's autonomy doctrine grants the EU its own jurisdictional sovereignty,[33] which resides on the premise that the relationship between the EU and its Member States takes place not under international law, but through a network of rules and principles that render individuals, and not only Member States, as relevant subjects.[34] These rules and principles replace the CJEU's need for recourse to customary international law under the VCLT in the interpretation and application of the EU Treaties.[35] While this point is beyond the scope of this chapter, the constitutional nature of the EU legal order may be taken for granted. The focus is rather on the limits of such constitutional dimension *vis-à-vis* international law, by reference to the principle of autonomy in the specific context of ISDS.

---

[31] See Barents (2004), pp. 252–253; Lenaerts et al. (2021), p. 49; Shuibhne (2019), pp. 22–38.

[32] CJEU Case C-294/83 *Les Verts v Parliament* ECLI:EU:C:1986:166, para. 23.

[33] Eckes (2020), p. 1.

[34] van Rossem (2009), p. 199.

[35] De Boeck (2022), p. 304. Article 19(1) TEU entrusts the CJEU with ensuring that 'in the interpretation and application of the [EU] Treaties, the law is observed.' Reference to 'the law' must be understood as the *sui generis* nature of the law created by the EU Treaties. See Opinion 2/13, supra note 21, para. 167: "These essential characteristics of EU law have given rise to a structured network of principles, rules and mutually interdependent legal relations linking the EU and its Member States, and its Member States with each other, which are now engaged, as is recalled in the second paragraph of Article 1 TEU, in a 'process of creating an ever closer union among the peoples of Europe'".

3 The Autonomy of EU Law in Case Law Concerning ISDS

3.1 CJEU Case Law

As a matter of principle, the CJEU's case law consistently claims the *prima facie* compatibility of international dispute resolution mechanisms with EU law.[36] The CJEU has even clarified that it lacks jurisdiction to hear potential infringements of EU law when they are ancillary to alleged failures to comply with arbitration agreements on an issue falling outside of the areas of competence of the EU.[37] However, in practice the CJEU has limited to a great extent the compatibility of international dispute resolution mechanisms with EU law when Member States or areas governed under EU law are involved. It has done so on the grounds that they conflict either with the CJEU's exclusive jurisdiction under Article 344 TFEU,[38] or with the EU judicial system in itself,[39] which comprises both national and EU courts and is articulated around the mechanism under Article 267 TFEU, allowing national courts to refer questions for a preliminary ruling on the interpretation or validity of EU law. The exclusive jurisdiction of the CJEU seems to be the most relevant criterion, as the CJEU has ruled that an international agreement that avoids breaching its exclusive jurisdiction would preserve the autonomy of the EU legal system.[40] In the particular context of ISDS, the CJEU has held that the respect for the autonomy of the EU legal order is the one and only condition that must be met for the EU's proposed investment court system and a future multilateral investment court.[41]

In this sense, Govaere points out that the CJEU seems to be concerned with a possible 'Trojan horse' effect under which international dispute settlement can erode the EU legal order and its autonomy.[42] In the context of investment arbitration, the CJEU has found arbitration clauses allowing for intra-EU ISDS to be incompatible with EU law because such disputes, which may concern the interpretation or application of EU law, are removed from the EU judicial system, calling into question the principle of mutual trust and the exclusive jurisdiction of the CJEU.[43] This is based on the premise that ISDS provisions in BITs fall under the shared

[36] Opinion 1/76, *supra* note 18, para. 5; CJEU Opinion 1/91 (*Draft EEA Agreement*) EU:C:1991:490, para. 40; CJEU Opinion 1/09 (*Unified Patent Court*) EU:C:2011:123, para. 74; Opinion 2/13, *supra* note 21, para. 181; *Achmea*, *supra* note 2, para. 57; Opinion 1/17, *supra* note 8, para. 106.

[37] CJEU Case C-457/18 *Slovenia v Croatia* ECLI:EU:C:2020:65, paras. 104–105.

[38] Opinion 2/13, *supra* note 21, para. 213.

[39] Opinion 1/09, *supra* note 36, para. 79.

[40] *Commission v Ireland*, *supra* note 25, para. 124.

[41] Opinion 1/17, *supra* note 8, para. 108.

[42] Govaere (2010), p. 187.

[43] *Achmea*, *supra* note 2, paras. 48–60; *PL Holdings*, *supra* note 3, para. 47; *Komstroy*, *supra* note 3, para. 62. The principle of mutual trust binds Member States *inter se* and *vis-à-vis* the EU. See in this sense Lenaerts (2017), pp. 805–840.

competences of both the EU and the Member States,[44] and thus, according to the CJEU, Member States cannot remove disputes in the field of EU law from the system of EU judicial remedies without eroding the principles of mutual trust and sincere cooperation.[45] It also results from the CJEU's refusal to allow investment arbitration tribunals to refer questions for a preliminary ruling on issues concerning the interpretation of EU law,[46] a solution that would ensure the uniform application of EU law, the principle of mutual trust, and the CJEU's exclusive jurisdiction under Article 344 TFEU if it were to bind the arbitral tribunal in dealing with matters of EU law.[47] The reason for this far-reaching doctrine is that contrary to commercial arbitration, investment arbitration is not based on the free will of the parties, but rather on an international treaty by which the Member States themselves remove disputes from the EU judicial system.[48] According to the CJEU, under EU law Member States cannot do so in intra-EU situations.

The *Achmea* judgment was delivered in a dispute concerning an intra-EU BIT and did not expressly consider all intra-EU ISDS mechanisms in violation of EU law, including the ECT. Dashwood argued in this sense that the arbitration clause under Article 26 ECT, even when actioned in an intra-EU context, would not be caught by *Achmea*.[49] However, the CJEU clarified in *PL Holdings* and *Komstroy* that the incompatibility of EU law with intra-EU ISDS is not limited to BITs and that, in practice, it is an incompatibility on a matter of principle. In *PL Holdings*, it even instructed national courts to uphold applications to set aside awards rendered on the basis of an arbitration agreement "infringing Articles 267 and 344 TFEU and the principles of mutual trust, sincere cooperation and autonomy of EU law".[50] This wording suggests that the autonomy of EU law is jointly and adversely affected in any intra-EU ISDS context when structural elements of the EU legal order, such as the preliminary ruling procedure, the CJEU's exclusive jurisdiction, and key principles relating to the constitutional framework of the EU legal order are impaired. In Opinion 1/17, the CJEU outlined two specific conditions ISDS tribunals must meet

---

[44] CJEU Opinion 2/15 *(Singapore FTA)* ECLI:EU:C:2017:376, para. 293.

[45] *Achmea, supra* note 2, para. 58.

[46] The CJEU in *Achmea, supra* note 2, paras. 46 and following, held that investment arbitration tribunals cannot be classified as 'courts or tribunals of a Member State' under Article 267 TFEU insofar as they do not have any links with the judicial systems of the Member States that signed the BIT. It also reasoned that the review of awards where national courts could examine fundamental provisions of EU law, and if necessary refer a preliminary ruling request, were precluded in the case of investment arbitration proceedings.

[47] On this aspect, see the Opinion of AG Wathelet in *Achmea* ECLI:EU:C:2017:699, paras. 85 and 126–131.

[48] *Achmea, supra* note 2, para. 55.

[49] Dashwood (2021), pp. 415–434.

[50] *PL Holdings*, supra note 3, para. 55.

in order not to undermine the autonomy of the EU legal order in relation to the CETA Agreement,[51] namely:

1. Tribunals must not be empowered to interpret or apply EU law other than provisions of an agreement that form part of EU law, having regard to the rules and principles of international law applicable between the Parties; and
2. Tribunals may not issue awards which have the effect of preventing the EU institutions from operating in accordance with the EU constitutional framework.[52]

With regard to the former, the CJEU held that CETA tribunals had no jurisdiction to interpret rules of EU law other than the provisions of the CETA, and that in applying domestic law as a fact, they were obliged to follow the prevailing interpretation given to that domestic law, which includes the CJEU as far as EU law is concerned.[53] With regard to the latter, according to the CJEU, the autonomy of EU law would be undermined if the EU or Member States were obliged to withdraw or amend legislation concerning the level of public interest established in accordance with the EU constitutional framework, but that this was not the case of the CETA since its tribunals were not entrusted with that power.[54] Moreover, in Opinion 1/20 the CJEU held that the principle of autonomy is enshrined in particular in Article 344 TFEU,[55] which confirms that the principle's core is the exclusive jurisdiction that the CJEU enjoys *vis-à-vis* other international courts or tribunals when the dispute concerns the interpretation or application of the EU Treaties. This amounts indeed to a 'structural' understanding of the principle of autonomy, albeit one which still presents flaws: there is no coherent reasoning on why EU investors and EU Member States are equated for the purposes of Article 344 TFEU, nor on why and how the autonomy of EU law is impaired where an intra-EU dispute does not concern the interpretation and application of EU law.

It is here submitted that the CJEU's case law concerning international dispute settlement in general, and ISDS in particular, is in line with a 'structural' understanding of the principle of autonomy insofar as it is undermined when it affects a structural element in the constitutional architecture of the EU legal order. This finding would not extend to other lines of case law on the autonomy of the EU legal order beyond ISDS, where the CJEU has claimed a breach of the autonomy of EU law on the grounds of the incompatibility with the normative content of provisions of EU law.[56] This 'structural' dimension of the principle of autonomy of EU

[51] Comprehensive Economic and Trade Agreement (CETA) between Canada, of the one part, and the European Union and its Member States, of the other part, OJ L 11, 14.1.2017, pp. 23–1079.

[52] Opinion 1/17, *supra* note 8, para. 119.

[53] Ibid., paras. 131 and 134.

[54] Ibid., paras. 148 and 156.

[55] Opinion 1/20, *supra* note 14, para. 47. See also *Commission v Ireland*, *supra* note 25, paras. 122–124.

[56] See *Kadi*, *supra* note 19, paras. 281–285.

law is in principle compatible with international law obligations as it does not amount to an upfront infringement of Article 27 VCLT, insofar as the principle of autonomy of EU law can be linked to treaty provisions concerning the structure of the EU and does not amount to an exception based on a norm of domestic law.

3.2 *International Tribunals' Case Law*

The case law of arbitral tribunals takes an opposite view. As a starting point, EU law does not entrust a duty upon investment arbitration tribunals to take EU law considerations into account *ex officio* when rendering an arbitral award as a matter of principle.[57] However, EU law might enter the tribunal's analysis when determining if the subject matter is arbitrable or whether the tribunal has jurisdiction, as well as in relation to substantive provisions concerning the legal framework of the case at issue. Furthermore, as noted by Broberg and Fenger, arbitral tribunals may nonetheless consider taking EU law into account, or at least not to disregard its fundamental provisions in order to prevent the setting aside of their award.[58]

The case law of arbitral tribunals engages with all of these issues and can be summarized in that it denies the relevance of EU law in determining jurisdiction on the grounds that arbitral tribunals operate within a public international law framework and derive their jurisdiction from treaty provisions. Tribunals also often interpret and apply EU law provisions, sometimes in ways not limited to treating them as a matter of fact.[59] Already before the *Achmea* decision, international tribunals had rejected the so-called 'intra-EU exception' to their jurisdiction in investment arbitration disputes.[60] In the specific case of disputes pursuant to the ECT, tribunals have also refused to extend the *Achmea* ratio on the grounds that the ECT was not an intra-EU BIT,[61] and have continued to do so even after the CJEU clarified that the *Achmea* doctrine extended also to Article 26 ECT.[62] In examining the intra-EU exception, tribunals do not examine the principle of autonomy of EU law as such, focusing instead on substantive provisions of the EU Treaties and on general norms of treaty interpretation under public international law.

When denying the relevance of EU law to the applicable intra-EU dispute, the tribunal in *RFEF v Spain* found EU law to be a matter involving EU Member States

---

[57] Broberg and Fenger (2022), p. 89.

[58] Ibid., p. 93.

[59] The CJEU requires, as a condition for the respect of the autonomy of EU law, that tribunals restrain themselves to consider EU law as a matter of fact and following its prevailing interpretation under its case law. See Opinion 1/17, supra note 8, paras. 130 and 131.

[60] *RFEF v Spain*, ICSID Case No. ARB/13/30, Decision on jurisdiction, 6 June 2016, para. 89.

[61] *RFEF v Spain*, Decision on Responsibility and on the Principles of Quantum, 30 November 2018, para. 211.

[62] *Infracapital v Spain*, *supra* note 4, paras. 108 and 113.

only (*res inter alios acta*) and that it did not extend to the signing and ratification of the ECT.[63] In its view, even in an intra-EU context under the ECT, EU law does not entrust the tribunal with jurisdiction to alter the nature of the ISDS clause in Article 26 so as to accommodate EU law concerns.[64] This line of case law has been followed by other tribunals under the reasoning that in the event of an inconsistency between EU law and the ECT concerning jurisdiction, the tribunal must accord priority to the ECT as the 'legal instrument' or 'constitution' governing tribunal's jurisdiction.[65] In other words, according to this line of case law, the tribunal's jurisdiction is determined by the given international treaty, EU law being irrelevant for such purposes.

Some tribunals have reasoned that under international law, EU law is 'a subsystem of international law' that has no ability to prevail with 'supremacy' over specific international obligations and that in any case, the ECT would prevail over EU law in a dispute pursuant to it,[66] in some cases as a matter of *lex specialis*.[67] Others have taken the opposite approach and claimed that tribunals are placed within the unique context of international law and thus cannot take into account norms of EU law and its system of hierarchy of legal rules to determine their jurisdiction,[68] and that in the event of an incompatibility between the ECT and EU law on the merits, the latter would prevail in an intra-EU context.[69] However, tribunals have also refused to apply EU law to the merits arguing that intra-EU BITs and the EU Treaties have different subject matter, [70] in some cases rejecting any 'material inconsistencies' between EU law and the ECT.[71] There is also a division within the case law as to whether a harmonious interpretation of EU law and international law should be pursued,[72] but even if so, there is consensus that any interpretation of EU law as a relevant rule of international law between the parties under the VCLT cannot prevail over the relevant international agreements subject to interpretation,

---

[63] *RFEF v Spain, supra* note 60, para. 74.

[64] Ibid.

[65] Ibid.; *Landesbank Baden-Württemberg and Others v Spain*, ICSID Case No ARB/15/45, Decision on the Intra-EU Jurisdictional Objection, 25 February 2019, para. 194; *PV Investors v Spain*, PCA Case No 2012-14 UNCITRAL, Preliminary Award on Jurisdiction, 14 October 2014, para. 175; UP *and CD Holding Internationale v Hungary*, ICSID Case No ARB/13/35, Award, 9 October 2018, para. 253; *Foresight Luxembourg and Greentech v Spain*, SCC Case No 2015/550, Final Award, 14 November 2018, paras. 218–219.

[66] *RFEF v Spain, supra* note 60, paras. 71, 75 and 87.

[67] *Vattenfall, supra* note 11, para. 229.

[68] *Electrabel S.A. v. Hungary*, ICSID Case No ARB/07/19, Decision on Jurisdiction, Applicable Law and Liability, 30 November 2012, para. 4.112; *Infracapital v Spain, supra* note 4, para. 107.

[69] *Electrabel v Hungary, supra* note 68, para. 4.189.

[70] *Marfin Investment Group Holdings S.A. et al. v Cyprus*, ICSID Case No ARB/13/27, Award, 26 July 2018, para. 591.

[71] *Electrabel v. Hungary, supra* note 68, para. 4.196.

[72] For the two opposing views, see *RFEF v Spain, supra* note 60, para. 76, and *Electrabel v Hungary, supra* note 68, para. 4.112.

even in an intra-EU context.[73] Tribunals thus deny the 'primacy' or 'supremacy' the CJEU claims that EU law has in *inter se* relations between its Member States.

In the cases where they have been called on to interpret or apply EU law, tribunals have claimed that they were doing so without interpreting the EU Treaties or reviewing the legality of acts of EU law.[74] They have claimed that the CJEU could carry on exercising its exclusive jurisdiction and fulfil its role as ultimate guardian of EU law under infringement proceedings against Member States for hypothetical violations of the EU Treaties.[75] Tribunals have also denied the applicability of Article 344 TFEU to disputes involving EU investors[76] and rejected an expansive reading of this provision so as to preclude ISDS proceedings that may relate to the interpretation or application of the EU Treaties. [77] It is in this kind of examination of EU law where tribunals have also taken into account the *sui generis nature* of the EU legal order. For instance, the *Electrabel* tribunal recognized the "special status of EU law operating as a body of supranational law within the EU" and concluded that EU law was applicable to the dispute both as part of the rules and principles of international law and as part of Hungary's national law, as a matter of fact.[78] In *Infracapital v Spain*, the tribunal however denied the relevance of the *Komstroy* judgment reasoning that "[t]he applicable law to jurisdiction and the merits of the dispute is international law, and not principles of sub-systems of international law such as EU treaties".[79] Some tribunals have also refused to follow the *Achmea* doctrine on the grounds that the seat of the arbitration was not in the EU, particularly in proceedings under the ICSID Convention.[80]

The case law of international tribunals therefore does not explicitly refer to the principle of autonomy of EU law as such because the intra-EU jurisdictional objection is presented by reference to substantive Treaty provisions. This leads to an examination following interpretative methods under public international law or to an upfront denial of the relevance or applicability of EU law to the dispute.

In contrast to this, the recent award in *Green Power v Spain* stands as the only example in which a tribunal upheld the intra-EU jurisdictional objection, after concluding that both the ECT and EU law should be considered in determining jurisdiction.[81] As regards the applicability of EU law, its reasoning is inspired by the

[73] *Vattenfall, supra* note 11, paras. 154–155; Declève and Van Damme (2021), para. 13.36.

[74] *Electrabel v. Hungary, supra* note 68, paras. 4.157 and 4.162.

[75] Ibid.

[76] *Greentech Energy Systems A/S, et al v. Italy*, SCC Case No. V 2015/095, Award, 23 December 2018, para. 350.

[77] *Charanne and Construction Investments v. Spain*, SCC Case No. V 062/2012, Award, 21 January 2016, para. 443.

[78] *Electrabel v. Hungary, supra* note 68, paras. 4.195 and 4.197.

[79] *Infracapital v Spain, supra* note 4, para. 107.

[80] *Landesbank Baden-Württemberg and Others v Spain, supra* note 65, para. 150; WA Investments Europa Nova v Czech Republic, PCA Case No 2014-19, Award, 15 May 2019, para. 438.

[81] *Green Power v Spain*, supra note 5, para. 412.

Electrabel award in finding that it is applicable both as international and domestic law.[82] Specifically, it held that EU law as domestic law is relevant to determine, under the Swedish Arbitration Act (the law governing the arbitration), the arbitrability of the dispute, the validity of the arbitration agreement, and its compatibility with public policy.[83] By considering EU law as relevant to determining the validity of Spain's offer to arbitrate, the tribunal accepts that under the CJEU's case law, Spain's offer to arbitrate in an intra-EU ECT dispute is precluded under Articles 267 and 344 TFEU, and thus the tribunal lacks jurisdiction 'as a result of the autonomy and primacy of the EU legal order'.[84] While the tribunal does engage with the notion of autonomy and the CJEU's case law, it declines jurisdiction through a line of reasoning centered on the primacy of EU law, under which EU law norms preempt incompatible national law norms.[85] This results in EU law overriding Article 26 ECT applied intra-EU given EU law's status as *lex superior*.[86] In the tribunal's view, the principle of primacy of EU law safeguards the autonomy of the EU legal order in an intra-EU context under an international agreement, precluding the validity of an act of a Member State that undermines the autonomy of EU law. This was also the approach taken by the German Federal Supreme Court in its judgment in the *Achmea* case, concluding that there was no valid arbitration agreement as a result of the primacy of EU law provisions that safeguard the autonomy of the EU legal order.[87] The applicability of the *Green Power* reasoning is however limited to arbitration proceedings where the tribunal is seated within the EU, insofar as it renders EU law applicable as *lex arbitri*.[88] It is also unclear, both in the CJEU's case law and in academic scholarship whether the principle of primacy constitutes a valid conflict rule under which the EU Treaties trump any opposing treaty provision.[89]

---

[82] Ibid., paras. 169, 172, 414; *Achmea*, *supra* note 2, para. 41.

[83] Ibid, para. 172.

[84] Ibid, para. 456.

[85] *Costa v ENEL*, supra note 15. See also CJEU Case C-573/17 *Popławski* EU:C:2019:530, para. 54: "[the principle of primacy] requires all Member State bodies to give full effect to the various EU provisions, and the law of the Member States may not undermine the effect accorded to those various provisions in the territory of those States".

[86] *Green Power v Spain*, supra note 5, paras. 468 and 469.

[87] German Supreme Court Case *I ZB 2/15* [2018] DE:BGH:2018:311018BIZB2.15.0, paras. 25–28.

[88] See, for example, *9REN v Spain*, ICSID Case No. ARB/15/15, Decision on Annulment, 17 November 2022, paras. 235 et seq., in which the Ad Hoc Committee refuses to follow the reasoning in *Green Power* on the grounds that it was not subject to the law of an EU Member State as *lex arbitri*. In this sense, the seat of an arbitral tribunal in an EU Member State may also render an extra-EU dispute (i.e. between a non-Member State and/or a non-EU investor) under the scope of EU law, cf. *Komstroy*, *supra* note 3, para. 34.

[89] In the author's view, the CJEU's case law is still premature on whether the principle of primacy of EU law results in EU law prevailing over any inconsistent treaty provision entered into by Member States. See for instance CJEU Joined Cases C-364/95 and C-365/95 *T Port and Others* EU:C:1998: 95, paras. 59–65 and CJEU Case C-435/22 PPU *Generalstaatsanwaltschaft München* EU:C:2022: 852, paras. 108 and 110. Some authors have claimed that primacy is indeed a special conflict rule,

It follows that while the case law of international tribunals (except for *Green Power*) does not explicitly refer to the principle of autonomy of EU law, it nonetheless examines the structural dimension of this principle and the *sui generis* nature of the EU legal order. This is a result of examining relevant Treaty provisions such as Article 344 TFEU and the different dimensions of the EU legal order as comprising norms of general international law or of a subsystem of the international legal order, as well as EU law as the applicable national law. Therefore, the CJEU and arbitral tribunals both analyze the autonomy of the EU legal order from a structural viewpoint and claim that the EU legal order has a *sui generis* and hybrid nature which manifests itself both as regards national and international law.

4 Autonomy as EU Public Policy

In his Opinion delivered in the *Achmea* case, Advocate General Wathelet made the following statement in advising the CJEU on whether the intra-EU ISDS clause in the Netherlands-Czechoslovakia BIT undermined the allocation of powers under the Treaties and the autonomy of the EU legal system:

> 244. [. . .] whatever the procedures, the courts and tribunals of the Member States of the Union are able to ensure the uniform interpretation of EU law and compliance with the European public policy rules, whether in a competition matter or in other areas of EU law.
>
> [. . .]
>
> 250. [. . .] The uniformity of application of EU law may be ensured on the basis of a number of reasons, the most relevant of which are the fact that the arbitral procedure was not in accordance with the agreement of the parties and that recognition and enforcement of the award would be contrary to public policy, including European public policy.[90]

The Advocate General further suggested that under applicable German law,[91] the award had been amenable to an action seeking its annulment before German courts, who were able to ensure the uniformity of interpretation of EU law and compliance with the EU public policy by referring a preliminary ruling request to the CJEU, as they in fact did.[92] He also pointed to the fact that all EU Member States have acceded to the New York Convention for the Recognition and Enforcement of Arbitral

see Georgaki (2023), p. 2, or that under this principle EU law trumps incompatible *inter se* agreements between Member States, see Hingelang (2012), p. 179. However, from an international law perspective, *lex superior* as special conflict rule of a hierarchical nature is questionable when applied between the EU Treaties and the ECT, moreover since the more accepted *lex specialis* canon would *prima facie* render the latter applicable. See Lavranos (2022), p. 170.

[90] Opinion of AG Wathelet in *Achmea*, *supra* note 46, paras. 244 and 250.

[91] The tribunal was seated in Frankfurt, Germany.

[92] Opinion of AG Wathelet in *Achmea*, supra note 46, para. 247.

Awards ('NYC'),[93] which enables national courts to deny recognition and/or enforcement of awards where it would be contrary to public policy, "including European public policy".[94]

The question that thus arises is whether and to what extent the autonomy of EU law is a norm of public policy and, if so, whether it may be relied as a defense in legal proceedings. This issue has not yet been clarified in the case law of the CJEU, domestic courts, and arbitral tribunals. There is only a recent example in which the Swedish Supreme Court set aside the award in *PL Holdings v Poland* on public policy grounds.[95] Neither the CJEU nor arbitral tribunals have substantially engaged with the public policy implications on account of breaches of EU law's autonomy. This is a relevant question because the concept of public policy can be found simultaneously in national, EU and international law, while public policy exceptions can also be raised directly before arbitral tribunals as well as domestic courts. As noted by Bermann, the EU's exclusive competence over foreign direct investment following the Lisbon Treaty further allows EU law imperatives to alter the international arbitration landscape, in particular by presenting EU law as a public policy defense.[96] If the autonomy of the EU legal order were to be presented as a public policy exception, the current incompatibilities between EU and international investment law could perhaps be smoothened or, at least, addressed under a uniform conceptual framework.

4.1 Public Policy in International Investment Agreements

In the context of international investment law, public policy exceptions may operate as a defense as a limit to investment protections and as a legal ground in the context of judicial or arbitral proceedings. As a limit to investment protections, they allow States 'to pursue regulatory objectives in ways that would otherwise be inconsistent with investment treaty obligations',[97] thus acting in a similar way to the general

[93] United Nations Convention on the Recognition and Enforcement of Foreign Arbitral Awards, signed in New York City on 10 June 1958 ('NYC').

[94] Opinion of AG Wathelet in *Achmea*, supra note 46, para. 250.

[95] Swedish Supreme Court Case T 1569-19 (2022). The Swedish Supreme Court held in paras. 52 et seq. that the invalidity of arbitration awards rendered under arbitration clauses in intra-EU BITs must be examined against Swedish procedural public policy rules, and held that such awards are unlawful because they are incompatible with the fundamental rules and principles governing the legal order of the EU and, therefore, of Sweden, *inter alia* because it undermines the autonomy of EU law.

[96] Bermann (2011), p. 1200.

[97] Henckels (2015), p. 81.

exceptions contained in Article XX GATT[98] or Article XIV GATS.[99,100] Thus, by examining public policy exceptions, arbitral tribunals examine whether host States have violated standards of investment protection under a given agreement. These standards, which are also modeled under WTO law, typically include fair and equitable treatment, full protection and security, national and most-favored nation treatment, and the prohibition of arbitrary and discriminatory measures.[101] However, under clauses incorporating general exceptions, international investment agreements allow States to adopt measures that would be normally inconsistent with their international obligations, but nonetheless necessary to protect their fundamental interests,[102] such as national security, public order, morality, the environment or public health.[103] That is the case, for instance, of Article 28.3 CETA, which includes a reference to Article XX GATT. In this sense, the CJEU has ruled that the autonomy of the EU legal order would be undermined if the EU would be prevented by ISDS tribunals from regulating the public interest in accordance with its constitutional framework.[104] Construed in international law terms, this means that the autonomy of the EU legal order would be undermined if the EU were prevented from relying on such general exceptions to regulate the public interest in accordance with its constitutional structure.

When operating as a defense, public policy exceptions enable parties to rely on them before a court or tribunal, whether it is before adjudicating arbitral tribunals or in the context of award enforcement and recognition proceedings.[105] Here they are normally not presented in relation to the substance of the dispute, but as a challenge to the legality of the dispute and/or of a rendered award. Thus, as a defense, public policy exceptions refer to a certain category of rules that relate to fundamental values and principles deemed to be essential to that legal order,[106] both of procedural and substantive nature,[107] their inobservance seriously imperiling the very foundations of that legal regime. In other words, public policy exceptions raised as a defense seek to ensure that foreign judgments or arbitral awards do not impair the fundamental characteristics of a given legal order. This is the relevant public policy dimension to examine whether a principle such as the autonomy of EU law may qualify as public policy, insofar as it relates to the structural dimension of the EU legal order.

---

[98] General Agreement on Tariffs and Trade (GATT), signed in Marrakesh on 15 April 1994.

[99] General Agreement on Trade in Services (GATS), signed in Marrakesh on 15 April 1994.

[100] Newcombe and Paradell (2009), pp. 500 *et seq.*

[101] See Dolzer et al. (2001), pp. 186–195. See also: Grierson-Weiler and Laird (2008), pp. 205–304.

[102] Garzini (2012), p. 114.

[103] See, for instance, Article 28.3 of the CETA Agreement.

[104] Opinion 1/17, supra note 8, para. 150. See in this sense, Hirsch (2008), pp. 154–181.

[105] Bermann (2012), p. 408.

[106] Corthaut (2014), p. 12. In this sense, the CJEU employs the concepts of public policy and *ordre public* indistinctly (see CJEU Case C-568/20 *H Limited* EU:C:2022:264, para. 41).

[107] Scheu and Nikolov (2020), p. 260.

In this sense, under the framework of the NYC and the UNCITRAL Model Law,[108] parties can challenge the award before the courts of the arbitration seat claiming a violation of the public policy of that State. On the contrary, under the ICSID Convention,[109] awards are binding on the parties and cannot be subject to appeal in domestic courts. They can only be challenged upon an ad hoc Committee and under grounds not including public policy. However, ICSID awards may be treated as final judgments of the host State for the purposes of recognition and enforcement,[110] although this seemingly would not include public policy.[111] This notwithstanding, public policy is also relevant *ratione materiae* in the pre-adjudication phase before an arbitral tribunal, as the content of arbitrability and jurisdictional objections may be the same as what at a later stage may be presented as a public policy defense. For instance, in the *Komstroy* case, the Paris Court of Appeal annulled the contested award on the ground of lack of jurisdiction of the tribunal, even though Moldova had challenged the lack of jurisdiction by claiming a breach of public policy.[112]

This signals that the seat of an arbitration within the EU legal order and whether the arbitration is administered under the ICSID Convention are important variables as regards the scope of review under EU public policy rules. Further, depending on the context in which public policy exceptions are presented as a defense, it is possible to identify three types: (1) domestic public policy, when it relates to the norms of a municipal legal order arising in a domestic context;[113] (2) international public policy, which concerns the norms of public policy of a municipal legal order projected *ad extra*, when the legal relationship takes place in an international context;[114] and (3) transnational public policy, which relates to rules that are only to be found in the international arena, for instance fundamental principles of natural law and universal justice, *jus cogens* norms, general accepted principles of law, international custom, or arbitral precedent.[115]

4.2 The Existence of EU Public Policy

As with any legal order, EU law has its own norms of public policy, even if the contours of what exactly constitutes EU public policy are still unclear and have not

---

108 United Nations Commission on International Trade Law (UNCITRAL) Model Law on International Commercial Arbitration, adopted in 1985.

109 Convention on the Settlement of Investment Disputes between States and Nationals of Other States, signed in Washington, D.C. on 18 March 1965 (ICSID Convention).

110 Article 54(1) ICSID Convention.

111 See *Micula and others v Romania* [2020] UKSC 5, para. 68.

112 *Komstroy*, supra note 3, paras. 13–14.

113 Scheu and Nikolov (2020), p. 260.

114 Bermann (2007), p. 3.

115 See, for instance, Lew (1978), p. 253; Gaillard (2001), p. 59; Zarra (2021), p. 319.

been defined by the CJEU.[116] In the case of the EU legal order, it is generally accepted that fundamental provisions of EU law may constitute norms of public policy, which in principle may arise in a domestic, international or transnational context.[117] The CJEU's case law can be read as validating the existence of EU public policy, but refusing to provide it with its own autonomous content.[118] In its *Eco Swiss* judgment, the CJEU noted that Article 85 of the EC Treaty was "a fundamental provision" and as such, "any agreements or decisions prohibited pursuant to that article are automatically void".[119] On that basis, it held that where national law provides the annulment of an arbitration award on grounds of breach of domestic public policy, it must also do so on account of a violation of Article 85 EC,[120] since that provision could be regarded as public policy within the meaning of the New York Convention.[121] In *Krombach*, the CJEU established that recourse to public policy bears a high threshold and must be construed narrowly, therefore only when recognition or enforcement of judgments

> would be at variance to an unacceptable degree with the legal order of the State in which enforcement is sought inasmuch as it infringes a fundamental principle [. . .] the infringement would have to constitute a manifest breach of a rule of law regarded as essential in the legal order of the State in which enforcement is sought or of a right recognised as being fundamental within that legal order.[122]

Using this narrow understanding of public policy as a starting point, the CJEU employs the principle of equivalence of EU law to allow for the possibility to rely on public policy exceptions when the infringed norm stems from the EU legal order and not from national law.[123] In *Diageo Brands*, it held that the fact that an alleged manifest error concerns a rule of EU law and not of national law does not alter the conditions for reliance on public policy.[124] Therefore, Member States must take EU

---

[116] Bermann (2011), p. 1211.

[117] See Corthaut (2014), pp. 20–21; Bermann (2011), p. 1215; Van der Haegen (2009), pp. 449–476.

[118] Van der Haegen (2009), p. 465.

[119] CJEU Case C-126/97 *Eco Swiss* EU:C:1999:269, para. 36. Article 101 TFEU (ex 85 EC) prohibits all agreements and collusive practices by undertakings that result in restrictive practices and in anti-competitive behavior, such as cartels.

[120] Ibid., para. 37.

[121] Ibid., para. 38.

[122] CJEU Case C-7/98 *Krombach* EU:C:2000:164, para. 37. For a different use of public policy, in relation to conditions on the loss of EU citizenship, the CJEU has held that public policy "presupposes, in any event, the existence, in addition to the disturbance of the social order which any infringement of the law involves, of a genuine, present and sufficiently serious threat affecting one of the fundamental interests of society." See CJEU Case C-118/20 *Wiener Landesregierung* EU:C:2022:34, para. 69.

[123] CJEU Case C-430/93 Van Schijndel v Stichting Pensioenfonds voor Fysiotherapeuten EU:C:1995:441; CJEU Case C-38/98 Régie Nationale des Usines Renault SA v. Maxicar SpA and Orazio Formento EU:C:2000:225, para. 32; *Eco Swiss*, *supra* note 119, para. 37.

[124] CJEU Case C-681/13 *Diageo Brands* EU:C:2015:471, para. 48.

law into account in determining what constitutes public policy within their legal orders,[125] and, pursuant to the principle of effectiveness, Member States' courts must raise EU law public policy provisions on their own motion.[126] Thus, the CJEU's case law imposes an obligation to set aside an arbitral award when fundamental rules of EU law are manifestly breached, and national courts must grant EU law a similar standard of protection in relation to national law.

4.3 The Principle of Autonomy as EU Public Policy in the Case Law of the CJEU

Considering the principle of autonomy of EU law as a functional principle that relates to the essential structural characteristics of the EU legal order, it is possible to claim that it amounts to a norm of public policy without impairing its narrow scope of application as a defense.[127] In the context of international arbitration, the recognition of an arbitral award would have to amount to a manifest breach of an essential rule of law of the Member State in which recognition and enforcement is sought, insofar as its recognition would be at variance to an unacceptable degree with its legal order.[128] As stressed in *Diageo Brands*, this applies invariably when it comes to manifest breaches of EU law and to the protection of the EU legal order.[129]

The principle of autonomy would seem to meet that test, insofar as it is directly linked to essential characteristics of the EU's legal order. In this sense, when the CJEU rules that the autonomy of EU law is undermined, it always does so on the basis of an infringement of specific provisions of the EU Treaties, namely Articles 344 and 267 TFEU. The CJEU treats the specific features enshrined in those provisions, namely the CJEU's exclusive jurisdiction and the preliminary ruling mechanism, as essential characteristics of the EU and its law.[130] As reasoned above, reference to these provisions underscore a structural understanding of the autonomy of EU law. A manifest breach of provisions such as Article 344 TFEU would undermine the *autonomous quality* of the EU legal order given that it precludes the EU institutions from carrying out functions that are essential to that legal order's structure. In the context of ISDS, this is the case of (1) situations where the EU is prevented by an ISDS tribunal from operating within its constitutional framework to regulate the level of public interest under general exceptions to investment protection standards (public policy as a limit to investment protections) and (2) situations

[125] Bermann (2011), p. 1201.

[126] CJEU Case C-168/05 *Mostaza Claro* EU:C:2006:675; CJEU Case C-40/08 *Asturcom Telecomunicaciones* EU:C:2009:615.

[127] Bermann (2011), p. 1208.

[128] *Krombach*, supra note 122, para. 37.

[129] *Diageo Brands*, *supra* note 124, paras. 48 and 50.

[130] See *Achmea*, *supra* note 2, paras. 33 and 60.

where the recognition of an arbitral award would constitute a manifest breach of a fundamental rule of law such as the exclusive jurisdiction of the CJEU (public policy as a legal ground).

In other words, autonomy is a fundamental principle of the EU legal order insofar as it preserves, in essence, the qualitative nature of that legal order vis-à-vis national and international law, and insofar as the undermining of that autonomy is directly linked to an infringement of essential norms of that legal order such as Article 344 TFEU. Autonomy can therefore be a norm of public policy insofar as, if the EU legal order were not autonomous, its very *sui generis* nature as a subsystem of international law with a constitutional dimension would be in peril.

4.4 Raising Autonomy as Public Policy

Insofar as autonomy is a fundamental principle of the EU legal order, it is here submitted that it may be raised as a public policy defense in legal proceedings, both before arbitral tribunals themselves as well as before national courts in enforcement and recognition proceedings. Given that the CJEU's case law on autonomy concerns fundamentally its external dimension and, above all, that ISDS necessarily takes place in an international context, if the principle of autonomy were to be raised as a public policy defense it would only be done as international or transnational public policy.

Raised as an international public policy defense, the infringement of the principle of autonomy would have to be in breach of the public policy of the State in which enforcement and recognition of an award is sought.[131] If EU law forms part of the applicable law because the seat of the arbitration is within the EU, then the international public policy of that Member State would naturally include the principle of autonomy of EU law. Based on this understanding, an award given in an intra-EU dispute or precluding the EU to act in accordance with its constitutional structure under the scope of general exceptions would undermine the structural elements underpinning the EU legal order, which are defined in Treaty-level provisions. In such circumstances, it seems plausible that a national court would uphold the public policy exception and annul the award or deny its execution. That indeed was the conclusion the Swedish Supreme Court arrived to in annulling the award of *PL Holdings v Poland*, reasoning that the undermining of the autonomy of EU law was incompatible with the fundamental rules and principles of the EU legal order, and therefore of Sweden.[132]

A different situation arises where the same award is challenged in a non-EU forum, such as before a non-EU court or in the context of an ICSID arbitration. When challenged before a non-EU court, EU law does not form part of the

[131] See Article V(2)(b) of the NYC.

[132] Case T 1569-19 [2022], paras. 58–59. See also *Green Power v Spain*, *supra* note 5, para. 172.

applicable law to the arbitration, but may still be considered by the tribunal even if the principle of autonomy would not form part of that third State's public policy *stricto sensu*. For instance, an award in an intra-EU dispute could be challenged in a third country on the grounds of violation of its procedural public policy by alleging that the tribunal lacked jurisdiction to adjudicate or that the dispute is non-arbitrable. In this case, the substance of the claim must be examined on account of the alleged infringement of the structural elements the EU legal order's autonomy. Claiming that autonomy is a norm of public policy of the EU legal order may result in higher degrees of deference and to affording 'legal comity',[133] in recognition that the EU has its own constitutional structure with sovereign implications from an international law perspective.[134]

In the context of an ICSID arbitration, awards may be reviewed through the procedure under Article 52 thereof, which includes a manifest excess of the tribunal's powers as grounds for review. On this basis, *ad hoc* review committees may examine whether a tribunal has exceeded its powers in a way that would deprive EU law of its autonomy. *Ad hoc* committees may thus examine whether a tribunal impaired the EU's permission to regulate a level of public interest in accordance with its constitutional structure under general exceptions to international investment agreements, or whether the EU was precluded from its ability to operate according to that constitutional structure, which is determined by norms of international law that are interpreted authoritatively by the CJEU. In so doing, *ad hoc* committees may apply EU law as interpreted by the CJEU as a fact. In this sense, a dispute pursuant to the ECT or to another investment agreement the EU is party to would mandate consideration of EU law norms, including the principle of autonomy, both as a matter of fact and as applicable principles of international law between the Member States *inter se* and with the EU.[135] Should it be clear to them that the autonomy of EU law, understood as a respect for the constitutional structure of the EU, is a norm of public policy from which neither its Member States nor other parties may derogate, it is likely that they would exercise restraint so as to not impair that autonomy. Alternatively, tribunals and *ad hoc* committees may consider the autonomy of EU law to be a norm of transnational public policy applicable in an intra-EU

[133] See the concept of 'legal comity' in D'Alterio (2011), pp. 394–424, defined as "the effect arising from the use of "common judge-made rules" regulating the relations between legal systems". See also: Crawford (1981).

[134] The Commission has implicitly taken such approach in a recent case in before a U.S. court supporting Spain's motion to dismiss a petition to enforce an intra-EU claiming the invalidity of the arbitration agreement. In its *amicus curiae* brief, the Commission submitted that 'the Court should afford the highest degree of deference to the CJEU's [*Komstroy*] ruling', as the issue there addressed remains 'one of immense importance to the EU legal order'. The Court, exercising high deference towards EU law and the CJEU, held there was no valid arbitration agreement and declined subject matter jurisdiction under the arbitration exception of the Foreign Sovereign Immunities Act. See Memorandum of 29 March 2023, *Blasket Renewable Investments LLC v. Kingdom of Spain*, U.S. DC for the District of Columbia, Civil Action No. 1:21-cv-03249-RJL.

[135] See, for instance, Article 26(6) ECT.

context.[136] Tribunals could therefore examine on their own motion whether delivering an award would run contrary to transnational public policy insofar as it would affect the autonomy of EU law and the integrity of the EU Treaties.[137]

While it is here submitted that autonomy of EU law may be raised as a public policy defense, the effectiveness of such a defense may be limited to recognition and enforcement proceedings where EU law forms part of the *lex arbitri* because the tribunal is seated in an EU Member State. In non-EU fora, international courts and tribunals in principle do not have an obligation to examine EU law *ex officio*. They may however still consider EU law as a fact or as rules of international law. In this sense, an explicit recognition by the CJEU that the autonomy of EU law is a fundamental norm covered by the notion of public policy would give a necessary authoritative argument for non-EU courts and tribunals to exercise a higher degree of deference towards the EU legal order, and would also clarify the scope of EU Member States' duty to review an arbitral award in breach thereof.[138] This is particularly the case for situations involving awards in ICSID arbitrations, which are automatically enforceable in the same conditions as domestic judgments. While the ICSID awards are not reviewable under public policy grounds, national courts could potentially deny enforcement of awards where such enforcement would result in a violation of a fundamental norm of EU law, such as the principle of autonomy.[139] The CJEU has so far refused to clarify the fundamental nature of the autonomy of EU law in relation to the nature of the ICSID Convention, while maintaining that intra-EU ICSID awards cannot be executed by Member States courts.[140] Indeed, the CJEU's *Achmea* case law is built around the premise that review of arbitral awards on the grounds of public policy under national law is insufficient,[141] which in turn justifies far-reaching consequences for ISDS mechanisms that undermine the autonomy of EU law.

An explicit and authoritative recognition that the autonomy of EU law is a norm of public policy would clarify the nature of what is generally understood to be a nebulous concept with a difficult application to the field of ISDS. For this, the CJEU

---

[136] It has been argued that EU public policy may qualify as transnational because it exceeds State boundaries, but would remain circumscribed to an EU context. See Van der Haegen (2009), p. 460.

[137] In this sense, contrary to De Brabandere's claims, transnational public policy is not limited to *jus cogens* norms, but as the tribunal in *World Duty Free v Kenya,* ICSID Case No ARB/00/7, Award, 4 October 2006, held in para. 138 that principles such as the prohibition of corruption may qualify as such. See De Brabandere (2020), pp. 847–866.

[138] See Broberg and Fenger (2022), p. 98.

[139] See *Costello v Ireland* [2022] IESC 44 Hogan J paras. 233–234. However, investors have claimed that enforcing ICSID awards in U.S. courts is also a matter of public policy, see Memorandum in support of petitioner's preliminary injunction, *9REN v Spain*, U.S. DC for the District of Columbia, Civil Action No. 19-cv-01871 (TSC).

[140] CJEU Case C-333/19 *Romatsa and Others* EU:C:2022:749, paras. 22 and 43.

[141] *Achmea, supra* note 2, para. 53.

would need to overcome its skepticism to define the content of EU public policy as more than a mere extension of the domestic public policy of Member States.[142]

5 Conclusion

The principle of autonomy is a fundamental norm of the EU legal order because it relates to its *sui generis* nature as both domestic and international law, specifically as a subsystem of international law with a constitutional dimension. In relation to ISDS, the CJEU has developed a line of case law that relates to the structural features of the EU legal order, notably the CJEU's exclusive jurisdiction under Article 344 TFEU. The choice of a structural view is preferrable from an international law perspective in order to avoid a violation of Articles 26 and 27 VCLT, insofar as the structural features of the EU legal order are established through Treaty provisions under international law. Arbitral tribunals have not substantially engaged with the principle of autonomy of EU law, a principle which sets the boundary between the EU legal order and public international law. Instead, they have resorted to different interpretative mechanisms under public international law to deny the relevance of EU law provisions in determining their jurisdiction in intra-EU disputes. However, in examining structural elements of the EU legal order, arbitral tribunals and the CJEU share a structural view of the autonomy that EU law enjoys.

Despite calls to redress violations of the autonomy of EU law through review on the grounds of public policy,[143] there is still no consensus on this. The award in *Green Power v Spain* and the judgment of the Swedish Supreme Court in *PL Holdings v Poland* are the only examples linking violations of the autonomy of EU law to public policy breaches. It has been argued here that the principle of autonomy is indeed a norm of EU public policy because it constitutes a fundamental provision of the EU legal order. In such circumstances, the autonomy of EU law is undermined where the EU is unable to operate according to its constitutional structure under general exceptions in investment protection agreements. It is also undermined by an arbitral award rendered in breach of a structural element in the constitutional architecture of the EU legal order, such as the exclusive jurisdiction of the CJEU or the functioning of the EU judicial system. This has implications for the recognition, enforcement and review of awards, although its effectiveness may be limited in international fora where EU law is not the governing law. However, presenting the principle of autonomy as a norm of public policy would clarify its fundamental nature and might increase deference towards EU law, as public policy is a concept present in most jurisdictions, if not all. In this sense, an authoritative interpretation of the principle of autonomy as a norm of EU public policy by the

[142] For a recent example of the CJEU's reluctance to define the content of EU public policy, see CJEU Case C-568/20 *H Limited* EU:C:2022:264, para. 42.

[143] Opinion of AG Wathelet in *Achmea*, *supra* note 46, paras. 244 and 250.

CJEU would clarify the scope, nature and limits of how this principle operates in national and international law.[144]

The relationship between the autonomy of EU legal order and its condition as a public policy norm is relevant because it enables the achievement of what some authors have referred to as a 'discursive' understanding of autonomy, under which the shape of EU law's autonomy would be defined by both internal and external processes.[145] In the absence of statehood, and given its *sui generis* legal nature, if the EU wants to become a responsible international actor and fulfil its guiding principle of ensuring respect for international law, it ultimately must respond to this question. This already is a reason for which arbitral tribunals, the CJEU and national courts should engage with the public policy framework: given the *sui generis* nature of the EU legal order, how much autonomy it is able to exert is a question that ought to be responded in a pluralistic way. Public policy can therefore serve as a vehicle for national and international tribunals to engage with the question of the autonomy of EU law, one that to date still presents many unanswered questions.

References

Barents R (2004) The autonomy of community law. Kluwer Law International, Alphen aan den Rijn

Bermann GA (2007) Introduction: mandatory rules of law in international arbitration. Am Rev Int Arbitr 18(1):1–20

Bermann GA (2011) Reconciling European Union law demands with the demands of international arbitration. Fordham Int Law J 34(5):1193–1216

Bermann GA (2012) Navigating EU law and the law of international arbitration. Arbitr Int 28(3): 397–446

Binder C, Hofbauer JA (2017) The perception of the EU legal order in international law: an in- and outside view. Eur Yearb Int Econ Law 8:139–203

Broberg M, Fenger N (2022) The law of arbitration and EU law – like oil and water? Eur Investment Arbitr Law Rev 7(1):87–112

Contartese C (2017) The autonomy of the EU legal order in the EJC's external relations case law: from the "essential" to the "specific characteristics" of the union and back again. Common Mark Law Rev 54:1627–1671

Convention on the Settlement of Investment Disputes between States and Nationals of Other States, signed in Washington, D.C. on 18 March 1965

Corthaut T (2014) EU ordre public. Kluwer Law International, Alphen aan den Rijn

Crawford J (1981) Execution of judgments and foreign sovereign immunity. Am J Int Law 75(4): 820–869

Cremona M (2018) Structural principles and their role in EU external relations law. In: Cremona M (ed) Structural principles in EU external relations law. Hart, Oxford

[144] As noted by Odermatt (2023), pp. 17–18, the CJEU applies the principle of autonomy in a relational way, taking into account the type of relationship between EU law with other international dispute resolution mechanisms. The CJEU has thus not defined a uniform understanding of the scope, nature and limits of this principle.

[145] Pirker and Reitemeyer (2015), pp. 168–188.

D'Alterio E (2011) From judicial comity to legal comity: a judicial solution to global disorder? ICON 9(2):394–424
Dashwood A (2021) Article 26 ECT and intra-EU disputes – the case against an expansive reading of Achmea. Eur Law Rev 46(4):415–434
De Boeck M (2022) EU law and international investment arbitration: the compatibility of ISDS in Bilateral Investment Treaties (BITs) and the Energy Charter Treaty (ECT) with the autonomy of EU law. Brill, Leiden
De Brabandere E (2020) The (ir)relevance of transnational public policy in investment treaty arbitration – a reply to Jean-Michel Marcoux. J World Invest Trade 21(6):847–866
Declève Q, Van Damme I (2021) Investment arbitration under intra-EU BITs. In: Mata Dona JR, Lavranos N (eds) International arbitration and EU law. Elgar, Cheltenham, pp 291–319
Dolzer R, Kriebaum U, Schreuer C (2001) Standards of protection. In: Principles of international investment law, 3rd edn. Oxford University Press, Oxford, pp 186–195
Eckes C (2020) The autonomy of the EU legal order. Europe World Law Rev 4(1). https://doi.org/10.14324/111.444.ewlj.2019.19.
Gaillard E (2001) Transnational law: a legal system or a method of decision making? Arbitr Int 17(1):59–72
Garzini T (2012) Bilateral investment treaties. In: Garzini T, De Brabandere E (eds) International investment law: the sources of rights and obligations. Nijhoff, Leiden, pp 99–132
Georgaki K (2023) Conflict resolution between EU law and bilateral investment treaties of the EU Member States in the aftermath of Achmea. Yearb Eur Law 0:1–27
Govaere I (2010) Beware of the Trojan Horse: dispute settlement in (mixed) agreements and the autonomy of the EC legal order. In: Hillion C, Koutrakos K (eds) Mixed agreements revisited: the EU and its Member States in the world. Hart, Oxford, pp 187–207
Grierson-Weiler TJ, Laird I (2008) Standards of treatment. In: Muchlinksi P, Ortino F, Schreurer C (eds) The Oxford handbook of international investment law. Oxford University Press, Oxford, pp 259–304
Henckels C (2015) Proportionality and deference in Investor-State arbitration. Cambridge University Press, Cambridge
Hingelang S (2012) Circumventing primacy of EU law and the CJEU's judicial monopoly by resorting to dispute resolution mechanisms provided for in inter-se treaties? The case of Intra-EU investment arbitration. Leg Issues Econ Integr 39(2):179–206
Hirsch M (2008) Interactions between investment and non-investment obligations. In: Muchlinksi P, Ortino F, Schreurer C (eds) The Oxford handbook of international investment law. Oxford University Press, Oxford, pp 154–181
Klabbers J, Koutrakos K (2019) Introduction: an anatomy of autonomy. Nordic J Int Law 88(1): 9–40
Lavranos N (2022) Green power K/S and SCE. Solar Don Benito APS v Kingdom of Spain: how EU law allegedly Trumps international investment law. Eur Invest Arbitr Law Rev 7(1): 166–174
Lenaerts K (2017) La vie après l'avis: exploring the principle of mutual (yet not blind) trust. Common Mark Law Rev 54:805–840
Lenaerts K, Gutiérrez-Fons JA, Adam S (2021) Exploring the autonomy of the European Union legal order. Heidelberg J Int Law 81(1):47–88
Lew JDM (1978) Applicable law in international commercial arbitration. Oceana Publications, New York
Newcombe A, Paradell L (2009) Law and practice of investment treaties. Kluwer Law International, Alphen aan den Rijn
Shuibhne NN (2019) What is the autonomy of EU law, and why does that matter? Nordic J Int Law 88(1):9–40
Odermatt J (2016) When a fence becomes a cage: the principle of autonomy in EU external relations law. EUI working paper MWP 2016/07. European University Institute. Available at: https://cadmus.eui.eu/bitstream/handle/1814/41046/MWP_2016_07.pdf?sequence=1&isAllowed=y

Odermatt J (2023) The Court of Justice of the European Union and international dispute settlement: conflict, cooperation and coexistence. Camb Yearb Eur Leg Stud, pp 1–23
Pescatore P (1970) International law and community law – a comparative analysis. Common Mark Law Rev 7(2):167–183
Pirker BH, Reitemeyer S (2015) Between discursive and exclusive autonomy – opinion 2/13, the protection of fundamental rights and the autonomy of EU law. Camb Yearb Eur Leg Stud 17: 168–188
Scheu J, Nikolov P (2020) The setting aside and enforcement of Intra-EU investment arbitration awards after Achmea. Arbitr Int 36:253–274
Schilling T (1996) The autonomy of the community legal order: an analysis of possible foundations. Harv Int Law J 37(2):389–410
United Nations Commission on International Trade Law Model Law on International Commercial Arbitration, adopted in 1985
United Nations Convention for on the Recognition and Enforcement of Foreign Arbitral Awards, signed at in New York City on 10 June 1958
Van der Haegen O (2009) European public policy in commercial arbitration: bridge over troubled water? Maastricht J Eur Comp Law 16(4):449–476
van Rossem JW (2009) Interaction between EU law and international law in the light of Intertanko and Kadi: the dilemma of norms binding the Member States but not the community. Netherlands Yearb Int Law 40:183–227
Zarra G (2021) 'From Paris with love': transnational public policy and the romantic approach to international arbitration. Italian Law J 7(1):303–331

Trajan Shipley is an Associate in Van Bael and Bellis' Brussels office, where he specializes in EU trade law, investment protection, and public international law. He holds an LL.M. in European Law from the College of Europe in Bruges. Trajan has authored several publications on EU law, international trade law, and investment arbitration.

MFN Dilemma in India's DTAAs Post Concentrix Ruling: A Ticking Time Bomb

Saurabh Sharma and Mukesh Rawat

Contents

Abstract Treaty interpretation has always been an arduous task for courts and scholars alike. The subject becomes even more confounding and contentious in the wake of the imprecise drafting of the terms within certain treaties. In one such instance, India was on the receiving end when the Most-Favour-Nation (MFN) clause in the Convention between the Republic of India and the Kingdom of Netherlands (Member States) for the avoidance of Double Taxation and the Prevention of Fiscal Evasion with respect to Taxes on Income and on Capital (Dutch-India DTAA or subject DTAA) was at the core of the adjudication in a Writ Petition namely the *Concentrix* ruling before Delhi High Court.

Concentrix's ruling had sent a strong shockwave in the corridors of power when the High Court summarily rejected India's Income Tax Department submission regarding the interpretation of the MFN clause of Dutch-India DTAA and ruled in favour of the taxpayer. The deconstruction of the condition, as provided for in the MFN clause, regarding the membership of a third state in the Organization of

S. Sharma (✉)
Rajiv Gandhi National University of Law, Patiala, Punjab, India
e-mail: saurabh_faculty@rgnul.ac.in

M. Rawat
Hemvati Nandan Bahuguna Garhwal University, Garhwal, Uttarakhand, India

M. de Amstalden et al. (eds.), *International Economic Law*, Special Issue,
https://doi.org/10.1007/978-3-031-41996-6_11

Economic Cooperation and Development either at the time of claiming the MFN benefit by the petitioner or at the time of treaty negotiation was the apple of discord. Many scholars have criticized the Concentrix ruling as the Delhi High Court, on the one hand, buttresses the principle of Common Interpretation for decrypting the given issue and, on the other, relies on the unilateral declaration made by the Directorate-General for Tax Affairs, International Tax Affairs (Netherlands Tax Department). The ruling also falls short of adherence to the principles entrenched within the Vienna Convention on the Law of Treaties (VCLT), 1969.

The ruling has challenged the normative underpinnings of the MFN clause under the Dutch-India DTAA, which has the potential to open the floodgates to litigation against the Department and an impending threat of erosion of India's tax base due to treaty shopping. It may have spillover effects on many developing countries following source-based tax principles and would warrant a reassessment of their DTAAs with developed nations. The present paper will reflect upon these issues by critically analyzing the Concentrix Ruling, rationalizing its legal consequences, and addressing the concerns it gives rise to by suggesting ways to narrow these legal gaps. It concludes by acknowledging the growing jurisprudence in this domain.

1 Introduction

The genesis of the MFN clause was found in Friendship, Commerce, and Navigation Treaties and MFN treatment was the core obligation the commercial policy parties undertook.[1] The principle requires the parties to uphold parity amongst the traders or investors of the trading partners by accentuating the commitment to ensure equitability for traders and investors.[2] In other words, the principle serves as an antidote to discriminatory measures undertaken by offering more favourable treatment to traders or investors of a particular nation(s) vis-à-vis others. With the growing acceptability of the MFN clause, it became a general practice to engrain the principle within bilateral, regional, and multilateral investment and trade-related agreements.[3]

Although a bit nuanced, the MFN clause has found its place within various Double Taxation Avoidance Agreements (DTAAs). In this context, it has captured the understanding amongst the relevant parties of DTAAs, which requires them to extend the same benefits (of the lower rate of withholding tax or a scope more restricted) to each other as those being offered to a third party under another tax treaty. That said, the scope of MFN in the given DTAA is subject to the benefits provided regarding specific income, the date of the relevant tax treaty, an association

[1] OECD (2004).

[2] METI (n.d.).

[3] Sharmin (2020), pp. 37–41.

of a third party to a particular organization, etc.[4] It also purports that provisions pertaining to MFN are usually the result of the negotiations carried out between parties to the DTAAs and should not be construed as an obligation of customary international law.[5] It is apparent that the benefits of the MFN obligation inscribed in DTAAs are restricted, though not legally, to capital-exporting countries, while developing countries are capital-importing countries seeking investment in their countries. Conversely, the duty to provide such benefit lies on countries following the source-based tax principle.[6] Due to variations in articulating such commitments, the obligations under the MFN clause could be effectuated through various mechanisms depending upon their wording. It could be a self-triggered clause which would entail automatic activation of the MFN clause, or a publication of a specific notification (with or without any intimation to another party) or carrying out necessary amendment through bilateral consultation/negotiations, or such DTAA being silent as to the procedure for the application of the MFN clause.[7]

Besides all its gradations, the interpretation of the MFN clause under Dutch-India DTAA (subject DTAA) became a bone of contention in the Writ Petition titled *Concentrix Services Netherlands B.v. & Others vs Income Tax Officer (TDS) & Anr.* (Concentrix Ruling or ruling)[8] before the Delhi High Court (High Court). In the said ruling, Concentrix Services B.v. is a parent company registered in the Netherlands and having its subsidiary company in India registered by the name Concentrix Services India Pvt. Ltd. The provision of Clause IV (2)[9] of the Protocol appended to Dutch-India DTAA contains the principle of MFN. The major thrust of this ruling

---

[4]For e.g., Convention Between the Government of the Republic of India and the Government of the French Republic for the Avoidance of Double Taxation and the Prevention of Fiscal Evasion with Respect to Taxes on Income and on Capital (India-France DTAA), Clause 7 of the appended Protocol. Available at: https://www.taxsutra.com/sites/taxsutra.com/files/dtaa/FRANCE%20DTAA.pdf.

[5]Nikièma (2017), p. 2.

[6]In a source-based tax principle, a country taxes the income, of its resident and non-resident alike, which have its source in that country itself. If such nations conclude a DTAA with a capital-exporting country having an MFN clause, then benefits of such less rate or restricted scope of tax are usually enjoyed by the taxpayers who are residents of capital-exporting countries at the expense of countries following source-based taxation. Due to this, there is growing scepticism regarding the prevalence of the MFN clause in DTAA as it may entail unforeseen obligations.

[7]Kapoor (2021), p. 7.

[8]W.P.(C) 9051/2020, W.P.(C) 882/2021, CM Appl. 2302/2021, Delhi High Court, (2021).

[9]Convention between the Republic of India and the Kingdom of Netherlands (Member States) for the avoidance of Double Taxation and the Prevention of Fiscal Evasion with respect to Taxes on Income and on Capital, 1989 [Dutch-India DTAA]. Clause IV (2) of Dutch-India DTAA provides that: '*If after the signature of this convention under any Convention or Agreement between India and a third State which is a member of the OECD India should limit its taxation at source on dividends, interests, royalties, fees for technical services, or payments for the use of equipment to a rate lower or a scope more restricted than the rate or scope provided for in this Convention on the said items of income, then as from the date on which the relevant Indian Convention or Agreement enters into force the same rate or scope as provided for in that Convention or Agreement on the said items of income shall also apply under this Convention*'.

lay in unravelling the phrase "*third State, which is a member of the OECD*"[10] as provided in the above-mentioned clause. For the petitioners, who favoured the literal interpretation,[11] the meaning of this phrase was axiomatic, while the Income Tax Department (Department), in its argument, furthered purposive interpretation.[12] The High Court, in its reasoning, relied on the tool of "common interpretation"[13] and gave primacy to the unilateral decree issued by Netherlands Tax Department.[14] It is pertinent to discuss these principles of interpretation in the context of the ruling and this will be dealt with in detail during later sections of this article.

1.1 Elucidating the Syntax of MFN Within DTAAs

Against this backdrop, the thematic analyses of the given subject were quite discernible. The available literature suggests that the relevance of the MFN clause under DTAAs is intrinsic within the contours of this ruling. The discourse has also directed attention towards the role of tools for interpreting tax treaties.

With great emphasis, Prof. Sanja Djajic conveys the importance of MFN—which, although not referred to in the VCLT, has emerged as a separate topic at the UN International Law Commission and is extensively used in the realm of economic and trade liberalization.[15] From the perspective of DTAAs, MFN intends to maintain the equilibrium between treaty partners vis-à-vis third parties.[16] Therefore, the principle of MFN is integrated within various DTAAs signed between India and other nations and it can be considered to be a core obligation of such treaties.

As opposed to this, a different perspective is postulated by Deepak Kapoor in his paper describing the MFN clause as an onerous obligation on developing nations.[17] The authors earmark the perils of the MFN clause, which encircles the possibility of reduced taxation, and developing countries following the principle of source-based taxation will always be at risk of losing a potentially significant part of their tax base.[18] Accordingly, author Dhruv Janssen-Sanghavi while critiquing the ruling in his research paper, brought a novel dimension wherein he submits that the High Court does not express cogent reasoning in its adoption of the "rule of common

[10] Ibid.

[11] Reddy (2011), pp. 1–7. See also: Chawla (2012), pp. 1–9.

[12] Awana (2020), p. 46.

[13] Vogel (1986), p. 37.

[14] Decree of 28 February 2012, No. IFZ 2012/54M, Tax Treaties. India February 28, 2012 No. IFZ 2012/54M (hereinafter Unilateral Decree/Decree).

[15] Djajic (2015), p. 323.

[16] Ghosh et al. (1998), p. 1.

[17] See *supra* fn. 7.

[18] Shah and Shah (2021), p. 4.

interpretation".[19] He further contended that the High Court has misconstrued the application of common interpretation by giving preeminence to this tool and overlooking Article 3(2) of the Dutch-India DTAA requiring reference to internal laws for interpreting those terms that remained undefined.[20] Aside from this critical assessment, others lauded the *Concentrix* ruling and hailed it as a landmark judgment[21] rationalizing the real intent of negotiators by affirming that the Protocol to the India-Netherlands DTAA forms an integral part of the DTAA and no separate notification is required to apply the MFN clause under the Protocol.[22]

The evolving literature on this subject is noteworthy; nevertheless, to fully appreciate it, there is a dire need to probe into five intricate issues specifically. Firstly, it is germane to study the need for the High Court to opt for the rules of common interpretation instead of purposive interpretation in its ruling. The topic assumes greater significance in light of the recent circular issued by the Central Board of Direct Taxes (CBDT)[23] clarifying India's stand on the MFN clause annexed within the protocols of its DTAAs. Secondly, the MFN clause dealt with under the Dutch-India DTAA must be perused meticulously to articulate the specific suggestions for addressing the legal anomalies arising from its drafting. Thirdly, the present deliberation evaluates the interplay between MFN and treaty shopping, which is crucial in a fair analysis of the vitality of MFN provisions in DTAAs. This interaction becomes all the more pertinent in the wake of the application of the Principal Purpose Test on Covered Tax Agreement as contained in Article 7 Paragraph 15(a) of the Multilateral Convention to Implement Tax Treaty Related Measures to Prevent Base Erosion and Profit Shifting (MLI).[24] Fourthly, after as many as 135 countries have participated in a new apparatus of international tax policymaking, i.e. Base Erosion and Profit Shifting,[25] involving rigorous negotiations, it necessitates those interpretations of tax treaties which invigorate full tax norms. The present research focuses on finding the policy to bridge the gap between the judiciary and diplomats by sensitizing them to the implication of tax base erosion in our country. In addition, these policies would be equally helpful for other countries currently facing the menace of tax-base erosion. Fifthly, the existing

---

19 Ibid.

20 Ibid.

21 Bheda et al. (2021), p. 1.

22 JMP Advisors (2021).

23 Government of India, Ministry of Finance, Department of Revenue Central Board of Direct Taxes, Circular No. 3/2022. Available at: https://www.incometaxindia.gov.in/communications/circular/circular-3-2022.pdf.

24 OECD (n.d.-a). It provides that "*For paragraph 1 not to apply to its Covered Tax Agreements on the basis that it intends to adopt a combination of a detailed limitation on benefits provision and either rules to address conduit financing structures or a principal purpose test, thereby meeting the minimum standard for preventing treaty abuse under the OECD/G20 BEPS package; in such cases, the Contracting Jurisdictions shall endeavors to reach a mutually satisfactory solution which meets the minimum standard*".

25 Brauner (2014), p. 57.

literature is silent on the delicate issue of tax disputes, often culminating in Investor-State Disputes.[26] The government of India must take a cautious approach to avoid any friction that results in the invocation of Investor-State Dispute Settlement clauses under Bilateral Investment Treaties.[27] These novel issues arising from the ruling shall be delved into in detail in other sections of this paper.

1.2 Research Methodology and Framework

The present research proposes to bring to the fore the detrimental effect of the not-so-precisely drafted MFN clause in the Dutch-India DTAA, which has remained unbridled for far too long. The trajectory of this research would also suggest the bearing of VCLT, 1969, on the DTAAs and various interpretative tools.[28] The focal point being the Concentrix ruling, it is also imperative to explore the outcomes reached when applying these interpretative tools in the ruling. To that end, the paper adopted non-empirical research for analyzing the ruling and lacing it with doctrinal analysis for identifying the role of relevant provisions of VCLT, 1969 in the selection of tools of interpretation and deriving argumentative support through a collection of secondary sources for theorizing the ramifications of shoddy drafting of tax treaties. The paper is bifurcated into four parts, wherein the first section was a prelude to the discussion explaining the fundamentals of the MFN clause in DTAAs; followed by the second section dealing with a thorough examination of the Concentrix ruling—particularizing certain legal greys; the third section underscores the legal consequences arising from poor drafting of the terms in the subject DTAA and the ruling; the fourth section, promulgates several submissions for going-forward in this regard, and the final section, acknowledges the growing jurisprudence to stimulate more scholarly work and academic discussion in the given regime.

2 Deconstructing the *Concentrix* Ruling

The ruling is a Writ Petition filed by deductees, namely *Concentrix Services Netherlands B.v. and Optum Global Solutions International B.v.*[29] (petitioner or deductees), which challenged the issuance of impugned certificates by the department stipulating a withholding tax rate/participation dividend rate of 10% on dividends receivable by the petitioners. The petitioners' argued that their request

[26] Anthony and Dumberry (2021), p. 225.

[27] Gazzini and Brabandere (2012), p. 14.

[28] Linderfalk (2007), pp. 133–159.

[29] See *supra* fn. 8.

to the department was rejected for the issuance of a certificate at a lower withholding tax rate of 5%. The deductees are the ultimate beneficiary of dividends, and the remitters are the Indian subsidiaries of the above-said deductees, respectively. The moot legal question which arose for consideration was what should be the withholding rate of tax in respect of the dividend. In light of that, the consequential relief requested by the petitioners was the quashing of the impugned certificate, whereby the withholding rate of tax was pegged at 10% and the issuance of a new certificate at the rate of 5%.

The treaty partners signed the Dutch-India DTAA on 21 January 1989. It was contended by the petitioners that as per the MFN clause, they are entitled to the same rate of withholding rate of tax as applicable in DTAAs between India and other OECD members, such as Slovenia,[30] Lithuania and Colombia.[31] By placing its reliance on the MFN clause, the petitioners argued that the aforementioned DTAAs aid deductees by entitling them to lower withholding tax or scope more restricted on a certain income if India offers similar benefits in another DTAA to a nation being a member of OECD. Since India had signed DTAAs with other countries which were members of the OECD, the lower rate or the restricted scope in the DTAA executed between India and such a country would automatically apply to the subject DTAA.

The reasons advanced on behalf of India's Income Tax Department primarily counters, in defence of the impugned certificate, by terming the petitioners' argument regarding membership of OECD as being completely misconceived. The Department endorses that the notion of OECD membership should be construed from the standpoint of the date on which the DTAA was signed. In other words, if the third state with which a DTAA is signed, on which reliance is made, has been a member of the OECD or becomes a member of OECD on the date when the subject DTAA was signed, then the benefits of MFN shall accrue and not otherwise.

To further its stance, the Department claimed that since there were many instances when amendments were made to DTAA in question and therefore if the benefits of a lower rate of withholding tax or scope more restricted as provided in DTAAs between India and members of the OECD is to be extended it could be done by amending the subject DTAA followed by the issuance of a notification. It is hard to side with the Department concerning this view as the High Court was accurate in bringing the appended protocol within the gamut of the Dutch-India DTAA. The idea that the protocol forms an integral part is well endorsed within the text of the subject DTAA itself, and as a result, it extinguishes the need for the issuance of a separate notification to carry out any such amendments.

---

[30] Convention Between the Government of the Republic of India and the Government of the Republic of Slovenia for the Avoidance of Double Taxation and the Prevention of Fiscal Evasion with Respect to Taxes on Income, 2009 (India-Slovenia DTAA).

[31] Agreement Between the Government of the Republic of India and the Republic of Colombia for the Avoidance of Double Taxation and the Prevention of Fiscal Evasion with Respect to Taxes on Income, 2005.

The dispute would remain undecided until it is judicially established that when a third state offered a lower rate of tax or a scope more restricted on a certain income, it is expected to be a member of the OECD. It would then be contextualized with the date on which the Dutch-India DTAA was signed to render any benefit under the MFN clause. As the benefits of MFN were made conditional upon the determination of such date, the legality of the impugned certificate issued by the Department to the taxpayer providing for the higher rate of tax was also at stake.

In its judgment, the High Court sided with the taxpayers, which resulted in the quashing of impugned certificates and the issuance of new certificates providing for a lower tax rate. The High Court, in its reasoning, opined that for the application of the principle of parity as provided for under the MFN clause, three conditions must be fulfilled: first, the third State with whom India signs a DTAA should be a member of the OECD; second India should have, in its DTAA, executed with the third State, limited its rate of withholding tax, on subject remittances, at a rate lower or a scope more restricted, than the rate or scope provided in the subject DTAA; and third, if both the above are satisfied then the benefits of MFN treatment under subject DTAA shall accrue from the date the DTAA relied upon has come into force. Taking into account these parameters, India had a DTAA with Slovenia, which entered into force on 17 February 2005. Subsequently, it became a member of the OECD on 21 July 2010, providing for a lower tax rate compared to the subject DTAA, i.e., 5% under India-Slovenia DTAA as opposed to 10% under Dutch-India DTAA. It demanded the retrospective operation of benefits accrued under the MFN clause with effect from 21 July 2010 at the rate of 5% to the participation dividend paid by Indian subsidiaries of such deductees. The forthcoming parts of this section shall deal broadly with this aspect of the judgment for the present paper.

2.1 Application of VCLT, 1969 & Principles of Interpretation in the Concentrix Ruling

The VCLT, 1969 represents the codification of customary international law and is tempered on the touchstone *pacta sunt servanda*, i.e., fulfilling international commitments as assumed under treaties in good faith.[32] As the cornerstone of treaty interpretation, it ingresses a lot of significance in coagulating various rules of interpretation that seeks a balance among the main schools of interpretation.[33]

To formalize the discussion on tools of interpretation substantially, Articles 31–32 of VCLT, 1969[34] must be relied upon. For brevity, Article 31 of VCLT, 1969[35]

[32] Binder et al. (2019), pp. 671–672.

[33] Gardiner (2015), p. 2.

[34] Vienna Convention on the Law of Treaties (VCLT), 1969, 1155 UNTS 331, Articles 31–32.

[35] Article 31 of VCLT, 1969 titled *General Rules of Interpretation* provides that: "*1. A treaty shall be interpreted in good faith in accordance with the ordinary meaning to be given to the terms of the*

stipulates general rules of interpretation wherein the terms of the treaty should be interpreted, in good faith, by giving it an ordinary meaning and considering the object and purpose of such treaty. It also emphasizes that any subsequent agreements/instruments made between parties relating to such treaties, preamble and annexes, subsequent practices existing amongst parties, and relevant rules of international law applicable amongst them as suitable material for interpretation. While Article 32 of VCLT, 1969[36] put forth supplementary means to be utilized for interpretation, such as *travaux préparatoires*, etc., when interpretation under Article 31 yields obscurity or manifestly absurd results.

Under VCLT, 1969, the above-said provisions provide a particular type of context to the treaty terms that require interpretation.[37] As opposed to an orthodox view where the parties' intent was given precedence, these provisions require an extensive perusal of the text of the treaty. Put in other words, the intent of the parties has to be gathered from the text of the treaties.[38] Nevertheless, the principle enshrined under Article 31(1) of VCLT, 1969 should not be projected as sacrosanct, given that it would cater to any situation. The orientation of this provision in its subsequent clause gives space to the special intent of the parties if it is established that the parties so intended.[39]

Within the broader scheme of things, DTAAs are international agreements wherein the concerned parties undertake obligations. The evolution and consequences of DTAAs are discerned through the lens of the VCLT, 1969, which act as a guiding force in the interpretation of DTAAs. The operational objective of any DTAA is to eliminate double taxation and foster an environment where global trade and investments could thrive.[40] Bearing in mind the object of the DTAAs, the

---

treaty in their context and in the light of its object and purpose. 2. The context for the purpose of the interpretation of a treaty shall comprise, in addition to the text, including its preamble and annexes: (a) any agreement relating to the treaty which was made between all the parties in connection with the conclusion of the treaty; (b) any instrument which was made by one or more parties in connection with the conclusion of the treaty and accepted by the other parties as an instrument related to the treaty. 3. There shall be taken into account, together with the context: (a) any subsequent agreement between the parties regarding the interpretation of the treaty or the application of its provisions; (b) any subsequent practice in the application of the treaty which establishes the agreement of the parties regarding its interpretation; (c) any relevant rules of international law applicable in the relations between the parties. 4. A special meaning shall be given to a term if it is established that the parties so intended."

[36] Article 32 of the VCLT titled *Supplementary means* of interpretation provides that "*Recourse may be had to supplementary means of interpretation, including the preparatory work of the treaty and the circumstances of its conclusion, in order to confirm the meaning resulting from the application of article 31, or to determine the meaning when the interpretation according to article 31: (a) leaves the meaning ambiguous or obscure; or (b) leads to a result which is manifestly absurd or unreasonable.*"

[37] Van der Bruggen (2003), p. 142.

[38] See *supra* fn. 13.

[39] See *supra* fn. 34 and Article 31(4) VCLT.

[40] Arnold (2020), p. 10.

purpose of interpreting the terms of the treaties is to identify the parties' common intention and for which reference must be made to the language of the treaty itself. The special intent of the parties, as propagated by Klaus Vogel, in the DTAAs could be authenticated from notes and letters exchanged at the time the treaty was signed along with subsequent agreements and state practices so developed amongst the parties.[41]

The *Concentrix* ruling presented an enthralling opportunity for the High Court to revisit the interface between the terms of DTAAs and the VCLT, 1969. In a highly contentious setup, the High Court grappled with the phrase "*third State which is a member of the OECD*"[42] under Clause IV (2) of Dutch-India DTAA, and to be even more specific, the interpretation of the word "is" was indispensable to glean the intent of the parties. In contrast to an autological word having an obvious connotation, the word "is" imbibes a wide array of meanings and, thus, heterological. It paves the way for a holistic reference to OECD membership as the High Court described the word "is" as a state of affairs that should exist not necessarily at the time when the subject DTAA was executed but when the taxpayers or deductees make a request for issuance of a lower rate withholding tax certificate. Even though petitioners vouched for literal interpretation, which gave an unadorned meaning to the word "is", without subjecting it with an underlying intent as well as objectives of DTAAs and other phrases of Clause IV (2) of subject DTAA.[43] In effect, both the High Court and the petitioners in their reasoning were aligned with the unilateral declaration made by the Netherland Tax Department.

The justification of the High Court's stance lies in applying Common Interpretation,[44] which necessitates consistency in the interpretation of the provisions by the tax authority and the courts by adopting a fair and efficient approach. Although its precepts are more protrusive within the domain of Private International Law, courts in various jurisdictions apply it in interpreting tax treaties. As such interpretation is backed by mutual acceptance of the parties.[45] In this ruling, the High Court cited some precedents and dictums[46] to legitimize the application of common interpretation.

As a result, it examined the unilateral decree issued by the Netherlands Tax Department, which updated the policy decision on the consequences of the MFN clause in the subject DTAA by juxtaposing it with India's commitments under the India-Slovenia DTAA and examining Slovenia's membership of the OECD. On a bare perusal of this decree, the Netherlands' interpretation of Clause IV (2) of the

---

[41] EU-Chi, par. 7.94, QURESHI, Asif H., op. cit., p. 9, note 15 as cited in Hallivis Pelayo (n.d.).

[42] See *supra* fn. 9.

[43] See *supra* fn. 18, p. 1034.

[44] See *supra* fn. 8, p. 19.

[45] Number 630 v. M.N.R., 59 D. TAX 300, 303 (1959); *Canadian Pacific Ltd. v. The Queen*, 76 D. TAX 6120, 6135 (1976); *Donroy, Ltd. v. United States*, 301 F.2d 200, 9th Cir. (1962).

[46] *Corocraft Ltd. vs. Pan American Airways Inc.*, 3 W.L.R. 1273, 1283 (1968); *Fothergill vs. Monarch Airlines*, 3 W.L.R. 209, 224 (1980).

Dutch-India DTAA allows a lower rate of withholding tax as set out in the DTAA between India and other OECD members to be applicable under the subject DTAA.[47] The High Court deems it in the fitness of things to apply the principle of common interpretation to maintain comity and ensure consistency and equal allocation of tax claims between the treaty partners.

In doing so, it rejected India's Income Tax Department Department's submissions that confronted the view of expanding the denotation of the word "is" within the MFN clause of the Dutch-India DTAA. The Department characterized the MFN clause as a contingent contract, and its benefits could be extended to deductees on the satisfaction of two conditions, which were (1) the other country should be a member of the OECD on the date when the subject DTAA was executed and when a claim for the lower rate of withholding tax is made by deductees; and (2) the more beneficial provisions should have been extended to the residents of countries who are members of the OECD post the execution of the subject DTAA. As Slovenia, Lithuania and Colombia had never been a member of the OECD when the subject DTAA was signed, the fact that these countries apply for the membership of OECD should not obliviate India's Income Tax Department in issuing a certificate for a participation dividend tax at the rate of 10%. It also vindicated the Department's stance that it was a deliberate decision to have a lower participation dividend rate under the India-Slovenia DTAA and not intended to have a spillover effect after taking the MFN clause under the subject DTAA into consideration.[48] It is evident that the above-said criteria point to the Department's inclination towards purposive interpretation, as it instils flexibility without disregarding legislative intent and permeates collective intentionality.[49] The Department, for one, advocated focusing attention on the object and purpose of the treaty to delineate the overall goals intended to be achieved through the MFN clause under the Dutch-India DTAA.

2.2 *Putative Legal Gray Areas: A Critical Analysis of the High Court's Reasoning*

The ruling has become the subject of scholarly/academic discussion primarily due to the various shortcomings and legal gaps left in the judgment. It would validate critical analyzes of the reasoning offered by the High Court, and in this part, such apprehensions shall be irradiated. The analysis of this ruling shall be limited to the principles of interpretation and other legal aspects required to be considered in respect of the reasoning made by the High Court.

As far as interpretation is concerned, the High Court surprisingly referred to common interpretation in discerning the ordinary meaning of the MFN clause by

---

[47] See *supra* fn. 14.

[48] See *supra* fn. 7, p. 8.

[49] Ammann (2020), p. 208.

relying on a unilateral decree issued by the Netherlands Tax Department. Generally speaking, the principle of common interpretation warrants that courts of one contracting state should look at decisions made by courts of the other contracting state when confronted with problems of interpretation and that they test whether their interpretation can be transferred. Any reference to this approach must be made cautiously, as it does not entail going a long way to acquiesce to the judgment and reasoning of a foreign court/authorities, much less that it is considered a binding authority on courts.[50] One of the significant problems that arise with common interpretation is that the judge may feel obliged to accept the decisions of the foreign court which are adduced before him by the parties. However, it must be factored in that the parties providing these decisions will be inclined to provide decisions that are favourable to their position.[51] With deference, there is some semblance of dichotomy in the High Court's reasoning as it applied to the tool of common interpretation by advertently accepting a unilateral decree issued by the Netherland Tax Department, without any critical review, to ensure equitable allocation of taxes between treaty partners. A contradiction lies in applying this supplementary means of interpretation without delving too deeply into the object and purpose of the subject DTAA as enshrined within Article 31(1) of the VCLT, 1969.[52] These means only have a persuasive value that could be applied when a manifestly absurd or unreasonable result ensues[53] and does not substitute the judiciary's role in interpreting the ordinary meaning of the terms used in such DTAA in light of the object and purposes of the treaty. On top of this, accepting a unilateral decree issued by the executive arm of the state and not involving any judicial adjudication appears to be a flawed approach, as it does not reflect the shared understanding between the parties to subject DTAA.[54] In other words, since the judicial authorities or the domestic court of the Netherlands have not deciphered the issue at hand, by providing an opportunity to hear both parties, this executive decree seems to manifest an opinion of the Dutch government regarding the relief from taxes that must be paid in India.[55]

The other problematic facet of the Concentrix ruling was the High Court abandoning the tool of purposive interpretation and, consequently, turning a blind eye to the basic objective and purpose of the MFN clause embodied within the Dutch-India DTAA. It ruled that the date on which Slovenia joined the OECD was the relevant date for the accrual of the benefits of MFN under the Dutch-India DTAA to the petitioners. If at the time of negotiating the India-Slovenia DTAA, India had been aware that Slovenia was vying to be a member of the OECD, it is highly

---

[50] *Ulster-Swift, Ltd. v. Taunton Meat Haulage Ltd.*, 1 W.L.R. 625, 631 (1977).

[51] Sixdorf (2016), pp. 590–607.

[52] See *supra* fn. 36.

[53] Polish Postal Service in Danzig Case (1967) Series B, No. 11, (1925) p. 39; McDougal et al. (1967), pp. 226–242.

[54] Mondaq (2022).

[55] Kumar (2022), pp. 4–6.

improbable that India would have agreed to a lower rate of withholding tax. Also, in the case of the India-Slovenia DTAA India being a net exporter of capital, it perceptibly envisioned an advantage for its resident taxpayers, and therefore the offering of a lower rate participation dividend tax was consciously included in the treaty.[56] Such a broad interpretation may have even violated the principle of good faith and the High Court failed to deliberate upon the principle of *pacta sunt servanda,* given such an interpretation exceeded the mandate of the parties collated under the concerned DTAAs.[57] In this way, it also squandered an opportunity to appreciate the arrangement of the word "is" in Clause IV (2) of the subject DTAA being placed after the phrase "*after the signature of this convention*", suggesting limiting the effect of MFN from the date when subject DTAA was signed. Thus, the High Court's interpretation gave leeway for defeating the object and purpose of the MFN clause under subject DTAA.[58]

The High Court failed to pay any heed to Article 3(2)[59] of the Dutch-India DTAA, which is instrumental in interpreting the provisions by defining terms with reference to the member state's internal laws, including tax laws, applying the VCLT, 1969. As per OECD commentary, the above-said provision provides for a general rule of interpretation applicable only if the context of an undefined term does not require an alternative interpretation, which then permits the application of common interpretation, and such context must be determined in accordance with the intention of the contracting parties.[60] It is pertinent to note that the member state's legislation concerning laws in force existing at the time of application of the Convention shall be applied to interpret the undefined terms. The High Court observed that tax treaties are negotiated and drafted by diplomats, and such treaties are an outcome of the bargaining process.[61] It is coupled with the fact that the indirect incorporation of those treaties into an Act of Parliament would impinge upon the treaty's terms and would create unnecessary hardship, hence, it did not even consider it fit to analyze the application of Article 3(2) of the subject DTAA. No persuasive reason was laid down for the non-application of this provision with statutory drafting.[62] Under the pretext of differences in the principles of interpretation of the treaty and act/statute, to give the context to contentious issues embedded

[56] See *supra* fn. 7, p. 6.

[57] See *supra* fn. 53.

[58] Taxsutra (2021).

[59] Article 3(2) of Dutch-India DTAA provides that *"As regards the application of the Convention by one of the States any term not defined herein shall, unless the context otherwise requires, have the meaning which it has under the law of that State concerning the taxes to which the Convention applies."*

[60] OECD (2017a).

[61] Davis (1985), p. 4.

[62] Bennion (1992), p. 461.

within the MFN clause; the High Court directly opted for common interpretation,[63] which altered the dynamics of the above-said contested phrases.

The MFN clause in DTAAs has portrayed itself as a potential tool for treaty abuse.[64] In the context of tax treaties, Treaty abuse involves a taxpayer, though complying with the wording of a given tax treaty provision(s), attempting to obtain advantages that are beyond the rationale of that or those provision(s).[65] There are many arrangements through which foreign-based taxpayers utilize the benefit of a lower rate of withholding taxation under different DTAAs and distort their tax obligations under the garb of the MFN clause mentioned in their respective DTAA.[66] It results in either escaping taxation altogether or being subject to inadequate taxation in a way the member states did not intend and modifies the balance of concessions that the parties to such a treaty made.[67] The decisive factor that needs to be gauged in such a distortion is the exploitation of inter-jurisdictional tax arrangements by investors.[68] It would not have been out of context in the given Writ Petition for the High Court to adjudicate whether deductees exploit the MFN clause as a tool for treaty abuse by claiming treaty benefits and thereby undermining tax sovereignty.

3 Familiarization with Potential Legal Consequences: On the Brink of a Disaster

The erratic interpretation made ominous signs evident, as the writing was on the wall that serious ramifications for the Department should ensue. The present section seeks to account for the potential unintended and unforeseen consequences of this judgment. The most obvious effect of this ruling in posterity is the binding value of this precedent on the courts or tribunals or quasi-judicial bodies lower in the hierarchy than the High Court. It will open the floodgates for numerous actions against the Department by taxpayers who, under their respective DTAA, are paying a higher rate of taxes. The possibility of new member states, with whom India has a DTAA, joining the OECD cannot be ruled out, and if India has signed a DTAA at a lower rate of withholding tax or scope more restricted, it will become a massive challenge to mitigate the claims made by taxpayers from another jurisdiction.

To build more upon this impending threat, it is equally important to highlight that the ruling has sown the seeds for the triggering of the MFN clause under other DTAAs by Multinational Enterprises (MNEs). MNEs leverage their omnipresence,

---

[63] See *supra* fn. 8, p. 10.

[64] West (2020).

[65] João (2020), pp. 252–264.

[66] Åkerman (2016).

[67] Blum and Seiler (2006), p. 5.

[68] Park et al. (2021), p. 1.

as their structure allows them to reduce their tax burden.[69] In other words, an MNE could have its taxable presence in a particular nation with which India has signed a DTAA containing the provisions of the MFN clause, and through calculated tax planning, it will end up paying less tax.[70] To put it succinctly, through these arrangements, taxpayers such as MNEs indulge in treaty shopping leading not only to an erosion of the tax base but multilateralization of bilateral tax treaties,[71] and constrain states' fiscal autonomy.[72]

The financial and economic disparity amongst the parties is contributing to mounting skepticism towards MFN clauses in DTAAs. In the context of the Dutch-India DTAA, the Netherlands, being a developed and capital-exporting country,[73] is at an advantage as its resident taxpayers would generally accumulate the benefits arising from the MFN clause vis-à-vis India. On the other hand, India follows the source-based taxation principle,[74] which would, in essence, require them under the subject DTAA and present ruling to forgo its taxing rights in favour of Dutch-based petitioners. Adding another dimension, losing out on such a substantial tax base might prompt India to counter the ill-effects of this ruling with an austerity measure, like those seen in the Cairn Energy[75] and Vodafone Ltd.[76] These measures run the risk of being subjected to judicial scrutiny in Investor-State Investment Dispute (ISDS) arbitration under Bilateral Investment Treaties (BITs). The foreign taxpayer, usually from developed nations, have deployed this strategy which allows them to challenge such measures for being in violation of the Fair and Equitable Treatment clause, or other clauses, under the respective BIT.[77] In hindsight, the MFN clause under these DTAAs might seem counterproductive for India, as there is hardly any bilateral obligation on its counterparts, i.e. to offer similar benefits to Indian taxpayers; rather, it cast a huge financial implication upon the Department.

Last but not least, the need for redrafting the MFN clauses is quintessential as its cascading effects are not just limited to subject DTAA but are also ostensible in India's Conventions with France, Switzerland[78] other European states, and OECD Members. To consolidate their stand, and High Court's reliance on the unilateral

---

[69] Arel-Bundock (2017), p. 349.

[70] Streng (1992), p. 6.

[71] Schill (2009), pp. 121–196.

[72] Ibid.

[73] Embassy of India (Netherland) (2021).

[74] Rao (2008), pp. 75–82.

[75] Vora (2021), p. 287.

[76] Goel and Goel (2020), p. 243.

[77] International Tax Review (2014).

[78] Convention Between the Government of the Republic of India and the Government of the French Republic for the Avoidance of Double Taxation and the Prevention of Fiscal Evasion with Respect to Taxes on Income and on Capital (1994). Agreement Between The Republic Of India and The Swiss Confederation for The Avoidance Of Double Taxation with Respect to Taxes on Income (1994).

decree issued by the Netherlands Tax Department in the ruling[79] giving much impetus, the tax department of other nations also published notifications[80] concerning the interpretation of the MFN clause *ex-post facto*. After the *Concentrix* Ruling, the Indian Income Tax Department was not much behind its counterpart in notifying a non-binding circular that clarifies the MFN clause in the protocol to certain DTAAs.[81] It vehemently disagreed with those decrees/official bulletins/ notifications issued by Netherlands, France, and Switzerland, as they stand in derogation of the rules of international treaties and should desist from selective import of concessional rates under the MFN clauses of the respective DTAAs. These notifications are unilateral as they echo any mutual understanding amongst the parties of such DTAAs and profess only the viewpoint favourable to such a nation. It even relegates the vitality of Article 31(3)(b) of VCLT, 1969,[82] which acts as a guiding beacon for uniform interpretation of international treaties by bestowing relevance on subsequent practices establishing mutuality amongst the parties. It is safe to infer that unless the ruling is overturned on appeal before the Supreme Court of India (Supreme Court), the existing scenario is a disaster in waiting as it would deter the achievement of the objectives and purposes of the subject DTAA.

4 The Way Forward

The incongruity and dichotomy in applying the tools of interpretation call for measures that would ameliorate these errors. The present section lists such measures along with their contours for remedying these concerns. These measures can be effectuated at the level of adjudication when the India's Income Tax Department files an appeal before the Supreme Court or during the comprehensive analysis by carrying out the impact assessment of the subject DTAA.

As per the hierarchy of the Indian judiciary, the Department still holds a chance to ensure that the High Court's decision in this ruling be reversed by filing an appeal with the Supreme Court.[83] The Supreme Court being an apex court of India could

---

[79] See *supra* fn. 14.

[80] For such notification, Application of the most favoured nation clause of the protocol amending the agreement between the Swiss Confederation and the Republic of India for the avoidance of double taxation with respect to taxes on income; Direction Générale Des Finances Publiques (2016), Official bulletin of public finances-taxes (Legal ID: BOI-INT-CVB-IND-20161104), France on November 4, 2016.

[81] CBDT Circular (2022), Clarification regarding the MFN Clause in the Protocol to India's DTAAs with certain countries (Circular No. 3/2022), India on 3 February 2022.

[82] See *supra* fn. 35.

[83] In accordance with Article 133 of the Constitution of India, 1950, if there is any substantial question of law or it is wrongly decided and it needs to be decided by the Court. In such cases, the High Court grants the certificate to make appeals to the Supreme Court. The appeal can only be made within 60 days from the grant of certificate of the High Court.

well be a torch-bearer in culling out the ordinary meaning of the MFN clause in the light of the objects and purposes of the subject DTAA. Going by the limited precedents available on the interpretation of DTAAs, the obiter dictum of the Supreme Court in the *Azadi Bachao Andolan* case[84] has gained a lot of traction when it reiterated the observation of the Federal Court in *John N. Gladden v. Her Majesty the Queen*:[85]

> Contrary to an ordinary taxing statutes... A literal or legalistic interpretation must be avoided when the basic object of the treaty might be defeated or frustrated insofar as the particular item under consideration is concerned.

Not only does the subject DTAA explicitly mentions the need for the elimination of double taxation, but at the same time it also augurs the commitments of the parties towards fiscal evasion. The reasoning of the High Court is found wanting on the aspect of fiscal evasion which forms part of the theme of the subject DTAA. This putative contention could reinforce the underlying intent of the treaty partners to ensure that taxpayers do not advance a mechanism to subvert their tax obligations under the guise of the MFN obligation of the treaty partners.[86]

The Department's representation can also reflect upon the principle of full taxation, which furthers its viewpoint. The over-compliance with the non-double taxation principle has created a huge possibility for non-taxation of income.[87] In return, it creates an opportunity for harmful tax competition wherein developed and developing countries lobby for corporate capital through their lenient tax policies.[88] Post the formulation of the Base Erosion and Profit Shifting (BEPS), various action plans to address such concerns have been brought under this framework. These action plans promoted certain minimum standards aiming for tax transparency and allowing for the growing acceptance of full taxation norms.[89] In an abstract sense, the principle serves as an antithesis to non-double taxation by requiring nations to prevent abusive and aggressive tax planning and closing loopholes or gaps in tax treaties.[90] The Indian Income Tax Department in its submission should reiterate the commitment of the judiciary towards the prevention of fiscal evasion and should also argue for an interpretation of the preamble of the subject DTAA that would enhance the implementation of full tax norms.

Apart from that, the OECD progress report on an 'Inclusive Framework on BEPS' while institutionalizing the norms of full taxation required nations to modify treaties to address treaty-shopping abuses under the second minimum standard.[91]

---

[84] Union of India v. Azadi Bachao Andolan, (2004) 10 SCC 1.

[85] The Estate of the late John N. Gladden (Plaintiff) v. Her Majesty the Queen (Defendant) 85 DTC 5188, Federal Court, (1985).

[86] Dürrschmidt (2006), p. 3.

[87] OECD (2013), p. 18.

[88] Rixen (2011), p. 197.

[89] OECD (2019), pp. 16–17.

[90] Parada (2018), p. 971.

[91] See *supra* fn. 89.

The causal link between full tax norms and measures for the avoidance of treaty shopping lies in the dissuasion of third countries endeavoring for access to treaty benefits that are otherwise not available to them.[92] To materialize these efforts, under the auspices of the BEPS framework, the MLI aids governments in reducing these gaps in existing international tax rules by transposing the results from the OECD/G20 BEPS Project into DTAAs worldwide.[93] The Department would relish taking advantage of the fact that India and the Netherlands being a signatory to MLI brings subject DTAA[94] within the ambit of the Covered Tax Agreements, thereby permitting the application of the Principle Purpose Test to it. Under Article 7 (15) (a) of Multilateral Convention to Implement Tax Treaty Related Measures to Prevent Base Erosion and Profit Shifting,[95] the nations are justified in acclimating to the Principle Purpose Test to keep a check on those arrangements whereby taxpayers intend to take a benefit that is not in accordance with the object of such Covered Tax Agreements.

Under this scenario, it is no gainsaying that there exists a divide between the two primary organs of the Indian government, i.e. the judiciary and the executive. This was self-evident when the High Court deciphered the terms of the treaty without gleaning the intent of the member states in reference to the object and purpose of the subject DTAA, which makes it self-evident that it intends to narrow down the instances of double non-taxation and further full-tax norms. The need to sensitize the judiciary about the working of the executive, while drafting and negotiating international agreements, is the need of the hour.[96] Although in sovereign states executives are free to enter into such international treaties, in the case of taxation, these treaties automatically become part of the domestic or municipal law.[97] This galvanizes the role of the judiciary to interpret those treaties and to give prominence to the real intent of its negotiators.

In the contemporary era, the content of international agreements frequently evolves. This allows the parties to carry out amendments and even issue joint notes concerning the interpretation of specific terms of such agreements.[98] This function reduces friction amongst parties and fosters mutual respect for the same. In the present context, it is pertinent that since the subject DTAA is more than three decades old, there is a dire need to revisit its terms by the member states. The impact

---

[92] OECD (2017b), p. 17.

[93] See *supra* fn. 24.

[94] OECD (n.d.-b).

[95] See *supra* fn. 24.

[96] Sehrawat (2021), p. 4.

[97] CBDT (2019), Notification No. So 2887(E) [Notification No. 57/2019/F.No. 500/71/2015-Ftd-I], Section 90 of The Income-Tax Act, 1961—Double Taxation Agreement—Multilateral Convention to Implement Tax Treaty Related Measures to Prevent Base Erosion and Profit Shifting, India on 9 August 2019.

[98] Moloo (2021), pp. 261–264.

assessment of the MFN clause in subject DTAA can be carried out to critically appreciate its relevance and curtail its spillover effects.

5 Conclusion

The *Concentrix* ruling has captured the imagination of academicians, lawyers, tax scholars, and policymakers alike. More than the ruling it is the interpretation that became the talking point as it sets a unique precedent for the lower judiciary. The High Court has acknowledged the jurisprudence of tax treaty interpretation yet its application has been off the mark. But before inferring the consequences of the ruling, it is equally important to highlight the detrimental effect of the poor drafting of the MFN clause. The word "is" should have been originally qualified with a clearer temporal qualifier so that it could not have become an apple of discord amongst the member states. It is obvious that the OECD being open to new members would have various nations applying for its membership and it could also be expected that such nations would have a DTAA with India.

Moving forward, the debilitated reasoning offered by the High Court in the application of the tool of common interpretation was a point of inflexion. Not only does the very application seem faulty but the validation in the form of a unilateral decree passed by the Netherlands Tax Department[99] was quite problematic. The deviation from the objects and purposes of the subject DTAA as entrenched within its text while reference being made to supplementary means cannot be in line with Articles 31–32 of the VCLT, 1969,[100] and was somewhat paradoxical.

Though this paper aimed to explore the daunting effects of poor drafting of the MFN clause from the context of the Concentrix Ruling, it would be fitting to visualize, those aspects related to the MFN clause within a DTAA, that go beyond the scope of the present paper. In this way, an intriguing discussion could be initiated to acknowledge the growing jurisprudence in the given domain and stimulate the contribution of more scholarly work. The dearth of academic work in the given realm makes it quite challenging to critically analyze this ruling and at the same time, it presents an opportunity to explore this domain by carrying an interdisciplinary approach, empirical research, critical analysis, comparative analysis, impact assessment study, etc.

The present research due to its limited scope did not delve into the basis behind the need for renegotiating the MFN clause in the subject DTAA as negotiation is inundated with several policy considerations of the member states including the interest of resident taxpayers. The drafting of the text of the DTAA is seemingly tedious but its revival would truncate the procedure to renegotiate the similarly drafted MFN clauses of other DTAAs that India has signed. Empirical research

[99] See *supra* fn. 14.

[100] See *supra* fn. 35.

could be carried out to justify the growing usage of the MFN clause under DTAAs by Developed countries. The study can focus not only on the ins and outs of such an emerging trend but could well be a tool for fostering the capacity building of developing nations. Eyeing the MFN clause with suspicion could be counterproductive for rapidly advancing developing countries. Despite recent experience, there should be no rush towards abandoning the standard MFN clause without careful analysis and reflection. These issues can instill a fresh perspective in the debate pertaining to the north-south divide and the pragmatic application of such laws for north-south economic integration.

References

Åkerman S (2016) Does the LOB clause in BEPS Action 6 violate the principle of MFN treatment in EU law? Graduate thesis, Lund University. Available at: https://lup.lub.lu.se/luur/download?func=downloadFile&recordOId=8897833&fileOId=8901304

Ammann O (2019) Domestic Courts and the Interpretation of International Law. Brill, Leiden

Anthony V, Dumberry P (2021) Investor-State Dispute Settlement. In: Vanduzer A et al (eds) Promoting and managing international investment: towards an integrated policy. Routledge, Abington

Arel-Bundock A (2017) The unintended consequences of bilateralism: treaty shopping and international tax policy. Int Organ 71(2):349–371

Arnold B (2020) An introduction to tax treaties. Available at: https://www.un.org/development/desa/financing/sites/www.un.org.development.desa.financing/files/2020-06/TT_Introduction_Eng.pdf

Awana V (2020) Jurisprudential aspects and significance of rule of purposive interpretation. Int J Leg Sci Innov 2(2):46–54

Bennion F (1992) Statutory interpretation, 2nd edn. Butterworths, Oxford

Bheda M et al (2021) India: Delhi High Court ruling on taxability of dividends under the India-Netherlands tax treaty. International Tax Review. Available at: https://www.internationaltaxreview.com/article/b1s3jtc74237jy/india-delhi-high-court-ruling-on-taxability-of-dividends-under-the-indianetherlands-tax-treaty

Binder C et al (2019) The Pacta Sunt Servanda principle or the limits of interpretation - The Gabčíkovo-Nagymaros case revisited. In: Forlati S et al (eds) The Gabčíkovo-Nagymaros Judgment and its contribution to the development of international law. Brill, Leiden, pp 315-342

Blum D, Seiler M (2006) Preventing treaty abuse, 1st edn. Linde Verlag, Vienna

Brauner Y (2014) What the BEPS? Fa Law Rev 16(2):55–115

Chawla A (2012) Interpretation of tax treaties: an art yet to be mastered! Natl Law Sch India Rev 23(2):1–9

Davis DR (1985) Principles of international double taxation relief. Sweet & Maxwell, London

Djajic S (2015) True purpose of the most-favoured-nation clause in international arbitration: substantive guarantee or only a cause of action? In: Harmonization of Serbian and Hungarian law with the European Union law, vol 3. University of Novi Sad Faculty of Law, pp 323-341

Dürrschmidt D (2006) Tax treaties and most-favoured-nation treatment, particularly within the European Union. Schriftenreihe Steuerinstitut Nürnberg Nr. working paper no. 2006-02, 6. Available at: https://www.steuerlehre.rw.fau.de/files/2017/03/Tax-Treaties-and-Most-Favoured-Nation-Treatment.pdf

Embassy of India (Netherland) (2021) Brief on India-Netherlands Bilateral Trade and Investment. Available at: https://indianembassynetherlands.gov.in/page/overview-of-indian-economy/#:~:text=The%20Netherlands%20is%20the%20third,36.28%20billion%20over%20the%20period

Gardiner R (2015) Treaty Interpretation, 2nd edn. Oxford University Press, Oxford
Gazzini T, Brabandere E (2012) International investment law: the sources of rights and obligations, International investment law series. Brill Nijhoff, Leiden
Ghosh M et al (1998) The value of MFN treatment. National Bureau of Economic Research working paper no. 6461
Goel A, Goel S (2020) The Vodafone-India capital gains tax controversy: the past and the future. Tax Notes Int 100(2):243–246
Government of India, Ministry of Finance, Department of Revenue Central Board of Direct Taxes, Circular No. 3/2022. Available at: https://www.incometaxindia.gov.in/communications/circular/circular-3-2022.pdf
Hallivis Pelayo ML (n.d.) Using the Vienna Convention on the laws of treaties for interpreting tax treaties. Revista Direito Tributário Internacional Atual. Available at: https://www.ibdt.org.br/RDTIA/en/1/using-the-vienna-convention-on-the-laws-of-treaties-for-interpreting-tax-treaties/
International Tax Review (2014) Indian dispute resolution under bilateral investment treaties. Available at: https://www.internationaltaxreview.com/article/2a698axyv1rz4d0lg1qf4/indian-dispute-resolution-arbitration-under-bilateral-investment-treaties
JMP Advisors (2021) Tax matters, issue no. 2021/05. Available at: http://www.itsgnetwork.com/pdf/taxNews/JMP_Tax.Matters-2021.05.pdf
João R (2020) Mechanisms to fight treaty abuse: an overview. Revista de Direito Tributário Internacional Atual 7:252–264
Kapoor D (2021) An Albatross around the neck of developing nations - MFN clause in tax treaties. Tax Cooperation Policy Brief 17:1–11
Kumar A (2022) Analysing the most-favoured-nation clause under tax treaty: is India's divergent view correct? The Law Blog, 19 November 2022. Available at: https://thelawblog.in/2022/11/19/analysing-the-most-favoured-nation-clause-under-tax-treaty-is-indias-divergent-view-correct/
Linderfalk U (2007) On the interpretation of treaties: the modern international law as expressed in the 1969 Vienna Convention on the Law of Treaties, 1st edn. Springer, Cham
McDougal S et al (1967) Interpretation of agreements and world public order. Yale University Press, New Haven
METI (n.d.) Most-favoured nations treatment principle. WTO Report: 2016. Available at: https://www.meti.go.jp/english/report/data/2016WTO/pdf/02_02.pdf
Moloo R (2021) Changing times, changing obligations? The interpretation of treaties over time. Am Soc Int Law 106:261–264
Mondaq (2022) India: CBDT clarifies the legal interpretation of the MFN clause. Available at: https://www.mondaq.com/india/tax-authorities/1159610/cbdt-clarifies-the-legal-interpretation-of-the-mfn-clause.
Nikièma S (2017) The most-favoured nations clause in investment treaties. IISD, Manitoba. https://www.iisd.org/system/files/publications/mfn-most-favoured-nation-clause-best-practices-en.pdf
OECD (2004) Most-favoured-nation treatment in international investment law. OECD working papers on international investment 2004/02, OECD Publishing. https://doi.org/10.1787/518757021651
OECD (2013) Action plan on base erosion and profit shifting. OECD Publishing
OECD (2017a) Commentaries on the articles of the Model Tax Convention 2017, Commentary on Clause IV (2). Available at: https://www.oecd.org/berlin/publikationen/43324465.pdf
OECD (2017b) Inclusive framework on BEPS (progress report). OECD Publishing. Available at: https://www.oecd.org/tax/beps/inclusive-framework-on-BEPS-progress-report-july-2016-june-2017.pdf
OECD (2019) Peer review report on treaty shopping, inclusive framework on BEPS, Action 6. OECD Publishing
OECD (n.d.-a) Multilateral convention to implement tax treaty related measures to prevent BEPS. OECD. Available at: https://www.oecd.org/tax/treaties/multilateral-convention-to-implement-tax-treaty-related-measures-to-prevent-beps.htm

OECD (n.d.-b) Signatories and parties to the multilateral convention to implement tax treaty related measures to prevent base erosion and profit shifting (status as of 10 May 2022). Available at: https://www.oecd.org/tax/treaties/beps-mli-signatories-and-parties.pdf
Parada L (2018) Hybrid entity mismatches and the international trend of matching tax outcomes: a critical approach. Intertax 46(12):971–993
Park SJ et al (2021) Navigating optimal treaty-shopping routes using a multiplex network model. PLoS ONE 16(8):1–16
Rao S (2008) Nexus matters: India's right to tax. Tax Notes Int 49(1):75–82
Reddy A (2011) Literally interpreting the law - a appraisal of the literal rules of interpretation in India, Manupatra Online. Available at: https://www.manupatra.com/roundup/338/Articles/Literally%20interpreting%20the%20Law.pdf
Rixen T (2011) From double tax avoidance to tax competition: explaining the institutional trajectory of international tax governance. Rev Int Polit Econ 18(2):197
Schill S (2009) The multilateralization of international investment law. Cambridge University Press, Cambridge
Sehrawat V (2021) Implementation of international law in Indian legal system. Fa J Int Law 31(1): 98–119
Shah S, Shah D (2021) Delhi High Court invokes most favoured national clause and applies 5% withholding tax on dividend income under India-Netherlands Tax Treaty. Direct Tax Alert, Dhruvaa Advisors. Available at: https://www.dhruvaadvisors.com/insights/files/Dhruva%20DT%20Alert%20-%20Delhi%20HC%20applies%205-percent-rate%20on%20dividend%20income%20under%20India-Netherlands%20DTAA.pdf
Sharmin T (2020) Application of most-favoured-nation clauses by investor state arbitral tribunals: implication for the developing countries, 1st edn. Springer, Cham
Sixdorf F (2016) Common interpretation as a method for interpreting double tax conventions in Germany: theoretical foundation and results of empirical research. Intertax 44(8):590–607
Streng W (1992) Treaty shopping: tax treaty limitation of benefits issues. Houston J Int Law 15(1): 789
Taxsutra (2021) Applicability of MFN clause on dividends - does Delhi HC settles the dust. Available at: https://www.taxsutra.com/dt/experts-corner/applicability-mfn-clause-dividends-does-delhi-hc-settle-dust
van der Bruggen E (2003) Unless the Vienna Convention otherwise requires: notes on the relationship between Article 3(2) of the OECD Model Tax Convention and Articles 31 and 32 of the Vienna Convention on the Law of Treaties. Eur Tax IFBD 43(5):142–157
Vogel K (1986) Double tax treaties and their interpretation. Int Tax Bus Law 2(1):4–85
Vora A (2021) Cairn Energy Plc and Cairn UK Holdings Private Limited v The Republic of India: retroactive tax legislation when it ceases to meet the fair and equitable treatment standard. Br Tax Rev 3:287
West C (2020) MFN dangers: the (potential) unraveling of tax treaty policy. Leiden Law Blog. Available at: https://leidenlawblog.nl/articles/mfn-dangers-the-potential-unravelling-of-tax-treaty-policy

Saurabh Sharma is a Guru Gobind Singh Indraprastha University, New Delhi graduate. He completed his Master's (LLM) in International Law from South Asian University and his dissertation topic involved perusing issues pertaining to Base Erosion and Profit Shifting specifically from developing countries perspective. He has cleared the UGC (NET) exam in the subject of Law in 2019. Prior to joining RGNUL as Assistant Professor in Legal Research, he worked as an Assistant Professor (Law) with Sheds College of Law (Affiliated with Himachal Pradesh University), Solan, Himachal Pradesh. He has taught Public International Law subject to the students of the 5th Semester and is currently teaching International Dispute Settlement Bodies to the 10th Semester of RGNUL. He is also a member of various Research Centres such as the Centre for Business Law and Taxation, Centre for Environmental Legal Studies and Centre for Advanced Studies in

International Humanitarian Law, along with being editor of RGNUL Law Review Journal and RGNUL Journal of Social Sciences. Saurabh has authored various Op-eds on issues ranging from domestic law issues like Telecommunication bill and GST on ODR Services to international law issues like WTO e-commerce moratorium and gender inclusivity in the United Nations on numerous platforms like SCC Online, The Leaflet, etc. He has undertaken various initiatives under the inter-disciplinary programme to deliberate upon dispute settlement body under trade law and was also invited by GLA University to teach synchronization of trade and health. His research interest includes Public International Law, International Economic Law, Dispute Settlement and Private International Law.

Mukesh Rawat is an Assistant Professor at the Department of Law, Hemvati Nandan Bahuguna Garhwal University. Presently, he is writing his doctoral thesis at Rajiv Gandhi School of Intellectual Property Law, Indian Institute of Technology, Kharagpur. He holds a bachelor degree in law from the University of Delhi. He has an LLM degree in International Law from South Asian University (SAARC University), Delhi. His research interests include International Trade Law, Procurement Law and International Sports Law. In the past, he has worked with organisations of international repute like United Nations High Commissioner for Refugees, National Anti-Doping Agency, All India Football Federation and FIFA (International Federation of Football Association).

Part IV
Trade Regulation

Energy Transit Under GATT Article V and Energy Transit Dispute Resolution at the WTO

Michail Skouzes

Contents

Abstract This chapter analyses Article V of the General Agreement on Tariffs and Trade (GATT) and its application to transit of energy related goods via fixed infrastructure with certain capacity, such as pipelines and power grids. Modern economy requires the passing of goods through the territory of more than two countries in order to reach their destination. This also applies to goods in the energy sector, since oil and natural gas producing countries are not their majority consumers. There is a nexus of pipelines, both on land and below the sea, that transport oil and natural gas through vast distances of land crossing several countries to connect producing and consuming countries. Transfer via pipelines is not the only mode of transportation in the energy sector. Sea carriage via specially designed ships, such as oil tankers or LNG carriers, is another common way of transporting energy commodities. Electric power can be internationally transported through power grids connecting neighboring countries. In an era, in which energy plays a strategic role, the transportation of energy related goods is essential to the welfare of countries. In the absence of a multilateral International Treaty regulating international trade in the energy sector, bilateral treaties proliferate in this sector. It is evident that the creators of the GATT did not intend to regulate energy matters.

M. Skouzes (✉)
I. Vassardanis & Partners Law Firm, Athens, Greece
e-mail: m.skouzes@outlook.com

M. de Amstalden et al. (eds.), *International Economic Law*, Special Issue,
https://doi.org/10.1007/978-3-031-41996-6_12

However, as will be discussed in this article, the World Trade Organization (WTO), with its Dispute Settlement System, can be a forum suitable to adjudicate disputes in the energy sector, concerning e.g. the transportation of natural gas, oil and electric power. Article V of the GATT ensures freedom of transit, with some limitations, from the territory of each contracting party for goods, vessels and other means of transportation. Should this Article be applied to the energy sector and it being interpreted so as to also provide for capacity establishment rights, it has the potential to liberalize the energy market for WTO Members and reshape the world economy.

Keywords World Trade Organization · GATT Article V · Energy · Energy transit · Routes most convenient · Fixed infrastructure · Capacity establishment rights · Third Party access · Dispute resolution · WTO dispute settlement system · Energy transit dispute resolution

1 Introduction

In the present era, where energy plays a strategic role for most countries, international trade proliferates in this sector. When reference is made to energy related goods, it is important for one to distinguish between the sources of energy and energy itself. Thus, in the context of the present chapter, energy related goods include all energy products (e.g. natural gas, oil shale, oil products, electricity from geothermal and solar thermal, etc.), whether primary or secondary and renewable or non-renewable,[1] whereas energy refers to heat and power,[2] generated through combustion, in the instance of fossil fuels, or through other methods, in the instance of renewable energy sources. Although energy from renewable energy sources has risen exponentially during the last decade, renewable energy sources are still far from being the primary source of energy. The consumption of traditional fossil fuels (i.e., coal, oil and natural gas) accounted for 84% of the world's primary energy consumption in 2019 and the global demand for hydrocarbons is expected to continue to grow until about 2040, albeit at a slower pace.[3] Natural gas comprises 16.4% of the world total energy consumption.[4] The demand for natural gas is expected to continue increasing until 2030 or 2040 in a scenario of Net Zero or Accelerated energy transition, before beginning to rapidly decline.[5]

---

[1] For more information on the categorization of energy products see Marhold (2021), pp. 15–17.

[2] OECD, IEA and Eurostat, Energy Statistics Manual (OECD/IEA 2005), p. 17.

[3] Zhukovskiy et al. (2021), p. 2.

[4] IEA, Global share of total energy supply by source, 2019, IEA, Paris. Available at: https://www.iea.org/data-and-statistics/charts/global-share-of-total-energy-supply-by-source-2019, IEA. Licence: CC BY 4.0.

[5] BP, Energy Outlook 2022 edition. Available at: https://www.bp.com/content/dam/bp/business-sites/en/global/corporate/pdfs/energy-economics/energy-outlook/bp-energy-outlook-2022.pdf.

Oil and solid fuels, such as coal, are easily stored and transferred across borders, whereas natural gas is traded across borders via pipelines, in its natural gaseous form. However, natural gas is increasingly being liquefied in order to transport it to remote regions via sea carriage and for storage.[6] Sea carriage is primarily regulated by the United Nations Convention on the Law of the Seas (UNCLOS), [7] which guarantees for ships of all states the rights of innocent passage through the territorial sea (UNCLOS Article 17)[8] and transit passage through straits used for international navigation (UNCLOS Article 38), [9] and will not be examined in this chapter. The only way to transport electricity is through power grids. Given that major fossil fuel reserves are situated far from their major consumers, they must be transported across thousands of kilometers crossing the borders of multiple states. Therefore, a state could take advantage of its location and hinder its transportation for its own purposes. In this context, the present chapter will examine how GATT Article V could ensure the freedom of transit of energy resources, with a focus on fixed infrastructure. It will examine the issues that may arise from the ownership status of infrastructure and whether third parties have a right to access the infrastructure. Then, it will present the dispute settlement system of the WTO and elaborate on its suitability to adjudicate disputes arising from transit in the energy sector.

This chapter is constituted of two parts. The first part will present freedom of transit in the WTO and will elaborate Article V and its implications to the transit of energy and energy related goods. It will examine the issues presented for the transit of energy related goods via fixed infrastructure with a limited capacity such as pipelines and power grids and how, in light of those issues, Article V should be interpreted. In the second part, the dispute settlement system of the WTO will be presented, as well as the reasons for which the WTO is a forum suitable to adjudicate disputes arising from the transit of energy.

2 Freedom of Transit in the WTO

Freedom of transit in the context of the WTO legal order is primarily regulated by two articles in different agreements: Article V of the GATT and Article 11 of the Agreement on Trade Facilitation (TFA). The former is more general while the latter primarily deals with the technical and economic aspects of transit, *e.g.* the advanced filing and processing of transit documentation and data prior to the arrival of

[6] Cottier et al. (2011), p. 214.

[7] United Nations Convention on the Law of the Sea (UNCLOS), 10 December 1982, 1833 U.N.T.S.

[8] UNCLOS Article 17.

[9] UNCLOS Article 38.

goods.[10] It is clearly stated in the Preamble of the TFA that Members intend to clarify and improve relevant aspects of GATT Article V, *inter alia*, with a view to further expediting the movement, release and clearance of goods, including goods in transit. Therefore, one may confidently claim that GATT Article V lays the principles/sets the general context of the freedom of transit, as recognized in the law of the WTO, whereas TFA Article 11, further elaborates and clarifies GATT Article V.

It is supported that the initial aim of the GATT or the WTO Agreement was not to regulate matters relating to trade in the energy sector.[11] Albeit there is no specific provision in the text of any of the WTO Agreements that excludes trade in the energy sector from its scope of application, *de facto*, Members regarded that energy trade fell mostly outside the scope of the GATT for decades.[12] However, an underlying reason for this practice is the fact that major fossil fuel producing countries were not Members, until recently, *e.g.* the Russian Federation gained Member status on 22 August 2012, Kazakhstan became a Member on 30 November 2015 and the Kingdom of Saudi Arabia on 11 December 2015.[13] Nevertheless, the practice of Members may not add or diminish any rights or obligations under the covered Agreements. In addition, the very preamble of the WTO Agreement states that the Parties agree to the expansion of the production and trade in goods and services. Thus, one cannot convincingly argue that the regulation of energy goods falls outside the scope of application of the GATT. The wording of the preamble allows the evolutionary interpretation of terms found in the GATT in light of the contemporary needs and issues of the Members.[14] It is logical, after all, that the law and interpretation of the law should pay due regard to the advancements of technology and the evolution of society. Therefore, since nowhere in the WTO Agreements is it stated that regulation of energy trade falls *a priori* outside the scope of the WTO, one cannot convincingly claim that the provisions of the various Agreements are not applicable in the energy sector.

2.1 GATT Article V

GATT Article V is a complex provision comprised of seven paragraphs designed to ensure the freedom of transit for goods through the territory of WTO Members (Members). This Article has not been invoked in many disputes and relevant jurisprudence is provided by Panel Reports in only two cases: *Colombia – Ports of*

[10] Agreement on Trade Facilitation (TFA) Article 11.9.

[11] Marceau (2012), p. 385.

[12] Marhold (2013), p. 2.

[13] WTO, Members and Observers of the WTO. Available at: https://www.wto.org/english/thewto_e/countries_e/org6_map_e.htm.

[14] Ugaz (2011), p. 280.

Entry[15] and *Russia – Traffic In Transit.*[16] According to GATT Article V:1, goods, vessels or other means of transport are in transit when the passage across the territory of a Member is only a portion of a complete journey beginning and ending beyond the frontier of the Member whose territory the traffic passes.[17] This traffic is termed in Article V as "traffic in transit".

Traffic in transit destined to or originating from another Member shall be guaranteed freedom of transit via the routes most convenient for international transit.[18] The use of the term 'or' in the first sentence of Article V:2 shall be construed as creating two separate obligations for each Member. A Member has an obligation to ensure transit through its territory to traffic entered from any other Member or exited to any other Member.[19] Considering the ordinary meaning of the word freedom is the unrestricted use of something, a Member may not, in principle, restrict the passage of traffic in transit. GATT Article V:2 first sentence limits this freedom to the routes most convenient for international transit.[20] However, there is no further elaboration either by the GATT or by a Panel on what constitutes a 'route most convenient for international transit'.

Article V:2 second sentence establishes a non-discrimination obligation stating that no distinction shall be made based on circumstances relating to the ownership of the goods or modes of transport, the point of entry or exit, the destination and origin of the goods or on the flag of the vessels carrying the goods.[21] Therefore, as noted by the Panel in *Colombia – Ports of Entry*, goods from all Members shall enjoy the same level of access and equal conditions when in international transit.[22]

Article V:3 stipulates that a Member has the right to require that traffic in transit through its territory be entered at the proper customs house. However, it cannot be subject to unnecessary delays or restrictions. Furthermore, Article 11.6 of the Agreement on Trade Facilitation (TFA) provides that formalities, documentation requirements and customs control shall not be more burdensome than necessary in order to: (a) identify the goods; and (b) ensure fulfilment of transit requirements. Traffic in transit is also exempt from all charges imposed in relation to the transit. Charges may only be imposed for transportation, to cover administrative expenses or the cost of services rendered. Charges and regulations imposed by Members shall be reasonable, having regard to the conditions of the traffic. Article V:5 contains a Most Favoured Nation (MFN) treatment obligation with respect to all charges, regulations

---

[15] Panel Report, *Colombia – Indicative Prices and Restrictions on Ports of Entry*, WT/DS366/R, adopted on 20 May 2009.

[16] Panel Report, *Russia – Measures Concerning Traffic in Transit*, WT/DS512/R, adopted on 26 April 2019.

[17] GATT Article V:1.

[18] GATT Article V:2 first sentence.

[19] Panel Report, *Russia – Traffic in Transit*, *supra* note 16, pp. 62–63.

[20] Panel Report, *Colombia – Ports of Entry*, *supra* note 15, pp. 174–175.

[21] GATT Article V:2 second sentence.

[22] ibid, 175.

and formalities on connection with transit. The Ad note to this Article provides that MFN treatment regarding transportation charges refers to like products being transported on the same route under the same conditions.[23] MFN treatment, which is entailed in GATT Article I, prohibits discrimination among like products originating in or destined for different countries.[24] The fundamental purpose of the MFN treatment obligation is to ensure the equality of competitive opportunities for like products from all Members.[25] Whether two products are 'like' has to be examined *in concreto*. In *Japan – Alcoholic Beverages II*, the Appellate Body took the following four elements into consideration: the product's end-uses in a given market, consumers' tastes and habits, the product's properties, nature and quality and their tariff classification on the basis of the Harmonized System established under the World Customs Organization (WCO).[26]

Article V:6 requires Members to accord MFN treatment to products which have been in transit through the territory of any other Member. The issue raised from this paragraph is whether it creates obligations for the Member whose territory a product passes or the Member whose territory is the ultimate destination of a product. The Panel in *Colombia – Ports of Entry* found that the obligations of Article V:6 apply to Members whose territory is the final destination for goods in transit.[27]

Article V:7 explicitly limits the scope of Article V to not cover aircraft in transit. However, Article V applies to the air transit of goods.

In summary, Article V contains two basic principles of international economic law: the principle of non-discrimination and the MFN treatment obligation. It provides for the equal treatment of traffic in transit regardless of its origin, destination or the ownership and origin of the goods. It exempts traffic in transit from all duties imposed in respect of transit and only allows the imposition of certain reasonable charges and regulations with regard to the conditions of traffic and it creates an obligation for Members to avoid causing unnecessary delays or restrictions to traffic in transit.

Regulating trade in the energy sector was not an intended target for the GATT. At the time it was negotiated, major energy producers were not contracting parties to the GATT, e.g. the Russian Federation (member since 22 August 2012), Saudi Arabia (member since 11 December 2005) and Kazakhstan (member since 30 November 2015). There are opinions that GATT Article V does not apply to transit of energy resources through fixed infrastructure, for the WTO is not suited to regulate trade in

---

[23] Panel Report, *Colombia – Ports of Entry*, *supra* note 15, p. 190.

[24] Appellate Body Report, *Canada – Certain Measures Affecting the Automotive Industry*, WT/DS139/AB/R, WT/DS142/AB/R, adopted on 19 June 2000, para. 27, Matsushita et al. (2015), p. 159.

[25] Appellate Body Report, *European Communities – Measures Prohibiting the Importation and Marketing of Seal Products*, WT/DS400/AB/R, WT/DS401/AB/R, adopted on 18 June 2014, para. 120.

[26] Appellate Body Report, *Japan – Taxes on Alcoholic Beverages*, WT/DS8/AB/R, WT/DS10/AB/R, WT/DS11/AB/R, adopted on 1 November 2006, pp. 20–21, Matsushita et al. (2015), p. 164.

[27] Panel Report, *Colombia – Ports of Entry*, *supra* note 15, paras. 186–192.

energy and at the time Article V was negotiated not a great many goods was transported by fixed infrastructure.[28] Thus, Article V may create various issues when it is applied to transit via fixed infrastructure, such as oil or natural gas transferred via pipelines and electricity transmitted via power grid.

The GATT, as opposed to the ECT,[29] does not contain a specific provision that defines energy products. In view of this, one must begin his analysis by defining what is to be considered an energy product. In the context of the GATT, it is clear that natural gas, oil and other fossil fuels are by definition considered goods and therefore fall within the scope of Article V:1. Although there was a debate on whether electricity is considered a 'good' or a 'service', this chapter maintains that based on the ordinary meaning of the word 'good' as something that has economic utility or satisfies an economic want, electricity should be considered a good. This position is further reinforced by the fact that the Court of the European Union has found that the Law of the European Union and the domestic legislation of its Member States treat electricity as a good.[30] In addition, the ECT treats electricity as a good, for it is included in Annex EM, where a list of the energy materials and products is provided. These present a clear example that international practice tends to treat electricity as a good rather than as a service. Electricity is, also, included in the Harmonized System of the WCO in Section V Chapter 27 under Heading 27.16, albeit this heading is optional for WCO Members. One more argument in favour of counting electricity as a good is the fact that it is generated from natural resources (*e.g.* coal, natural gas, etc.). Thus, one may convincingly claim that it is a manufactured good.[31] In addition, in the negotiating text of the TFA one may notice that Members intended to explicitly include in the goods covered by GATT Article V and TFA Article 11 goods transferred via pipelines and electricity grids.[32] In contrast, it is argued that electricity cannot be considered a good as it cannot be stored in large quantities, as opposed to 'traditional' goods.[33] However, due to advancements in technology, storage of electricity has been made possible in recent times and it is estimated that in a Net Zero Emissions scenario battery storage capacity will reach 680 GW by 2030, compared to 16 GW in 2021.[34] Therefore, electricity should be regarded as 'goods' and fall within the scope of GATT Article V.

---

[28] Lei (2020), p. 261; Konoplyanik (2009), p. 466.

[29] ECT Article 1(4).

[30] Case C-393/92—*Gemeente Almelo and Others v Energiebedrijf IJsselmij* [1994] ECR I-01477, para. 28.

[31] World Trade Organization, World Trade Report 2010 (2010) p. 55. Available at: https://www.wto.org/english/res_e/booksp_e/anrep_e/world_trade_report10_e.pdf.

[32] World Trade Organization—Negotiating Group on Trade Facilitation, Draft consolidated negotiating text, [23 October 2013] TN/TF/W/165/Rev.18, p. 16.

[33] Ibid, p. 55.

[34] International Energy Agency (2022), Grid-Scale Storage. Available at: https://www.iea.org/reports/grid-scale-storage.

2.2 *The Issues in GATT Article V:2*

2.2.1 The Routes Most Convenient for International Transit

Article V:2 limits the freedom of transit to 'the routes most convenient for international transit'. However, it does not elaborate on what constitutes a convenient route or what are the criteria which determine convenience. In order to resolve this issue, one must first define the term route and, more specifically, whether or not it covers both fixed infrastructure, such as a pipeline, or just a land, sea and air corridor. This is quite important for the transit of energy and energy related goods, since electricity can be transported only through power grids, whereas natural gas is primarily transported through pipelines. It is supported that, by its ordinary meaning, the term route is broad enough to cover fixed infrastructure as well as land, sea or air corridors.[35] In addition, this view is supported by the fact that the wording of GATT Article V:1 refers generally to 'means of transport' without excluding any mode, except for aircrafts in transit.[36] Plain access to the territory of another is, also, considered a route.[37]

On the issue of convenience, the answer is not simple and may not be uniform for all cases. It has been maintained that the text of GATT Article V:2 provides that convenience is linked to the "international transit" as opposed to a 'party'.[38] The wording of GATT Article V:2 ("via the routes most convenient for international transit") supports this opinion. However, little to no explanation is given as to what and who determines convenience. In view of the principle of territorial sovereignty, it is the position of this Article that the transit state shall determine which route is convenient. This position is, also, supported by the fact that the transit state is better situated to determine convenience.[39] However, it cannot do so arbitrarily.

In order for a transit state to not violate its obligations under GATT Article V:2, it must take into account several criteria. Indeed, convenience is greatly dependent on the geographical position of the consumer and the producer.[40] The shortest route entails less costs. However, when determining convenience, the transit state shall, also, take into account the interests of the international community in general; a route that passes through a protected and fragile ecosystem is not convenient on the sole basis that it is the fastest route. Therefore, environmental aspects shall be considered as well. Furthermore, the transit state should consider the economic feasibility this particular route has for the entity that intends to use it. It should, also, be taken into account whether the suggested route might be prejudicial to the peace, good order, or security of the transit state. It is evident, that there one Member shall consider a

---

[35] Pogoretskyy (2017), p. 133.

[36] Cossy (2012), p. 297; Ugaz (2011), p. 258.

[37] Willems and Li (2014), p. 37.

[38] Ibid, p. 38.

[39] Pogoretskyy (2017), p. 135.

[40] Azaria (2009), p. 572.

plethora of criteria to ensure it does not violate its obligations under GATT Article V:2. Thus, the optimal way to ensure compliance is via bilateral (or plurilateral) negotiations with the interested parties.

In a scenario, where negotiations are not successful and an agreement is not reached, the transit state shall weigh all the aforementioned criteria and, most likely, even more. However, it is the position of this article that, in light of the general principles of good faith and the prohibition of abuse of rights, a transit state shall not be found to be obstructing freedom of transit when it has taken all the possible considerations into account, but has decided to give more importance to some of them when determining convenience, to the extent this decision is reasonable and justified by the available data.

In light of the above, a pipeline or a power grid may be the most convenient route on the sole principle of its existence. As *Pogoretskyy* notes, albeit in a different context, in liberalized energy markets a pipeline (or a power grid) is similar to a highway, where any entity may utilise it (for a fee), but in an instance where the pipeline is owned and operated by a single entity, access to a third party is not always permitted, thus resembling a private railway line.[41] Thus, as regards to the transit of energy via fixed infrastructure, when determining convenience one must, also, examine whether or not he is permitted to utilise the existing infrastructure and what rights one has when the existing infrastructure for various reasons cannot be utilised. These issues will be examined in the following paragraphs.

2.2.2 Capacity Establishment Rights

When a fixed infrastructure with a certain capacity, such as a pipeline or a power grid is concerned, the issue of convenience becomes more complex. A pipeline may become convenient on the sole basis of its existence, but then congestion problems may arise rendering its utilization not feasible in a technical aspect. Therefore, an alternative solution must be found: either the construction of a new pipeline or the expansion of the existing one or the use of another pipeline. Constructing a new or expanding an existing pipeline or power grid and, thus, creating new capacity is defined as capacity establishment.[42]

It is maintained that GATT Article V:2 alone does not impose an obligation to Members to construct or permit the construction of new routes.[43] Article 11.5 of the Agreement on Trade Facilitation (TFA) stipulates that Members are encouraged to make available, where practicable, physically separate infrastructure (such as lanes, berths and similar) for traffic in transit. One cannot convincingly argue that TFA Article 11.5 imposes an obligation for capacity establishment. This is based on the wording of the Article, which states "encouraged" instead of legally binding treaty

[41] Pogoretskyy (2017), pp. 234–235.

[42] Ibid., p. 54.

[43] Azaria (2009), p. 572.

language such as "shall". It is the position of this article that, when read in conjunction with TFA Article 11.5, and in accordance with the principles of good faith and the prohibition of abuse of rights, a Member may not arbitrarily hinder the construction of new or the expansion of existing fixed infrastructure. Instead, the transit state shall have an obligation to conduct negotiations with the interested parties to address this matter. This obligation should not be construed as an obligation to achieve a certain result (e.g., construct a new pipeline), rather as a behavioral obligation to hold negotiations in good faith to examine whether it is possible for the parties to reach an agreement.

It should be noted that there are other international treaties, that certain Members have signed, which specifically provide for capacity establishment.[44] Primarily, the United Nations Convention on the Law of the Sea (UNCLOS) and the Energy Charter Treaty (ECT). The former stipulates in Article 125 that land-locked States, in order to exercise the rights provided for in the UNCLOS, shall enjoy freedom of transit through the territory of transit States by all means of transport. In the context of UNCLOS, 'all means of transport' does not entail transport pipelines and gas lines, unless land-locked States and transit States agree otherwise. ECT Article 7 (4) stipulates that, if transit of energy materials and products cannot be achieved by means of energy transport facilities, then the contracting parties shall not, in principle, place obstacles in the way of new capacity being established. In addition, it is supported that in an instance, where the transport capacity is limited, the transport company may be required to reduce the capacity it has allocated to every user, in order to fulfill the requirements of non-discriminatory treatment. This reduction will, most likely, either be not possible or the transport company will be obliged to pay an excessive amount of damages to the users. Thus, ECT Articles 7(1) and 7(3) may indirectly compel it to expand its pipeline capacity.[45] In addition to these treaties, there are other soft law documents, such as the UN GA Resolution 63/2010, which welcomes international cooperation in developing transportation systems and pipelines and recognizes the need for extensive international cooperation in determining ways of ensuring the reliable transportation of energy to international markets through pipelines and other transportation systems.

The fact, that other international treaties, whether addressing specifically energy matters (in the case of the ECT) or create more general provisions for transit (in the case of UNCLOS) may provide for capacity establishment rights or simply encourage cooperation to ensure the reliable transportation of energy (such as the UN GA Resolution 63/2010) is of little to no significance in the context of obligations assumed under the GATT. However, when these treaties are read in conjunction with TFA Article 11, they constitute a convincing argument that the denial of a Member to establish new capacity will be done in bad faith and will constitute an abuse of right, provided of course that the Member is a contracting Party to the other

[44]For more information regarding the International Treaties on energy transit, see Azaria (2015).
[45]Liesen (1999), pp. 64–65.

treaties (or one of them). Therefore, a Member will be in breach of its obligation under Article V:2 to provide freedom of transit through its territory.

One has to consider the systemic implications to which such an interpretation of the Law might lead to. Could this argument, also, be applied to impose an obligation to the transit state to construct other infrastructure, e.g., a railroad, a highway, or even a new port? This argument is not uniform. It has to be examined on a case-by-case basis, taking into account the circumstances and the obligations a Member has assumed under other international treaties or soft law documents.

2.2.3 Ownership and Third-Party Access

The obligation, under GATT Article V:2, for a Member to provide the same level of access and equal conditions to goods from all Members when in international transit can be problematic, when an infrastructure with limited capacity, such as a pipeline or a power grid, is concerned. There are two main issues arising in such a scenario. The first one concerns the ownership of the infrastructure. It is not uncommon for a private entity to be the owner of a pipeline. Second, should the same level of access to a pipeline/power grid be given to all Members, then congestion issues would arise and the infrastructure might not be able to handle the volume of all goods passing through.

Should the owner of the infrastructure be a private entity, then it will not be bound by WTO rules and obligations. The WTO is an international organization comprised of states and three separate customs territories that possess full autonomy in the conduct of their external commercial relations.[46] It should be noted that all the agreements under the WTO are integral parts of one agreement: the WTO Agreement.[47] Therefore, the WTO Agreements should be regarded as an international treaty between subjects of international law.[48] A third state has an obligation from an international treaty only if it consents to it in writing.[49] The WTO Agreements do not concern, in principle, private entities, for they only apply to Members. It is possible, in certain instances, for a private entity to be deemed as a 'public body' and, therefore, be subject to WTO law. A 'public body' is an entity that is vested with governmental authority and exercises governmental functions.[50]

It is maintained that the provisions of GATT Article V:2 establish an obligation to achieve a certain result and, thus, Members incur responsibility when this result is

[46] Van den Bossche and Zdouc (2013), p. 105.

[47] Appellate Body Report, *Brazil – Measures Affecting Desiccated Coconut*, WT/DS22/AB/R, adopted on 20 March 1997, para. 18.

[48] Willems and Li (2014), p. 39.

[49] Konstantinidis (2011), p. 387.

[50] Appellate Body Report, *United States – Definitive Anti-Dumping and Countervailing Duties on Certain Products from China*, WT/DS379/AB/R, adopted on 25 March 2011, paras. 122–123.

not achieved.[51] It should be noted, that the actions of a private entity will be attributable to a Member if said Member directs in any formal way a private entity to act inconsistently with WTO Law or if the private entity acts on behalf of the government of the Member.[52] In a scenario where infrastructure is owned by a private entity, freedom of transit could be reduced to inutility as Members would have the ability to circumvent their obligations by allowing private entities to be the sole owners or operators of their infrastructure. It would be inconsistent for GATT Article V:2 to impose an obligation to the Members, only for them to circumvent this obligation by allowing a private entity to operate the infrastructure. Consequently, Members must enact binding measures in their national legislation to regulate the practices of private entities in order to be in conformity with their obligations under the WTO regime.[53]

A second issue regarding freedom of transit via fixed infrastructure concerns the limited capacity such an infrastructure has. A pipeline or a power grid can transport a finite volume of goods, before congestion problems arise. In order to ensure identical level of access to every interested party the infrastructure's owner should grant access to every party that requests it. This essentially constitutes an obligation to allow third-party access. However, it is supported that Article V does not provide a legal basis for third-party access.[54] Were it the case, the obligation to allocate capacity to a third-party could lead to energy security problems and demand would be less fulfilled, since each party would be allocated less capacity for its goods. This would lead in a restricted energy market rather than a liberalized one and jeopardize the energy security of States. A valid argument against the compulsory third-party access obligation is that in certain States, the pipelines were financed, built and operated by private investors for their private use. A mandatory third-party access obligation would infringe on the property rights of these investors.[55] This could be considered as expropriation and the transit State may be found liable to pay damages to the investors. Therefore, a mandatory allocation of capacity to third-parties would not be practically feasible.

As mentioned above, GATT Article V:2 does not by itself create an obligation for a Member to construct or permit the construction of new infrastructure. In order to reject the establishment of new capacity, the transit state's rejection should be in accordance with the principles of good faith and the prohibition of abuse of rights. Therefore, the only way to guarantee an identical level of access in infrastructure with limited capacity is to set up a mechanism by which they regulate capacity allocation between exports, imports, transit, and domestic transport in a non-discriminatory manner.[56] This can be done through the establishment of a

[51] Azaria (2015), p. 65.

[52] Pogoretskyy (2017), pp. 236–237.

[53] Willems and Li (2014), pp. 40–41.

[54] Azaria (2009), p. 572.

[55] Pogoretskyy (2017), p. 234.

[56] Azaria (2015), p. 65.

fixed set of procedures, in accordance with the principles of non-discrimination and national treatment, to allow interested parties to negotiate access to the infrastructure on the same basis through transparent procedures. This will provide equal opportunities to access the infrastructure and protect the interests of all interested parties. Consequently, in the case of infrastructure with limited capacity, such as power grids and pipelines, the obligation to provide the same level of access, set by the Panel in *Colombia – Ports of Entry*,[57] shall be interpreted to mean the provision of same opportunities to access the infrastructure through transparent procedures.

3 Dispute Resolution

3.1 The WTO as a Forum to Adjudicate Disputes

The WTO has three institutions to adjudicate trade disputes: the Dispute Settlement Body (DSB), the Appellate Body and the Panels established by the DSB. The DSB has the authority to establish Panels and a standing Appellate Body, adopt Panel and Appellate Body reports, supervise the adoption of these reports and authorize suspension of concessions under the covered agreements. The Appellate Body is comprised of seven members, which shall have a demonstrated experience in the fields of law and international trade, and has the competence to hear appeals from panel cases. The Panels are comprised of three (or five if the parties to a dispute agree so within 10 days from the establishment of the panel) well qualified individuals, selected with a view on ensuring the independence of the members and they may not be a citizen of a Member who is a party to the dispute the panel adjudicates. A panel is established, if a complaining party requests it, at the latest DSB meeting which follows the one in which the request first appeared as an item to its agenda. The DSB retains the authority to decide by consensus to not establish a Panel.

As per DSU Article 20, the period between the establishment of a panel until the date the DSB considers the Panel or Appellate Body report for adoption shall not exceed 9 months where the panel report is not appealed or 12 months where the report is appealed.[58]

Any dispute that arises from any of the WTO Agreements can be adjudicated, pursuant to the rules and procedures of the DSU. The aim of the dispute settlement system is to provide security and predictability to the multilateral trading system.[59] Hence, the DSB may not add to or diminish the rights and obligations provided in the WTO Agreements.[60] The Panels and the Appellate Body when interpreting a covered agreement are guided by the customary rules of interpretation of public

[57] Panel Report, *Colombia – Ports of Entry*, *supra* note 15, para. 175.

[58] DSU Article 20.

[59] DSU Article 3.2.

[60] Ibid.

international law.[61] However, their interpretation is not definitive as the Ministerial Conference and the General Council have the authority to adopt definitive interpretations.[62]

3.2 Energy Transit Disputes in the WTO

The WTO's dispute settlement system, in contrast to the ECT does not contain any procedures specifically designed to resolve energy transit dispute. ECT Article 7 (7) establishes a conciliation procedure for disputes in energy transit. However, this procedure is subject to the previous exhaustion of any contractual or otherwise dispute resolution mechanisms (including ECT Articles 26 and 27) that have been agreed by the parties to the dispute.[63] Therefore, a (WTO) Member before resorting to the conciliatory process found in ECT Article 7(7) shall, also, submit the dispute to the DSB. In light of this, the conciliatory process should be viewed as the last step to the settlement of the dispute and the party to the dispute shall assess what the most suitable forum to adjudicate the dispute is.

It should, also, be noted that the ECT is ratified by 52 Contracting Parties, including the European Union and Euratom, and certain EU Member-states have expressed their intention to withdraw from the ECT. It would be safe to claim that the ECT is a regional agreement. The US-Mexico-Canada Free Trade Agreement (USMCA), the follow up agreement to NAFTA which as of July 2020 is no longer in force, does not contain an energy specific chapter.[64] Consequently, the only multilateral forum that remains to settle disputes and safeguard the rule of law, while keeping the delicate balance in international relations, is the WTO.

When addressing the issue of suitability, one has to consider that the WTO has managed, among other to establish the rule of law among its members and to establish a certain set of procedures that guarantee transparency.[65] Transparency, as mentioned earlier, is key in ensuring the same level of opportunities to access infrastructure with limited capacity. Therefore, it is safe to assume that the WTO is an impartial forum.

Furthermore, during the past years there have been many Panel/Appellate Body Reports regarding energy related disputes. Primarily, these disputes relate to subsidies in the renewable energy sector, pursuant to the provisions of the Agreement on Subsidies and Countervailing Measures (SCM).[66] One of the reasons that only renewable energy subsidies have been challenged, may be that they include a

---

[61] Ibid.

[62] Matsushita et al. (2015), p. 87.

[63] Azaria (2009), p. 582; Stănescu (2018), Article 7 para. 7.31.

[64] Marhold (2021), p. 145.

[65] Marceau (2012), p. 388.

[66] See Asmelash (2022), p. 459.

Feed-In Tariff (FIT) with domestic content requirements, in order to generate domestic jobs or promote the national manufacturing industry. Thus, a Member may be found in breach of its obligations under GATT Article III:4, Article 2.1 of the TRIMS Agreement and Article 3.1(b) of the SCM.[67] There have, also, been two GATT/WTO cases relating to petroleum that have been initiated by OPEC members against US domestic measures.[68] Consequently, one can convincingly claim that the WTO can adjudicate energy disputes in general, having done so a number of times in the past.

In view of the above, it is evident that the WTO is not only an impartial forum with an organized set of procedural and substantive rules, but also the various Panels and the Appellate Body have significant expertise in adjudicating energy dispute. The main issue, however, is whether the WTO has the necessary substantive rules to regulate energy transit. As it was stated, the provisions of the various WTO Agreements were not specifically intended to regulate energy matter. The provisions of the ECT are largely based on those of the GATT and are better adapted to the needs of energy trade.[69] Thus, and in accordance with the provisions of the Vienna Convention on the Law of Treaties,[70] when interpreting the various provisions of the GATT, the ECT may provide a guideline to the Panels or the Appellate Body, when interpreting the provisions of the GATT.

4 Conclusion

When GATT Article V was negotiated, transit via pipelines could hardly had been envisioned by its creators. However, the law and its interpretation should not remain stagnant throughout the years, but it should follow the advancements in technology and society. In this context, GATT Article V, when interpreted in light of the principle of good faith could provide the legal basis for the construction and the improvement of fixed infrastructure, necessary to transport energy related goods. Each Member should set transparent procedures in order for the interested parties to access its fixed infrastructure, thus fulfilling its obligation to provide identical level of access to interested parties. The WTO as a universal Organization has a set of rules and procedures established in the DSU, in order to adjudicate disputes arising by any of the Multilateral Agreements that are listed in Appendix 1 of the DSU, including the GATT. Therefore, since traditional energy resources are considered goods, electricity is treated in international practice as a good and there is nothing in the WTO Agreements that *a priori* excludes energy trade from the scope of the WTO, it is a forum competent to resolve disputes in the energy trade sector. What

[67] Asmelash (2015), pp. 279–280.

[68] See Desta (2004), pp. 388 *et seq.*

[69] Marhold (2013), p. 5.

[70] United Nations Vienna Convention on the Law of Treaties, 23 May 1969, 1155 UNTS.

makes the WTO a forum suitable to adjudicate energy transit disputes is the composition of the various Panels and the Appellate Body by individuals, who are experts in the field of international trade law, the fact that it has managed to establish the rule of law, while maintaining the balance in international relations and that its general provisions, when interpreted in light of the principle of good faith and the more specialised provisions of the ECT can ensure that energy transit is guaranteed for all Members. The WTO has the potential to completely liberalize trade in the energy sector and promote energy security, should Members be willing to apply its provision to this sector and not resort to the isolationism of the past years.

References

Asmelash H (2015) Energy subsidies and WTO dispute settlement: why only renewable energy subsidies are challenged. J Int Econ Law 18:261–285

Asmelash H (2022) The first ten years of WTO jurisprudence on renewable energy support measures: has the dust settled yet? World Trade Rev 21:455–478

Azaria D (2009) Energy transit under the Energy Charter Treaty and the general agreement on tariffs and trade. J Energy Nat Resour Law 27:559–596

Azaria D (2015) Treaties on transit of energy via pipelines and countermeasures. Oxford University Press, Oxford

Cossy M (2012) Energy trade and WTO rules: reflexions on sovereignty over natural resources, export restrictions and freedom of transit. In: Herrmann C, Terhechte J (eds) European yearbook of international economic law 2012, European yearbook of international economic law, vol 3. Springer, Heidelberg. https://doi.org/10.1007/978-3-642-23309-8_9

Cottier T et al (2011) Energy in WTO law and policy. In: Cottier T, Delimatsis P (eds) The prospects of international trade regulation: from fragmentation to coherence. Cambridge University Press, Cambridge, pp 211–244

Desta M (2004) The GATT/WTO system and international trade in petroleum: an overview. J Energy Nat Resourc Law 21:385–398

Konoplyanik A (2009) Gas transit in Eurasia: transit issues between Russian and the European Union and the role of the energy charter. J Energy Nat Resour Law 27:445–486

Konstantinidis A (2011) The law of international treaties. In: Antonopoulos K, Magkliveras K (eds) The law of the international society, 2nd edn. Nomiki Bibliothiki, Athens, pp 361–400

Lei Z (2020) The applicability of GATT rules to gas transit against the backdrop of the Belt and Road Initiative: China's pipeline transit transport. Asian J WTO Int Health Law Policy 15:259–284

Liesen R (1999) Transit under the 1994 Energy Charter Treaty. J Energy Nat Resour Law 17:56–73

Marceau G (2012) The WTO in the emerging energy governance debate. Am Soc Int Law Proc 106: 385–389

Marhold A (2013) The World Trade Organization and energy: fuel for debate. ESIL Reflections 2(8):1–6

Marhold A (2021) Energy in international trade law: concepts, regulation and changing markets. Cambridge University Press, Cambridge

Matsushita M et al (2015) The World Trade Organization: law, practice and policy, 3rd edn. Oxford University Press, Oxford

Pogoretskyy V (2017) Freedom of transit and access to gas pipeline networks under WTO law. Cambridge University Press, Cambridge

Stănescu CG (2018) Article 7 – transit. In: Leal-Arcas R (ed) Commentary on the Energy Charter Treaty. Edward Elgar, Cheltenham, pp 95–113

Ugaz P (2011) Prospects for a transit regime on energy in the WTO. Año XVIII. Agenda Internacional, pp 247–298
Van den Bossche P, Zdouc W (2013) The law and policy of the World Trade Organization, 3rd edn. Cambridge University Press, Cambridge
Willems A, Li Q (2014) Using WTO rules to enforce energy transit and influence the transit fee. Eur Energy J:34–42
Zhukovskiy YL et al (2021) Fossil energy in the framework of sustainable development: analysis of prospects and development of forecast scenarios. Energies 14. MDPI AG: 5268

Michail Skouzes is a LL.M. candidate in International and European Energy Law in the Democritus University of Thrace, where he also earned his LL.B. He is an Associate at I. Vassardanis & Partners Law Firm. His practice mainly focuses on energy and corporate law issues, as well as dispute resolution. His research interests include international trade in energy and protection of investments in the energy sector.

EU Imported Biodiversity Loss: The Gaps and Overlaps Between Trade Impact and Provisions on Biodiversity in EU Free Trade Agreements

Justine Muller

Contents

Abstract Trade and biodiversity are connected in many ways. One of them is the negative impact of trade itself on biodiversity. This chapter focuses particularly on whether the integration of environmental provisions, including some relevant to biodiversity, in EU Free Trade Agreements could mitigate this negative impact of trade on nature. To do so, the chapter aims to expose the gaps and overlaps between the impact of trade on biodiversity and the core biodiversity-related provisions of EU trade agreements' Trade and Sustainable Development chapters. Firstly, by considering the negative impacts that trade may have on biodiversity, directly or through embedded biodiversity loss, and that trade agreements may enhance. The chapter thus brings a rationale behind the inclusion of biodiversity-related provisions in EU trade agreements to the fore. Secondly, the chapter presents the main goals of the relevant environmental clause in EU trade agreements and what kind of protection

J. Muller (✉)
European University Institute, Florence, Italy
e-mail: justine.muller@eui.eu

M. de Amstalden et al. (eds.), *International Economic Law*, Special Issue,
https://doi.org/10.1007/978-3-031-41996-6_13

they can provide for biodiversity. Based on these two elements, the chapter identifies, in a third and final section, the gaps and overlaps between these negative impacts of, or enhanced by, EU trade agreements on biodiversity and the main goals of environmental provisions.

Keywords Environment · Biodiversity · FTA · EU · Sustainable development

1 Introduction

'People assume that we can carry on destroying biodiversity without consequence. This is not the case. It's bad news for people, economies and business'.[1] Biological diversity encompasses the diversity within species (genetic), between species (variety) and of ecosystems[2] and it is currently experiencing a crisis.[3] Despite a growing awareness of the issue, biodiversity is widely misunderstood and negative impacts from human activities, including international trade, are often underestimated. For the last decade, mentions of the environment have been growing in Free Trade Agreements (FTAs) between the European Union (EU) and partner countries. Since the development of the so-called EU 'New Generation' FTAs, new EU trade agreements contain dedicated chapters on sustainable development that are more and more detailed and may include provisions on specific areas of environmental protection such as biodiversity. Much thought has been given to their enforceability but little to their content. Hence, many questions about their potential and actual effect remain. One of them asks whether the environmental provisions could mitigate the negative influence of the FTA itself on the environment.

Focusing on biodiversity, this chapter aims to answer this question by exposing the gaps and overlaps between the impact of trade on biodiversity and the core biodiversity-related provisions of EU trade agreements' Trade and Sustainable Development (TSD) chapters. It does so, firstly, by exposing the negative impacts of trade on biodiversity and presenting the rationale behind the inclusion of biodiversity-related provisions in EU trade agreements (Sect. 2). Secondly, by presenting the main goals of the relevant environmental clause in EU FTAs (Sect. 3). Taking archetypal examples from the EU's most recent FTAs, the chapter undertakes a textual analysis of clauses relevant to the protection of biodiversity. Thirdly, the chapter identifies the gaps and overlaps between these main goals and the negative impacts of, or enhanced by, trade on biodiversity (Sect. 5). Gaps are

[1] Ogwal (2020), Speech at the Post-2020 Open-ended Working Group, UN Convention on Biodiversity Negotiations. Available at: https://enb.iisd.org/events/2nd-meeting-open-ended-working-group-post-2020-global-biodiversity-framework/summary-report.

[2] Convention on Biological Diversity (CBD) (adopted 5 June 1992, entered into force 29 December 1993) 1760 U.N.T.S. 69.

[3] IUCN monitors (2022) Gland, Suisse. Available at: https://www.iucn.org/our-work/biodiversity.

identified when an EU FTA exerts or enhances a negative effect on biodiversity (directly or through embedded biodiversity loss) but no biodiversity-related provision in the FTA aims to mitigate this effect. On the contrary, overlaps are found when such provisions may be capable of countering this negative effect of the FTA on biodiversity.

2 The Rationale Behind Addressing the Biodiversity Crisis in EU Free Trade Agreements

2.1 The Direct and Indirect Impacts of EU Trade on Biodiversity

Direct Impacts of Trade

International trade can have direct negative impacts on biodiversity mainly through trade in endangered or overexploited species, transportation, and the spreading of alien invasive species. [4] Firstly, illegal activities necessary for wildlife trafficking, such as poaching, threaten biodiversity directly. [5] In addition, trade in overexploited species is damaging despite being legal. It occurs when a species is not included by a CITES party in the relevant appendix despite scientific evidence that the species is overexploited. Trade in fish products from overfished species is a straightforward example of this.[6] Secondly, transportation linked to international trade is directly impacting biodiversity in two ways: the development of necessary infrastructures (e.g. roads and ports)[7] together with collisions during transport, [8] and the cumulated pollution (air, land, water and noise) from transport.[9] Thirdly, international trade increases the spread of alien species that often become invasive when introduced to their non-native habitat.[10] The cumulative damage of these direct impacts makes trade one of the drivers of change in nature identified by the Intergovernmental Science-Policy Platform on Biodiversity and Ecosystem Services (IPBES).[11]

Indirect Impacts of Trade

Human, environmental, or resource footprint are all terms used to define the negative impact of anthropogenic activities on nature and the environment.[12] Using different

[4] Bellora et al. (2020), pp. 11–13.

[5] IPBES (2019), p. 116.

[6] For example, EU import of overexploited fish and fish products see: Bureau (2012), pp. 171–176.

[7] IPBES (2019), p. 113.

[8] Abdulla and Linden (2008), pp. 33–41.

[9] Bellora et al. (2020), p. 11.

[10] Ibid., p. 12 and IPBES (2019), p. XVII.

[11] IPBES (2019), p. XVI.

[12] Weinzettel et al. (2013), p. 433.

indicators (e.g., extraction of raw material, water consumption or emissions of GHGs),[13] the aim of the environmental footprint is to reveal the pressure created by a country, a specific good or any human activity. This approach considers the assessment of a product's environmental impact throughout its 'life', including all the processes necessary for its production.[14] Hence, it incorporates the biodiversity loss embedded in a product.[15] Embedded, or embodied,[16] biodiversity loss means, for instance, the consequences of land-use changes from agriculture on mammals' habitat, and the diminution thereof of their population.[17] Hence, the impact on biodiversity does not come directly from the good but derives from its production.

The environmental impact due to the production of goods can be domestic when the product is consumed in the same country where it was produced. Due to the telecoupling effect of international trade, however, the impact can also occur in another country.[18] The increase in international trade in commodities leads to a shift in the environmental burden.[19] This shift creates a situation of inequality in which one country (the producing/exporting country), often a low-income country, will bear the environmental burden of the other one (consuming/importing country), often a high-income country.[20]

As Dittrich et al. put it, some countries, including the EU Member States, "enjoy the consumption of imported goods, while the exporting countries carry the environmental burden caused by the production of those goods".[21] This is confirmed by Europe's resource deficit.[22] The EU has a negative import/export balance when considering all embedded resources needed to produce its imported commodities.[23] This means that it has an important ecological footprint on the biodiversity of countries outside its territory. It is paramount for the EU to reframe biodiversity protection as a trade policy objective and aim to reduce its footprint on partner countries through its FTAs. Each good imported into the EU has its own impact on biodiversity across the value chain.

For clarity, this chapter uses two examples of commodities imported to the EU that have embedded biodiversity loss. The first example is the import of bananas (fresh or dried) which are among the most imported agricultural products in the

[13] Giljum et al. (2018), pp. 94–99.

[14] Finnveden et al. (2009), p. 1.

[15] Wiedmann and Lenzen (2018), p. 314.

[16] Scott (2020), p. 66.

[17] de Baan et al. (2015), p. 2237.

[18] IPBES (2019), p. 87 but also many scientific sources such as Yu et al. (2013), p. 1178.

[19] Ibid.

[20] Ibid.

[21] Dittrich and Bringezu (2010), p. 1838.

[22] Wood et al. (2018), p. 553. Also Tukker et al. (2016), p. 171. And Scott (2020), p. 67.

[23] Ibid.

EU.[24] The leading cause of impacts on biodiversity from banana production is its reliance on agrochemicals which deteriorate the quality of water and soil.[25] Pesticides and fungicides are used in every step of the production phases in large quantities. [26] Another source of negative environmental impact on water and soil quality is the large production of waste that is often left in open dumps.[27] In addition, despite not being limited to banana plantations, the expansion of the fruits and vegetables sector is causing a critical land conversion from natural ecosystems to agricultural ones, often leading to deforestation.[28] The second example is the import of hake. Hake is among the most consumed wild fish species in the EU. [29] In addition to overfishing, the fishing of hake can damage biodiversity in two main ways. First, the technique of bottom trawling is destroying benthic habitats,[30] notably by causing high mortality of non-targeted species which changes ecosystems' structure.[31] Second, the long lines used in bottom trawling are the cause of seabird mortality.[32]

It is the production of bananas or the fishing of hake and not their international trade *per se* that impacts biodiversity, but these impacts are embedded in the product. Indirect impacts of trade might be more challenging to define and especially the causal link between the damage and trade. However, this link has been identified by the scientific community[33] and recognised to some extent by the EU in some of the most recent impact assessments.[34]

2.2 *Putting Biodiversity Protection and Conservation in EU Free Trade Agreements*

Since the Treaty of Lisbon, the promotion of sustainable development has been included in the EU's external trade policy. [35] This promotional approach[36] is at the

---

[24]Resource Trade.Earth (2020) Chatham house, The Royal Institute of International Affairs. Available at: https://resourcetrade.earth/?year=2020&importer=euu&units=value&autozoom=1.

[25]For example, Barraza et al. estimate that the use of pesticides by Costa Rican banana plantations in 2019 represented 22% of all pesticide usage in Costa Rica. Barraza et al. (2020), p. 52.

[26]Ibid., p. 52.

[27]BKP Economic Advisors (2022), Annexes G-H, p. 54.

[28]Ibid., Annex D2, pp. 207–225.

[29]EUMOFA (2015), p. 16.

[30]Farriols et al. (2015), p. 245.

[31]Antsygina (2021), p. 311.

[32]Barnes et al. (1997), p. 227.

[33]See, for example, Chaudhary and Brooks (2019), pp. 178–187; Hong et al. (2022), p. 597; Wood et al. (2018) and Tukker et al. (2016).

[34]BKP Economic Advisors (2022), Annex D2, pp. 207–225; Bureau et al. (2012), pp. 171–176.

[35]Articles 3(5) and 21 TEU; Article 207(1) TFEU.

[36]Bronckers and Gruni (2021), p. 1.

heart of the EU's 'value-based' trade policy [37] and has been opposed to the USA's more sanction-based approach.[38] In its latest communication the European Commission states that

> The EU is strongly committed to ensuring that its trade agreements foster sustainability, so that economic growth goes together with the protection of human rights, decent work, the climate and the environment, in full adherence with the Union's values and priorities.[39]

At the bilateral level,[40] the promotion, or fostering, of sustainability is essentially realised in trade and sustainable development chapters (TSD chapters). These TSD chapters have two main purposes. A commercial purpose to ensure a level-playing for EU companies[41] by providing for consistency with international environmental and labour standards, a high level of environmental protection and labour standards as well as the prohibition to lower the level of protection.[42] TSD chapters also have a political purpose to enhance the enforcement of non-trade rules and objectives. TSD chapters are distinct from the rest of the FTA as the obligations contained within are considered to be non-trade policy objectives.[43] As such, in case of conflicts regarding the provisions in the TSD chapters, a special dispute settlement procedure is established to resolve the matter.[44] As detailed below, the promotion of sustainability by the EU principally pushes the international environmental agenda and only a few provisions are evoking any link to trade.

The protection of biodiversity is amongst the prominent environmental issues on the international scene.[45] Biodiversity is also one of the environmental topics included by the EU in the TSD chapters of its most recent free trade agreements. As described further below, the EU and its partners have incorporated biodiversity protection and conservation, either broadly or specific to certain ecosystems, in their FTAs. They have done so chiefly by referring to two multilateral agreements: the CBD and the CITES. Notwithstanding the various level of details and of protection afforded in those provisions they mostly follow the political purpose of enhancing the enforcement of multilateral environmental agreements. The direct and indirect impacts of trade on biodiversity described above prompt, however, to question

---

[37] Commission Communication (2015), p. 15.

[38] Bronckers and Gruni (2021).

[39] Commission Communication (2022), p. 1.

[40] As opposed to the multilateral level the bilateral level includes trade agreements between the EU and a limited number of partners.

[41] Commission Communication (2015), p. 10.

[42] For a discussion of these three obligations in EU TSD chapters see Marín Durán (2020).

[43] Borchert et al. (2021), p. 1.

[44] Bartels (2013), p. 297.

[45] Several multilateral environmental agreements focus on the protection and conversation of biodiversity. Some are generalists, such as the Convention on Biological Diversity (CBD) while others focus only of certain species or ecosystem, for example the Convention on the Conservation of Migratory Species of Wilf Animals (CMS) or the Convention on Wetlands of International Importance Especially as Waterfowl Habitat (Ramsar Convention).

whether this boost of the parties' international commitments is enough. Products imported in the EU generate direct and indirect impacts on biodiversity outside of its borders. Hence, this biodiversity loss is generated by EU's international trade and consumption. Because this loss is linked to trade it could justify the introduction of further biodiversity provisions aiming more precisely at mitigating the impact of trade. The following section describes in detail the core provisions related to biodiversity and assess whether they have the potential to alleviate trade-related biodiversity loss.

3 The Main Goals of Biodiversity-Related Clauses in EU FTAs' TSD Chapters

Since the conclusion of the EU-South Korea Free Trade Agreement (FTA) in 2011,[46] the EU has been shaping its model of TSD chapter. Despite evolutions and differences amongst the EU FTAs signed since then there are several archetypal clauses which can be connected, with varying proximity, to biodiversity. This section teases out the core obligations found in three types of clauses that are the most closely related to biodiversity issues: the Biological Diversity clauses (1), the Trade in Forest Products (2) and the Trade in Fish Products clauses (3). Nine of the eighteen FTAs the EU signed since 2011 contain a Biological Diversity clause, [47]

---

[46] Free trade Agreement between the European Union and its Member States, of the one part, and the Republic of Korea, of the other part [2011] OJ L 127, 14.5.2011, pp. 1–1426.

[47] Trade Agreement between the European Union and its Member States, of the one part, and Colombia and Peru, of the other part (EU-CPE FTA) [2012] OJ L 354, 21.12.2012, pp. 3–2607; Association Agreement between the European Union and the European Atomic Energy Community and their Member States, of the one part, and Georgia, of the other part (EU-Georgia FTA) [2014] OJ L 261 30.8.2014, p. 4; Association Agreement between the European Union and the European Atomic Energy Community and their Member States, of the one part, and the Republic of Moldova, of the other part (EU-Moldova FTA) [2014] OJ L 260 30.8.2014, p. 4; Comprehensive and enhanced Partnership Agreement between the European Union and the European Atomic Energy Community and their Member States, of the one part, and the Republic of Armenia, of the other part (EU-Armenia FTA) [2017] OJ L 23, 26.1.2018, pp. 4–466; Economic Partnership Agreement between the European Union and Japan (EU-Japan FTA) [2018] OJ L 330, 27.12.2018, pp. 3–899; EU-Mexico trade agreement—agreement in principle (EU-Mexico FTA) [2018] Provisional text available at: https://policy.trade.ec.europa.eu/eu-trade-relationships-country-and-region/countries-and-regions/mexico/eu-mexico-agreement_en. EU-MERCOSUR trade agreement—agreement in principle (EU-MERCOSUR FTA) [2019] Provisional text available at: https://policy.trade.ec.europa.eu/eu-trade-relationships-country-and-region/countries-and-regions/mercosur/eu-mercosur-agreement/text-agreement_en. Free Trade Agreement between the European Union and the Socialist Republic of Viet Nam (EU-Viet Nam) [2019] OJ L 186, 12.6.2020, pp. 3–1400; EU-Chile Advanced Framework Agreement—agreement in principle (EU-Chile FTA) [2022] Provisional text available at: https://policy.trade.ec.europa.eu/eu-trade-relationships-country-and-region/countries-and-regions/chile/eu-chile-agreement/text-agreement_en.

while almost all FTAs (13/18) since then have enshrined the two ecosystem-specific clauses.[48] Clauses on Trade in Forest Products and Trade in Fish Products have a limited scope as they lay down goals of conservation and sustainable use of specific biological resources but incorporate obligations that are often stronger upon the parties than in biodiversity clause. They are, in addition, paramount to the present analysis considering they are the main doorway for biodiversity protection in the no less than the thirteen agreements without a biodiversity clause.

3.1 Biological Diversity Clauses

The first occurrence of a Biological Diversity, or Biodiversity, clause is found in the EU-Colombia, Ecuador, and Peru (EU-CPE) FTAs. It was not followed by a constant inclusion in EU trade agreements. The EU FTAs that include a Biodiversity clause have been signed with dissimilar countries, both geographically and economically. Despite this heterogeneity of partners, there are some core features in the biodiversity clauses that can be found in each occurrence.[49] As shown in Table 1, most of these features relate to Multilateral Environmental Agreements (MEAs). The parties restate their commitment to protect biodiversity 'in accordance'[50] with the CBD[51] and other biodiversity-relevant MEAs. They also 'commit to'[52] cooperating in other fora to promote the 'conservation and sustainable use of biological diversity'.[53] Such acknowledgement of obligations under biodiversity-relevant MEAs in EU FTAs is seen by optimistic authors as a way to mutate international environmental rules into a stronger and more enforceable law.[54] This idea is mainly based on the fact that respect for MEAs' obligations, or provisions restating them, could now be enforced under the TSD chapter's dispute settlement mechanism. All EU FTAs with a TSD chapter exclude conflicts regarding the TSD provisions from the general

---

[48] Ibid. and Agreement establishing an Association between the European Union and its Member States, on the one hand, and Central America on the other (EU-Central America FTA) [2012] OJ L 346, 15.12.2012, pp. 3–2621; Association Agreement between the European Union and its Member States, of the one part, and Ukraine, of the other part (EU-Ukraine FTA) [2014] OJ L 161, 29.5.2014, pp. 3–2137; Comprehensive Economic and Trade Agreement (CETA) between Canada, of the one part, and the European Union and its Member States, of the other part (CETA) [2017] OJ L 11, 14.1.2017, pp. 23–1079; Free Trade Agreement between the European Union and the Republic of Singapore (EU-Singapore FTA) [2019] OJ L 294, 14.11.2019, pp. 3–755.

[49] The present paper focuses only on common elements and will not discuss the differences.

[50] For example, in EU-Moldova FTA, article 368.1.

[51] CBD (1993).

[52] For example, in EU-Georgia FTA, article 232.2(d).

[53] Ibid.

[54] See for example: Stockhaus (2017), pp. 208–222; Jinnah and Morgera (2013) pp. 324–339.

Table 1 Core provisions found in Biological Diversity Clauses of EU FTAs

Provision	Language	EU partner
Importance of conversation and sustainable use of biodiversity	Acknowledgement	All
Conserve and sustainably use biodiversity in accordance with MEAs	Acknowledgement	All
Promote the inclusion of species in CITES' appendices	Hortatory	Georgia, Moldova, Vietnam, Mexico, MERCOSUR, Armenia, Chile
Adopt and implement effective measures to reduce illegal trade in wildlife	Mandatory	Japan, Vietnam, Mexico, MERCOSUR, Armenia, Chile
Encourage trade in natural resource-based products obtained through a sustainable use of biodiversity	Hortatory	Georgia, Moldova, Japan, Vietnam, Mexico, MERCOSUR, Chile
Promote access to genetic resources and the fair and equitable sharing of benefits arising from their utilisation	Hortatory	CPE, Japan, Vietnam, Mexico, MERCOSUR, Armenia, Chile
Exchange information and cooperate at bilateral, (regional) and multilateral levels on matters of relevance to the biodiversity clause	Hortatory	All (except CPE)

FTA dispute settlement mechanism and include instead a three-steps resolution process which include, as a last resort, recommendations from a Group of Experts.[55]

Two provisions reiterate already existing obligations from the CBD and the Convention on International Trade in Endangered Species of Wild Fauna and Flora (CITES).[56] For the CBD, the obligation echoes its article 15 only. The provision is formulated using hortatory language[57] to exhort the parties to 'promote'[58] access to genetic resources and the fair and equitable sharing of benefits arising from their utilisation. This provision and its implementation remain rather vague. Reiteration of the existing obligation found in the CITES is more precise. The parties are urged to 'promote the listing of species'[59] under the CITES appendices. The CITES aims at controlling the international trade of selected species notably by

[55]The FTA between the EU and the CARIFORUM is the only EU bilateral trade agreement that include biodiversity provisions falling under the jurisdiction of the general FTA dispute mechanism and thus could be sanctioned with trade remedies. Environmental provisions of this FTA are not however in a TSD chapter and it this hence outside of the scope of this chapter. See Economic Partnership Agreement between the CARIFORUM States, of the one part, and the European Community and its Member States, of the other part [2008] OJ L 289, 30.10.2008, pp. 3–1955.

[56]Convention on International Trade in Endangered Species of Wild Fauna and Flora (adopted Washington, DC, 3 March 1973, entered into force 1st July 1975).

[57]Rajamani (2016), pp. 337–358.

[58]For example, in EU-MERCOSUR FTA, article 7.2(d) of the TSD chapter.

[59]For example, in EU-Moldova FTA, article 368.2(c).

pressing its parties to designate species in different appendices, namely lists, depending on the level of protection they require.[60] Precise or not both provisions do nothing more than encouraging the FTAs' parties to act accordingly to their international obligations.

Another core provision is the obligation to 'adopt and implement appropriate effective measures [...] leading to a reduction of illegal trade in wildlife'.[61] This provision is often linked to the CITES but is formulated in a stronger language than other provisions referring to international environmental agreements. The trade agreements that include this obligation provide that 'each party shall' followed by several provisions on biodiversity issues that may change depending on the FTA. All these provisions use hortatory words such as 'encourage' or 'promote'[62] while the obligation to take and implement measures against illegal trade in wildlife is formulated with a mandatory language.[63] This type of language makes the obligation stand out in the Biodiversity clauses. Moreover, the obligation goes beyond the implementation of the CITES, and may also affect 'other endangered species'[64] as mentioned in the EU-Japan FTA. In other FTAs, such as the EU-Mexico agreement in principle, the CITES is not even mentioned in the provision.[65] This thus creates a new, independent, obligation on the parties to combat illegal trade in wildlife even when species are not listed under the CITES.

Among the core obligations found in EU FTAs' Biological Diversity clauses, there is another provision that is not connected to any MEAs. The parties 'commit to'[66] the promotion of the 'trade in natural resource-based products obtained through a sustainable use of biological resources and contributing to the conservation of biodiversity'.[67] The EU FTAs themselves do not favour trade in products based on their process and production methods by, for example, reducing tariffs further for goods that were produced through sustainable use of biodiversity or contributed to its conservation.[68] Instead, the provision found in the Biodiversity clauses exhorts parties to bolster trade in such products without specifying how this is to be achieved.[69] Such a vague obligation does not warrant much. It is unfortunate that

[60] CITES (2015) How CITES work. Available at: https://cites.org/eng/disc/how.php.

[61] EU-Viet Nam FTA, article 13.7.3(d).

[62] Rajamani (2016).

[63] Ibid.

[64] EU-Japan FTA, article 16.6.2(b).

[65] EU-Mexico FTA article 6.3(a) of the TSD chapter provides that 'each party shall [...] implement effective measures to combat wildlife trade, including through cooperative activities with third countries, as appropriate.'

[66] For example, EU-Moldova FTA, article 368.2.

[67] Ibid., article 368.2(a).

[68] This has been done in the EFTA-Indonesian trade agreement, see Bürgi Bonanomi and Tribaldos (2022), pp. 359–385.

[69] Only the EU-Japan FTA lays out an example of how to encourage the use and not the trade of such products. Its article 16.6.2(a) provides that such encouragement can be done through 'labelling schemes.'

a trade agreement would not deal itself with such a trade matter with provisions such as tariffs or quotas.

3.2 *Trade in Forest Products Clauses*

Since the EU-Colombia-Peru-Ecuador trade agreement, all EU FTAs that have a TSD chapter have enshrined a clause on Trade in Forest Products. The length and content of these Trade in Forest Products clauses differ but five core provisions can be extracted (see Table 2).

Table 2 Core provisions found in Trade in Forest Products clauses of EU FTAs

Provision	Language	EU partner
Recognition of importance of and cooperation on the conservation of forests	Acknowledgement/ hortatory	All
Improve forest law and governance	Hortatory	CPE, Central America, Georgia, Moldova, Ukraine, Armenia, Singapore, Mexico, Vietnam, MERCOSUR
Combat illegal logging and trade in illegal forest products	Mandatory	All (except Central America)
Effective implementation of CITES	Hortatory	CPE, CA, Georgia, Moldova, CETA, Armenia, Singapore
Promote and exchange information on trade in timber and timber products from sustainably managed forests	Hortatory	All (except Central America)

Using the language of acknowledgement, the EU FTAs' parties recognise the importance of the conservation and sustainable management of forests which are the two key concepts throughout the Trade in Forest Products clauses. They are linked to all the other core provisions. In addition, the parties are exhorted to cooperate 'at the regional and global level with the aim of promoting the conservation of forest cover'.[70] There is no agreement at the international level focusing on forests only, the conditions of this cooperation are thus not explicit. Moreover, the parties 'shall' 'exchange information to improve'[71] or 'promote'[72] forest laws and governance. While this obligation is sometimes limited to 'global' governance this is not always the case. In the absence of any specific geographical scope, the parties are arguably encouraged to discuss how to improve national forest law and governance as well.

[70] For example, EU-Armenia FTA, article 278.2(f).

[71] For example, EU-Vietnam FTA, article 13.8.2(d).

[72] For example, EU-Singapore FTA, article 12.7(b).

Two other core provisions of the Trade in Forest Products clauses are connected to the legality of timber. Firstly, in provisions similar to those found in the Biodiversity clause, the parties are encouraged to 'promote the effective use of'[73] CITES and promote the 'listing of timber species'.[74] This ensures that the trade of timber species that are endangered is illegal. Secondly, the parties commit to 'adopting measures to [...] combat illegal logging and related trade'.[75] This mandatory obligation is sometimes followed by an encouragement to exchange information on policies to exclude illegal timber from trade flows.[76]

Lastly, the promotion of trade in 'timber and timber products derived from sustainably managed forests'[77] is enshrined in a similar fashion as natural resource-based products in Biodiversity clauses. Likewise, there is no further tariff reduction for timber and products coming from sustainably managed forests and the circumstances of this promotion are not described.

3.3 *Trade in Fish Products Clauses*

All EU FTAs that have a TSD chapter since the EU-CPE trade agreement (2012) have enshrined a clause on the Trade in Fish Products. The length and content of these Trade in Fish Products clauses differ but four (4) core provisions can be extracted (see Table 3).

Table 3 Core provisions found in Trade in Fish Products clauses of EU FTAs

Provision	Language	EU partner
Recognition of the importance of conserving and sustainably managing marine resources	Acknowledgement	All
Cooperate in context of RFMOs and promote good governance	Hortatory	CPE, Georgia, Moldova, Ukraine, CETA, Japan, Mexico, Vietnam, MERCOSUR, Chile
Combat IUU fishing and exclude its products from trade	Hortatory/ mandatory	All
Take effective measure to monitor and control fishing activities	Mandatory	All

[73] For example, EU-Singapore, article 12.7(d).

[74] For example, EU-Georgia, article 233.2(e).

[75] For example, EU-Georgia FTA, article 233.2(c).

[76] For example, EU-Armenia FTA, article 278.2(d).

[77] For example, EU-Mexico FTA, article 7.2(a) of the TSD chapter.

The Trade in Fish Products clauses all include recognition by the parties of the 'importance of ensuring the conservation and sustainable management of living marine resources'[78] or 'the conservation and sustainable management of fish stock'.[79] As for the Trade in Forest Products clauses, the Trade in Fish Products clauses are more centred on sustainable management than conservation. While this was done by introducing an obligation to combat illegal trade and promoting products from sustainable forests in the Trade in Forest Products clauses, the Trade in Fish Products clauses only focus on controlling fishing activities.

The conditions under which the fishing activities would be considered sustainable are not explicit in the FTAs texts but are not left entirely to the parties' domestic laws either. In almost all EU FTAs with a TSD chapter,[80] the parties commit to cooperate 'as widely as possible'[81] in the context of Regional Fisheries Management Organisations (RFMOs). RFMOs play a key role in the regulation of fishing activities on the high seas[82] by, for example, setting catch limits.[83] The parties are thus strongly encouraged to cooperate at the regional level to determine what sustainable fishery entails. In some EU FTAs, the parties also commit to ensuring 'full compliance' with the measures adopted by RFMOs.[84]

RFMOs are also central to addressing illegal, unreported, and unregulated (IUU) fishing activities. The obligation upon the EU FTAs' parties to take and 'implement policies and measures'[85] to exclude from trade products originating from IUU fishing is another core obligation of the Trade in Fish Products clauses. There are two main criteria to determine if a product comes from an IUU fishing activity.[86] The first relates to domestic and international law. It can be illegal if the fishing activity is contrary to the law, or unreported if the activity did not respect legal reporting duties. [87] The second is linked to the RFMOs directly. Fishing activities are considered unregulated if they do not follow the rules set out in the relevant RFMO.[88] RFMOs are science-based[89] and their mandate is to reach sustainability.[90] Thus, excluding

---

78 For example, EU-Vietnam FTA, article 13.9.1.

79 For example, EU-Singapore FTA, article 12.8.

80 See Table 3.

81 For example, EU-Moldova FTA, article 370 (c).

82 European Commission (2021), Regional fisheries management organisations (RFMOs). Available at: https://ec.europa.eu/oceans-and-fisheries/fisheries/international-agreements/regional-fisheries-management-organisations-rfmos_en.

83 Ibid.

84 For example, EU-Moldova FTA, article 370 (c).

85 For example, EU-Armenia FTA, article 279 (e).

86 Rosello (2020), pp. 33–47.

87 FAO (2001) International Plan of Action to Prevent, Deter and Eliminate Illegal, Unreported and Unregulated Fishing, para. 3, pp. 2–3. Available at: https://www.wto.org/english/tratop_e/rulesneg_e/fish_e/2001_ipoa_iuu.pdf.

88 Rosello (2020), p. 34.

89 European Commission (2021).

90 Haas et al. (2021), p. 133.

products from IUU fishing activities from trade goes beyond simply promoting trade in sustainably fished products. In fact, the parties are under the obligation to only authorize the export of fish products that have been caught following domestic, regional, and international rules. This differs from the provisions in the Trade in Forest Products clauses which only banned illegal timber and aimed, somehow loosely, at favouring trade in products from sustainably managed forests.

The last core provision of the Trade in Fish Product clauses is a general obligation to monitor and control fishing activities, but it can also be linked to RFMOs rules in some cases.[91] Some EU FTAs do not give details on how this monitoring and controlling should take place while others provide examples. These examples mostly concern vessel monitoring.[92] This last core provision is linked to the obligation to exclude IUU fish products from trade. Only through such monitoring and control can the parties make sure that they do not allow such products to enter the market.

4 The Gaps and Overlaps in the Response to Direct and Indirect Impacts of Trade in EU Free Trade Agreements' Trade and Sustainable Development Chapters

In face of the different negative impacts of trade on biodiversity, what are the responses provided in the EU FTAs TSD chapters core provision described above? Table 4 summarises the direct and indirect impacts of the trade of the two examples, banana and hake, on biodiversity in its left column.[93] In the right column, core provisions from the three clauses described above which could answer, or mitigate, these impacts are proposed. Only clear and direct answers to biodiversity issues are considered here. Core provisions that are acknowledgements of broad commitment such as the recognition of the importance of conservation and sustainable use of biodiversity are regarded as too general to be responses to trade impacts. Gaps are identified between an EU FTA's negative effect on biodiversity (direct or indirect, produced or enhanced) but no biodiversity-related provision in the FTA aims to mitigate this effect. These gaps are represented by the ∅ sign in the right column of Table 4. Inversely, overlaps are identified when biodiversity-related provisions can theoretically lessen this negative effect of the FTA on biodiversity.

---

[91] For example, EU-Ukraine FTA, article 295(b).

[92] For example, EU-Vietnam FTA, article 13.9.2(b) or CETA, article 24.11.2(a).

[93] For the indirect impacts only the impacts from the example provided are used.

Table 4 Direct and indirect impacts of trade on biodiversity and corresponding core provisions from Biological Diversity, Trade in Forest Products, and Trade in Fish products clauses

Negative impact on biodiversity	Related core provision in selected clauses
Direct impacts	
Trade in endangered or overexploited species	• Biological Diversity clauses – Promote the inclusion of species in CITES' appendices – Adopt and implement effective measures to reduce illegal trade in wildlife • Trade in Forest Products clause – Combat illegal logging and trade in illegal forest products – Effective implementation of CITES • Trade in Fish Products clause – Combat IUU fishing and exclude its products from trade – Take effective measure to monitor and control fishing activities
Transportation	• Biological Diversity clauses ∅ • Trade in Forest Products clause ∅ • Trade in Fish Products clause – Take effective measures to monitor and control fishing activities
Alien invasive species	• Biological Diversity clauses ∅ • Trade in Forest Products clause ∅ • Trade in Fish Products clause ∅
Indirect impacts (from banana production and hake fishing)	
Pollution of soil	• Biological Diversity clauses ∅ • Trade in Forest Products clause ∅ • Trade in Fish Products clause ∅
Pollution of water	• Biological Diversity clauses ∅ • Trade in Forest Products clause ∅ • Trade in Fish Products clause ∅
Land-use changes/deforestation	• Biological Diversity clauses ∅ • Trade in Forest Products clause – Improve forest law and governance • Trade in Fish Products clause ∅
Destruction/modification of habitats	• Biological Diversity clauses ∅ • Trade in Forest Products clause ∅

(continued)

Table 4 (continued)

Negative impact on biodiversity	Related core provision in selected clauses
	• Trade in Fish Products clause – Cooperate in context of RFMOs and promote good governance – Take effective measure to monitor and control fishing activities
Bycatch mortality	• Biological Diversity clauses ∅ • Trade in Forest Products clause ∅ • Trade in Fish Products clause – Cooperate in context of RFMOs and promote good governance – Take effective measure to monitor and control fishing activities

Table 4 shows clearly that there are more gaps than overlaps between the negative impact of trade and the core provisions of the Biological Diversity, the Trade in Forest Products, and the Trade in Fish Products provisions. The direct impact of trade in endangered or overexploited species is the issue that has the highest number of provisions connected to it. In all three clauses analysed there are provisions that exhort the parties to combat illegal trade and to promote the implementation of CITES. If the trade in endangered or overexploited species is causing, without any doubt, considerable damage to biodiversity, it remains nevertheless an issue related to global illegal trade. This means that, overall, EU FTAs are not adding any new obligations for the parties and are not mitigating impacts caused or enhanced by the FTAs themselves.[94]

Three other provisions can be identified as responding to a trade-related biodiversity issue. First, the obligation to take effective measures to monitor and control fishing activities from the Trade in Fish Products clauses can arguably help reduce impacts from transportation by, for example, checking that the vessels are following rules regarding emissions levels. This provision could also answer some of the indirect impacts of the trade in hake. Control and monitoring of vessel nets and the content of their catch could reduce bycatch for example. The second and third provisions deal with good governance. The obligation to improve forest law and governance may alleviate deforestation from land-use change by, for example, creating protected areas or limiting zones that can be deforested for agricultural uses. In the same way, the obligation to cooperate in the context of RFMOs and promote good governance could mitigate the impact of fishing on ecosystems by, for instance, taking technical measures on vessels' nets or setting catch limits on overfished species.

[94]The only exception to this would be that arguably the interdiction to put fish products from IUU fishing activities goes beyond the question of legality.

Answers to trade-related impacts in EU FTAs have hence been stealth. For most of the direct and indirect impacts of trade, there is no real answer in the core biodiversity-related provisions of the EU FTAs. This is due to the broadness of the provisions enshrined. The core biodiversity-related provisions, as identified, largely reiterate international obligations and/or promote cooperation.

5 Conclusion

The core provisions found in biodiversity-related clauses among the Trade and Sustainable Chapters of recent EU trade agreements strongly emphasize already existing international obligations. By referring to or repeating provisions found in multilateral environmental agreements the TSD chapters do not do much more than create a tactical linkage[95] between the trade and biodiversity regimes. This might foster political gain and answer some of the dissident voices against free trade agreements, but it will unlikely mitigate the negative impacts trade can have on biodiversity. The big gaps and little overlaps between the most salient direct and indirect impacts of trade and the relevant core biodiversity provisions enshrined in EU FTAs demonstrate that mitigation is indeed not the goal of the TSD chapters.

However, there is reason to believe that it should be their goal. Biodiversity, as for the rest of the environmental issues in the TSD provisions, is considered a non-trade policy objective. Non-trade policy objectives seem to be add-ons to an otherwise pure trade agreement. Yet, there are biodiversity impacts that are caused or enhanced by trade, and this could justify that relevant biodiversity loss be approached as a trade issue. How else should one endeavour to prevent damage if not by looking at its cause? Answers to this trade issue should hence be dealt with by trade law. One solution would be to have provisions tailor-made for the mitigation of the negative impacts of trade, enhanced by these FTAs, on biodiversity. The European Commission's 15-Point Action Plan puts forward a new approach for the TSD chapters that will be 'more tailored and targeted' to countries' specific situations.[96] The objective of this country-specific approach would be to strengthen the implementation of specific field where needed. This is paramount for biodiversity loss. Indirect impacts from trade are diversified depending on the types of products imported by the EU. Beyond the examples set in this piece, bananas and hake, other commodities such as ores or manufactured products can have dire effect on ecosystems. Ecosystem-specific or activity-specific provisions have however been limited to forest (or forestry) and marine (or fishing) thus far. Hopefully, this new tailor-made approach by the European Commission can foster new types of biodiversity-related clause that aim at mitigating the direct and indirect impacts of trade.

---

[95] Laurens and Morin (2019), p. 533.

[96] Commission Communication (2015), p. 6.

References

Abdulla A, Linden O (eds) (2008) Maritime traffic effects on biodiversity in the Mediterranean Sea: review of impacts, priority areas and mitigation measures. IUCN Centre for Mediterranean Cooperation, Malaga, pp 33–41

Antsygina E (2021) Prohibition of bottom trawling on extended continental shelves: creeping jurisdiction or enforcement of sovereign rights? Int J Mar Coastal Law 36:311

Barnes KN, Ryan PG, Boix-Hinzen C (1997) The impact of the Hake Merluccius spp. longline fishery off South Africa on Procellariiform Seabirds. Biol Conserv 82:227

Barraza D, Jansen K, Wesseling C, van Wendel de Joode B (2020) Pesticide risk perceptions among bystanders of aerial spraying on bananas in Costa Rica. Environ Res 189:109877

Bartels L (2013) Human rights and sustainable development obligations in EU free trade agreements. Leg Issues Econ Integr 40:297

Bellora C, Bureau JC, Bayramoglu B, Gozlan E, Jean S (2020) Trade and biodiversity. European Parliament's Committee on International Trade (INTA) 2020. EP/EXPO/INTA/FWC/2019-01/Lot5/1/C/03

BKP Economic Advisors (2022) Ex-post evaluation of the implementation of part IV of the Association Agreement (Trade Pillar) between the EU and its Member States and Central America – Draft Interim Report. Available at: https://policy.trade.ec.europa.eu/analysis-and-assessment/ex-post-evaluations_en

Borchert I, Conconi P, Di Ubaldo M, Herghelegiu C (2021) The pursuit of non-trade policy objectives in EU trade policy. World Trade Rev 20:623

Bronckers M, Gruni G (2021) Retooling the sustainability standards in EU free trade agreements. J Int Econ Law 24:25

Bureau JC, Jean S, Albagly M, Foster WE, Fuentes Espinosa C, Furche C, Gohin A, Piña J, Ramos P, Tromben C, Valdés A (2012) Evaluation of the economic impact of the trade pillar of the EU-Chile association agreement. Final report. For the European Commission, Directorate General for Trade, pp 171–176

Bürgi Bonanomi E, Tribaldos T (2022) PPM-based trade measures to promote sustainable farming systems? What the EU/EFTA-Mercosur agreements can learn from the EFTA-Indonesian Agreement. In: Bungenberg M et al (eds) European yearbook of international economic law 2020, vol 2022. Springer, Cham, pp 359–385

Chaudhary A, Brooks TM (2019) National consumption and global trade impacts on biodiversity. World Dev 121:178–187

Commission Communication (2015) Communication from the Commission to the European Parliament, the Council, the European Economic and Social Committee and the Committee of the Regions. Trade for all towards a more responsible trade and investment policy. COM(2015) 497 final, 14/10/2015

Commission Communication (2022) Communication from the Commission to the European Parliament, the Council, the European Economic and Social Committee and the Committee of the Regions. The power of trade partnerships: together for green and just economic growth. COM(2022) 409 final 22/06/2022

de Baan L, Curran M, Rondinini C, Visconti P, Hellweg S, Koellner T (2015) High-resolution assessment of land use impacts on biodiversity in life cycle assessment using species habitat suitability models. Environ Sci Technol 49:2237

Dittrich M, Bringezu S (2010) The physical dimension of international trade. Ecol Econ 69:1838

EUMOFA (2015) The EU fish market. Available at: https://www.eumofa.eu/home.

Farriols MT, Ordines F, Hidalgo M, Guijarro B, Massutí E (2015) N90 index: a new approach to biodiversity based on similarity and sensitive to direct and indirect fishing impact. Ecol Indic 52:245

Finnveden G, Hauschild MZ, Ekvall T, Guinée J, Heijungs R, Hellweg S, Koehler A, Pennington D, Suh S (2009) Recent developments in life cycle assessment. J Environ Manag 91:1

Giljum S, Bruckner M, Lutter S (2018) Resource footprints. In: Bleischwitz R et al (eds) Routledge handbook of the resource nexus. Routledge, Oxford, pp 93–104
Haas B, Haward M, McGee J, Flemming A (2021) Explicit targets and cooperation: regional fisheries management organizations and the sustainable development goals. Int Environ Agreements Polit Law Econ 21:133
Hong C, Zhao H, Qin Y, Burney JA, Pongratz J, Hartung K, Liu Y, Moore FC, Jackson RB, Zhang Q, Davis SJ (2022) Land-use emissions embodied in international trade. Science 376:597
IPBES (2019) In: Brondizio ES, Settele J, Díaz S, Ngo HT (eds) Global assessment report on biodiversity and ecosystem services of the Intergovernmental Science-Policy Platform on Biodiversity and Ecosystem Services. IPBES Secretariat, Bonn
Jinnah S, Morgera E (2013) Environmental provisions in American and EU free trade agreements: a preliminary comparison and research agenda - environmental provisions in FTAs. Rev Eur Comp Int Environ Law 22(3):324–339
Laurens N, Morin JF (2019) Negotiating environmental protection in trade agreements: a regime shift or a tactical linkage? Int Environ Agreements Polit Law Econ 19:533
Marín Durán G (2020) Sustainable development chapters in EU free trade agreements: emerging compliance issues. Common Mark Law Rev 57:1031
Rajamani L (2016) The 2015 Paris Agreement: interplay between hard, soft and non-obligations. J Environ Law 28:337–358
Rosello M (2020) Illegal, unreported and unregulated (IUU) fishing as a maritime security concern. In: Otto L (ed) Global challenges in maritime security: an introduction. Springer, Cham, pp 33–47
Scott J (2020) Reducing the European Union's environmental footprint through 'territorial extension'. In: Mauerhofer V, Rupo D, Tarquinio L (eds) Sustainability and law: general and specific aspects. Springer, Cham, pp 65–85
Stockhaus H (2017) The EU-Vietnam free trade agreement – a successful attempt to protect Vietnam's environment while pushing for economic integration? J Eur Environ Plann Law 14(2):208–222
Tukker A, Bulavskaya T, Giljum S, de Koning A, Lutter S, Simas M, Stadler K, Wood R (2016) Environmental and resource footprints in a global context: Europe's structural deficit in resource endowments. Glob Environ Change 40:171
Weinzettel J, Hertwich EG, Peters GP, Steen-Olsen K, Galli A (2013) Affluence drives the global displacement of land use. Glob Environ Change 23:433
Wiedmann T, Lenzen M (2018) Environmental and social footprints of international trade. Nat Geosci 11:314
Wood R, Stadler K, Simas M, Bulavskaya T, Giljum S, Lutter S, Tukker A (2018) Growth in environmental footprints and environmental impacts embodied in trade: resource efficiency indicators from EXIOBASE3. J Ind Ecol 22:553
Yu Y, Feng K, Hubacek K (2013) Tele-connecting local consumption to global land use. Glob Environ Change 23:1178

Justine Muller is a PhD researcher at the European University Institute in Florence, Italy. Her work focuses on the intersections between biodiversity science, biodiversity law, and international trade law. Her thesis concentrates on the European Union's Free Trade Agreements, particularly those signed with South and Central American countries. She holds Master degrees in International Business Law and in Biodiversity, Environment and landscape (Geography) from Université Paris 1 Panthéon-Sorbonne, France, as well as an LLM in International Law and Sustainable Development from the University of Strathclyde, Scotland.

Multilateral and Bilateral Trade Agreements at the Service of 'Common Interest'

Inebu Agbo-Ejeh

Contents

Abstract Common interest or community interest is a term that is frequently used in contemporary international law. Undoubtedly, there is a shift from the traditional international law concept of co-existence to cooperation. Due to a shared interest in other areas of inter-state relations and concerns, like eradication of poverty, and development, common interest has become a central focus. As a result, the international trading regime, which was integrated into the World Trade Organization, has gone beyond reciprocity to addressing issues of development in less developed countries. It is believed that common interest is addressed by two principles in the World Trade Organization—reciprocity and special and differential treatment. Common interest is also addressed in bilateral agreements, for example, the Economic Partnership Agreement between the EU and countries in Africa. It is maintained that reciprocity correlates with a common interest in the context of ensuring mutual benefits to all WTO Members and at the same time assisting less developed countries that are also members of the WTO. This work underscores the importance of special

I. Agbo-Ejeh (✉)
Baze University, Faculty of Law, Abuja, Nigeria
e-mail: Christiana.Agbo@bazeuniversity.edu.ng

M. de Amstalden et al. (eds.), *International Economic Law*, Special Issue,
https://doi.org/10.1007/978-3-031-41996-6_14

and differential treatment, notwithstanding its controversial origin and hortatory provisions.

1 Introduction

'Common interest' is usually used interchangeably with 'community interest', collective interest, common concerns or common values.[1] These terms are rarely defined, and if they are conceptualised, they carry varied meanings.[2] According to Bruno Simma, community interest is: '. . .a consensus according to which respect for certain fundamental values is not to be left to the free disposition of States individually or *inter se*, but it is recognised and sanctioned by international law as a matter of concern to all states'.[3] Peter-Tobias Stoll viewed common interest in the context of World Trade Organisation (WTO) relations among countries. According to him, the WTO is an international organisation that promotes trade liberalisation and cooperation among its members.[4] Its aim is to help governments create more open and predictable trading systems, which it believes can contribute to economic growth and development.[5] To achieve this goal, the WTO seeks to establish common rules and standards for international trade and to resolve disputes between its members.[6] It does this through negotiations and by providing a forum for governments to discuss trade-related issues and find mutually beneficial solutions.[7] To Stoll, the WTO, on the face of it, represents the pursuit of personal advantage, in other words, the WTO does not seems take into account other matters not related to reciprocal trade.[8] However, some aspects of global economic law are not far removed from serving the common interest of all or certain groups.[9] In other words, international economic law is not all about reciprocity *stricto sensu* because, notwithstanding the nature of its dispute settlement, its roots can be traced to Article 55 of the United Nations Charter,[10] later discussed in this chapter.

The WTO aims to promote trade and cooperation in order to help create a more prosperous and stable world economy in which all members can benefit from

[1]Kritsiotis (2002), pp. 961–992.

[2]Villalpando (2010), p. 385.

[3]Rao (2011), pp. 334–335.

[4]Stoll (2011), p. 174.

[5]Stoll (2011), p. 179.

[6]Stoll (2011), p. 179.

[7]Stoll (2011), pp. 173–178. Cottier and Ahmad (2021), pp. 195, 446; Van den Bossche and Zdouc (2017), p. 3.

[8]Stoll (2011), p. 173.

[9]Stoll (2011), p. 173.

[10]Article 55 Charter of the United Nations and Statutes of the International Court of Justice (San Francesco 1945), https://treaties.un.org/doc/publication/ctc/uncharter.pdf.

economic growth.[11] This was reflected in the EU-Africa partnership joint vision 2030[12] and past agreements.[13] It was declared in the joint vision that the EU-Africa partnership is aimed at promoting 'our common priorities, shared values, international law, and preserving together our interests and common public goods'.[14] Thus, the proponents of the renewed EU-Africa partnership believe there is much that holds the two continents together, hence, the promotion of common public goods.[15] The EU-Africa relationship is metamorphosed into a two-level common interest as identified by Stoll—reciprocity and special treatment that can be extended to the less powerful countries in the trade arrangement.[16]

Therefore, the expression 'common interest' is widespread in contemporary discourse.[17] Both multilateral and bilateral agreements point to common interest and international law as guiding principles.[18] As such, it has been argued that reciprocity correlates with a common interest in the world economic order in the context of ensuring mutual benefits and assisting less developed countries.[19] However, Stoll did not dwell on Special and differential treatment (SDT) being a common interest but agreed that it is part of the international trade structure. This paper takes the argument forward by contending that SDT represents common interest, notwithstanding its controversial origin. However, it needs strengthening for the benefit of countries in need. The terms common interest or community interest shall be construed broadly in this chapter. It shall not be translated to mean the exclusive interest held by the international community as a whole but a common interest shared on a non-universal level and protected by law that binds a group of people or states.[20]

Practical illustrative examples can be found in the Economic Community of West African States (ECOWAS) Trade Liberalisation Scheme and non-reciprocal trade

---

[11] Preamble to the Marrakesh Establishing the WTO. Available at https://www.wto.org/english/docs_e/legal_e/04-wto_e.htm.

[12] The Agenda 2030 was originally formulated by the United Nations (2022). See United Nations, Transforming Our World: The 2030 Agenda for Sustainable Development A/RES/70/1, 10 May 2022. https://sustainabledevelopment.un.org/content/documents/21252030%20Agenda%20for.

[13] European Economic Community (EEC) and African, Caribbean and Pacific (ACP) countries (1975) Lomé Togo.

[14] European Council, Sixth European Union-African Union Summit: A Joint Vision for 2030, European Council Press Release, 18 February 2022, pp. 1–6, 1. https://www.consilium.europa.eu/media/54412/final_declaration-en.pdf.

[15] Id. 1.

[16] Stoll (2011), pp. 182–183 (emphasis added). See, European Council Decision, Interim Agreement Establishing a Framework for an Economic Partnership Agreement between the Eastern and Southern African States, on one Part and the European Community and its Members States on the other Part Official Journal of the European Union L 111 VOLUME 55, 24 April 2012 available at https://eur-lex.europa.eu/legal-content/EN/TXT/PDF/?uri=OJ: L:2012:111:FULL.

[17] Kritsiotis (2002).

[18] Villalpando (2010), p. 385.

[19] Rao (2011), pp. 334–335.

[20] Feichtner (2007); Rao (2011), pp. 334–335. Simma (1994), pp. 217–384.

opportunities provided under the Africa Growth and Opportunity Act (AGOA).[21] Contrary to the Yaoundé Convention,[22] the Lomé Agreement granted preference based on non-reciprocity.[23] According to the ACP-EU Courier, under Lomé Conventions,[24] several protocols produced a significant profit by allowing export products such as bananas, beef, rum, and sugar into the EU market.[25] Another point evident in the spirit of the New International Economic Order (NIEO) was aid, which formed a substantial component of the Lomé Convention, funded through the European Development Fund (EDF).[26] Furthermore, a mechanism was put in place to provide indemnity for countries that had experienced losses due to fluctuations in the prices of raw materials through the Stabilisation of Commodity-export earnings (STABEX).[27] EU-Africa relations Must continue in some form. The argument here is that the developing countries must continue to argue constructively for SDT with a robust legal commitment on the side of the developed countries. As Stoll posits, where a system is established by states, usually it does not focus mainly on strict bilateral or contractual 'exchange'; by implication a 'measure of justice' will be introduced into the regime for the benefit of less powerful countries.[28] Instructively, the Lomé Convention is a trade and aid agreement because it is meant to increase foreign aid to African, Caribbean and Pacific (ACP) countries

[21] OECD (2015), p. 152.

[22] see Article 3 (3) of the second Convention of Association between the European Economic Community and the African and Malagasy States Associated with that Community and Annexed Documents (hereinafter Convention of Association) (May 1970). The first Yaoundé Convention was signed on 20 July 1963 in Yaoundé, Cameroon. The European Economic Community and 18 Associated African States and Madagascar (AASM), which was valid for 5 years. The association was founded on free trade and financial aid from the Six.

[23] The Yaoundé Convention, Article 3 (3) Convention of Association between the European Economic Community and the African and Malagasy States Associated with that Community and Annexed Documents (herein after Convention of Association) (May 1970).

[24] European Parliament 'Relations with the Africa, Caribbean and Pacific Countries: From Yaoundé and Lomé to Cotonou Agreement' 'Economic development cooperation started between EU and West Africa in 1963 with leading successive agreements: First Lomé Convention (1975–1980)' signed between 9 EU States and 46 ACP States, following the foundation of the ACP group in Georgetown (Guyana); 1979, Second Lomé Convention (1980–1985), signed between 9 EU States and 58 ACP States; 1984, Third Lomé Convention (1985–1990) signed between 9 EU States and 58 ACP States; and 1990, Fourth Lomé Convention (1990–2000) signed between 12 EU States and 68 ACP States. The Fourth Lomé Convention was in two stages, 1990–1994 and 1995–2000. Lomé IV bis was signed between 15 EU Members and 70 ACP States. The ACP group is presently composed of 78 states (46 African, 16 Caribbean and 14 Pacific). Available at www.europarl.europ.eu/facts_2004/6-4-5-en.htm. Accessed: 17 June 2018; DeLong and Eichengreen (1991), p. 3.

[25] The ACP-EU Courier (1996).

[26] Regulation (EEC) No 1598/75 of the Council 24 June 1975, https://eur-lex.europa.eu/legal-content/EN/TXT/PDF/?uri=CELEX:31975R1598&qid=1680503731575&from=EN. Bretherton and Vogler (2006), p. 116.

[27] Articles 23 (1) and (2), 24 and 25, Second ACP-EEC Convention, 1979 available at https://edit.wti.org/app.php/document/show/8a201121-e8e8-4722-9657-9db3ef9f46ee.

[28] Stoll (2011) pp. 182–183.

by European Community; and to enable the former export goods duty free to latter based on the agreement that they do not compete with European products.[29]

The rest of the chapter is divided as follows: Section 2 discusses reciprocity to unpack its nature in the trading system and whether the system of special and differential treatment has a marked effect or influence on its operation in the trading regime. Section 3 explores special and differential treatment and common interests. Section 4 looks at the EU-Africa trade relationship and common interests, and Sect. 5 concludes the chapter.

2 Reciprocity

Bruno Simma, a prominent international legal scholar and former judge of the International Court of Justice (ICJ), advocated that the principles of reciprocity and common interest are important factors in developing and maintaining the international legal system.[30] Reciprocity refers to the idea that states will be more willing to comply with their legal obligations if they believe that other states will do the same.[31] In other words, states will be more likely to comply with their obligations if they believe that other states' actions will protect their interests.[32]

Simma maintains that common interest dictates that states have a shared interest in maintaining the stability and predictability of the international legal system.[33] Simma argues that these principles are closely linked and that the effectiveness of the international legal system depends on the extent to which states are willing to act in both their own self-interest and the collective interest of the international community.[34] According to Stoll, it is debatable if this idea propounded by Simma is in tandem with international trade law. Nevertheless, according to Isabel Feichtner, the interpretation of common interest resembles the WTO's common good because it ensures 'security and predictability in international trade relations.'[35] It is noted that while the first paragraph of the WTO preamble refers to raising standards of living, the third paragraph of the preamble dwelt on the mutuality of reduction of trade barriers and non-discrimination. To a large extent, this third point on the agenda has been realised. It may seem that WTO is about reciprocity and as such, has no affinity with other global concerns,[36] but as demonstrated below, there is a meeting point for

[29] See Articles 49,53, 54, 1 of the Second Lomé Convention.

[30] Simma (1994), p. 261.

[31] Simma (2008), para. 1.

[32] Id.

[33] Id. also Paulus (2011), p. 118.

[34] Paulus (2011), pp. 114–115.

[35] Feichtner (2007).

[36] Paulus (2011); Stoll, supra note 28, questioning whether treaty arrangements without mutual exchange can be termed 'law'.

reciprocal common interest and common concern or interest for less developing countries in the trading system.[37]

While the international legal order focused on sets of rules meant to protect and respect state sovereignty into the future, there has been a change in focus.[38] This shift has altered certain social relations between states. In other words, there was a transformation in international law that considers the protection of public goods to fulfil common interests.[39] On that note, Stoll asserts that the WTO may appear to be founded on strict reciprocity; however, on closer examination, the WTO does not strictly follow the principle of reciprocity to promote a common interest.[40] Consequently, Stoll conceives that the WTO seems to be driven by absolute self-interest in situations where the state acts as an 'accountant' and seeks any possible advantage.[41] He acknowledged that WTO cases depicted the trading system that operates purely 'by sheer interest' and nothing more.[42] But the WTO does dilute the first kind of common interest, reciprocity, to promote the second type of common interest through special and differential treatment briefly mentioned in Stoll in the concluding section of his work.[43]

2.1 *From Reciprocity to Common Interest*

Some scholars of international relations attribute the Peace of Westphalia, 1648 with paving the way for the foundation of the modern state system.[44] Arguably, the treaties articulated mainly territorial integrity.[45] Thus, the society of states, stemming from the Peace of Westphalia was founded on strict repartition jurisdiction based on territory.[46] The partition between states was quite restrictive and did not envisage cooperation.[47] Nonetheless, Leo Gross maintained that international norms went beyond repartition by providing for co-existence between Protestants and Catholics through safeguards for religious minorities, including freedom of conscience.[48]

[37] Scotchmer (2008), p. 2 (emphasis added). James (1965) and Brummer (2007–2008).

[38] Pauwelyn (2003), pp. 17–20.

[39] Stoll (2011), pp. 172–173.

[40] European Communities-Customs Classification of Frozen Boneless Chicken Cuts WT/DS269/AB/R, WT/DS286/AB/R (12 September 2005). Mexico-Anti-Dumping Investigation of High-Fructose Corn Syrup (HFCS) WT/DS132/R, (28 January 2000).

[41] Stoll (2011), pp. 172–173.

[42] Id.

[43] Id., p. 182.

[44] Patton (2019), pp. 91–92.

[45] Croxton (1999), p. 574.

[46] Id pp. 569–591.

[47] Id., p. 589. Villalpando (2010), p. 390.

[48] Ward (1934), pp. 20–41.

Similarly, to an extent due to the increase in international interconnectedness, particularly due to inter-state trade and the transnational movement of individuals, social connections were promoted to mutual contract to fulfil positive reciprocated obligations in the context of compromise of interest of the individual state.[49]

Regarding common values and institutions, the Australian political scientist Heley Bull differentiates between three orthodox lines of thinking of states' relationships.[50] First, the Hobbesian concept demonstrated that states are either in a cold or hot war. It is entrenched in power politics, brief alliances and national interest.[51] However, according to Samantha Besson, states are not mainly 'self-interested' because nations can pursue both domestic 'collective' and global interests.[52] The second view of the state is the Kantian or universalist, who 'sees at work in international politics a potential community of mankind'.[53] This group sees the state as temporary; it is not an end.[54] They underscore international civil society, multinational cooperation and non-governmental organisations.[55] These authors focus on promoting justice and equity, which call for community interposition, sometimes for protecting persons against the state to which they belong.[56] The third group is what Bull referred to as the Grotian or internationalist view. It conceives of international society as made up of states and individuals.

A core neo-Grotian[57] thinks of the international system as an 'organised state community' with particular importance placed on the common interest of all states. Therefore, there is support for Wolfgang Friedmann's 'Law of cooperation' of collective security of the international legal order.[58] According to Christian Tomuschat, it would be wrong to assume that states constitute the international community as the only propinquity of individual units. Instead, the concept denotes an overarching system that embodies all states' common interests and, indirectly, humanity.[59] This, to writers, is the current state of affairs.[60]

John Jackson's view aligns with the third position mentioned above. According to Jackson, the extensive adjustment precipitated by globalisation, with a focus on 'market economic ideas' and its adverse reaction, had watered down the traditional theory of co-existence of international law.[61] Therefore, as a result of correlating

---

[49] Villalpando (2010), p. 390.

[50] Bull (2002), p. 23; Hedley (2002).

[51] Morgenthau (1948), pp. 14–17; Carty (1991), p. 66.

[52] Samantha (2018), p. 39.

[53] Bull (2002), p. 23; Slaughter (1995), p. 6; Teson (1992), p. 92.

[54] Simma (1994), p. 217. See Giorgio (2011).

[55] Bull (2002).

[56] Id.

[57] Verdross and Simma (1984), pp VII–VIII. Cited in Paulus (2011), p. 114.

[58] Haq (2018), pp. 74–85.

[59] Tomuschat (1993), p. 241.

[60] Id.

[61] Jackson (2006), p. 3.

interests in other fields of inter-state relations, such as eradicating poverty, development, telecommunications, and disease control, the discussion of common interest has taken centre stage.[62] Thus, the international trade regime integrated into the WTO is more than a set of written works and agreements.[63] The global trading system's regulation goes beyond the definitive and traditional gains to the direct parties in a separate agreement to ensure that issues of development concerns are addressed due to interdependence identified at the global level.[64] While McRae strictly defined international law as a law of 'co-existence', Joost Pauwlyn states that international law has been expanded to include the law of cooperation to tackle common problems.[65] To Pauwelyn, international law has 'shifted' its focus to other areas to protect the common interest.[66] Scholars seem to agree that common interests connote the interdependence of two or more states with shared values.[67]

When Tony Blair addressed the Economic Club of Chicago in April 1999, he declared that: by the 'new doctrine of the international community,' it is believed there is an 'explicit recognition that today more than ever before, we are mutually dependent, that national interest is to a significant extent governed by international collaboration. . . .'[68] In 2001, Blair revisited the idea of countries coming together. In a speech at the Annual Labour Conference in Brighton. He made it known that the ' power of community is asserting itself' globally.[69] The community has become the 'lesson' of 'the financial markets, climate change, international terrorism, nuclear proliferation [and] world trade' because 'our self-interest and our mutual interests' are indivisible.[70] Thus, the relationship between the EU and Africa, or other WTO members, or the EU can be located in the neo-Grotian and Kantian ideas.[71]

According to Bruno Simma, community interest calls for a consensus for respect for specific 'fundamental values' due to these intense connections or globalisation.[72] To him, a common interest is a shared objective or goal that is pursued by two or more states. Common interests can be based on a variety of factors, such as economic, political or security considerations. States may have a common interest in maintaining regional stability, promising economic development, or preventing the spread of nuclear weapons, for example. In international relations, states often

---

[62] Id.

[63] Stoll (2011), pp. 172–173. Jobim (2013), p. 55. Tasioulas (1996), p. 88.

[64] Alessandrini (2011), p. 168. Cited in Jobim (2013), p. 55.

[65] Pauwelyn (2003), p. 31.

[66] Id., pp. 17–18.

[67] Keohane and Nye (2011), p. 221. Rao (2011).

[68] Blair (1999) Speech by Prime Minister Tony Blare to the Economic Club of Chicago on 22 April 1999. Available at: http://www.britishpoliticalspeech.org/speech-archive.htm?speech=279.

[69] Blair (2001) 'A Moment to Seize: Let Us Reorder this World Around Us', The Guardian. Available at: https://www.theguardian.com/politics/2001/oct/02/labourconference.labour7.

[70] Id; also Cottier and Ahmad (2021), pp. 3–4.

[71] Slaughter (1995), p. 526.

[72] Id.

work together to achieve common interests through cooperation and coordination. Common interests can also be used to build trust and strengthen relationships between states. Thus, industrialisation, the advancement of modern economies, and globalisation have led to a rapid paradigm shift in international relations.

Common interest found a niche in Article 55 mentioned above. It provides that for peaceful co-existence among nations, the United Nations (UN) should encourage the promotion of a 'higher standard of living, full employment, and conditions for economic and social progress and development.'[73] Although economic law does not have the key concepts that could be considered 'values'.[74] However, as mentioned earlier, the WTO contains some language for raising standards of living.[75] It states that trade relations should be carried out to raise the standard of living through full employment, and this only happens with the expansion of the production and exchange of resources—reduction of barriers to trade and non-discrimination.[76] To a large extent, the second paragraph has realised that the first part of common interest and the second part of common interest represented in the first paragraph of the WTO preamble is yet to produce a satisfactory result.[77] Special consideration for developing countries as provided by the WTO is explored next to demonstrate whether it serves common interest.

3 Special and Differential Treatment and Common Interest

SDT in the WTO refers to the provision of special consideration for developing countries in the rules and operations of the organisation.[78] This treatment is intended to help these countries participate more effectively in the global trading system and to take into account their special needs and difficulties.[79] The principle is embodied in various WTO agreements, including the General Agreement on Tariffs and Trade (GATT), the Agreement on Trade-Related Aspects of Intellectual Property Rights

---

[73] Article 55 Charter of the United and Statute of International Court of Justice 24 October 1945. Available at https://treaties.un.org/doc/publication/ctc/uncharter.pdf.

[74] Stoll (2011), p. 174.

[75] Preamble para 1 of the Marrakesh Agreement Establishing the World Trade Organisation (adopted 15 April 1994, came into force 1 January 1995); Stoll (2011), p. 174.

[76] General Agreement Tariffs and Trade 1994 (GATT), Marrakesh Agreement Establishing the World Trade Organisation (adopted 15 April 1994, entered into force 1 January 1995) Annex 1A1867UNTS4,190ArtXIIGATT.

[77] Stoll (2011), pp. 174–175.

[78] Fukasaku (2000), pp. 156–170. Hoekman et al. (2003), pp. 562–565.

[79] Fukasaku (2000), pp. 156–170.

(TRIPS),[80] and the Agreement on Agriculture.[81] Examples of special and differential treatment provisions include more extended implementation periods for trade agreements, flexibility in meeting certain obligations, and technical assistance to help developing countries implement and benefit from WTO agreements.[82] SDT provisions are intended to ensure that developing countries are not disadvantaged by the rules and procedures of the WTO and provide them with additional support to help them take advantage of the opportunities provided by the global trading system.[83]

According to Trebilcock and Howse, at the time of the negotiation in Bretton Woods, developing countries have little or no influence shaping the agenda and design of the regime that would govern international trade over the decades that followed.[84] As such, at any given opportunity, developing countries sought more preferential treatment.[85] These demands developed gradually into a central focal point in the United Nations Conference on Trade and Development (UNCTAD) as part of the innovation in the international trading system in the 1960s and 1970s.[86] However, according to Hudec[87] and Lamp,[88] it was far from the intention and plan of the developing countries to be treated in a special way. Nevertheless, they requested to be able to fashion their GATT obligations in a manner consistent with their needs—which turned out not to be compatible with developed countries' preferences in certain areas. Consequently, SDT for developing countries as it is known today was crafted by 'developed countries to preserve their preferred design of the trade regime, and to stick to their favoured method of making trade law, while keeping developing countries within the system.'[89] In essence, Lamp argued that the main reason for the provision of special treatment for developing countries was to placate them without changing anything fundamental about the trading system.[90]

As mentioned above, in 1964, the first UNCTAD took place in Geneva where the idea of a special section on trade and development to be added to the GATT was developed.[91] Consequently, part IV—Trade and Development was made part of the

---

[80] Articles 65.2 and 65.4 provides for transition periods for the implementation of the agreement; 67, technical and financial assistance and 66.2, encouraged technology transfer to least developed countries. See Michalopoulos (2003), Special and Differential Treatment of Developing Countries in TRIPS. TRIPS Issues Paper, Quaker United Nations (QUNO) Geneva. Available at, https://quno.org/sites/default/files/resources/Special-Differential-Treatment-in-TRIPS-English.pdf.

[81] E.g. Articles 15.2. 6.2. 6.4. 9.4 and 12.2 of the Agreement on Agriculture. Available at, www.wto.org/english/docs_e/legal_e/14-ag_01_e.htm.

[82] Id.

[83] Edwini (2007), pp. 12–18.

[84] Trebilcock and Howse (1995), p. 518.

[85] Id.

[86] Id; Pauwelyn (2003), pp. 17–18.

[87] Hudec (1987), p. 4.

[88] Lamp (2015), pp. 743–771.

[89] Id.

[90] Id., p. 745.

[91] UNCTAD (1964), pp. 18–25.

GATT to consider the concerns of developing countries.[92] The principle was expressed in the Generalised System of Preference (GSP), which was politically adopted at UNCTAD II in New Delhi in 1968 and technically accepted by UNCTAD's Trade and Development Board in 1970 to create a generalised, non-reciprocal, non-discriminatory system of preferences to favour developing countries.[93]

There are many angles to the idea of SDT. It embraces non-reciprocity, permissive protection and a general preference system—the focus of this chapter. It is essential to give a brief overview of this to find out how efficiently the mechanisms worked in practice and if advocating for it—whether it has served the common interest of the members of the multilateral trading system.

3.1 Non-reciprocity Mechanism

Non-Reciprocity is provided for in part IV of the General Agreement on Tariff and Trade (GATT). Article XXXVI considers the concerns of developing countries. Article XXXVI provides that the contracting parties are not expected to trade reciprocally with less developing countries in negotiations regarding reducing or removing tariffs.[94] This idea is further amplified in Article XXXVII:3 (c). The provision requires that developed countries give special attention to the trade interest of developing countries when measures are being applied. Developed countries are enjoined to explore all possibilities of constructive remedies before taking such measure, especially if they would affect essential interest of the less developed countries. It encouraged developed countries to remove certain obstacles that may prevent products of developing countries from accessing their markets. However, this provision has been criticised; for instance, according to Alessandrini, the imprecise requirements on non-reciprocity and the lack of legal commitments remain the foremost obstacle to bringing about positive results for developing countries.[95] According to this author, the reason for this vagueness is that developed countries are not willing to concretise the SDT in legal terms as there are no reciprocal benefits.[96]

[92] Part IV of the General Agreement on Tariff and Trade, entitled, Trade and Development. Available at, https://www.wto.org/english/res_e/booksp_e/gatt_ai_e/part4_e.pdf.

[93] UNCTAD (1968), pp. 11-12,200-2.

[94] Article XXXVI:8 Part IV of the GATT.

[95] Alessandrini (2011), pp. 174–176.

[96] Id.

3.2 Import Substitution and Protection of the Infant Industry

Under the GATT, certain protections are granted to developing countries. Regarding GATT responsibilities, developing countries are granted special treatment in Articles XI, XII, and XVIII. Article XVIII was the GATT's first try to assist developing countries' concerns. The article comprises three components. Article XVIII, Section A permits developing countries to renegotiate tariff bindings to encourage the establishment of industry. If a developing country decides to use this provision, the expectation is that it must offer compensation or face retaliation.[97] Article XVIII, Section B provides for a balance of payment escape clause for developing countries. The provision in Article XVIII, Section B basis for imposing such restrictions is less burdensome than the criteria that apply to developed countries under Article XII. Article XVIII, Section C allows developing countries to impose quantitative restrictions for infant industry protection. Similar to Article XVIII: A tariff renegotiation, Article XVIII, Section C provides compensation and retaliation in the absence of a negotiated agreement.

Article XXVIII: bis (3), which appeared for the first time in the 1955 Review Session, provides that developing countries provide that negotiations shall take into account "the needs of less-developed countries" to use tariffs for economic development and fiscal purposes. At the time of the reviewing of the GATT Articles, the Contracting Parties were urged to increase capital flows to developing countries to facilitate the objectives of the General Agreement by stimulating the economic development of these countries while at the same time rendering it less necessary for them to resort to import restrictions.'[98]

During the 1960s, 1970s and 1980s, many African countries adopted import substitution policies as a way to promote industrialisation and economic development.[99] Some examples of African countries that experienced gains from import substitution during this period include Ghana, Tanzania, Kenya, Côte d'Ivoire, Senegal, and many other African countries; import substitution policies led to the growth of domestic industries, particularly in the manufacturing sector.[100] This helped diversify the economy and create jobs, contributing to economic growth and development.[101] On the contrary, others argued that import substitution was uncertain and only favoured the mining industry for the most part; this sector was focused on due to the small nature of the market size and poor infrastructure.[102]

[97] Article XVIII: A GATT; Governmental Assistance to Economic Development. Available at https://www.wto.org/english/res_e/publications_e/ai17_e/gatt1994_art18_gatt47.pdf.

[98] Id.

[99] Mendes et al. (2004), pp. 128–131.

[100] Huq and Tribe (2018), p. 17. Gulhati and Sekhar (1982), pp. 949–972.

[101] Herbst (1990), pp. 494–958; Stein (1992), pp. 86–86.

[102] Supra note 98, p. 125.

3.3 Generalised Systems of Preference

One of the most concrete outcome in the SDT concerned the GSP. At the initial stage, the GSP was designed under the aegis of UNCTAD,[103] and it included differential treatment among developing countries, depending on their stage of development. At the preparatory stage, the intention was for the developed countries to grant preferences to their former colonies.[104] The scope of the GSP was then expanded. For the GSP to come into force, a waiver had to be obtained according to Article XXV of the GATT.[105] It was created to mitigate the MFN clause in GATT Article I permitting the implementation of a preferential system within the global trade system. In 1979, the rule of preferences became fully established, introducing the Enabling Clause.[106] The Enabling Clause has given developed countries optional powers to direct and design their systems of preferences.[107] Developing countries could choose products they prefer to import and provide incentives for primary product industries, which provided 'perverse incentives' against manufacturing in poor countries.[108]

It is noted that when differential treatment has been granted, Europe and the US would impose several conditions to its being granted, then adopting a controversial 'graduation policy', which was designed according to their needs.[109] Thus, preferences are conditional gains that could be withdrawn at any time, depending on the benchmark used by the granting country.[110] Uncertainty and unpredictability inherent in preferential treatment have become an obstacle for developing countries, and the infant industries seeking to be protected; this, in the long term, is an obstacle to prevents economic growth.[111] For example, market access in sectors such as textiles, manufacturers, agriculture, and tropical products, sectors of interest to developing countries, remained uncertain.[112] It is not in doubt that GSP has advanced export growth in developing countries, but the system was used as a political and economic weapon. For example, the US Trade Act of 1974 gave the US President power to

[103] UNCTAD (1972) Proceedings of the United Nations Conference on Trade and Development, Third Session, Santiago de Chile, 13 April to 21 May 1972, United Nations, New York. https://unctad.org/system/files/official-document/td180vol1_en.pdf/.

[104] Patterson (1996), pp. 1945–1965.

[105] Article XXV:5 GATT. Available at, https://www.wto.org/english/res_e/publications_e/ai17_e/gatt1994_art25_gatt47.pdf.

[106] 'Differential and More Favourable Treatment Reciprocity and Fuller Participation of Developing Countries' Decision of 28 November 1979 (L/4903), https://docs.wto.org/do12fe/Pages/SS/directdoc.aspx?filename=Q:/JCR/TOKYO/ENABLEING.pdf&Open=True.

[107] Trebilcock and Howse (1995), Third edn, pp. 630–631.

[108] Thomas and Trachtman (2009), pp. 1–21; Id. Trebilcock and Howse (1995), p. 561.

[109] Whally (1990), pp. 1324–1325.

[110] Id., p. 1320.

[111] Id; Trebilcock and Howse (1995), p. 518. Franck (1998), p. 12. Also Trachtman (2011), pp. 3–4.

[112] Id.

waive GSP status if the recipient country failed to provide 'reasonable access' to its markets and commodities and failed to afford sufficient and adequate protection of intellectual property rights.[113]

3.4 The Merit and Demerit of SDT

Undoubtedly, the GSP has supported and encouraged relatively modest gains in developing countries.[114] However, there has been a broader argument against the adoption of preferences than the inadequacy of SDT.[115] The proponents of expeditious liberalisation direct attention to the fact that developing economies persistently seek to advance their own interests by development policies that have adverse consequences for other developing countries.[116] Another argument put forward is that SDT promotes protectionist trade policies, which do not create a system for achieving maximum productivity in developing countries.[117] Therefore, an exception from the WTO discipline would rather heighten the disadvantageous position of developing countries because it promotes protectionism and excludes them from the worldwide economy.[118] In other words, every country's compliance with the reciprocity and non-discrimination principle will become competitive, notwithstanding the differences in their level of development.[119] However, according to Chang's argument, supported with evidence, the United Kingdom and the United States engaged in trade protectionism and government support for industries during their own development processes.[120]

The principle of reciprocity, which became the foundation of the GATT, originates in sovereign equality under international law. The idea of sovereign equality is premised on the supposition that states are identical in identity and abilities.[121] Article I of the GATT, or MFN treatment, transfers the concept of equality from international law into the economic field.[122] This assumption was challenged by

[113] Id. p. 528.

[114] Kleen and Page (2005), pp. 2–4.

[115] Trump, (2019) Reforming Developing Country Status in the World Trade Organisation. Available at: https://www.presidency.ucsb.edu/documents/memorandum-reforming-developing-country-status-the-world-trade-organization.

[116] Stiglitze and Charlton (2005), p. 13.

[117] Cottrel and Trubek (2012-2013). Sutherland et al. (2004). 'The Future of the WTO: Addressing Institutional Challenges in the New Millennium', Report by the Consultative Board to the Director General Supachai Panitchpakdi Geneva. Available at https://www.wto.org/english/thewto_e/10anniv_e/future_wto_e.pdf. Hoekman and Howse (2005), pp. 13–14.

[118] Stiglitze and Charlton (2005), p. 85.

[119] Isard (1995), p. 95.

[120] Chang (2007) pp. 125–122, 41–42.

[121] Yanai (2004).

[122] Espiell (1971), p. 29.

developing countries from the 1950s to the 1970s. They contended that the idea took no cognisance of inequality between states in terms of development. Thus, it was from this argument that SDT in the form of the Enabling Clause emerged. SDT is founded on the position that 'equal treatment could secure equality only among identical parties',[123] and it was believed that only SDT could alleviate the negative impact of economic and power asymmetries between developing and developed countries. The argument is widely accepted that the MFN principle is not an adequate or convenient means of attaining development, especially in developing countries.[124] Thus, arguably the SDT has some benefits and has not been a total failure. For example, the GSP of the United States and the EU gave their leaders the discretion to extend beneficiary status to any country that conforms to stipulated conditions.[125] countries such as South Korea, Singapore, Malaysia, and Hong Kong used the scheme, and after they became successful exporters and achieved 'high income' positions, they 'graduated'.[126] However, according to Stiglitz and Charlton, the Asian countries did not rely on GSP or free trade or non-interference policies by the government but benefitted from government involvement and tackling difficult internal reforms were largely responsible for the success of the of the above-mentioned countries.[127] Notwithstanding that Stiglitz and Charlton encourage developing countries to focus on reforms internally,[128] the SDT can be of substantial benefit if it is genuinely targeted at assisting developing countries.

The United States recognised the second aspect of common interest by extending assistance to Europe through the Marshall Plan. The former United States Secretary of State, George C Marshall, gave a speech at Harvard University and emphasised the need for substantial aid to Europe to stop economic and political retrogression.[129] He declared, 'our policy is directed not against any country or doctrine but hunger, poverty, desperation, and chaos'.[130] Between 1948 and 1953, the Marshall Plan made a huge contribution of more than $13 billion dollars in economic and technical assistance for the recovery of 16 countries.[131] The Marshall Plan was described as a 'politics of prosperity'[132] and a clear case of the 'principle of solidarity' between advanced countries to eliminate poverty and prevent the threat of war. The effort was to achieve industrial productivity in Europe by creating international agreements among actors for economic growth.[133] It has been argued that this similar solidarity

[123] Supra note 113, p. 88.

[124] Supra note 89, p. 29.

[125] Grossman and Sykes (2005), pp. 45, 56.

[126] Id, p. 45.

[127] Stiglitze and Charlton (2005), p. 89.

[128] Id, p. vii.

[129] OECD (1947); see DeLong and Eichengreen (1991).

[130] Id, OECD.

[131] Supra note 93. Supra note 118, DeLong and Eichengreen (1991), pp. 3–5.

[132] Lakshmi (2005).

[133] Stiglitze and Charlton (2005), p. 118; DeLong and Eichengreen (1991), p. 55.

should be extended to developing countries that exist in the vicious cycle of poverty.[134]

4 EU-Africa and Common Interests

By 1960, most overseas territories had gained independence, and Guy[135] notes that it became imperative to renegotiate the 'Associate Status' between the six European Economic Community (EEC) and 18 African Associate and the Malagasy States.[136] The second Yaoundé Convention from January 1971 to March 1975 brought some minor improvements.[137] However, it maintained the fundamental structure of the earliest agreement.[138] It is important to note that the series of trade arrangements has its background in the European post-colonial settlement after World War II, what Minta referred to as an 'unbroken historical continuum.'[139] A commercial imperialism which began in the sixteenth to the mid nineteenth centuries, moving through to the Commonwealth period and to the series of Lomé Conventions, and preferential arrangement yet no substantial advantage has accrued to the latter from the former which has been the dominant party in their trading relations.[140] The EU's way forward with Africa in terms of advancing the 'economic integration' and development in the recent Economic Partnership Agreement has resulted in uncertainty.[141] Desta Melaku expressed the view that the EU-Africa has developed gradually over time from colonialism to serpentine relations, outlined as a 'partnership'.[142] However, there has been reconditioning of the Europe-Africa relationship since the Lomé conventions—an evolution in the relationship from the colonial period.[143] Fundamentally, the relationship is still asymmetrical, but some positive elements in the Lomé and Cotonou Agreements are built on to advance the interests of African countries.[144] The Cotonou Agreement succeeded the Lomé Convention, which heralded a new era of Economic Partnership Agreements (EPAs).[145]

The early part of the year 2000 heralded a fundamental policy change to the preferential non-reciprocal trade arrangements between the EU and ACP

[134] Id Stiglitze and Charlton (2005), p. 3. See footnote 3 of the book.

[135] Martin (1982).

[136] Nwobike (2006), pp. 87–124.

[137] Twichett (1974), pp. 51–63.

[138] Id.

[139] Minta (1980), p. 954.

[140] Id, pp. 943, 974. Luke et al. (2020).

[141] Id Luke et al. (2020)

[142] Melaku (2021).

[143] Supra note 24. See, Ravenhill (1979–1980), pp. 151–157.

[144] Grossman and Sykes (2005), p. 41.

[145] Ravenhill (2002), p. 6.

countries[146] The reasons put forward by the European Union for the controversial[147] EPAs are mainly twofold: (1) compliance with Article XXIV of the World Trade Organisation (WTO) rules,[148] and (2) sustainable development and active participation of the developing countries in the world trading system. In other words, the EU and Africa are to trade based on reciprocity, and the former would offer some flexibility to the latter countries. The new relationship considers the two levels of common interest: reciprocal trade arrangements for the mutual benefit of both parties and special treatment provided to the African partners due to their lack of development. This point is further discussed later in this work. Brown argued that the circumstances that inform the relationship between Africa and the EU could only be critically understood from the point of view of cooperation between developing countries in Africa and 'Western' developed countries.[149]

According to a World Bank report, Sub-Saharan Africa is home to more than one billion people, with the largest free trade area in the world.[150] If well implemented, the African Continental Free Trade Area (AfCFTA) has great prospects to eliminate extreme poverty on the continent. The World Bank identified the great potential of the region but also listed the woes that are likely to betide Africa. For example, it states that economic growth in SSA slowed down from 4.1% in 2021 to 3.3% in 2022, partially due to sluggish growth globally. This is bound to be exacerbated due to the war in Ukraine, worsening debt related distress.[151] These problems undermine the vision of eradicating extreme poverty. It is forecasted to remain high at 59.5% of GDP in 2022 in SSA. The Bank further states that 8 out of 38 IDA-eligible countries on the continent are in debt distress, and 14 are at a very high risk of falling into similar distress.[152] A 2023 IMF report is not so different in outlook to the World Bank. It states that 'rising food and energy prices are impacting the region's most vulnerable, and public debt and inflation are at levels not seen in decades.'[153] According to an UNCTAD report, 'forty-five African economies are commodity dependent [. . .] [w]ith highly volatile revenue due to price boom and bust nature of the market'.[154] Commodity dependence is when commodities represent more than 60% of total merchandise exports. 83% of African countries are commodity

[146] European Commission (2010).

[147] Ramdoo and Bilal (2011), p. 3.

[148] Smith (2005). Mandelson Peter, is quoted as saying "to end the grinding poverty which is the daily experience of so many ACP citizens". Oxfam International (2006), p. 13.

[149] Brown (2002), p. 368.

[150] The World Bank, (2023) The World Bank in Africa. Available at https://www.worldbank.org/en/region/afr/overview.

[151] Id.

[152] The World Bank (2022).

[153] International Monetary Fund (n.d.).

[154] UNCTAD (2022).

dependent, accounting for 45% of the commodity-dependent worldwide.[155] It further noted the struggle by African countries to diversify their export of goods and services is doable but with a serious challenge.[156]

The United Nations Economic Commission for Africa (UNECA) reported that in Africa, approximately 60% of the poor live in acute poverty, and 40% live in temporary poverty. 'In countries with comparable data, an estimated 33% of poor households live in chronic poverty, with variations across countries. The Democratic Republic of the Congo has more than twice that proportion, and Rwanda, Mozambique, Malawi and Madagascar have 1.5–2 times that proportion'.[157] According to the report, the African share of global exports reduced from 2010 to 2019 but increased in other regions. The trade share of the continent fell from 2.48% in 2019 to 2.14. It states, 'Africa has shown a merchandise trade deficit since 2013, reflecting continued dependence on exports of low-value-added commodities and imports of high-value manufactured goods, reinforcing its vulnerability to external shocks during a crisis'.[158] The HIV/AIDS shocks in the 1990s, and intermittent drought reduced and affected learning outcomes and caused huge losses.[159] However, some progress has been made in reducing poverty in Africa. For instance, Cabo Verde, Gabon, the Gambia, Lesotho, Mauritania, Morocco, Namibia and Tunisia halved poverty and are on track to eradicate poverty as set in the Agenda 2030 for sustainable development. Nevertheless, poverty has increased tremendously in many other countries, such as Angola, Cote d'Ivoire, Sao Tome and Principe, Senegal, etc.[160]

On the other hand, the EU, which operates a single market, is comprised of 27 countries.[161] The total value of goods and services, which was produced (Gross Domestic Product) in the EU in the year 2021 amounted to €14.5 billion. The EU 27 accounts for about 14% of the trade in goods—making the region one of the largest trade and player in the global trading system.[162] in the same year, 2021, accounted for €4.3 billion in total world trade. In trading among its members, it was valued at EUR 6786 billion in 2021[163] In 2016 Africa's share of world GDP shrank from 3.3% to 3.1%. In 2006, the EU-28's share of world GDP was 29.7%, but in

[155] UNCTAD (2022), pp. 3–6. UNCTAD (2001), Trade and Development: From Recovery to Resilience: The Development Dimension. Available at, https://unctad.org/system/files/official-document/tdr2021overview_en.pdf.

[156] Id.

[157] ECA (2022), p. 4.

[158] Id p. 26.

[159] Id p. 30.

[160] Id p. 87.

[161] EU, Facts and Figures on the European Union Economy. Available at, https://european-union.europa.eu/principles-countries-history/key-facts-and-figures/economy_en; see, EU (2019), p. 14.

[162] Id.

[163] Id. Eurostat, Share of European Union EU27 (From 2020) in the World Trade. Available at https://ec.europa.eu/eurostat/databrowser/view/EXT_LT_INTROEU27_2020__custom_3351101/default/bar?lang=en.

2010, due to the worldwide economic crisis, the share came down to 25.2%; in 2016 EU's share was 21.7 %.[164] In terms of trade between the continents, the gap is wide. In 2013, the EU reported that the EU recognised these differences in development level and has provided development assistance in the form of aid for many years.[165] Also, it offered non-reciprocal trade arrangements for ACP countries from 1975 until the new Cotonou trade agreement of 2000, which heralded reciprocity between the continents.[166] The motivating force behind aid has been a subject of debate. According to Whitefield,[167] aid is given by the donor for the transfer or projection of its 'moral values' or it can be intended to increase the donor's power or influence. For Carol Lancaster, countries give assistance for the purpose of diplomatic relationships and to advance their mercantile interests, such as better access to raw materials in developing countries.[168] The EU has been criticised for the 'political conditionality' of aid. Development assistance has been used to promote human rights and democracy, and there may also be a sanction if there is a breach of the principles mentioned above.[169] The ideas of human rights, good governance and democracy are clearly reflected in the Cotonou agreement.

As mentioned above, many developing and least developed countries have benefitted from preferential access to markets in developed countries. The initial preferential arrangement set up by some countries was the GSP, where an indefinite waiver from the fundamental principle of non-discrimination at the WTO was granted under the Enabling Clause. Other arrangements have included, for example, the African Growth and Opportunity Act (AGOA), the EU's Everything But Arms (EBA) initiative which was meant for least-developed countries, and the Caribbean Basin Initiative of the United States.

4.1 SDT in the EU-ACP Economic Partnership Agreement

Special and differential treatment (SDT) refers to measures taken to recognise the unique needs and challenges developing countries face in negotiating and implementing international trade agreements.[170] These measures are intended to ensure that these countries are not disadvantaged and can fully participate in and benefit from the WTO Agreements.[171] Common or community interest refers to the shared goals and objectives of a group of countries that are not disadvantaged by the

---

164 Id.

165 EU (n.d.), pp. 8–10.

166 WTO (2001).

167 Whitefield (2009), p. 28.

168 Lancaster (2007), p. 15.

169 Hurt (2003), p. 171. See Crawford (1997), p. 70.

170 Stevens et al. (2008), pp. 1–3, 6.

171 Id.

agreements. This can include provisions for longer implementation periods, special flexibilities, and technical assistance to help these countries implement the agreements, as mentioned above.[172]

In 1996, an EU green paper recommended the replacement of non-reciprocal trade arrangements in the Lomé Convention between the EU and African Caribbean and Pacific (ACP) countries with a reciprocal free trade agreement.[173] The Cotonou Partnership Agreement clearly defines the new framework for relations between the EU and ACP countries.[174] During the preparations for the EPA negotiations and at the time it was formally launched in West Africa in September 2002, the attention was on reciprocity and how common interest beyond reciprocal arrangements could be achieved.[175] The concerns were centred on the development dimension of the EPAs and their impact on poverty, as well as the strengthening or weakening of the integration of the regions in Africa.[176] Addressing these issues in the context of EPA negotiations proved to be difficult—due to the complexity of African challenges.[177] Notwithstanding the complex nature of the African problem, such as lack of capacity to assess and manage their challenges, administrative dysfunctionality and challenges of governance, poverty and poor infrastructure.[178] African exports like many other developing countries since independence has been focused on raw material.[179] Special treatment was included in the EPAs.

Regarding the protection of infant industry, it provides that tariffs may increase due to a significant surge in the quantity of EU imports. Before this can apply, it must be shown that the EU import surge caused or threatened to cause serious injury, and safeguards may apply if the disturbance continues. The period of time that safeguards may apply is limited at first to eight years. For example, the SADC-EU EPA limits this to 8 years within the first 12 years,[180] CARIFORUM limits the application of safeguards to 8 years within the initial 10 years, Ghana is 8 years within the first

[172] WTO, Special and More Favourable Treatment Reciprocity and Fuller Participation of Developing Countries, Decision 28 November 1979 (L/4903). Available at, www.wto.org.

[173] Commission of the European Communities (1996), p. iii.

[174] Article 95 (1), Partnership Agreement between the members of the African, Caribbean and Pacific Group of States of the one Part, and the European Community and its Member States, of the other Part, (23 June 2000) (hereinafter Cotonou Agreement). Available at https://eur-lex.europa.eu/resource.html?uri=cellar:eebc0bbc-f137-4565-952d-3e1ce81ee890.0004.04/DOC_2&format=PDF.

[175] Supra, Hurt (2003), p. 173.

[176] Id. Mandelson P European Commissioner for Trade, 'Economic Partnership Agreements: progressive trade policy into practice' SPEECH/05/241 ACP—EU Joint Parliamentary Assembly Bamako, Mali, 19 April 2005, p. 5. Available at, https://ec.europa.eu/commission/presscorner/detail/en/SPEECH_05_241.

[177] Stevens et al. (2008), pp. 1–9. Bilal and Dan (2009).

[178] Malik and Teal (2008), pp. 248–252. Commission of the European Communities (1996), p. xii.

[179] Wilkinson (2014), p. 32.

[180] Articles 33, 34, 35 and 36 SADC-EU EPA. Available at, https://trade.ec.europa.eu/doclib/docs/2015/october/tradoc_153915.pdf.

10 years, with the option of an extension for Ghana.[181] Finally the EAC EPA with the EU provides for 8 years of infant industry protection within the first 10 years.[182]

It has been argued that the scope of the safeguards measures is limited.[183] The position of the EU is that the limited flexibility on safeguards is to meet the requirement of 'substantially all trade.'[184] It was further noted in critiques that the definition of 'serious injury', was borrowed from WTO rules. This has resulted in some countries in the ACP fearing that its meaning could be influenced by GATT Article XIX, the WTO Safeguards Agreement,[185] and the Appellate Body's strict interpretation of this concept.[186] The phrase 'serious disturbance' seems to have been imported from EC GSP.[187] In the same way the EPA included the WTO idea of 'such increased quantities' which 'cause or threaten to cause' without a specific reference to the volume or price that could trigger this effect.[188] For instance, data on import volumes may be collected with much less rigour in developing countries. Safeguards may be hard for ACP countries to make use of effectively, which could hamper their effectiveness without, among other things, advances in observing trade flows and new rules.[189] As a result of a lack of capacity in these areas, it has been observed that many African countries cannot take advantage of the safeguard measures as provided for in the agreement's text.[190]

However, it should be noted that the EU is bound by international obligations, such as the WTO agreements, which determine the extent to which the EU could take action to a large degree. The EU, for instance, is obligated to observe its WTO obligations in a variety of areas including MFN tariffs, safeguards, technical barriers to trade (TBT), sanitary and phytosanitary (SPS) measures, the GATT (1994), and the General Agreement on Trade in Service (GATS) all of which constrain the scope

---

[181] Articles 25 (8) and (7) (b), 16; Ghana-EU EPA Ghana-EU EPA Annex 2. Available at https://eur-lex.europa.eu/legal-content/EN/TXT/PDF/?uri=CELEX:22016A1021(01)&rid=4. Berthelot (2016).

[182] Articles 50 (5) (b), 49, Economic Partnership Agreement Between the East African Community Partners States, and the European Union, (hereinafter EAC-EU EPA) Available at, http://repository.eac.int/bitstream/handle/11671/1699/EAC%20-%20EU%20EPA%20AGREEMENT.pdf?sequence=1&isAllowed=y. Article 21 ESA-EC Interim EPA.

[183] Ratna and Gupta (2018), pp. 20–48.

[184] Article XXIV: 8 GATT.

[185] Supra, Ratna and Gupta (2018).

[186] Argentina-Safeguard Measures on Imports of Footwear WT/DS121/AB/R 14 December 1999 para. 96. Korea-Definitive Safeguard Measure on Imports of Certain Dairy Products, WT/DS98/AB/R Para. 86 14 December 1999.

[187] Article 22 Council Regulation (EC) No 980/2005 of 27 June 2005 Official Journal of European Union (27 June 2005). Available at https://eur-lex.europa.eu/legal-content/EN/TXT/PDF/?uri=CELEX:32005R0980&from=EN.

[188] Sykes (2003), pp. 2–6. Trebilcock and Howse (1995), pp. 330–331. See The WTO (n.d.), Article XIX, of the WTO Agreement on Safeguard Measure. Available at https://www.wto.org/english/tratop_e/safeg_e/safeint.htm.

[189] Id, Trebilcock and Howse (1995), p. 334.

[190] Agbo-Ejeh (2022), p. 103.

of EU policy. The Commission has argued extensively that GATT Article XXIV constrains the scope of its flexibility towards ACP countries.[191] Nevertheless, Woolcock observed that EU policy towards African countries is shaped by 'normative factors' such as the EU debate on policy space and institutional factors that move the focal point of EU policy-making between the EU Director General for Trade and the EU Director General for Development (DG INTPA today).[192] Normative issues and trade rules, no doubt, shape market access.[193]

It is important to note that the kernel of EU trade policy is provided in the Common Commercial Policy (CCP). Article 206 of the Treaty on Functioning of the European Union (TFEU) states: ' the EU shall contribute, in the common interest, to the harmonious development of world trade, the progressive abolition of restrictions on international trade and on foreign direct investment, and the lowering of customs and other barriers'.[194] This CCP must comply with the external objectives of the EU provided in Article 21 of the Treaty on EU.[195] The general aims include the promotion of democracy, the rule of law and human rights, the preservation of peace and good governance, trade and investment 'and fostering of sustainable economic, social and environmental development of developing countries to eradicate poverty and also 'to encourage the integration of all countries into the world economy', including prevention of barriers to trade liberalisation. The EU also acknowledged a common interest in its CCP to promote developing countries' welfare. However, it remains to be seen the extent to which this special treatment will truly benefit African countries.

5 Conclusion

This chapter addressed common interest against a backdrop of special and differential treatment in the GATT/WTO law and the EU-African relationship including EPAs and the renewed vision for the EU-Africa Partnership, agenda 2030. This limited assessment demonstrated attenuated reciprocity in the WTO. It is recognised that reciprocity remains the key principle of the world trading system.[196] Fundamentally the focal point is the balance of rights and obligations of each member as well as among all WTO members.[197] However, to enable less developed countries to trade and level up with more advanced economies, they were allowed to deviate from the non-discrimination principle and given allowances based on SDT.

[191] Koroma and Deep Ford (2006), pp. 25–30.

[192] Woolcock (2014), pp. 36–48.

[193] Woolcock (2014), pp. 36–48.

[194] Article 206, TFEU, https://knowww.eu/nodes/5c35a63bc76ed6738667ee38.

[195] Id.

[196] Stoll (2011), pp. 181–182.

[197] Id.

Thus, this work recognised the positions from which scholars[198] view common interest: first considered was reciprocity and non-discrimination with a view to advancing the interests of all WTO members through mutual tariff reduction. The second is the gains that accrue as a result of trade negotiation in 'terms of rights and obligations' benefitted by or 'owed to any member'. The third debatably is the idea that where a system is put in place by states, justness and equity is implied, as such the relationship can no longer be based purely on bilateral exchange.[199] The provision of SDT is a recognition of developing countries' current lack of capacity to compete effectively with advanced countries. Hence such concerns become a common interest of all members. As such, it is reflected in the SDT to enable these countries to level up. This chapter explored the various provisions of SDT and found that developing countries have benefitted from SDT but not sufficiently to solve their problems. As noted by Lamp, there is no benefit in the SDT provisions that is the intention, but any gain by the developing countries is 'accidental' or incidental because the arrangement was made for a different purpose: to keep developing countries within the system. SDT is perceived as the 'second best solution, and it turns developing countries 'quest for market access into a begging operation'.[200]

An examination of some provisions of the Economic Partnership Agreement between the EU and various African groups revealed minimal flexibility; indeed, the flexibilities granted to the African countries run both ways because they are extended to the EU. This is not to say there are no other flexibilities provided for the African countries in the EPA, but fundamentally, there are widespread beliefs that these countries have no capacity to take advantage of the special treatment provisions or deviations from the core agreement.[201] As noted Jones, maintains that EU leaders should put aside 'grand plans and framework' to give relevant and significant strategy.[202] The focus, according to her should be 'alliance' and not 'partners of equals' because of the realities faced by African countries.[203]

Since SDT does not yield the desired outcome for the targeted countries, per se, should it be discarded? As noted in the conceptualisation of common interest, the ability of developing countries to participate or take advantage of the provisions of WTO law should indeed be a common concern. This should encompass a substantial commitment being made by advanced economies with a view to attaining the objectives and respecting the principles underlying SDT. However, it is important to note that SDT is not the only solution. The common interest expressed in the African Continental Free Trade Area provides a great opportunity for moving Africa forward to trading more robustly with the rest of the world.[204]

---

[198] Rao (2011), Stoll (2011), and Simma (1994).

[199] Stoll (2011), pp. 182–183.

[200] Lamp (2015), p. 765.

[201] Lopes (2019).

[202] Jones (2020), p. 7. See Ismail and Grunder (2019), p. 19.

[203] Id.

[204] Supra note 129.

The global trading system can adopt a well-informed plan of action to accommodate many of its developing members to reduce disparities in global living standards. This should be genuinely made a common interest to curb and eliminate acute poverty and all forms of lack of capacity in Africa and other parts of the world; this can only be achieved by moving away from a hortatory declaration concerning SDT. Efforts must be made to reconcile competing interests at different levels of development for equity in the world order.[205]

References

Agbo-Ejeh C (2022) Asymmetrical power relations: a legal analysis of the European Union and economic community of West African states economic partnership agreement. Thesis submitted to University of Cape Town

Alessandrini D (2011) Developing countries and the multilateral regime. Hart, Oxford, pp 174–176

Berthelot J (2016) The contradiction of Ghana's Interim EPA, 7 August 2020. www.sol-asso.fr

Bilal S, Dan L (2009) Contentious issues in the negotiations ECDPM discussion paper no 89, Belgium. p 3. http://ecdpm.org/WP-content/uploads/2013/11/DP-89-contentous-issues-interim-EPAs-Flexibility-negotiationand-2009.pdf

Blair T (1999) Doctrine of the International Community. Speech to the Economic Club of Chicago on 22 April 1999. http://www.britishpoliticalspeech.org/speech-archive.htm?speech=279

Blair T (2001) A moment to seize: let us reorder this world around us. The Guardian, London, 3 October 2001, p 4. https://www.theguardian.com/politics/2001/oct/02/labourconference.labour7

Bretherton C, Vogler J (2006) The European Union as a global actor, 2nd edn. Routledge, London

Brown W (2002) The European Union and Africa: the restructuring of North-South relations. IB Tauris, London, p 368

Brummer C (2007–2008) Regional integration and incomplete club goods: a trade perspective. Chic J Int Law 8:535–560

Bull H (2002) The anarchical society. a study of order in world politics, 3rd edn. Palgrave, New York

Carty A (1991) Critical international law: recent trends in the theory of international law. EJIL 2:66

Chang H-J (2007) Kicking away the ladder: the 'real' history of free trade. In: Shaikh A (ed) Globalisation and the myths of free trade: history, theory, and empirical evidence. Routledge, London, pp 125–29; 41–2

Commission of the European Communities (1996) Green paper on relations between the European Union and the ACP Countries on the Eve of the 21st century: challenges and options for a new partnership, 20 November 1996, COM (96) (570 Final), p iii. https://eu-lex.europa.eu/legal-content/EN/TXT/pdf/?uri=CEL

Cottier T, Ahamd Z (2021) The prospects of common concern of humankind in international law. Cambridge University Press, Cambridge, p 111

Cottrell, Trubek (2012-2013) Law as problem solving: standards, networks, experimentation, and deliberation in global space. Transnat'l & Contemp. Prob. 359

Crawford G (1997) Foreign aid and political conditionality: issues of effectiveness and consistency. Democratisation 4(3):70

Croxton D (1999) The peace of Westphalia of 1648 and the origins of sovereignty. Int Hist Rev 21(3):569–591

[205] Rao (2011), pp. 336–337.

DeLong, Eichengreen (1991) The Marshall plan: history's most successful structural adjustment program. NBER working papers series, no 3899. pp 3-5. www.ssrn-id226738.pdf

ECA (2022) Addressing poverty and vulnerability in Africa during the Covid-19 Pandemic economic report on Africa 2021, 12 May 2022, p 4. www.uneca.org

Edwini K (2007) The legal status of special and differential treatment provisions under the WTO agreement. In: George AB, Petros CM (eds) WTO law and developing countries. Cambridge University Press

Espiell HG (1971) The most favoured nation clause: its present significance in GATT. J World Trade Law 5(29):35

EU (2019) The European Union and the African Union: a statistical portrait, 2019 edition. Publications Office of the European Union, Luxembourg, pp 17–19. https://ec.europa.eu/eurostat/documents/3217494/9767596/KS-GQ-19-001-EN-N.pdf

EU (n.d.) Europe in the World: the future of the European Financial Architecture for Development, Council of the European Union General Secretariat, pp 8–10. http://www.consilium.europa.eu.media/40967/efad-report_final.pdf

European Commission (2010) Economic Partnership Agreements (EPAs), New ACP-EU Trade Partnerships, July, 2010. https://eu.europa.eu/trade/wider-agenda/development/economic-partnerships

Feichtner I (2007) Community interest. In: Wolfrum (ed) The Max Planck encyclopedia of public international law. Oxford University, online. http://www.mpepil.com

Franck TM (1998) Fairness in International Law and Institutions. Oxford University Press, pp 10–12

Fukasaku K (2000) Special and differential treatment for developing countries: helping those who helped themselves. In: Murshed SM (ed) Globalisation, marginalisation and development. Routledge, London

Giorgio G (2011) The protection of general interests in the international community. Gen Course Public Int 364

Grossman G, Sykes A (2005) A preference for development: the law and economics of GSP. World Trade Rev 4:41–45

Gulhati R, Sekhar U (1982) Industrial strategy for late starters: the experience of Kenya, Tanzania and Zambia. World Dev 10(11):949–972

Haq UM (2018) Negotiating the future. In: Falk R, Kim SS et al (eds) Toward a just world order, vol 1. Routledge, New York, p 350

Hedley B (2002) The anarchy society: a study of order in world politics, 3rd edn. Palgrave, New York, p 23

Herbst J (1990) The structural adjustment in Africa. World Dev 18(7):494–958

Hoekman B, Howse S (2005) Economic responses to preference erosion: from trade as aid to aid for trade. Paper presented at the symposium, preferences erosion: impact and policy responses, Geneva, June 13–14

Hoekman B et al (2003) More favorable and differential treatment of developing countries: toward a new approach in the World Trade Organization. World Bank Publications

Hudec R (1987) Developing countries in the GATT legal system. University of Cambridge Press, New York

Huq M, Tribe M (2018) The economy of Ghana: 50 years of economic development. Palgrave Macmillan, p 17

Hurt SR (2003) Cooperation and coercion? The Cotonou agreement between the European Union and the ACP states and the end of Lomé Convention. Third World Q 24(1):161–176

International Monetary Fund (n.d.) Regional outlook: sub-Saharan Africa. IMF Data Access to Macroeconomic and Financial Data. www.data.imf.org

Isard P (1995) Exchange rates economics. Cambridge University Press, Cambridge, p 95

Ismail F, Grunder J (2019) Making Britain great again! for what purpose? Implications for South Africa's future relations with the UK Post-Brexit! Trade & industrial policy strategies working paper 19

Jackson JH (2006) Sovereignty, the WTO, and changing fundamentals of international law. Cambridge University Press, Cambridge, p 3
James B (1965) An economic theory of club. Economica 32:1
Jobim ML (2013) Drawing on the legal and economic argument in favour and against 'reciprocity' and special and differential treatment for developing countries within the WTO system. https://doi.org/10.5539/jpg.v6n3p55
Jones E (2020) Will this time really be different? Twenty years of trying (and failing) to reset Europe-Africa relations, global policy, 7 April 2020. https://www.globalpolicyjournal.com/articles/world-economy-trade-and-finance/will-time-really-be-different-twenty-years-trying-and
Keohane RO, Nye J (2011) Power and interdependence, 4th edn. Pearson, Chattanooga, p 276
Kleen P, Page S (2005) Special and differential treatment of developing countries in the world trade organisation. Overseas Development Studies, UK
Koroma S, Deep Ford JR (2006) The agricultural dimension of the ACP-EU economic partnership agreements, FAO commodities and trade technical paper 8, pp 25–30. https://www.fao.org/3/a0676e/a0676e00.pdf
Kritsiotis D (2002) Imagining the international community. EJIL 13:961–992
Lakshmi P (2005) Towards a new trade 'Marshall Plan' for least developed countries: how to deliver on the Doha Development promise and help realize the UN millennium development goals, UNCTAD trade, poverty and cross-cutting development tissues study series no. 1, p 1
Lamp N (2015) How some countries became 'Special': developing countries and the construction of difference in multilateral trade Law making. J Int Econ Law, pp 743–771, 744
Lancaster C (2007) Foreign aid: diplomacy, domestic politics. University of Chicago Press, Chicago
Lopes C (2019) Why Africa should revise its agreement with the EU. https://www.cnbcafrica.com/media/6178041844001/. Accessed 31 Jan 2023
Luke D et al (2020) EU-Africa trade arrangement at a crossroads: securing Africa's external frontier, Global Governance Spotlight 3/2020. https://www.sef-bonn.org/fileadmin/SEF-Dateiliste/04_Publikationen/GG-Spotlight/2020/ggs_2020-03_en.pdf
Malik A, Teal F (2008) Towards a more competitive manufacturing sector. In: Collier P et al (eds) Economic policy options for a prosperous Nigeria. Palgrave Macmillan, New York, p 247
Martin G (1982) Africa and the ideology of Eurafrica: neo-colonialism or Pan-Africanism. J Mod Afr Stud 20(2):226
Melaku GD (2021) The normative mess governing Africa-EU trade relation granted a new lease of life: a preliminary reflections on the trade-related aspects of the negotiated between the EU and OACPS, 16 November 2021. Volkerrechts blog. https://voelkerrechtsblog.org/the-normative-mess-governing-africa-eu-trade-relation-granted-a-new-lease-of-life/
Mendes P A et al. (2004) Industrialisation in Sub-Saharan Africa and Import Substitution Policy. Brazilian J Polit Econ vol 134 (1) pp 120-138. pp 125 128-131
Michalopoulos C (2003) Special and differential treatment of developing countries in TRIPS. TRIPS Issues Paper, Quaker United Nations (QUNO) Geneva. https://quno.org/sites/default/files/resources/Special-Differential-Treatment-in-TRIPS-English.pdf
Minta IK (1980) The Lomé Convention and the new international economic order. Howard Law J 27:953
Morgenthau HJ (1948) Politics among nations: the struggle for power and peace, 1st rev edn. Afred A. Knopf, INC, pp 14–17
Nwobike JC (2006) The emerging trade regime under the Cotonou partnership agreement its human rights implication. J World Trade 40(2):291–314. https://doi.org/10.54648/TRAD2006015
OECD (1947) The 'Marshall Plan' speech at Harvard University, 5 June. www.oecd.org
OECD (2015) Investment policy reviews: Nigeria 2015. OECD Publishing, Paris, p 152. http://dx.doi.org/10.1787
Oxfam International (2006) Unequal partners: how EU-ACP Economic Partnership Agreements (EPAs) could harm the development prospects of many of the world's poorest countries.

Briefing Note, p 13. https://policy-practice.oxfam.org/resources/unequal-partners-how-euacp-economic-partnership-agreements-epas-could-harm-the-115057/
Patterson D (1996) Discrimination in international trade: the policy issues 1945–1965
Patton S (2019) The peace of Westphalia and it affects on international relations, diplomacy and foreign policy. Histories 10(1), Article 5
Paulus A (2011) Reciprocity revisited. In: Ulrich F et al (eds) From bilateralism to community interest: Essay in honour of judge Brunno Simma. Oxford University Press, Oxford
Pauwelyn J (2003) Conflict of norms in public international law: how WTO law relates to other rules of international law. Cambridge University Press, Cambridge
Ramdoo I, Bilal S (2011) EPA negotiations: the honeymoon is over. Briefing note 31. www.ecdpm.org/publications
Rao SP (2011) The concept of international community' in international law and the developing countries. In: Ulrich F et al (eds) From: bilateralism to community interest: essay in Honour of Judge Bruno Simma. Oxford University Press, Oxford, pp 334–335
Ratna RS, Gupta RK (2018) A handbook on safeguard rules for least developed countries. United Nations Economic and Social Commission for Asia and the Pacific, United Nations Publication 2018. https://www.unescap.org/sites/default/files/handbook%20on%20safeguard%20rules%20for%20LDCs.pdf
Ravenhill J (1979–1980) Asymmetrical interdependence: renegotiating the Lomé convention. Int J 35(1):150–169
Ravenhill J (2002) The three bloc world? The new east Asian regionalism. Int Relat Asian Pac 2 (2):167–195. p 180
Samantha B (2018) Community interest in international law: whose interest are they and should we best identify them. https://core.ac.uk/download/pdf/159157428.pdf
Scotchmer S (2008) Club. In: Nurlauf SN, Blume LE (eds) The new Palgrave dictionary of economics, p 2. https://doi.org/10.1057/978-1-349-95121-5_660-2 P 2
Simma B (1994) From bilateralism to community interest in international law. Recueil des Cours de I'Academe de Driot International 250:217, 232 et passim
Simma B (2008) Reciprocity. In: Wolfrum R (ed) The Max Planck encyclopaedia of public international law. Oxford University Press, online. https://opil.ouplaw.com/display/10.1093/law:epil/9780199231690/law-9780199231690-e1461
Slaughter AM (1995) International law in a world of liberal states. EJIL 6
Smith N (2005) The European Commissioner for trade's speech to civil society dialogue group in Brussels. The Guardian, 20 January 2005. www.theguardian.com/politics/2005/jan/development.internationalaidanddevelopment
Stein H (1992) Deindustrialisation, adjustment, the World Bank and the IMF in Africa. World Dev 20(1):83–95
Stephen W (2014) EU Policy on preferential trade agreements in the 2000s: a reorientation towards commercial aim. p 180. https://doi.org/10.1111/eulj.12101
Stevens C, Meyn M et al (2008) The new EPAs: comparative analysis of their content and the challenges for 2008. ODC ECDP. http://www.odi.org.uk/iedg/Projects/0708010_The_new_EPAs.html and www.ecdpm.org/pmr14
Stiglitze JE, Charlton A (2005) Fair trade for all. New York University Press, p 13
Stoll PT (2011) The WTO as a Club: rethinking reciprocity and common interest. In: Ulrich F, Rudolf G, Daniel EK et al (eds) From bilateralism to community interest: essays in Honour of Judge Bruno Simma. Oxford University Press, Oxford, p 179
Sutherland P et al. (2004) The Future of the WTO: Addressing Institutional Challenges in the New Millennium Report by the Consultative Board to the Director-General Supachai Panitchpakdi World Trade Organisation https://www.wto.org/english/thewto_e/10anniv_e/future_wto_e.pdf
Sykes A (2003) The safeguard mess: a critique of the WTO jurisprudence. John M Olin Program in law and economic working paper no 187
Tasioulas J (1996) In defence of relative normativity: communitarian values and the Nicaragua case. Oxf J Leg Stud 16:88

Teson FR (1992) The Kantian theory of international law. Columbia Law Rev 92(1):53–102
The ACP-EU Courier (1996) Special issue on the revised Lomé Convention, No 155, 6 the Lomé Convention. http://www.acp.int
The Agenda 2030 was originally formulated by the United Nations. See United Nations, transforming our world: The 2030 Agenda for sustainable development A/RES/70/1, 10 May 2022. https://sustainabledevelopment.un.org/content/documents/21252030%20Agenda%20for
The Sixth European Union-African Union Summit: A Joint Vision for 2030, 18 February 2022. https://www.consilium.europa.eu/en/press/press-releases/2022/02/18/
The United Nations Charter 24 October 1945 Article 55. https://www.icj/cij/org/en/charter-of-the-united-nations
The World Bank (2022) The World Bank in Africa overview: development news research. Data/ World Bank. www.worldbank.org
The WTO (n.d.) Agreement on safeguard measures article XIX. https://www.wto.org/english/tratop_e/safeg_e/safeint.htm
Thomas C, Trachtman JP (2009) Editors' introduction. In: Thomas C, Trachtman JP (eds) Developing countries in the WTO legal system. Oxford University Press, New York, pp 3–10
Tomuschat C (1993) Obligation arising for states without or against their will. RdC 241:195, 216, 211
Trachtman J (2011) Introduction: the crisis in international law, pp 3–4. https://doi.org/10.2139/ssrn.1905946
Trebilcock DM, Howse R (1995) The regulation of international trade, 3rd edn. Routledge, New York, p 518 ttps://www.theguardian.com/politics/2001/oct/02/labourconference.labour7
Twichett KJ (1974) Yaoundé Association and the enlargement European community. World Day 30(2):51–63
United Nations (2022) Energy crisis poses threat to Europe's industrial sector, monthly briefing on the World economic situation and prospects, No 167, 1 December 2022. https://www.org/development/desa/dpad/wp-content/uploads/sites/45/publication/Monthly_Briefing_167.pdf
United Nations Conference on Trade and Development (UNCTAD) (2022) Rethinking the foundations of export diversification in Africa: the catalytic role of business and financial services, economic development in Africa Report 2022. https://unctad.org/system/files/official-document/aidcafrica2022_en.pdf
United Nations Conference on Trade and Development, Geneva, 23 March–16 June (New York, 1964) Final Act and Report, pp 18–25. https://unctad.org/system/files/official-document/econf46d141vol1_en.pdf
United Nations Conference on Trade and Development, Second Session New Delhi, 1 February 29 - March (1968) Volume I report and annexes 11-12,200-2
Van den Bossche P, Zdouc W (2017) The law and policy of the World Trade Organisation, 4th edn. Cambridge University Press, Cambridge
Verdross A, Simma B (1984) Universelles Volkerrecht Theorei Und Praxis. Unveranderter Nachdruck der dritten Auflage. Duncker & Humblot, Berlin
Villalpando S (2010) The dimension of the international community: how community interests are protected in international law. Eur J Int Law 21(2):387–419
Ward AW (1934) The peace of Westphalia, the Cambridge modern history [Cited in: Gross L (1948) The peace Westphalia, 1648–1948. Am J Int Law 42(1):20–41 at 22]
Whally J (1990) Non-discriminatory discrimination: special and differential treatment under the GATT for developing countries. Econ J 100:1318–1328
Whitefield L (2009) The politics of aid: African strategies for dealing donor. Oxford University Press, Oxford, p 28
Wilkinson R (2014) What's wrong with WTO and how to fix it. Polity Press, Cambridge, p 32

Woolcock S (2014) Differential Within Reciprocity: The European Union Approach Preferential Trade Agreement. Contemp Polit 20 (1) P 39. https://doi.org/10.1080/13569775.2014.88/603
WTO (2001) The generalised system of preferences: a preliminary analysis of the GSP scheme in the Quad. WT/COMTD/W/93, 5 October 2001. www.docs.wto.org
Yanai A (2004) Legal frameworks for north-south RTAs under the WTO System. APEC Study Centre, working paper series 03/04 – No 6, p 8

Inebu Agbo-Ejeh is a Lecturer in Law at Baze University, Nigeria. Inebu holds a doctorate (PhD) in commercial law from the University of Cape Town, South Africa; a Master of Laws in International Economic Law from the University of Warwick, United Kingdom, and a Bachelor of Laws (LLB) from the University of Jos, Nigeria. Inebu is a Barrister & Solicitor of the Supreme Court of Nigeria and has practised law with the prestigious law firm of Kanu Agabi & Associates. She is a principal partner at Chrisnate & Associates.